Basis Administration for
SAP®

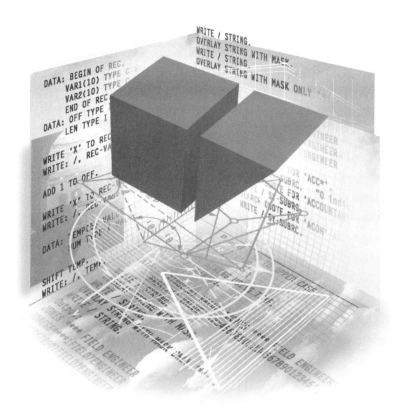

Robert E. Parkinson
Johan Marneweck

With

Kay Tailor
Victor Wood

SERIES EDITORS &
CERTIFIED SAP R/3
APPLICATION CONSULTANTS:

Gareth M. de Bruyn
Robert Lyfareff

Basis Administration for
SAP®

A Division of Prima Publishing

A Division of Prima Publishing

Prima Publishing and colophon are registered trademarks of Prima Communications, Inc. PRIMA TECH is a trademark of Prima Communications, Inc., Rocklin, California 95765.

"SAP" is a registered trademark of SAP Aktiengesellschaft, Systems, Applications and Products in Data Processing, Neurottstrasse 16, 69190 Walldorf, Germany. The publisher gratefully acknowledges SAP's kind permission to use its trademark in this publication. SAP AG is not the publisher of this book and is not responsible for it under any aspect of press law.

ABAP, ABAP/4, BAPI, ALE/WEB, Management Cockpit, R/2, R/3, SAP (Logo), SAP (Word), SAP ArchiveLink, SAP Business Workflow, SAP EarlyWatch, SAPPHIRE, and TeamSAP are trademarks or registered trademarks of SAP Aktiengesellschaft, Walldorf, Germany.

Windows, Windows Explorer, and Microsoft are registered trademarks of Microsoft Corporation.

ISBN: 0-7615-1887-8
Library of Congress Catalog Card Number: 98-068773
Printed in the United States of America

99 00 01 02 03 HH 10 9 8 7 6 5 4 3 2 1

Publisher:
Stacy L. Hiquet

Associate Publisher:
Nancy Stevenson

Managing Editor:
Dan J. Foster

Senior Acquisitions Editor:
Deborah F. Abshier

Project Editor:
Kevin Harreld

Copy Editor:
Laura Gabler

Technical Reviewers:
Victor Wood
Johan Marneweck

Interior Layout:
Marian Hartsough

Cover Design:
Prima Design Team

Indexer:
Johnna VanHoose

Dedication

This book is dedicated to my mother Ann,
and the loving memory of my father, Robert.
Their guidance and support over the years
has been an inspiration to me throughout my life and career.
Thank you for your unconditional love.

—RP

I dedicate this book to the people in the U.S.,
who allowed me to work and learn in their great country.

—JM

I dedicate this book to my patient wife, Anita,
first for encouraging me to do this book
and letting me stay up all hours of the night writing,
and most importantly, for looking after our two beautiful girls,
Shereene and Jade, while I was cooped up in my office.
Also, big thanks to my mum and dad for being there for me — the early years!

—KT

I graciously dedicate my portion of the book to my loving wife Eldore,
and my family Jordynn Lee and Rayne.
I thank them for their sacrifices,
so that I could be in a position to share the knowledge
and experience I have gained over the last few years.
I would like to thank my parents, my parents in-law and
Michelle and Herman for their support.

—VW

Acknowledgments

I would like to thank Prima Tech's Debbie Abshier, for the opportunity to contribute to this book, and Kevin Harreld for his excellent QA of my work. Also, I would like to acknowledge John Southcott and Peter Smith of Deloitte and Touche for giving me the opportunity to become involved in the SAP world, Timothy Rogers for his drive, Victor Wood for being my reality check, and also Micheal Doane, Mark Dendinger, Jeannie Browing, Keith Anderson, Jim Wilson, Steve Lewis, Bart Hughes, and all the clients I have been involved with and everyone else who has touched my life in a positive manner.

—KT

I would like to thank my co-authors Johan, Kay, and Robert for their valuable input into this manuscript.

I would like to thank Mark Sincliar, for giving me the opportunity to experience the amazing world of SAP Basis. I would like to thank Peter Smith, Martin O'Brein and the dream team of Lucent Denver for making me part of their teams. I would further like to thank Prima Publishing for their patience and support while guiding and enabling us to turn this minefield of technical data into a readable format.

—VW

About the Authors

Robert E. Parkinson is an accomplished SAP R/3 Basis Consultant who has held leadership roles in successfully implementing SAP R/3 at several Fortune 50 and 500 companies. With over 19 years of computer experience working for industry giants such as IBM, Oracle Corp. and SAP America, he is well versed in client/server technology. He began acquiring his R/3 knowledge when SAP was first introduced into the U.S. in 1992, and has received extensive training at SAP's headquarters in Walldorf, Germany. He now heads an independent consulting firm with plans for expansion. Robert can be contacted at his Web site URL address of **http://hometown.aol.com/robertpark** or by email at **robertpark@aol.com.**

Born and educated in South Africa, **Johan Marneweck** graduated in 1990 at the University of Pretoria in Mathematics and Computer Science. His primary focus initially was scientific computing, voice recognition, signal analysis, and laboratory systems until 1995 when he decided to get involved with SAP R/3. His SAP R/3 experience has allowed him to work in the U.S. since April 1996. His Oracle, Informix, SQLServer Unix VMS, and Windows NT experience assisted him with most of the big challenges the U.S. has provided, and every day he is still learning more. Currently he lives in Granite Bay, California, with his lovely wife and four kids.

Kay Tailor has been working in the SAP world for over five years as a Basis consultant, then as an SAP project manager, and now as an SAP practice lead. Kay has been involved in SAP projects in Canada, U.S., Europe, and Latin America for a number of global Fortune 500 companies and several medium-size companies.

Victor Wood is a technical Basis specialist with over 14 years experience in the IT industry, including 5 years of SAP experience. This SAP experience has come in the form of global SAP implementations in which he has played a key role in Basis administration. He believes that his years spent as a Basis consultant for Fortune 100 companies has given him the ability to interact with the client on a professional as well as technical level.

Contents at a Glance

Introduction. xxi

Part I **Overview** **1**

   1   An SAP Primer for Administrators. 3

Part II **Planning.** **19**

   2   The Administrator's Role in Installation Planning. . . 21
   3   R/3 System Strategies for Basis Administrators. 49

Part III **Installation** **59**

   4   An Administrator's Guide to Installing R/3. 61

Part IV **Configuration.** **121**

   5   Creating and Administrating Clients. 123
   6   Security Administration 155
   7   Spool Administration 193
   8   Correction and Transport System 221
   9   SAP Performance Tuning 239

Part V **Administration** **315**

   10   System Monitoring and Administration 317
   11   Performance Monitoring and Administration 339
   12   Database Administration. 355
   13   Data Archiving for Administrators 289
   14   An Administrator's Troubleshooting Guide 429
   15   The Internet and SAP 447

Part VI   **Upgrading. 467**

16   The Administrator's Role in Upgrading R/3 469

17   Pre-Production for Administrators 499

Part VI   **Appendixes 519**

A   Understanding the EDI Architecture. 521

B   Understanding Ready-to-Run R/3 547

Index 561

Contents

Introduction xxi

PART I   OVERVIEW 1

Chapter 1   An SAP Primer for Administrators 3

In This Chapter 4
SAP Architecture 5
The Basis Layer 6
Client/Server Architectures. 7
SAP's Tiered Architecture. 7
Homogeneous SAP Systems. 8
Heterogeneous SAP Systems 8
Graphical User Interface (SAPGUI) 9
SAP's Flexibility and Scalability 9
SAP R/3 Standard 9
ABAP Development Workbench 15
Data Dictionary 16
Problem Resolution. 17

PART II   PLANNING. 19

**Chapter 2   The Administrator's Role in
Installation Planning 21**

In This Chapter 22
Hardware Requirements 22
Selecting Your Hardware Platform 22
Sizing Your Hardware. 27
Server Requirements. 27
Planning for Future Growth 28
Software Requirements 29
Operating System Considerations 29

Selecting Your Database Server 29
Sizing Your Database 30
Laying Out Your Database 30
Selecting Your Application Server 32
Selecting Your Presentation Server 32
Networking Requirements. 33
LAN Considerations. 33
WAN Considerations 35
Remote Support Connections 36
Resource Requirements. 37
Identifying Personnel Roles. 38
Outsourcing 43
Installation Planning Checklist 44
Complete Technical Questionnaire 44
Size Hardware 44
Determine Technical Infrastructure Needs. 45
Procure Hardware and Network Connections 45
System Landscape. 45
System Purpose. 46
System Names 46
Client Strategy 46
Transport System Strategy 47
SAP Software Release Strategy. 48
Summary 48

Chapter 3   R/3 System Strategies for Basis Administrators **49**

In This Chapter 50
System Landscapes 51
Single-System Landscape 51
Two-System Landscape 52
Three-System Landscape 52
Client Strategy Best Suited for the System Landscape. 53
The Development Environment 53
How to Manage "Rolling Releases" 57

PART III **INSTALLATION** **59**

Chapter 4 **An Administrator's Guide**
to Installing R/3 . . . . **61**

In This Chapter 62
UNIX Operating System and Hardware Preparation 62
  Installation Steps 63
  ORAINST Pre-Execution Requirements 67
  ORAINST Procedure 69
  R/3 Installation Tools 71
  Installing the Database Software 80
  Installation Example 80
  Network Installation 86
  The Languages Your System Will Speak 87
  Preparing the SAP Online System 108
  SAP OSS Messages 112
  SAP OSS Administration 112
  SAP Service Connection 113
  General Functions 114
  Online Correction Support 116
  Steps for Installing Hot Packages 117
  Distributing Patches 119
Summary 119

PART IV **CONFIGURATION** **121**

Chapter 5 **Creating and Administrating Clients** **123**

In This Chapter 124
The R/3 Client Concept 124
Client Usage 125
Client Creation Tools 126
  Logical System 126
  Category 128
  Changes and Transports for
    Client-Dependent Objects 128
  Client-Independent Object Changes 129
  Restrictions 129

Local or Remote Client Copy SCCO 130
Local Client Copy SCCL 130
Remote Client Copy SCC9. 130
Copying a Client per Transport Request SCC1 131
Client Copy and Transport
    (Import and Export) SCC2. 131
Client Export SCC8 132
Client Import-Post-processing SCC7 132
Client Copy Log Analysis SCC3. 132
Deleting a Client SCC5 133
Client Import per Transport Request SCC6 133
Client Copy Profiles 133
Client Copy Prerequisites 136
Client Copy Utilities. 138
A Client Copy in Action. 140
Check Disk Space 142

Chapter 6   **Security Administration 155**

In This Chapter 156
Methodology 157
Authorizations 159
Authorization Classes and Objects 159
Special User Accounts. 168
Passwords 169
Table Authorizations. 171
ABAP Authorization 175
Authority-Checks 177
Profile Generator 177
Activity Group Creation and Assignment 178
Other Tools and Security Issues. 180
Transaction SU53—Authorization Check. 180
Transaction ST01—Trace. 180
Transaction ST05—SQL Trace 183
Security Roles and Responsibilities 184
The SAP Security Administrator. 186
Audit Information Systems (AIS) 187
System Audit and Business Audit 187

Critical Authorizations Combinations 191
Summary 192

Chapter 7 Spool Administration 193

In This Chapter 194
Printing. 194
    Printer Installation 197
Faxing. 208
    Faxing Using Delrina/Winfax at the Workstation 208
    Faxing Using SAPcomm/TOPCALL at the Server . . . 211
    Using SAPconnect (Replacing SAPcomm) 219

Chapter 8 Correction and Transport System. 221

In This Chapter 222
Repairs 222
Correction. 223
System Change Option 223
Transport Types 223
    C Type 225
    T Type 225
    K Type 225
Common Scenarios in a CTS Environment. 226
Object Types Related to the Correction
    and Transport System 226
Transport Management System (TMS). 227
    TMS Concepts. 227
    Configuring TMS. 228
Setting Up Correction and Transport System
    at UNIX Level 229
    Examining Unix Users, Groups, and Permissions. 231
    Verify Control Tables and Parameters Files for CTS . . 231
    Examine Control File TPPARAM 231
    Additional Entries to be Verified. 232
CTS Initialization. 233
    SE06. 234
    TPPARAM 234
    TSYST. 234

TDEVC 234
TASYS 234
RDDIMPDP 236
Maintenance of the CTS Environment 236

Chapter 9   SAP Performance Tuning 239

In This Chapter 240
Planning Considerations 240
SAP Services 241
System Layout, Distribution, and
Network Architecture 242
Hardware Architecture 249
Storage Devices and File System 249
Software and Database Layout 251
Operating System Tuning 257
Database Performance Considerations 264
SAP Performance Considerations 282
Memory Management 283
Buffer Management 304
Summary 313

PART V   ADMINISTRATION 315

**Chapter 10 System Monitoring and
Administration 317**

In This Chapter 318
Monitoring SAP R/3 318
Lock Manager (Enqueue) (SM12) 320
The SAP R/3 System Log (SM21) 321
Performance (ST03) 322
Buffers (ST02) 322
ABAP Errors (ST22) 322
Roll and Paging (ST02) 323
Trace Switch (ST05) 324
Batch Jobs (SM37 or SM39) 324
Updates (SM13) 325

Process (SM50)................................ 325
Load Balancing (SMLG) 326
Active and All Logged on Users (AL08).......... 326
Gateway (SMGW)............................. 327
Hot Package and Kernel Patch Level............. 327
Operating System 328
Database.................................... 330
Alert Monitor.................................... 333
Global (AL01-SAP System & AL02-Database) 333

**Chapter 11 Performance Monitoring
and Administration.................. 339**

In This Chapter 340
CCMS Monitoring Transactions..................... 340
Monitoring Transactions 341
Determining Performance Goals 342
User Response Time 343
Identifying Performance Bottlenecks 344
Tuning Rules of Thumb 348
ABAP Runtime Analysis........................... 349
With Subroutines 349
With Internal Tables........................... 349
With Technical Database Information.............. 350
Display Filter 350
Hit List 352
Tables...................................... 352
Group Hit List 353
Hierarchy 354

Chapter 12 Database Administration 355

In This Chapter 356
Roles and Responsibilities of a
Basis Administrator as DBA.................. 356
Installing and Upgrading the Database 357
Assisting and Managing the Development Process ... 357
Database Security 359

Backup and Recovery Strategies 361
Scheduled Database Maintenance and Support 370
Summary 388

Chapter 13 Data Archiving for Administrators 289

In This Chapter 390
Archiving Concepts. 391
Developing an Archiving Strategy 392
Archiving Authorizations 392
Identifying the Archive Objects. 393
Performing the Archive 398
Step 1: Parameters Setup. 398
Step 2: Configuring the Archiving Object 407
Step 3: Performing the Actual Archiving 407
Application Archiving Objects 408
Financial Archive Objects 409
Accounting Documents (FI_DOCUMNT);
Archive Customizing Example 411
Controlling Archive Objects 413
CO Cost Center Line Items (C0_CCTR_EP);
Archiving Example 414
Material Management Archive Objects 414
MM—Purchasing Documents (MM_EKKO):
Archiving Example 416
Sales and Distribution Archive Objects 417
SD—Sales Documents (SD_VBAK);
Archiving Example 417
Data Retention Tool (DART) 420
Summary 423
Archive. 424
Deletion 425
Post Processing 425
Other Options 426
ArchiveLink 426

**Chapter 14 An Administrator's
Troubleshooting Guide 429**

In This Chapter 430
Analysis Tools 431
   The System Log 431
   The System Process Overview (SM50) 434
   The ABAP Dump Analysis 435
   The Update Records Monitor 438
   The Lock Entries Monitor 440
   System Trace Files 441
   Online Service System 444
   The Database Alert Log 444
Diagnosing the Problem 445
   Is the Problem Reproducible? 445
   Problem Rectification 446

Chapter 15 The Internet and SAP 447

In This Chapter 448
Architecture 448
Installation Summary 449
Administration 450
The Internet Application Components (IAC) 450
ITS and Components 451
ITS Project Directory and Service File 454
   Creation of WebTransactions 455
   Creation of WebRFC and WebReporting 457
WebReporting 460
WebReporting Browser 461
   User Administration 462
Security 462
   Controlled Access 462
   Encryption Technology 463
SAP@Web Studio 464
Summary 465

PART VI   UPGRADING. **467**

**Chapter 16 The Administrator's Role in
               Upgrading R/3** **469**

In This Chapter 470
The Upgrade Process. 470
    When to Upgrade 471
    Planning Your Upgrade 471
    The Technical Upgrade 487
Summary 498

Chapter 17 Pre-Production for Administrators **499**

In This Chapter 500
Resource Planning. 500
Test and Measurement 501
    Volume Test 501
    Stress Test. 502
    System Administration Tests 504
Job Scheduling Management. 504
Database Management 506
Database Backup and Recovery Management 507
    Verify Data Written to the Backup Medium 507
    Backup and Recovery 508
Transport Management System (TMS) 508
SAP System Alerts and Logs 508
Printing and Fax Management 509
Daily Monitoring Activities. 509
    Daily Transactions. 509
    SAP R/3 System Administration. 511
Disaster Recovery 512
    Disaster Recovery Procedure 512
    Recovery and Test. 513
    Document Findings 513
Pre-production Data Migration and Data Loads 513

Pre-production Checklist. 515
Stabilization of the Production System 516
Summary 517

PART VI   APPENDIXES. 519

Appendix A   Understanding the EDI Architecture 521

Appendix B   Understanding Ready-to-Run R/3 547

Index 561

Introduction

SAP controls more than one-third of the client/server market, but not enough experienced resources are available to meet the high demand. Currently, there are a few books that discuss SAP R/3 concepts, but none of these books discretely addresses the concept of providing ongoing support for an SAP R/3 environment.

To date, the pool of more than 5,000 industries that have implemented SAP R/3 has had to pay high dollars to independent consulting firms for this information or has faced the arduous task of learning how to support SAP R/3 over time, through trial and error. Those industries have been waiting for a book like this one to speed their learning curve. Consulting firms are also eager to locate and enlist individuals with this highly sought-after experience, so those pursuing a career in SAP consulting also will benefit from reading this book.

The SAP phenomena continue to sweep the globe, with SAP en route to maintaining a superior market share through the year 2000 and beyond. The demand for SAP implementations remains strong because SAP streamlines the business operations of any company, with no restrictions to any particular industry. Companies realize that the long–term cost-saving benefits of SAP far outweigh the initial investment of time and money.

The Purpose of This Book

This book will provide comprehensive real-world beginning and intermediate technical information regarding Basis Administration of SAP R/3. There are relatively few books like this in the marketplace. SAP installations are growing at a fast pace, but Basis administrators lack valuable information and available resources in supporting these environments.

Basis Administration for SAP is written by Basis administrators and is aimed at the technical professional who desperately needs to understand how to effectively support SAP R/3. *Basis Administration for SAP* serves as a "technical cookbook" to enable comprehensive, real-world Basis Administration of an SAP R/3 installation. This book includes actual Basis Administration strategies that are in use at existing SAP R/3 installations.

SAP is not for the faint hearted; its complexity at times can overwhelm even a seasoned professional. Hands-on experience is the best teacher of SAP. Unfortunately, for those professionals who do not have the opportunity to gain on-the-job experience, there are only a limited number of formal training programs and technical publications available. The hands-on approach and real-world experiences involving various SAP implementations that are shared in this book will prove invaluable to the R/3 Basis professional.

For those who are just beginning to jump on the SAP bandwagon and for the seasoned professional alike, Basis Administration for an SAP R/3 system offers tremendous challenges.

Business and technical professionals are hungry to learn from the experiences of other SAP installation sites. Individuals new to the administrator role will value the real-world information this book provides. Experienced support professionals will value the information that helps them to migrate to an SAP environment.

As accomplished consultants with extensive experience in SAP R/3 Basis Administration involving several implementations with Fortune 50 and Fortune 500 companies, the authors provide pertinent guidance for everyday situations you're likely to encounter.

Intended Audience

There currently exists a large and ever-increasing market for this book, as corporations and individuals seek firsthand knowledge and experiences related to supporting SAP installations. This book's content is actively being sought by the following market segments:

> Businesses already using SAP
>
> Businesses eager to use SAP
>
> Individuals wanting marketable knowledge of and insight about SAP
>
> Universities attempting to meet the industry's demands for SAP knowledge and practical experience
>
> Corporate trainers

With each new release of SAP, the challenges of supporting and administering R/3 greatly increase. It is vital as an SAP Basis consultant, manager, or administrator to keep your skill set current and progressive in the latest technologies.

How This Book Is Organized

This book will cover the following major elements:

Reasons to support SAP R/3

Integrating business and technical needs

Effective organization structure

Training issues

Documenting for support

When and when not to use consultants

Managing customizations

SAP R/3 security

Reporting techniques

Satisfying your business customers

Managing changes

Managing functional aborts

Disaster recovery planning

Using job scheduling tools

This book is structured in a series of chronological sections:

Part I, "Overview" includes an SAP primer for administrators.

Part II, "Planning" includes the administrator's role in installation planning and R/3 system strategies for Basis administrators.

Part III, "Installation" includes an administrator's guide to installing R/3.

Part IV, "Configuration" includes creating and administrating clients, security administration, spool administration, the correction and transport system, and SAP performance.

Part V, "Administration" includes system monitoring, performance monitoring, database administration, SAP data archiving, an administrator's troubleshooting guide, and the Internet and SAP.

Part VI, "Upgrading" includes the administrator's role in upgrading, and pre-production preparation for administrators.

Part VII, "Appendixes" include understanding the EDI architecture and Ready-to-Run R/3.

How to Use This Book

Although this is a reference guide useful for professionals who support an SAP R/3 installation, it will also serve novices who are interested in learning more about working with SAP in a variety of situations.

Combining technical and business-based knowledge, this book arises from an in-depth understanding of both R/3 and the user (customer) base that utilizes it daily. This book includes SAP R/3 screen captures to illustrate the functionality to be used in particular situations, as well as custom spreadsheets, templates, and so on, which can be employed to provide a more efficient and consistent SAP R/3 support environment.

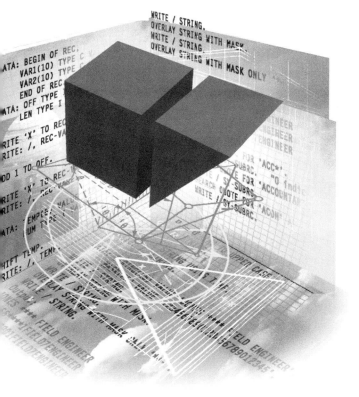

PART

I

Overview

1 An SAP Primer for
   Administrators

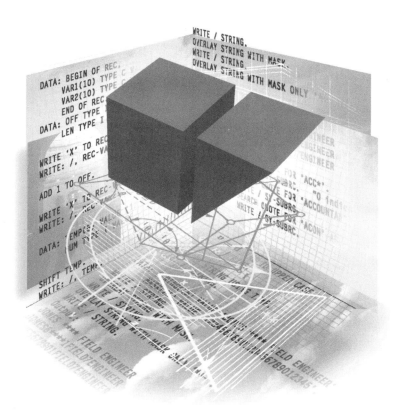

Chapter 1

An SAP Primer for Administrators

In This Chapter

Today's successful corporations depend on a sound and reliable infrastructure of enterprise-wide computing solutions on which to run their businesses. This infrastructure may include the sophisticated management of financial, manufacturing and logistics, sales and distribution, and human resources planning functions.

SAP R/3 (referred to as SAP from now on) is a suite of integrated applications, known as an enterprise resource planning (ERP) application that provides company-wide support of these critical functions. It is commercial software that has been utilized globally by many companies to meet their needs for core transaction processing systems.

The SAP system is *not* a "one size fit all" solution, but a highly flexible system application which will require configuration (SAP refers to it as "Customizing") to allow the software to function to your company's business processes.

SAP is implemented in a number of phases, and using SAP's implementation methodology, are broken down into the following stages:

◆ Project Preparation
◆ Business Blueprint
◆ Realization
◆ Final Preparation
◆ Go-Live & Support

Each of these phases will shape the way your company will do business in the future using the SAP software, and thus the project becomes a team effort between the experienced SAP consultants and your company's employees. The phases will identify which business areas (SAP Modules) will require customizing and which business transactions (also SAP Transactions) will be used.

The SAP modules are generally broken down into the following categories, with each module then broken down into sub-modules.

◆ **Financial Management.** A unified and integrated financial management solution including functions such as financial and cost accounting, activity-based costing, fixed asset accounting, treasury, and much more.

◆ **Manufacturing and logistics**. A comprehensive suite of functions from production planning and control to material management to quality assurance—in fact, the complete global supply chain management (SAP's SCOPE, Supply Chain Optimization, Planning and Execution, initiative).

◆ **Sales and Distribution**. A real-time tool for tracking sales and managing distribution channels to provide the best customer service.

◆ **Human Resources**. A flexible management solution from personnel planning development to personnel administration.

◆ **Basis**. A flexible environment to make enhancements to SAP programming functionality and set up your technical environment to support the SAP applications.

SAP's strength lies in the integration of all these business applications. As data is added, changed, or deleted within one application, all related functions and applications are immediately updated to reflect the new changes.

This book will primarily focus on the SAP Basis environment and the technologies involved to ensure a smooth and worry-free implementation.

SAP Architecture

The SAP architecture is said to be "open" in that SAP runs on the hardware platforms of many leading hardware vendors, and will blend smoothly with the client's technology infrastructure. It is "open" to allow interoperability with third-party solutions and services through business application programming interfaces (BAPIs).

SAP is said to be "integrated" as it overcomes the limitations of traditional hierarchical and function-oriented structures by integrating financial accounting, sales and materials planning, production planning, warehouse management, and human resources management into a workflow of business events and processes across departments and functional areas.

The SAP system consists of the SAP application running on one or more servers, which may include the S390 mainframe, or one of the different versions of UNIX or Windows NT. The Users access SAP through a graphical user interface referred to as the SAP GUI. The SAP GUI runs on Intel/Windows or Macintosh workstations and communicates with the servers via TCP/IP over the client's internal network. SAP uses a wide range of relational databases (Informix, Oracle, DB2 and MS-SQL) to manage configuration information, transactional data, and many other aspects of its operation.

At the heart of SAP R/3 is the SAP kernel, which is a collection of executable files that reside in a couple of directories "/sapmnt/<SID>/exe" and "/usr/sap/<SID>/SYS/exe/run". The existence of these executable files in all SAP systems provides a consistent interface between the SAP Basis and Business modules and operating system. SAP developed a set of executables for each operating system.

The Basis Layer

SAP can be thought of as a "middleware" layer (known as the Basis layer) that is separate from the underlying hardware/operating system/database, and from the SAP applications it interfaces.

The Basis layer consists of the following components:

BC-ABA	ABAP Runtime Environment
BC-BE	Business Engineer
BC-BMT	Business Management
BC-CCM	Computing Center Management System
BC-CI	Component Integration/Installation Windows Components
BC-CTS	Change & Transport System
BC-DB	Database Interface, Database Platforms
BC-DWB	ABAP Workbench
BC-FES	Front End Services
BC-INS	Installation Tools
BC-KRN	Kernel Components
BC-OP	Operating System Platforms
BC-SEC	Security
BC-SRV	Basis Services/Communication Interfaces
BC-UPG	Upgrade - general
BC-SRV-ARL	SAP Archive Link
BC-SRV-COM	Communication Interfaces
BC-SRV-KPR	SAP Knowledge Provider

BC-SRV-OFC	SAP Office: Mail and Archive System
BC-SRV-QUE	ABAP Query
BC-SRV-REP	Reporting
BC-SRV-SCR	SAP Script
BC-BMT-WFM	SAP Business Workflow

Each of these topics will be discussed in greater detail in the following chapters.

Client/Server Architectures

The client/server architecture is a breakdown of the system components to optimize the hardware and software components of the application. For the SAP environment, this would include the Database server (where the data resides), the Application server (where the logic resides), and the Presentation Server (the user's workstation). The term client/server refers to the communications between each component and the role they play in each communication. For example, a user requests to see a list of parts in a warehouse and inputs the information at the presentation PC (acting as a client); the application server then interprets the request (acting as a server). The Application (acting as a client) then sends the request to the database server (acting as the server) to fulfill the request. The Database then queries the database and forwards the data back to the Application, which in turn forwards the data to the Presentation server.

Some of the advantages of Client/Server include:

- ease of maintenance of host-based systems
- cost effective to purchase a specialized server than a host-based system
- flexible architecture
- workload distributed among several servers

SAP's Tiered Architecture

SAP uses client-server technology with three distinct layers, though the layers may reside in one or more servers. These layers are the following:

- The Presentation layer—This is where SAP users submit input to the SAP system for the processing of business transactions. It is also where the output from these transactions appears as output fields, reports, tables, and spreadsheets, plus interfaces to common PC applications.

◆ The Application layer—After a user initiates a request at the presentation level, application logic is invoked to service and process the inquiry.

◆ The Database layer—SAP exclusively uses a relational database to store and retrieve configuration, transactional, and master data.

Please note that an additional two layers have been added for accessing the SAP system via the Internet, discussed in detail in Chapter 15.

SAP uses client-server technology in two ways:

◆ To manage communications between the three layers (presentation, application, and database)

◆ To manage communications between the different SAP processes that run on the servers *(application server)*

This allows SAP application processing to be divided among two or more servers. When an SAP system has all its processing on a single server, it is referred to as a two-tier system. When processing is divided among multiple servers, it is referred to as a three-tier system.

A three-tier system provides additional scalability beyond a two-tier system through this division of application processing and allowing different servers to be tuned for specific SAP application functions. For example, one application server can be used for Human Resources users, another for Finance users, and so on.

Homogeneous SAP Systems

A *homogenous* system is where all the servers within the SAP cluster are running the same operating system—more specifically, the database server(s) and application server(s) are running the same flavor of UNIX or Windows NT. The presentation servers would typically be running windows-based workstations.

Heterogeneous SAP Systems

Conversely, a *heterogeneous* system is where the database server is running one operation system and the application servers another. An example of this is a database server running UNIX, the application servers running Windows NT, and again the presentation servers would be running windows-based workstations.

This ability of SAP to be heterogeneous makes it highly adaptable to existing and new computing environments.

Graphical User Interface (SAPGUI)

The SAPGUI, or presentation server, looks and acts the same on UNIX, MAC OS, OS/2, Motif and all the Microsoft products to provide consistency between all platforms. The goal of the SAP Graphical User Interface is to provide a user-friendly, intuitive, and consistent interface to users and react the same way for all users, using any hardware platform, operating system, database and SAP module.

The SAPGUI has all the features of other GUI's on the desktop: pull-down menus, tool bars, application bars, buttons, check boxes, scroll bars, selection lists, and World Wide Web features.

SAP's Flexibility and Scalability

Thanks to its design, SAP offers a great deal of flexibility/scalability:

- ◆ SAP fits a wide variety of organizations in a number of industries ranging from the largest, multi-billion dollar companies to the smallest.
- ◆ SAP applications can be accessed through a LAN, WAN, dial-up connection, or the Internet.
- ◆ SAP uses leading vendors' databases to allow third-party tools to access information or use SAP's new Business Warehouse tool (a data warehouse solution).
- ◆ SAP allows external programs to query SAP and its functions using Remote Function Calls (RFCs) and BAPIs.
- ◆ SAP supports Electronic Data Interchange (EDI) for intercompany exchange using Intermediate Documents (IDocs).
- ◆ SAP supports distributed application connectivity using Application Linking and Enabling (ALE).

SAP R/3 Standard

The SAP R/3 standard system is one to which no customizing, enhancements, or dictionary object changes are made. "Out of the box" SAP R/3 comes pre-configured (separate from customizing) and is theoretically configured extensively enough to accommodate most business environments. Alas, customers usually adapt the system to their own requirements and make changes to screens, programs, and dictionary objects.

Changes to standard SAP functionality require a consistent management environment to control these changes and to make upgrades to future SAP releases more manageable. Fortunately, for the Basis Administrators, SAP has adopted a standard and developed a set of functions to support this standardization. Adhering to these standards ensures compatibility with future SAP releases.

Industry Specific Solutions (IS Solutions)

SAP partnered with several industry sectors to develop solutions enhancing SAP to support these specialized industries and thus change the SAP R/3 standard. There are a number of minor disadvantages in implementing the IS solutions, which include an IS solution not being available for all releases and thus keeping your system on an older SAP release and introducing more administrative tasks when applying Hot Packages, OSS Notes, and upgrades.

However, the advantage that Industry Specific Solutions bring to the business should be the only consideration in implementing it. Listed below is a number of Industry Specific Solutions that are available at the time of this book going to print. SAP is updating this list on a regular basis.

SAP AEROSPACE

SAP AUTOMOTIVE

SAP BANKING

SAP CHEMICALS

SAP CONSUMER PRODUCTS

SAP ENGINEERING AND CONSTRUCTION

SAP HEALTHCARE

SAP HIGHER EDUCATION AND RESEARCH

SAP HIGH TECH

SAP INSURANCE

SAP MEDIA

SAP MILL PRODUCTS

SAP OIL AND GAS

SAP PHARMACEUTICALS

SAP PUBLIC SECTOR

SAP RETAIL

SAP SERVICE PROVIDER
SAP TELECOMMUNICATIONS
SAP TRANSPORTATION
SAP UTILITIES

Customizing

Companies are individual and unique entities, each wanting to deliver a product or service better and less expensive than its competition. SAP allows companies to customize their system to their own unique requirements to redefine their work processes to become more efficient and responsive to its customers' requirements. Customizing defines the way SAP reacts with its users to provide real-time data with complete data integrity. The IMG-implementation guide (IMG) tool assists customizing teams to configure the SAP system.

Basis administrators do not usually get involved with customizing except for some Basis functionality and regenerating the IMG after an upgrade. A Basis Administrator will typically configure users, printers, CTS, and be involved with the creation of some data dictionary object definition. SAP R/3 controls the customizing process and does not overwrite settings when the system is upgraded or changed by standard SAP tools.

Changes to SAP

Changes to standard SAP objects introduce the most amount of overhead in supporting and maintaining a consistent SAP environment. Changes to SAP R/3 entail changing objects in the SAP name range. An example is adding customer specific code into SAP proprietary ABAP. An SAP upgrade usually takes about three to six months depending on the complexity of the system and the amount of changes made to the system. "Rewriting" SAP will cause costly upgrade projects that will last for much longer periods.

OSS notes also introduce changes to SAP objects. These changes should be few if you keep installing the most recent Hot Packages or Legal Patches. If customers do implement OSS notes and later Hot Packages contain these notes, upon applying the Hot Package, the system will warn the user about the changes and usually return a changed object back to standard.

The SAP Workbench Organizer keeps track of all and any changes made to the system through version management. Another "Monitor for Modifications"

[handwritten: transport organizer]

utility will report on all changes made to SAP objects and can be accessed by executing transaction SE03. *[handwritten: SPDD]*

Transactions, such as SPAD and SPAU, will report all changes made to a system during an upgrade and Hot Package installations.

Enhancements

Enhancements are separate, added functionality to SAP objects allowed by SAP. Typically, without changing standard SAP objects, SAP defined special structures, such as user-exits for programs and append-structures for tables that assist developers to make consistent manageable changes to the SAP environment. These changes can then be migrated through the SAP release upgrade process. However, a large amount of testing will be required to ensure the enhancement functions as it was designed.

Added Custom Solutions *[handwritten: (create new objects)]*

Companies often develop their own custom solutions for SAP. Once again, SAP provides tools and structures to assist developers managing their projects. Custom projects are grouped together using development classes. These projects can then be migrated as single coherent entities using the Correction and Transport System to the QAS and PRD environment. These custom added enhancements will not be overwritten during the upgrade process, given that the developers did not create objects in the SAP name range. (Customer name ranges either begin with the letters Y or Z.)

Customer Exits

SAP provides user-exits throughout its code to enable developers to add additional functionality to SAP code without changing the standard SAP code. A user-exit is an empty program shell that developers can use to add their new code.

Application Exits *[handwritten: (SD)]*

Application exits are part of customizing to enable developers to enhance custom functionality. To view these exits, execute transaction **SPRO**, then follow menu path **Sales and Distribution, System Modifications, User Exits**. This will list a group of exits in the Sales and Distribution IMG. Selecting the user-exit—for example, credit checking—allows the developer to implement new methods to check the credit of an individual or company.

CTS—Correction and Transport System

The mechanics of the correction and transport system is discussed in much more detail in Chapter 8. This section will provide a brief overview of concepts related to CTS and how it relates to changes within the SAP system.

Multiple Development

SAP is a highly integrated system in which modules share objects, data, and functionality. A very simple example is one in which an object change in Sales and Distribution (SD) will likely be shared by the FI Financial Module. How do you coordinate multiple developments?

The CTS system is an attempt to coordinate this development process. When a developer changes an object, a lock is placed on the object with the name of the developer. This lock prevents other developers from changing it unless the owner of the lock allows another developer to share the lock using the CTS system. Thus, the CTS system coordinates multiple development changing shared objects in an orderly and consistent fashion.

Change Control

Change control is a set of procedures and rules put in place to manage changes in a production environment. In other words, it keeps track of who, how, when, and most importantly why changes were made to a system. It serves to protect the integrity of the application environment.

Users/Developers may not introduce uncoordinated changes into a production system directly. SAP uses three systems to manage change in the SAP environment: Integration (Development), Consolidation (Test/Quality), and Production. All new development is performed on the Integration system and these changes are registered in a change request under a developer's name. All the change requests are grouped together in a transport request. This transport containing all the changes is migrated to the Consolidation system, where it is tested. When all the errors are corrected, the changes migrate to the production system.

Some companies developed their own change control software within SAP to different degrees of success. A change control system should be able to document:

Who requested a change

The severity and priority of the change

Who analyzed this change and made suggestions on possible solutions

Who approved the solution

Who was assigned to make the changes

Who made the actual changes

Who tested the solution

How the solution was tested

Who approved that the solution should move to production

Version Management

SAP keeps versions of objects when changes are made, except when a system is upgraded or when Hot Packages are applied. The SAP owned objects will lose their versions and return to SAP standards. However, custom developed objects will keep versions during an upgrade or a Hot Package installation.

Version management facilitates change control and more importantly allows the system to revert to an older version of a changed object.

Naming Conventions—Customer Name Range

SAP ensures that any objects that adhere to the Customer Name Range will not be deleted or changed during an upgrade. As new naming conventions are continuously introduced by SAP in order to accommodate new structures and functionality, please check OSS for any notes.

Developer Registration

Only registered developers can make changes to SAP objects and create new objects. SAP keeps track of registered developers in the OSS system. This feature adds more security to the SAP system because it restricts the number of users that can make changes.

Object Registration (for SAP object)

SAP also keeps track of changes made to a customer system by forcing developers to register the changes they make to standard SAP objects. Registration of objects in the customer name range is not required. This feature also increases security and makes changes to the system visible.

ABAP Development Workbench

As mentioned previously, customers can take advantage of the tools provided by SAP to either enhance and extend the features of SAP functionality by using SAP provided "user-exits" or to develop and create their own application functionality.

The ABAP Development Workbench is a complete environment for developing and implementing SAP software, and it covers all stages of the software development lifecycle.

The ABAP Development Workbench includes:

◆ **ABAP Data dictionary.** Dictionary structures are described in the ABAP data dictionary as metadata. The metadata includes table and field definitions, value ranges and descriptions of the relationships between tables, internal structures of programs and their interfaces. The ABAP data dictionary is itself contained within the ABAP Repository. The ABAP Data dictionary is "active" in the sense that any changes made in the ABAP data dictionary automatically take effect immediately.

◆ **ABAP Repository.** Development objects such as ABAP programs, dictionary data, dynpros, documentation, and so on, are stored in the ABAP repository.

◆ **ABAP Repository information system.** All of the ABAP Development Workbench objects are stored in the ABAP repository. The ABAP repository information system is a collection of reports programs for viewing and evaluating these objects.

◆ **ABAP development tools:**

Screen Painter. The screen painter is used for displaying, modifying deleting or creating "dynpros" or screens. This tool supports field designation and arrangement, their attributes, and processing logic.

Menu Painter. The menu painter is used to assign functions implemented in programs to menus, push-buttons, and function keys.

ABAP Editor. The editor is not only used to edit and create programs, but it also offers other functions such as "where-used" functionality, data dictionary object navigation, yntax check, and online help.

Interactive program debugger. The debugger can be used to locate and rectify errors in programs and dynpros. It can also be used to insert interrupts or breakpoints within a program at execution. See the contents of fields, tables, and list any substitute values for these objects.

Computer Aided Test Tool (CATT). The CATT contains create, change, and delete functions to automate test procedures, including a record function to manually or automatically run and rerun test scenarios with variants and other variables.

Data Dictionary

As mentioned earlier, the data dictionary is made up of a number of objects to describe the structure of the data and views. Listed below are a number of the key objects with short descriptions.

◆ **Tables.** The idea of tables is central to the data dictionary, and the makeup of these structures can be envisioned as three layers. The upper-most layer being the table or structure, the next being the fields and data elements, and the final layer being the domains.

◆ **Fields and Data Elements**. A table is made up of a number of fields, and each of these fields refers to data elements, which describe the meaning of the field, such as headings, keywords, text, and so on.

◆ **Domains.** The data element is assigned to a domain which specifies the technical characteristics of the data element, such as data type, value, ranges, lengths, and so on.

◆ **View Tables.** The logical view of the tables and not the physical view as stored within the database Pool and Cluster Tables.

◆ **Pool tables.** A collection of logically related tables combined to create a larger table at the database level using table and field relationships. All records of all the tables are stored in the pool table.

◆ **Cluster tables.** A collection of logically related tables combined to create a larger table in the ABAP Dictionary. Logical rows from different cluster tables are linked in a single physical record. The records from the cluster tables are thus stored in a single cluster table.

◆ **Data Structures.** Data structures are very similar to tables except that they are created within programs, perhaps for internal calculations, data manipulation, and so on. The only difference is that no physical database tables exist or are generated—they only last the lifetime of the executed programs. However, the same domains and data elements can be used as utilized in tables.

◆ **Matchcodes.** Matchcodes are used as quick searches for one or more tables; for example, vendor and customer tables. The matchcodes are indexes to the original data, and can hold fields from one or more tables to provide quick and efficient searches.

Problem Resolution

Problem resolution is the action of finding the cause to a problem within SAP.

Problem resolution is an art, based on experience (knowledge of the system) and using the SAP OSS tools as your only tools used to assist with troubleshooting. For the extremely difficult problems, SAP provides the Remote Support and Early Watch services.

The *Remote Support* service is where SAP experts (with in-depth knowledge of the specific problem area) log onto your system and try to resolve problems. Depending on System type (i.e Production) and on the impact of your company's business, SAP will get involved as soon as possible.

◆ Ensure you have tried to solve the problem yourself by checking that the system is configured as SAP suggests, you have searched OSS and implemented potential fixes.

◆ Contact SAP and inform them of your problem as well as all the potential fixes you've implemented. This will assist them in making a decision to escalate a problem to a higher level of support.

◆ Use change control to implement the potential solutions.

The *Early Watch* service is a service SAP provides to identify potential system problems before they occur. The SAP "Experts" will log onto your system and gather statistics from the system for approximately a week. They will then analyze the data and prepare a report with recommendations for changes. Examples include adding more dialog processes, adding more memory, changing start-up profiles, changing your database file distribution, and so on.

Do not stop with an Early Watch report! SAP is a live and dynamic system, continuously tune and improve the system as needed.

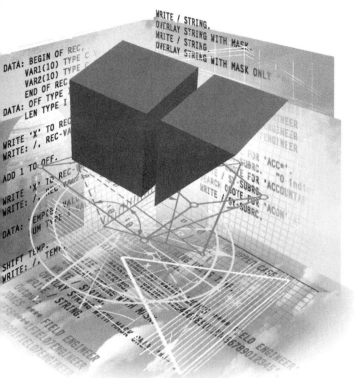

PART

II

Planning

2 The Administrator's Role in Installation Planning

3 R/3 System Strategies for Basis Administrators

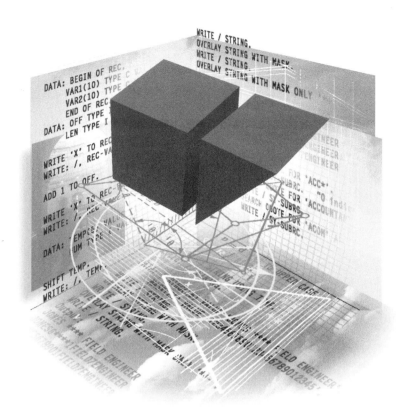

Chapter 2

The Administrator's Role in Installation Planning

In This Chapter

This chapter should pose some of the questions that you should ask yourself before selecting your hardware, operating system, and database to run the SAP application. Upon completion, you'll answer whether your selection is a scaleable, robust, and an SAP lifetime solution supported with the correct technical skill-set from your vendors and your Basis support team.

Hardware Requirements

Typically, the initial cost of the hardware is the first to impact the project budget and therefore the most visible upon the start of the SAP project. It is also the area in which the project will try to save money by under-sizing the machine in terms of CPUs, disk space, memory, application servers, raid/mirror setups, and so on.

The under-sizing of these machines is also a ploy used by *some* hardware vendors for you to purchase their hardware. For example, the more physical disk drives you have in your SAP hardware, the better performing system you will support as the data can be read or written on several disks simultaneously. So, hardware vendor A will provide you with a 10 x 3GB disk drive configuration that will perform to the machine's optimum capacity. However, vendor B will sell you a 5 x 6GB configuration and save you money. This would be a bad choice. Why? Even though the total capacity of the disk space is equal, the number of disk drives provided by vendor A will cost more, and when the system performs poorly and response times run into multiple seconds, the Basis administrator will be asked to perform miracles. All for a few hundred dollars savings!

It is in your best interest to be present when the hardware vendors present their SAP hardware solutions—you will be asked to support it!

more disk drives → better performance

Selecting Your Hardware Platform

The process of selecting hardware is analogous to purchasing a vehicle. Everyone has an opinion and everyone has a personal favorite. Also, you purchase a vehicle for specific needs and within your budget, but ultimately you (or your company) select what is right for your particular situation.

We will answer the question of which hardware is appropriate in typical consulting fashion by saying, "It depends!" Indeed, it depends on several factors.

Scope of the Implementation

Is SAP being implemented with a one-time "big bang" approach? Or are there a number of "phased" roll outs? If you are using the big bang approach, then you need most of your hardware capacity installed prior to the "go-live" date; but with the phased approach, you can upgrade the hardware as each phase is implemented.

Modules Being Implemented

The modules implemented also have an impact on the performance of the SAP system. For example, Sales and Distribution (SD) functions, reports, interfaces, and so on, all impact the performance of the system to a far greater extent than finance users due to the shear volume of data processing. You should talk to existing SAP customers about how they chose their hardware. Another possible resource is SAP and the QuickSizer tool.

Hardware Scalability & Lifetime

Is the hardware scaleable for future expansion and subsequent roll out of SAP and its "bolt-on" software?

Does the hardware vendor provide support once the hardware is no longer manufactured, and do they provide migration paths to larger and powerful servers?

Number of Users

If the implementation has users that total a couple hundred, then Windows NT will suffice; but for larger installations, UNIX/AS400/OS390 should be considered. In either case, as the number of users increases, you will need to add additional hardware.

Required System Landscape

Will the project require, as SAP recommends, a three-tier, three-system landscape (DEV, QAS, and PRD) or only a two-system landscape (DEV/QAS and PRD)? And will all servers need to be equal in capacity?

It is most probable that the development server (DEV) will not be the most powerful machine, as typically it is only accessed by the SAP technical and functional configurators (approximately 1 to 50 users would normally access this server).

QAS and PRD typically are comparable in size (DB) (except QAS does not have as many application servers as PRD). The QAS server is used to ensure that untested code, objects, and configuration changes do not enter the production environment without first being fully tested. A copy of the PRD system moved over to the QAS system should be performed on a regular basis to ensure that testing in QAS is comparable to making changes in PRD.

Figure 2-1 shows changes C+1, C+2, and C+3 moved from DEV to QAS, but only changes C+1 and C+3 are moved to PRD because C+2 did not function correctly. PRD is now out of synchronization with QAS. As more changes are moved to QAS and not to PRD, testing in the QAS environment will not reflect how the changes will behave in the present PRD environment. Therefore, a database copy is performed from PRD to QAS.

 NOTE

This operation does *not* have to be performed every time a change does not move to PRD—it is a judgment call. You can either perform this on a regular basis (weekly, monthly or quarterly) or on an ad-hoc basis.

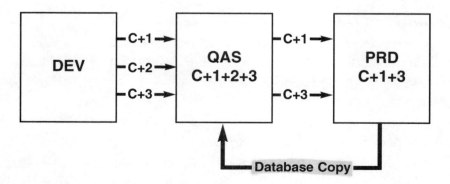

FIGURE 2-1 *Database copy procedure from PRD to QAS*

Selection of All Three Hardware Tiers

You may select a heterogeneous strategy, which means, for example, the presentation level may be any of the popular front-end operating systems (Windows based, MAC-OS, UNIX or Java) while the application servers are Microsoft Windows NT and the database servers are UNIX servers.

This may be a more cost-effective infrastructure as Windows NT servers as application servers are more economical than UNIX-based application servers.

Table 2-1 illustrates the types of hardware, operating systems, architecture, and databases supported by SAP for the presentation, application, and database servers.

Table 2-1

Presentation Java	Microsoft	OSF/Motif	Internet Browser Windows
Language	ABAP Objects	C / C++	
Database Informix	Microsoft SQL	Oracle	IBM DB2
Operating system Midrange	Microsoft NT	UNIX	
Hardware Architecture	Alpha / Intel	Compaq/ Digital UNIX	AS/400
/ Vendors IBM	ACER	HP-UX	
	Amdahl Bull	IBM-AIX	
	Compaq	Siemens UNIX	
	Data General	SUN - Solaris	
	DELL		
	Fujitsu		
	Hitachi		
	HP		
	Intergraph		
	IBM		
	ITAUTEC		

Table 2-1 *(Continued)*

Presentation Java	Microsoft	OSF/Motif	Internet Browser Windows
	Mitsubishi		
	NEC		
	NCR		
	Sequent		
	Siemens		
	Unisys		

Backup Solutions

What backup solutions are available for your backups? For example, HP-UX provides OmniBack and NetBackup solutions, whereas Windows NT has ArcServe and its own solutions. Determine which solutions are the most cost effective, reliable, and timely for your environment.

Vendor Support

You need to keep in mind a couple of questions: What levels of support does the vendor provide should a critical hardware component break down? What are the Service Level Agreements (SLA) the vendor provides?

Desire to Access SAP over the Internet

SAP provides an Internet transaction server (ITS), which will be used as a server to be accessed over the Internet. Taking advantage of this requires an additional Windows NT server for the ITS and hardware/software to provide firewall protection.

Skills of the IT Department

If your company is a UNIX shop, there's no reason why you should select the AS/400 as your hardware platform of choice. You should build upon the existing skills of the IT personnel.

Sizing Your Hardware

SAP has a number of simple formulas that will assist in sizing and establishing your hardware. SAP also provides a tool, the QuickSizer, which will assist in sizing the hardware and also provide details on the performance and workload expected on the servers. A detailed explanation of the QuickSizer tool is provided in Appendix B, "Understanding Ready-to-Run R/3."

Server Requirements

As mentioned earlier, each of the three-tier servers will have different requirements; for example, a UNIX database server should have large amounts of memory and CPU capacity as this is where the bulk of the work is performed. The CPU will be used to execute the code and the database will perform the reads/writes. These reads/writes are held in memory buffers to speed up the performance of the system. Another very important factor is disk space and disk access times.

The application server should also have large amounts of memory, as it will be used as a memory buffer for application-specific data. The application servers only require disk space for SAP operational overhead such as log, roll, and page files. The type of application server you define will determine the CPU resources you will require.

Dedicated batch servers typically require more CPU resources than a Dialog Application server. Presentation servers are standard PC, Macintosh, or UNIX workstations. SAP has recently announced that they plan to only support WIN32 and Java front-ends!

Obviously, if you set up standard workstations, it will be easier to support in terms of a familiar environment, office software connectivity, and SAPGUI maintenance.

 TIP

Ideally, you would like to get all the finance users to log on to a common application server so that all business logic and execution related to the finance users are buffered into the memory of that particular application server. Otherwise, data will be rolled in or out of the memory buffers for each application, degrading the performance of the server and consequently response times to the end users.

Please refer to Chapter 9 for more details on the setting up of logon and application balancing.

Presentation	Microsoft Windows	OSF/Motif	Internet Browser	Java	Mackintosh
Language	ABAP Objects		C/C++		Java
Database	Microsoft SQL1	Oracle	IBM DB2	Informix	Adabase
Operating System	Microsoft NT	UNIX		Midrange	Mainframe
Hardward Architecture/ Vendors	Alpha/Intel ACER Amdahl Bull Compaq Data General DELL Fujitsu Hitachi HP Intergraph IBM ITAUTEC Mitsubishi NEC NCR Sequent Siemens Unisys	Compac/Digital HP-UX IBM-AIX Siemens UNIX SUN-Solaris	UNIX	AS/400 IBM	S/390 IBM Amdahl Fujitsu Comparex Hitachi

FIGURE 2-2 *The database and application servers and the types of users logging on to the application servers*

Planning for Future Growth

The best method to plan for growth is to chart (record and graph) on a regular basis the amount of disk space usage and availability, CPU, batch processing, memory usage, number of users, and so on. This can be used as evidence that parameters require changing or more hardware may be required to speed up processes.

For example, if you see that certain buffers are continually paging data in and out and the parameters are set to their maximum limit and also that more new users are being added, it may be time to install a new application server. This will also assist in the logon-balancing procedure. Please see chapters 11 and 12 on system monitoring and performance to reveal usage and increase of resources requirements.

Software Requirements *(OS release)*

Software requirements need to be adhered to strictly, whether on the servers or the client, otherwise the SAP software will not perform as designed, and more importantly, not be supported by the SAP help desk. Typically, if you have functionality or technical problems and the SAP help desk reveals that you have incorrect software releases or patches, they will ask you to change the operating system and then reinstall the SAP software before they even look at the original problem.

Operating System Considerations

In SAP's installation manuals, you will see that each of the hardware has operating systems with certain release levels and kernel patches. You should also check OSS to see if there have been any changes made since the publication of the installation manual.

SAP may not support the latest release levels, and installing SAP on unauthorized release levels may cause errors during the installation process, and it will not be supported by SAP. For example, SAP for HP-UX, until recently, was supported for release level 10.x only, but now release 11.x has been approved for SAP operational use despite release 11.x being available for a number of months. SAP is also in the process of approving Windows NT 5 for operational use.

Selecting Your Database Server

Selecting your database, again, is a personal choice. If you have Informix skills in-house, select it as your database. There are minimal differences between the types of databases as far as the SAP software functionality is concerned; however, one database may have some advantages over others in terms of database through-put, administration, backups, and recovery.

If you (or your company) have decided that the SAP systems are to be outsourced or that you do not have any in-house database skills, the determining factor for the selection of your database will be your hardware selection and hardware vendor. For example, if you have selected HP/UNIX hardware, typically, you would select either the Oracle or Informix database. If you have selected the SP2/AIX hardware platform, you could select the DB2 or Oracle database. If you had selected the Windows NT environment, you could select the Microsoft SQL server or Oracle database.

Once you have selected your database and you begin your installation, you are required to use the SAP database CDs that were shipped with your SAP installation kit. These are the *only* release levels and versions that will function correctly with the SAP software. You are *not* to install or upgrade your database using CDs shipped by the database manufacturer (if you have done so, you will not be supported by SAP until the situation is rectified). Also, some of the available database functionality may not be used by SAP and therefore, should not be activated until you have checked on OSS or with your SAP Basis consultant.

Sizing Your Database

The disk space requirements are pretty strict during the UNIX/Oracle/SAP installation or upgrade, so you will have to check the installation or upgrade manuals for specific requirements. The installation manual may refer you to the SAPFS.TPL file in one of the installation or upgrade CDs for these requirements.

The other items that need to be factored when considering disk space requirements include the following:

◆ The amount of legacy system data migrated to the SAP system

◆ The amount of SAP activity on the system (transactions)

◆ The amount of nightly, weekly, and monthly batch processing

◆ The number of reports being produced nightly, weekly, and monthly

◆ The number of print jobs kept online within the SAP system

Laying Out Your Database

The layout of your database is another factor that will adversely affect your performance and response times if not configured correctly, and more importantly, might hinder a database recovery should a database crash occur.

In the ideal situation, each of the Sapdata files, Index files, control files, Saparch files, redo logs, and so on would be located on separate disk drives. For example, when data was written to a file, the corresponding index file could be written and/or updated on another disk drive and the logs written on yet another drive, thereby increasing performance.

Another item to consider before installing the SAP database is how to build adequate redundancy to prepare for the possibility of a database crash. SAP provides guidelines in the installation guides, which files should be mirrored, and which files should be Raid 5. The requisite redundancy may be achieved either at the database, the hardware, or the operating system level. Refer to Chapter 10 on the configuration of the database for more details.

Table 2-2 The file systems required for the Oracle database installation

File System Name	Description
/oracle/stage/stage_<xyz>	Installation and upgrade directory for database software
	(do not delete—used for ORACLE upgrades)
/oracle/<SAPSID>	Directory for ORACLE instance <SAPSID>
/oracle/<SAPSID>/origlogA	Original set A of redo logs
/oracle/<SAPSID>/origlogB	Original set B of redo logs
/oracle/<SAPSID>/mirrlogA	Mirrored set A of redo logs
/oracle/<SAPSID>/mirrlogB	Mirrored set B of redo logs
/oracle/<SAPSID>/saparch	Backup of redo logs
/oracle/<SAPSID>/sapreorg	Work direcory for database administration
/oracle/<SAPSID>/sapdata1	SAP data
/oracle/<SAPSID>/sapdata2	SAP data
:	SAP data
/oracle/<SAPSID>/sapdata<n>	SAP data

(Handwritten margin notes: "redo log" bracketing the origlog/mirrlog rows; "archive log" next to saparch; "data file" bracketing the sapdata rows)

As seen in Figure 2-3, and knowing that redo logs are written synchronously producing the highest I/O activity of all the database files, the redo logs (mirrored and non-mirrored) are placed on separate disk drives.

Also, it is recommended that /oracle/<SAPSID>/saparch should be placed on a separate disk as well. This is where the SAP/database logs are written if the archive log mode option has been set up. This option should be set in the production environment.

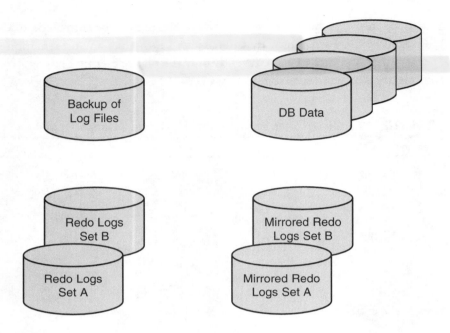

FIGURE 2-3 *Optimal SAP file system setup and distribution*

Selecting Your Application Server

If your application server is of the same type as the database server, the setup is referred to as Homogenous System, but if it is another hardware/operating system, it is referred to as a Heterogeneous System. For example, an HP-UX database and application servers are a Homogenous System setup, but if the database is HP-UX and the application server is Windows NT, then it is a Heterogeneous System setup.

Whatever your choice, you can set up the application servers to perform specific tasks; for example, online users, batch processing, background processing, application specific users, and so on. The most important factor is to have a very large amount of memory to optimize performance and load-balance.

Selecting Your Presentation Server

You have several options for your presentation server (desktop PCs), which may be incorporated with your corporate standards.

SAP adopted the strategy to only support the SAPGUI written for JAVA and WIN32. The GUI written in JAVA enables you to select any presentation server platform that supports JAVA. Currently only the platforms that have a GUI interface specifically developed for it—Windows based systems, Macintosh systems and UNIX based workstations.

Networking Requirements

For any SAP system setup, there is a number of networking requirements to ensure optimum network through-put for your Local Area Network and Wide Area Network, but also connectivity to the SAP OSS system.

LAN Considerations

For optimum performance and response times, it is wise to follow SAP's recommendations for your SAP system's LAN setup. For example, provide SAP with its own LAN, and have the database and application servers reside in close proximity, connected by the LAN and fiber optic (FDDI) or Fast Ethernet—as most network traffic occurs between the database and application server, it makes sense that a larger capacity connection be used.

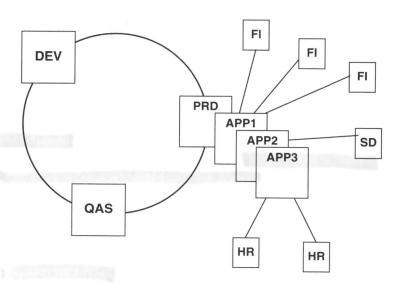

FIGURE 2-4 *A conceptual LAN setup in which the presentation servers log on to a specific application server, which in turn optimizes SAP execution and response times*

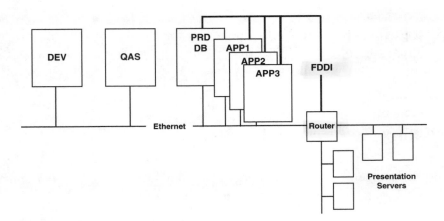

FIGURE 2-5 *An actual LAN server setup*

The LAN components of the SAP system are the following:

- ◆ **TCP/IP.** A network protocol is required to route network traffic and give each piece of equipment a unique address. These will be used during the setup of the SAP systems and are in the form xxx.xxx.xxx.xxx (for example, 141.234.22.12).

- ◆ **Ethernet.** This is the infrastructure used to transport the network data. However, there are limitations to the capacity that Ethernet can support—regular Ethernet has a capacity of 10MBps (megabytes per second) but new technology breakthroughs have allowed the development of Fast Ethernet, which runs at speeds up to 100MBps.

- ◆ **FDDI** or **Fiber Optic.** FDDI / Fiber Optic cables have an upper transfer rate of 100MBps, similar to the 100MBps Ethernet, but have an overwhelming advantage over Ethernet in that it is immune to electromagnetic interference that can occur with copper Ethernet cables. FDDI is typically used to connect the database server and application server for a large amount of data transfer that occurs between these servers.

Commonly, the presentation servers are connected to the application servers using 10MBps Ethernet, and the application server is connected to the database using either FDDI or the 100MBps Ethernet (your router will need to support either one of these connections). You may even opt to use Dual FDDI ring, in which if one of the FDDI LAN rings has an error, the other LAN will take over the communication between the servers.

WAN Considerations

Access to the SAP systems may be configured using either dial-up connections or through the Internet. For dial-up connections, users will have to input a network identification name and password before they are allowed access to the SAP systems. This network protection creates a certain amount of protection to the SAP environment. For Internet connections, the SAP systems will be required to be accessible over the Internet, which may make them vulnerable to attack from hackers. To provide protection against these types of attacks, firewalls must be placed between the SAP systems and the Internet. When configured correctly, the SAP system will be inaccessible to unwelcome visitors but readily available to your company's employees.

Figure 2-6 shows three methods to access SAP over large distances: a dial-up line, the Internet, and a dedicated line for remote offices.

SAP has introduced several new technologies that may require additional WAN bandwidth. One of the technologies is ALE (application link enabling), which allows separate SAP systems running different modules to communicate and update each system's respective data and databases. Anticipated ALE transfers need to be taken into account when sizing your WAN connections.

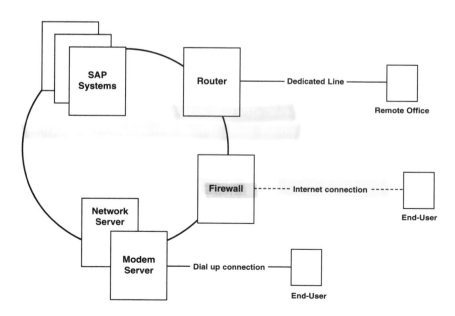

FIGURE 2-6 *The three methods to access SAP*

SAP also supports Idoc/EDI technology (with SAP-certified third-party software from Harbinger, Sterling, and other vendors), which requires special EDI connectivity from EDI VAN (value-added network) providers, such as GEIS (General Electric Information Service) from General Electric. These technologies are discussed in great detail in Appendix A.

Remote Support Connections

As part of the installation of your SAP system, you are required to provide a connection from your SAP systems to either SAPSERV4 in the United States or SAPSERV3 in Europe. The line is installed on one of your SAP systems (usually DEV) and is used to do the following:

◆ Log on to Online SAP Services (OSS) to check SAP corrections (OSS Notes), availability of SAP courses, log SAP problems, and so on.

◆ Download SAP Hot Packages or Legal Patches (you may only apply Hot packages OR legal patches—not both). They are a collection of SAP corrections that need to be applied to your SAP system after the completion of the SAP software.

Business Information Warehouse patches are applied to the separate BIW server independent of the SAP system.

◆ Allow SAP access to your SAP system for remote consulting. If there is a problem that cannot be rectified by applying OSS notes, you may open the line to allow SAP into your environment to examine the problem and provide a solution.

The most common type of wide area connection that is used and recommended by SAP is either through a Frame Relay connection or ISDN connectivity, available from most long distance telecommunications carriers. Support for X.25 connections is slowly being phased out by SAP in certain countries.

The Internet may be used as a connection but is not recommended by SAP because not all of the functions are supported. If you use the Internet, you will be required to input an ID and password. (This ID can only be created using a regular Frame Relay or ISDN connection!)

Resource Requirements

From an SAP Basis standpoint, the number of Basis resource requirements on the projects is subject to the number of SAP systems, the time frame of the project, the amount of data migration required before the go-live date, and the internal workings of your company.

For example, if the project is an **SAP ASAP** implementation, then the OS, database, and SAP administration may be performed by one person and the security by another person. On the other hand, if the project is a global implementation, then each activity may be performed by a different person or a team of administrators.

Figure 2-7 shows an implementation team for an ASAP implementation: a module expert for each SAP application being implemented, an ABAP resource, and a Basis resource all being managed by the project manager. This team setup can also be used to support the SAP system post implementation.

Figure 2-8 shows an implementation team for a large or global SAP implementation. Each application and technical area has a team leader and a number of people reporting to that leader, depending on the size of the implementation. The Basis roles may be broken down the following way:

- ◆ Operating system administrator
- ◆ Database administrator
- ◆ R/3 administrator
- ◆ Security administrator

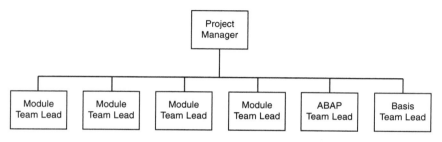

FIGURE 2-7 *Implementation team for an ASAP implementation*

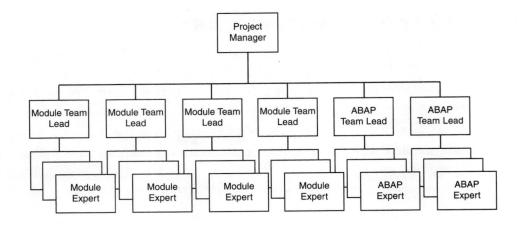

FIGURE 2-8 *Implementation team for a large or global SAP implementation*

Identifying Personnel Roles

Roles and responsibilities may be broken down and defined to whatever level your company's resources are able to support. For example, in a small SAP pre/post implementation support team, a single Basis resource would perform operating system, database, and SAP duties. In larger support teams, the previous activities may be performed by three separate individuals. The following is a breakdown for some of the activities performed by administrators.

Operating System Administrator

The SAP operating system administrator's primary role is to manage and support the UNIX operating system and to ensure that all operating system tasks perform to their optimal capacity. The administrator should also apply patches and releases only when they are supported by the SAP software (please check OSS for release and patches release levels)

The following courses are recommended for the SAP operating system administrator:

Course	Description
SAP020	SAP Overview
SAP040	SAP Architecture

SAP050	SAP Basis Overview
BC310/14/17/60/61/70	Technical Core Competence
BC315	SAP Workload Analysis
BC325	Workbench Organization and Transportation System
BC505/10/11/20/25	Database Administration

The necessary skills for the operating system administrator:

◆ Expert knowledge of the operating system (UNIX, Windows NT, AS400, etc.)

◆ Good knowledge of databases (Oracle, Informix, Windows SQL, DB2, etc.)

◆ Good SAP Basis knowledge

◆ Good knowledge of SAP system administration

◆ Good knowledge of SAP correction and transport

The major responsibilities of the operating system administrator:

◆ Assist in SAP upgrades

◆ Design, implement, and test SAP backup and recovery procedures

◆ Monitor and tune SAP, the operating system, and the hardware

◆ Document SAP operating system standards, policies, and procedures

◆ Document SAP operating system security policies and procedures

SAP Database Administrator

The SAP database administrator's primary role is to manage and support the SAP database system.

The administrator should also apply patches and releases only when they are supported by the SAP software (please check OSS for release and patches release levels).

The following courses are recommended for the SAP database administrator:

Course	Description
SAP020	SAP Overview
SAP040	SAP Architecture

SAP050	SAP Basis Overview
BC310/14/17/60/61/70	Technical Core Competence
BC315	SAP Workload Analysis
BC325	Workbench Organization and Transportation System
BC505/10/11/20/25	Database Administration

The necessary skills for the SAP database administrator:

◆ Good knowledge of the operating system (UNIX, Windows NT, AS400, etc.)

◆ Expertise with databases (Oracle, Informix, Windows SQL, DB2, etc.)

◆ Good SAP Basis knowledge

◆ Good knowledge of SAP system administration

◆ Good knowledge of SAP correction and transport system

◆ Good knowledge of SAP system monitoring and tuning

The major responsibilities of the SAP database administrator:

◆ Perform table and tablespace maintenance

◆ Assist in SAP upgrades

◆ Provide support for new table definitions

◆ Provide support for the data dictionary

◆ Provide support for archiving and database reorganization

◆ Design, implement, and test SAP backup and recovery procedures

◆ Monitor and tune SAP, operating system, database, and hardware

◆ Document SAP database standards, policies, and procedures

◆ Document SAP database security policies and procedures

SAP System Administrator

The SAP system administrator's primary role is to manage the operation and support of the SAP system and its peripheral components, such as interfaces and data migration. The administrator should also apply patches and releases provided by the SAP software.

The following courses are recommended for the SAP system administrator:

Course	Description
SAP020	SAP Overview
SAP040	SAP Architecture
SAP050	SAP Basis Overview
BC305	System Administration
BC310/14/17/60/61/70	Technical Core Competence
BC315	SAP Workload Analysis
BC325	Workbench Organization and Transportation System
BC340	Going Live
BC505/10/11/20/25	Database Administration

The necessary skills for the SAP System Administrator:

◆ Good knowledge of the hardware (HP, Compaq, AS400, etc.)

◆ Good knowledge of networking (TCP/IP, Novell, etc.)

◆ Good knowledge of the operating system (UNIX, Windows NT, AS400, etc.)

◆ Good knowledge of databases (Oracle, Informix, Windows SQL, DB2, etc.)

◆ SAP Basis knowledge

◆ Good knowledge of SAP system administration

◆ Good knowledge of SAP correction and transport

◆ Good knowledge of SAP system monitoring and tuning

The major responsibilities of the SAP system administrator:

◆ Install and maintain server hardware

◆ Establish and maintain network configuration and communication

◆ Install and maintain peripheral devices (dial-up, Internet, etc.)

◆ Perform operating system install, upgrades, and patches

◆ Maintain file systems

◆ Install, upgrade, and maintain SAP servers for the complete landscape

◆ Install and configure SAP printers

◆ Create initial user IDs for operating system, database, and SAP

◆ Create and maintain SAP clients

◆ Design, implement, and test SAP backup and recovery procedures

◆ Install third-party hardware/software interfacing with SAP

◆ Monitor and tune SAP, operating system, database, and hardware

◆ Design, set up, and support the SAP correction and transport system

◆ Document SAP administration standards, policies, and procedures

◆ Create and publish forms and change documents

◆ Provide technical support to business process teams

◆ Develop problem resolution procedure for application and technical problems and become single point of contact for SAP hotline

SAP Security Administrator

The SAP security administrator's primary role is to assist in the development and to manage SAP and its components' security.

The following courses are recommended for the SAP security administrator:

Course	Description
SAP020	SAP Overview
SAP040	SAP Architecture
CA010	SAP Authorization Concepts
BC310/14/17/60/61/70	Technical Core Competence
BC325	Workbench Organization and Transportation System

The necessary skills for the SAP security administrator:

◆ Basic knowledge of the hardware (HP, Compaq, AS400, etc.)

◆ Basic knowledge of networking (TCP/IP, Novell, etc.)

◆ Basis knowledge of the operating system (UNIX, Windows NT, AS400, etc.)

◆ SAP Basis knowledge

◆ SAP system administration

◆ SAP system monitoring

◆ SAP authorizations concepts

The major responsibilities of the SAP security administrator:

- ◆ Document SAP security policies and procedures
- ◆ Create and publish forms and change documents
- ◆ Create and maintain operating system user policies
- ◆ Create and maintain network, dial-up, or Internet access policies
- ◆ Create and maintain database user policies
- ◆ Create and maintain SAP user policies
- ◆ Create and maintain SAP authorizations and profiles
- ◆ Create and maintain interface/data files policies and procedures
- ◆ Analyze and resolve security issues

Outsourcing

Outsourcing is an option that many companies have taken in recent months. You can outsource your SAP environment in a number of ways, including the following:

- ◆ **Outsourcing the hardware.** The SAP systems may reside either in your data center or on a vendor's site, whereas the day-to-day activities are managed by the outsourcing company. These activities include maintenance of the hardware, operating systems, patches and upgrades; database administration (backups and restores), SAP system performance data capture, and so on.

- ◆ **Outsourcing the hardware and Basis support.** This is an extension to the previous scenario except that the outsourcing company also provides Basis support. The Basis resources are responsible for installing and upgrading servers, installing and upgrading all software, applying SAP Hot Packages, applying OSS notes, system backups and recovery, resolving performance issues, and monitoring the systems—basically, all Operating System, database and SAP administration. Ideally, SAP security should be controlled (access) by the client, but the mechanics (profile setup) may be part of the SAP administration.

- ◆ **Outsourcing the hardware as well as technical and application support.** The most extensive option is not only to outsource the hardware but also your technical and application support. This option allows clients to focus on core competence (their business) without having to worry about training and transferring their staff from their business into an SAP support role. This option also provides clients with the knowledge that employees, once trained on SAP, will not be recruited away by SAP headhunters.

Installation Planning Checklist

The following is a checklist of steps you will be required to perform for the planning of the hardware installation. Several of these operations will be covered in subsequent chapters in greater detail. However, they have been included in this checklist, with a small description, to provide a sequence of events.

Complete Technical Questionnaire

Create a technical questionnaire to size the SAP system in advance with your hardware vendors. Also, ask for a Ready to Run solution if your project fits the model. Refer to Appendix B for more details on Ready-to-Run solutions.

When sizing hardware, consider the following parameters:

◆ Scalability

◆ Current life cycle for the hardware

◆ Conditions and deliveries for urgent hardware patches, fixes, and enhancements

◆ Hardware Support and Service Level Agreement with the hardware vendor

Size Hardware

With assistance from your hardware partner, begin to size the systems using data gathered from the project manager. Each system (DEV, QAS, PRD, TRN, etc.) will have different requirements. The hardware may also be delivered at different phases of the project. Consider the following:

◆ Presentation Level:

Workstation configuration for network connectivity and office products

◆ Application Level:

Scalability (memory, CPU, disk space)

Memory sizing

◆ Database Server Level:

Scalability (memory, CPU, disk space)

Memory sizing

Database disk distribution

Growth path for the database server

Backup utility and media

Language and time zone dependencies

SAP software customizing requirements

SAP enhancement requirements

Data migration requirements

SAP interface requirements

SAP system growth

Migration paths to more powerful servers

Determine Technical Infrastructure Needs

Determine the technical requirements for your implementation at all three levels—presentation, application, and database server—including the network load in the system and on the various network, remote OSS, and printing components.

Procure Hardware and Network Connection

After you have determined your system and infrastructure needs, and the project has been approved by your project manager and checked by your hardware provider, go ahead and order the initial hardware (you may add components later or have systems delivered at different times during your project) and your remote network connection.

System Landscape

Determine the type of landscape required for implementation, following SAP's recommendation of a three-tier, three-system landscape, with presentation, application, and database servers for each of the development, quality assurance, and production systems.

System Purpose

You also may include other systems in the mix, such as a training system, a sandbox system, or a fire-fighting system.

System Names

Define the names of each system; for example, DEV, QAS, and PRD, or you could use a mix of alphanumeric characters such as TR1 (train1) or SB2 (sandbox2) or FF1 (fire-fighting 1). The choice is mainly yours to make, but there are certain three-character names reserved, which you may not use, such as C11 and SAP. A complete list of reserved names is provided in the Installation guide.

Client Strategy

Define client architecture for the system landscape:

A *client* is an organizationally independent unit within an system. Clients have their own separate data environment, including the following:

- Global, client-independent customizing settings
- Client-dependent customizing settings
- Repository objects
- Application data (such as master data and transactional records)
- User master records

Client types (commonly required client types):

- Development client
- Quality assurance and testing client
- Client for pre-production data
- Production client
- Fire-fighting client
- Training client
- Sandbox client

Distribute clients to the system landscape:

Clients within the same system share certain central resources, such as a number of global customizing settings and the ABAP repository, so care must be taken with the following:

- Changing of client-independent customizing settings
- Development and modification of repository objects
- Security of critical data

Client numbers:

Each client within a single system is required to have a unique, three-digit client number for identification purposes. Reserved clients are the following:

- **Client 000** is the standard SAP client used to store defaults for all tables and sample organizational data. This client is updated during every system and release upgrade, and because of this you must not work in this client.
- **Client 001** is also a standard SAP client and is simply a copy of client 000. Client 001 should be *copied* to generate other clients.
- **Client 066** is used for EarlyWatch services only (logins are disabled).

Client attributes (attributes that need to be established for each client):

- Category
- Changes and transports for client-dependent objects
- Client-independent object changes
- Restrictions

Transport System Strategy

Chapter 8 provides more details on the setup and configuration of the Transport system.

Formalize the process between the developers, application experts, and the Basis staff on the transporting of changes and development. Change request management is the only procedure for maintaining any system landscape, both for the importing of changes into each client and for the testing and quality assurance verification in each client or system.

There are four stages for the transport process, with an additional stage included for control and change management process:

- Release of a change request
- Import into the quality assurance environment
- Verification of quality assurance testing
- Import into other clients or systems
- Imports into production are performed with the correct sign-off from the module lead and project manager.

User authorization and ownership prevents others from releasing change requests for which they are not responsible.

SAP Software Release Strategy

Even though SAP may have that last release of software available, typically companies do not use that release until it has been tried and tested. For example, Version 4.0 was released, followed by release 4.0A, 4.0B and 4.5A in relatively short time. Therefore, a number of companies decided that they would implement 3.1I first and upgrade to version 4.5B when it stabilizes.

Therefore, it is important to anticipate, plan for, and define a strategy for the projected timeline for installations, maintenance, and major release upgrades (which would include both correction and functionality release upgrades). You should define a detailed strategy that includes the following:

- ◆ Understanding the type of installs and upgrade
- ◆ Understanding installing and upgrading of all systems within the system landscape
- ◆ Understanding the projected downtime
- ◆ Understanding the project application and post application activities
- ◆ Understanding the appropriate skill sets required for an installation and upgrade

Summary

This chapter should assist you in the decision-making process of selecting your hardware platform, operating systems, database type, SAP system setup, SAP landscape, and helped you understand the consequences for selecting that particular hardware. Also, it should provide you with a sequence of events that need to be followed to set up your SAP environment, including Dev, QAS, and PRD systems.

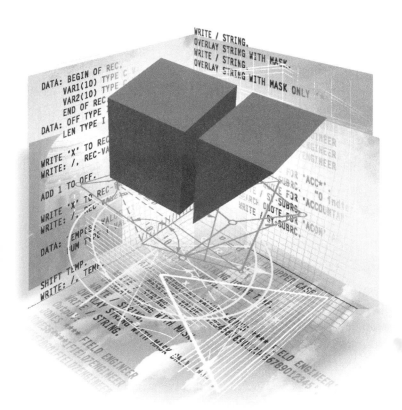

Chapter 3

R/3 System Strategies for Basis Administrators

In This Chapter

◆ System Landscapes

◆ Client Strategy Best Suited for the System Landscape

◆ How to Manage "Rolling Releases"

As a Basis administrator you will be called upon to design and implement an R/3 system landscape and architecture with varying hardware resources. You will be faced with decisions to distribute different data environments to different clients in the system landscape and will have to decide on a one-, two-, or three-system landscape. This chapter considers the decisions you will need to make to plan the architecture of the various R/3 system environments. It also discusses the management of a multi-release implementation.

The questions you are faced with initially are as follows:

◆ How many R/3 systems will be needed and what function will each perform in the system landscape?

◆ How many clients will be needed by each R/3 system?

◆ What role will each client play in the system landscape?

The implementation of SAP must first begin with the definition of the SAP systems and clients. This is done in order to bring an implementation to a productive state. The systems themselves form what is called the *system landscape*. Clients are then distributed in this landscape. It is recommended that the three-system landscape—dedicating one system to development activities, another to quality assurance testing, and another for the actual production environment—be used as the model for all implementations. In some installations where more than one phase of the implementation is taking place simultaneously, more systems are necessary.

The setup of the system landscape requires a well-defined strategy. Once the system landscape has been established and all the clients exist, all changes need to be distributed utilizing the correction and transport system (CTS).

When you are establishing a landscape strategy, the following issues need to be considered:

- How secure will the productive data need to be?
- What system performance will be expected?
- Will system administration and downtime be a concern?
- Will there be a need for extensive quality assurance and testing?
- Will there be ongoing development after reaching a productive state?

System Landscapes

To answer these questions, this section will review the three different landscape options:

- Single-system
- Two-system
- Three-system

Single-System Landscape (3 Clients)

In this scenario you will have a client dedicated to development and customizing. There will be a separate quality assurance client and production client. This might appear to be a cost-effective configuration, with lower hardware cost and fewer administrative costs. But in the long term, because of the problems and limitations associated with this configuration, the initial savings will be lost.

The following limitations will apply:

- Changes to client-independent or repository objects will affect the whole environment, regardless of where the changes are made. Therefore, changes are tested in the run-time environment of the production environment.
- The performance of the system affects all clients.
- The system administrator is unable to upgrade a non-production system.
- The production data is assessible from the development environment.

This scenario places many limitations on further development and the possible upgrade to a higher release of SAP.

Two-System Landscape

A *two-system landscape* allows development and production to be formed on two separate instances. The two instances should be on two separate machines separating the two environments.

TIP

It is possible to run two instances of SAP on the same UNIX platform, but this is not recommended.

There's one significant disadvantage:

◆ The development and quality assurance testing must still take place on the same development environment. This presents a problem, as all objects transported to production immediately become productive.

There are also a couple of distinct advantages:

◆ Production performance is not affected by the other clients.

◆ Development activities take place independent of the production environment.

Three-System Landscape

A *three-system landscape* meets the needs of most environments and is the landscape most commonly used. In a three-system landscape like the one shown in Figure 3-1, new development can take place without affecting the production environment. Upgrades can be performed without restrictions, and the quality assurance system allows for integration testing of developments before they are promoted to production.

Advantages include:

◆ Production data is secure, because security will prevent access to sensitive data and client settings will prevent the unauthorized changing of data.

◆ Production performance is not affected by other clients, because there is only one production client.

◆ Development is verified before being transported to production.

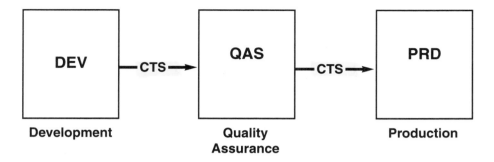

FIGURE 3-1 *The three-system landscape*

Disadvantages include:

◆ There is an increase in hardware requirements.

◆ There is tremendous system maintenance overhead.

Client Strategy Best Suited for the System Landscape

Once the system landscape has been established, you have to decide on the *client strategy*. For the purposes of this discussion, you should assume that the three-system landscape has been chosen.

The Development Environment

The *development environment* will essentially always be the first system to be implemented when a project is started. The development box will be the sandbox for the project, where most users will get their first hands-on experience before an implementation of SAP.

The Development System (aka consolidation)

There are two conventions used to describe the system layout in SAP: the SAP AG convention and the SAP USA convention. The three systems in the SAP AG convention are known as the Integration, Consolidation, and Recipient systems.

(delivery)

The SAP USA convention uses Development, Quality Assurance, and Production to identify the three systems in the landscape. The SAP USA version is used by the authors in this book.

The first step in creating a development environment is to copy client 001 to a user—defined client. For the purpose of this chapter, choose client 700 as the first customer—defined client. As most of the development work, customizing, and initial unit testing is performed in the development environment, the best approach is to separate these activities into separate clients. The four-client development environment is ultimately the most effective combination. Create a new client 700 via a client copy and use client 001 as the source client. This new client will become known as the Customizing client. Once client 700 has been created, you will create the other three clients, which will form the basis of your development environment. The clients will be known as client 725 quality assurance client, 750 ABAP development client, and 775 business process client.

Because a client represents a commercially and organizationally independent unit, with its own customizing, master data, and user master records, a four-client approach like this allows the different areas of the project to pursue their own goals in there own independent environments.

Client 700—Customizing

Golden client

This client is where all the client independent customizing and client settings should take place. This client is where all change requests will originate and eventually be used to seed the quality assurance and production environment in your three-system landscape. No transactional or master data should be loaded into this client. Figure 3-2 illustrates a typical client setup for this client.

Client 725—Quality Assurance

This client is where all unit testing will take place before a unit of work is promoted to the quality assurance system. The data conversion team will use this client to exercise dry runs of their conversion programs. The Basis team would typically use this client as a source client to refresh the development and business process clients as required. The configuration leads would be responsible for keeping the configuration up to date by copying their configuration down from client 700, utilizing internal client copies. Only business process transactions should be performed in this client.

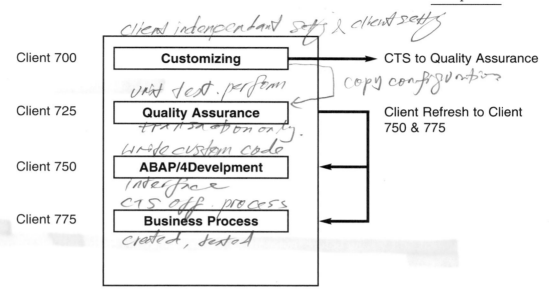

FIGURE 3-2   *A client setup for a development environment*

Client 750—ABAP Development

This client is provided for the development team to write custom code and inter-faces that will be used to interface with the legacy systems. This client will be refreshed from client 725 on a regular basis. This will ensure that the development team will have the latest version of the configuration with which to test their development. The decision as to how often the client is refreshed should be made by all the players on the project team.

If the developers should require client-independent system changes to be made, the designated configuration lead should perform these changes in client 700. As most development work is client-independent, the reports and conversion pro-grams can be unit tested in the quality assurance or business process client.

 TIP

The Basis team leads should try to have a process in place as soon as possible so that the development teams are aware of the advantages of regular refreshes.

Client 775—Business Process

This client is utilized by the business process team and is where all the different business processes are created and unit tested. The CTS is switched off so the system does not generate any change requests.

Once the business process has been agreed upon, the configuration lead will configure the relevant IMG changes in the customizing client 700 and manually transport the changes to the quality assurance client.

Essentially, the above-mentioned client strategy will give the development and business process team the ability to develop and test their processes in independent environments. The suggested client strategy will, however, allow for integrated unit testing before transporting the developments to the quality assurance system. This is also a means of keeping the various environments updated with the latest agreed-upon business process.

The Quality Assurance Environment (aka Consolidation)

Once the integration testing phase of the project has been entered, an environment to test the development needs to be established. The quality assurance environment is where acceptable levels of quality assurance and testing can be achieved. The quality of proposed customer developments can be validated for consistency, and the effect on performance can be assessed before promoting work to the production environment.

The quality assurance system typically is built from a copy of the customizing client in the development environment. The recommendation here is to have at least two clients: a master copy client and a quality assurance client. The master copy client will have no user master records and will be used to refresh the quality assurance client. The quality assurance client would be refreshed during integration testing phases before promoting a logical unit of work to production. An extra client can be utilized if conversion testing is needed.

The Production Environment (aka Recipient)

The production environment is the final system in your landscape. This is where the company actually conducts its business transactions. This environment will consist of only one client, and all transactions will take place here. The production environment is built by installing SAP on the system that will support the production environment. The development and customizing that was created in the development environment and tested in the quality assurance environment will be transported via CTS, into the production system. The data conversion team will run any data conversions needed, the interface team will connect any legacy interfaces. The security team will ensure that the relevant user profiles have been created. This will conclude the phases needed to bring an SAP system productive.

How to Manage "Rolling Releases"

In larger organizations in which the company has decided to implement SAP, the approach of implementing SAP in one huge project is undesirable. The organization will probably be broken up into separate business units, and a small portion of the business will be chosen as the initial introduction point of the SAP implementation. This approach presents a number of challenges to the system administrator.

Typically, the project will be divided into phases, and the first phase of the implementation will go productive. Phase 1 consists of the three-system landscape, which becomes the production support environment. If a problem is experienced in production, it is fixed in the development environment, tested in the quality assurance environment, and finally moved to production.

As the second phase of the project gets underway, a dilemma may arise—namely, the scope of the second phase may require that new functionality and more master data be added to the existing productive system. If these changes are introduced to the current production support environment, you will not have a stable development environment to fix any current production problems.

The suggested approach to this problem is to create an additional development and quality assurance environment. These environments will be seeded from the current production system to ensure that the second phase is based on the current production environment. These two new systems form part of the CTS landscape. To ensure that the two environments are kept separate, the CTS bridge is not switched on between the Phase 2 development environment and the current production environment. The Phase 2 developers and configuration team continue with their second-phase work in the development environment. They have a quality assurance system to do integration testing of the Phase 2 work. Once the project team is satisfied that Phase 2 is ready to move to production, the development and configuration can be moved to the production support

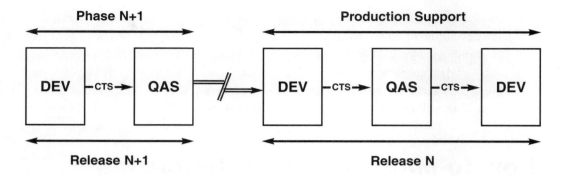

FIGURE 3-3   *System and client layout for rolling release*

environment on the designated go-live date. Once the production system is upgraded with the second phase, the third phase can be started on the development stream once again, and the whole process can be repeated until all the phases of the project have been completed. Figure 3-3 illustrates the system and client layout for rolling releases.

In conclusion, this model will be costly to administer and you will essentially need two teams of support personnel to support this model. The advantage of using this strategy is that it will accommodate the phasing in of SAP into a company as opposed to the big bang approach. The experience gained by the initial project team can be leveraged to improve and speed up the implementation of the remaining phases. This approach allows for changes and improvements in the initial process design. These changes will only affect a small part of the company's daily business operations and can be remedied before the whole organization is moved onto SAP.

To ensure that data is consistent in all environments, Application Link Enabling (ALE) can be used to keep all the development and quality assurance clients with all the latest production data. As the production environment grows, the ability to refresh the development environment via client copies will become increasingly difficult. The "database copy" process discussed in Chapter 11 will have to be utilized to refresh the clients.

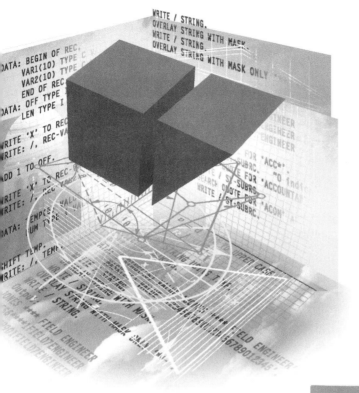

PART III

Installation

4 An Administrator's Guide
to Installing R/3

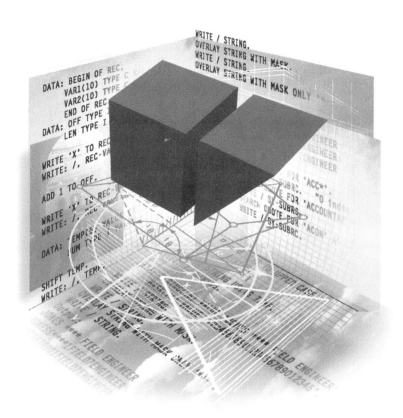

Chapter 4

**An Administrator's
Guide to Installing
R/3**

In This Chapter

- UNIX Operating System and Hardware Preparation
- R/3 Installation Tools
- Installing the Database Software
- Network Installation
- The Languages Your System Will Speak
- SAP OSS Messages
- SAP Service Connection
- Online Correction Support

In this chapter we'll discuss real-world experiences that the Basis Administrator may encounter during the installation of an SAP system. We'll attempt to list the steps involved in installing SAP on some of the many hardware platforms supported by SAP, but please be aware that differences will exist based upon each new release.

UNIX Operating System and Hardware Preparation

This section will primarily cover installations performed on UNIX based platforms. Please keep in mind that the steps required to perform an installation could vary greatly depending upon each new SAP major or minor release, and each vendor's specific hardware platform. This is not meant as a substitute or replacement for SAP provided installation documentation.

Always review the SAP provided documentation carefully, as well as any SAP recommended OSS notes before beginning the installation. It's advisable to also consult and engage an SAP Basis consultant for any installation that might be complex or difficult. SAP Basis consultants can provide a direct link to the developers in Waldorf for assistance in resolving difficult installation issues.

Installation Steps

In this section you'll learn some of the installation steps required to install SAP. You'll begin by looking at the major areas listed here:

- Choose SAP System Name (SID)
- Copy SAP Installation Software
- Set up SWAP Space
- Describe SAP System in /etc/sapconf
- Prepare File Systems
- Check Available Space in File Systems
- Create Unix Groups and Users
- Copy R/3 and Oracle Software from CD
- Modify Profiles and File Permissions
- Check and Modify UNIX Kernel

Choose SAP System Name

Choosing the SAP system name can be any alphanumeric, three-character name, with a few exceptions. Try to select something meaningful for your specific system environment. The system ID may not begin with a numeric character, and any alpha characters have to be uppercase (i.e. <SID> may be chosen as SAP System name).

Some reserved names that you may not use are:

ADD	ALL	AND	ANY	ASC	B20
B30	BCO	BIN	FOR	GID	INT
KEY	NOT	OFF	OMS	P30	RAW
SHG	SID	UID	SAP	COM	EPS
MON	SET	SGA	VAR	DBA	END

Copy Installation Software from CD

The steps for copying the installation software from the CD remain fairly consistent across platforms. SAP has created a format called CAR for compressing the installation software. During the SAP installations I was involved with, copying the CDs to disk gave me the advantage that all the data is available, and you do not have to swap CDs every once in a while. This is only true if you are able to mount only one CD. Some companies have hardware that can mount multiple CDs at the same time.

The following example shows the steps required for installing on a HP-UX platform. While logged on as root, issue the following commands to mount the CD and begin running the install:

```
mkdir/tmp/install
chmod 777/tmp/install
mkdir/sapcd
mount/dev/dsk/ctd0/sapcd
ll/sapcd
cd/tmp/install
/sapcd/KERNEL/UNIX/HPUX/R3INST
```

NOTE

/tmp/install/README file has CD contents listing:

- +/- 50 MB required in /tmp/install
- SUN +/- 50 MB required in /temp/install
- (/tmp is reserved for O.S.)

SAP Installation Tools are copied to /tmp/install during the step "Copy SAP Installation Software."

Set Up SWAP Space

Setting up SWAP space requirements for the system will vary between hardware platforms. Generally speaking, the following guideline should be met:

- ◆ At a minimum, 3 X RAM
- ◆ In some cases, 3 X RAM + 500MB
- ◆ On larger systems, depending on the amount of memory, install at least 1GB
- ◆ Systems with huge amounts of memory, such as 8GB, SAP recommends RAM + 2GB
- ◆ Use an entire disk for SWAP space if possible.

◆ For an AIX operating system, SWAP/Paging space creation is generally performed via Smitty, a system administration tool. SWAP space can be checked using the AIX command lsps −a.

◆ For all HP, file system SWAP is created via SAM.

Describe SAP System in /etc/sapconf:

The file known as sapconf resides in the /usr/sap/trans directory. When you do a normal SAP installation, you run R3SETUP and this utility will create and update sapconf with your environment settings.

Prepare File Systems

File systems during an installation can be created using each hardware vendor's system administration tools. Careful planning should be executed to ensure proper disk location and file system size before installing the SAP software.

◆ For AIX, use smit, or smitty

◆ For OSF/1:
  No LVM Support
  Standard file systems
  Advanced File Systems
  Disk-Shadowing is OK

◆ For HP-UX:
  SAM may be used to create file systems because it can assign 8K Fragment size

◆ HP 9000:
  File systems on standard disk partitions or File systems on logical volumes per LVM

◆ SUN:
  Manual disk and file system configuration using O.S. commands or system administration tools

Check Available Space in File Systems

Refer to the installation manual for each specific hardware vendor to determine file system sizes.

Verify that all file systems are mounted and large enough using the following Unix commands:

◆ df   *df − k*

◆ mount

◆ bdf   *(HP)*

Create Unix Groups and Users

Add Unix users and groups manually (i.e. using vi editor) or use O.S. specific utilities. In the following example, the ora<SID> and the <SID>adm users are shown.

Name	Group(s)	Home Directory
ora<SID>	dba	/oracle/<SID>
<SID>adm	sapsys and dba	Default $HOME

Copy R/3 and Oracle Software from CD

Manually copy files per /tmp/install/README using car, uncompress, and tar, or execute CDINST from /tmp/install.

On some platforms you can copy all SAP software proposed by the utility CDINST.

Modify Profiles and File Permissions

Always check to ensure that the installation utility has properly modified the user profiles and set the correct file permissions. Check the potential problem areas below for proper group and file permission ownership. Manual intervention using the UNIX commands chown and chgrp can be used to correct problems during the installation process. Use Unix chown and chgrp for:

ora<SID> owner and dba group for /oracle/stage, /oracle/<SID>, and $ORACLE_HOME <SID>adm owner and sapsys group for /sapmnt/<SID> and <SID>adm $HOME.

For some releases, execute SYSPROF and USERPROF to modify Oracle parameter files.

Check Created Users (AIX ONLY)

For earlier SAP releases, enter the lsuser command to check for the following user parameters on the AIX platform:

lsuser <SID>adm   (and ora<SID>)

The values should be set as listed below:

core=100000

cpu= -1

If not, change as necessary using the following AIX commands:

chuser cpu=-1 core=100000 <SID>adm   (and ora<SID>)

Check and Modify UNIX O.S. Kernel

UNIX kernel parameters may need to be modified during the installation process, depending upon the hardware platform.

A partial listing of platform specific changes that may need to be performed is listed below.

- ◆ AIX: No explicit user action necessary (kernel extensions done per Oracle ROOTPRE.SH execution)
- ◆ OSF/1, HP-UX, SINIX: Manual kernel config. per O.S. tools/commands
- ◆ OSF/1, HP-UX: kinst–info builds new Unix kernel

 NOTE

Kinst is no longer supported as of 3.0F.

- ◆ HP-UX, SINIX: kcheck checks existence of R/3 kernel requirements; verifies kernel values. R/3 should not be running when kcheck is executed.

Reboot UNIX to implement new kernel!

ORAINST Pre-Execution Requirements

Before running the ORAINST utility check, the Oracle DB Administration Unix user (ora<SID>) must exist with CSH, /bin/csh, as login shell. The Unix group, dba, must exist with Oracle DBA user as a member. $ORACLE_HOME must be /oracle/<SID>, (/oracle/<SID>), or there may be problems with R3INST.

During the installation process, the Unix login profiles for the sid<adm> and ora<sid> users must be modified before installing Oracle. These profiles are:

- ◆ .cshrc
- ◆ .login

On earlier SAP releases, the correct terminal type must be set for the curses inter-face screen. If not set correctly, the ORAINST window may crash if the window is resized during execution.

Pre-ORAINST Action

Before installing Oracle, verify that the following pre–ORAINST steps have been completed by the installation script, or manually carry them out yourself. In the following example, you'll look at preparations needed in an AIX environment.

◆ For earlier SAP releases on AIX, make sure that the ROOTPRE.SH script has been run.

◆ ROOTPRE.SH installs the necessary kernel extensions needed by AIX prior to the installation of the Oracle database.

◆ ROOTPRE.SH must be executed by root, with Oracle DBA Unix envi-ronment, prior to ORAINST.

◆ Environment variable LANG = en_US should be set before ROOTPRE.SH execution.

◆ Asynchronous i/o is activated by ROOTPRE.SH if not already acti-vated. Tests availability of asynchronous i/o after activation.

◆ The following files are copied from the Oracle staging area to /etc directory:

> adspc
>
> adspcinit
>
> pw_syscall
>
> loadext

Entries for these files are made in /etc/inittab to be loaded at system boot.

◆ Kernel extensions are activated by ROOTPRE.SH during execution.

◆ If a kernel extension is already installed (/etc/loadext exists), then ROOTPRE.SH prompts user to reboot so the current versions of the extension files may be installed.

◆ Reboot is mandatory to deactivate the previous versions!

◆ ROOTPRE.SH requires that AIX/BOSX messages are in English (unsetenv LANG, or setenv LANG En_US).

ORAINST Procedure

◆ The default values supplied when executing ORAINST are correct and should be used.

◆ Do not change any values unless specified by R/3 Installation Handbook.

◆ The R/3 Installation Handbook does not show every ORAINST screen. The default values should still be taken for all the screens, which do not appear in the Installation Handbook.

◆ ORAINST must be executed by Oracle DBA (ora<SID>).

◆ ORAINST must not be run as root!

◆ If ORAINST must be restarted, every product must be reinstalled.

◆ AIX specific prompts:

> The installer is asked whether install log information should be displayed on another xterm.

> Log file will be displayed in additional xterm window.

> The installer is prompted whether ROOTPRE.SH has been executed.

> The installer is asked whether shared versions of Oracle should be installed. Answer = NO.

◆ OSF/1 specific prompt:

> Installer is prompted for a "tmp" directory where +/- 70 MB is free. /usr/tmp or another directory may be entered.

Post-ORAINST: ROOT.SH Execution

This section deals with the steps that in most cases should have automatically been performed by the ORAINST installation script, but on occasion may still need to be completed manually at the end of running the ORAINST script.

◆ ROOT.SH is a Unix shell script generated by ORAINST. ROOT.SH must be executed by Unix user root in the C-shell using the Oracle DBA Unix environment:

ORACLE_HOME	/oracle/<SID>
ORACLE_OWNER	ora<SID>
ORACLE_SID	<SID>

- ROOT.SH copies three files to /usr/local/bin:

  oraenv

  coraenv

  dbhome

- ROOT.SH creates the following /etc/services entries:

orasrv	1525/tcp	oracle
tcptlisrv	1527/tcp	oracle

- ROOT.SH modifies and or creates /etc/oratab.
- ROOT.SH modifies the ownership and the following file permissions:

Directory:	$ORACLE_HOME/bin			
oracle	6751	owner=ora<SID>	group=dba	
orasrv	4751	owner=root	group=dba	
orapop	4711	owner=root	group=dba	(OSF/1)

 NOTE

If $ORACLE_HOME/bin/oracle is not correctly set up, the Oracle Admin user, ora<SID>, and R/3 Admin user, <SID>adm, will not be able to start the database.

Post-ROOT.SH Actions

The following steps should be verified as having been completed, or manually carried out after executing the ROOT.SH script. Some HP-UX specific steps are shown in the following:

- chmod o+x $ORACLE_HOME/bin/orasrv
- Copy: /oracle/stage/rdbms/admin/terminal/dbachp.res

  To: /oracle/<SID>/rdbms/admin/terminal/dbachp.res
- Copy: /oracle/stage/rdbms/lib/oracle.mk

  To: /oracle/<SID>/rdbms/lib/oracle.mk
- If SQLDBA issues warnings concerning codesets, the LANG environment variable must be correctly set for Local Language Codeset support.

- ◆ See: NLSINFO - Overview of installed Locale support. LOCALE—Current Locale environment
- ◆ Test to see if ora<SID> can start SQLDBA without errors: sqldba lmode=y

Database Startup Problems after ORAINST

Some common problems seen when trying to start the database after running ORAINST are:

- ◆ SQLDBA does not start after ORAINST.
- ◆ SETUID bit for ORACLE or ORASRV may be incorrect.
- ◆ AIX kernel extension files may be leftover from a previous version of Oracle (/etc/pw_syscall, ...).
- ◆ Insure that filesystems are not mounted with "-o nosuid" option.
- ◆ INIT<SID>.ORA parameters, shared_pool_size and db_block_buffers, may be incorrect.
- ◆ ORAINST execution aborted and won't restart until the partial installation is cleaned-up.
- ◆ AIX async i/o not permanent after O.S. reboot because it was not configured to be activated after reboot.
- ◆ Solaris execution of ROOT.SH checks for existence of /var/opt and will not execute until the file is created.
- ◆ Redo the ORAINST procedure from the beginning.

R/3 Installation Tools

In this section, you'll learn about some of the more common tools used during the installation process of the SAP software. The SAP Installation Tools are copied to /tmp/install during the step "Copy SAP Installation Software."

OSINST

- ◆ The log file for OSINST is: /tmp/install/OSINST.log.
- ◆ It is typically the installation preparation tool for execution on Central System.

- Execution time: +/- 1 Hour
- OSINST must be executed by root.
- Some of the functions it performs are:

  Describes SAP System in /etc/sapconf

  Prepares file systems

  Checks available space in file systems

  Creates Unix groups and users

  Copies R/3 software from CD

  Modifies profiles and file permissions

- OSINST calls other executables for various functions (fsinst, CDINST, sysprof, userprof).
- OSINST cannot check or modify SWAP space.
- OSINST does not recognize symbolic linked directories and will not be able to "find" any of the required directories if they are linked. Once the /etc/sapconf has been created, the rest of the functions done by OSINST may be done using standard Unix commands.
- /etc/services must be accessible for updates during the OSINST execution. Unix permissions 755 during OSINST.
- May be restarted and allows skipping steps, which may have already been done.
- May not be used to delete an SAP System. This must be done manually. OSINST is a screen interface based on the curses library.
- Changing the XTERM xindow size during OSINST will sometimes cause a program crash!
- Terminal types (TERM) as follows:

AIX and BOS/X	aixterm or xterm
OSF/1	vt100
HP-UX	hpterm
SINIX	97801, xterm, vt100

- AIX: OSINST is sensitive to Unix LANG environment setting. Set LANG variable to En_US or Gr_GR before OSINST.
- AIX: Ignore sna.sna.obj warning messages during OSINST.

◆ The OSINST screen is split into 3 sections:

    Menu Section

    Edit/Message/Input Section

    Info Section

The Menu Section shows buttons in reverse video. Buttons are activated with <CR>, L/R arrows, and TAB keys. The Edit/Message/Input Section is navigated by using the TAB and up/down arrow keys. The Info Section displays messages.

FSINST

FSINST performs an automatic setup of file systems according to the restrictions and requirements in its parameter files.

◆ FSINST parameter files:

    fsinst.pieces

    fsinst.restrictions

◆ FSINST.COMMANDS: fsinst.commands is executable script created by FSINST to perform the actual allocation of disk space into file systems. fsinst.commands must be closely examined before execution to verify that all LVM structures and file systems will be correctly created.

◆ FSINST Log Files:

    fsinst.log

    fsinst.log1, ...

◆ FSINST must not be used in a system environment using raw disk partitions.

◆ FSINST is intended for use on Unix systems supporting the Logical Volume Manager (LVM).

◆ FSINST should not be restarted after fsinst.commands has been executed.

◆ The FSINST parameter files use default R/3 SID values of <SID>. These files should be corrected if the SID will be anything else.

◆ FSINST.PIECES may be edited to increase the file system sizes, i.e., the sizes for the Oracle data file systems, to better fit the customers' hardware.

◆ Changes in FSINST.PIECES should also be done in the ORABUILD.PAR.TMPL parameter file.

◆ The sizes listed in FSINST.PIECES must not be reduced or the CD files will not fit on the disks, and the DB tablespaces will not fit.

◆ The FSINST.RESTRICTIONS file lists the restrictions that apply when allocating file systems to disks. The restrictions must be kept to insure data security.

◆ When installing more than one SAP System on a computer, the FSINST.PIECES.TMPL file must have the /usr/sap entry changed to /usr/sap/<SID> before FSINST execution for the second system.

◆ FSINST.COMMANDS functions:

Creates a volume group with a set of disks or adds disks to an existing empty group

Creates one logical volume for each file system per its parameter files

Creates file system mount point directories

Creates file systems on the logical volumes

Mounts the new file systems

CDINST

◆ Automatically imports R/3 software from CD.

◆ Input File: EXTRACT.TOC

◆ Contains CD contents information, label, size, and default directory destinations for the copy.

◆ Prerequisites:

root authorization

CD is mounted

◆ File systems have been created and are mounted.

◆ Proposed directories may be changed by the installer.

◆ Components may be selectively installed.

◆ Status bar displays elapsed time and which components have already been installed.

◆ README file on the CD supplies information on how to install using Unix commands rather than using CDINST.

SYSPROF

◆ Automatically maintains profiles for Oracle installations.

init<SID>.ora

init<SID>.sap

init<SID>.dba

◆ Log File: sysprof.log

◆ Command line options:

-H   specifies ORACLE_HOME

-S   specifies ORACLE_SID

-M   specifies maximum amount of RAM to be used for R/3
Instance and Oracle parameterization

◆ Template files are copied from /sapmnt/<SID>/exe/oraadm_templates to
$ORACLE_HOME/dbs. Return codes are supplied upon program execution.

USERPROF

◆ Automatically installs or upgrades user profiles in the home directories
of R/3 related users.

◆ Creates CRON jobs for the Oracle DB Administrator.

◆ Log File: userprof.log

◆ Command Line Parameters:

-u adm|ora specifies R/3 System Administrator, <SID>adm or
Database Administrator, ora<SID>.

-h <$HOME of R/3 Admin user> specifies $HOME of R/3
Admin user

-H <ORACLE_HOME> ORACLE_HOME of Oracle
Admin user

-S <ORACLE_SID> specifies Oracle DB SID

◆ Copies Admin user templates and modifies them for use.

◆ Previous files are renamed to ".old" versions.

◆ Return codes supply status of program execution.

KCHECK

◆ Lists available IPC resources at execution time.

◆ All processes that use IPC resources and are not running concurrently with R/3 should be inactive while executing KCHECK.

◆ KCHECK should only be used when the system is not available to users.

◆ Command line option:

-v   Verbose list of program output

◆ KCHECK is not supported on all supported Unix platforms.

◆ KCHECK should not be used on OSF/1 systems

ORABUILD

◆ ORABUILD is an SAP provided tool to assist you in building an ORACLE database.

◆ It is integrated into the R/3 installation tool, R3INST.

◆ It creates a new empty DB with all tablespaces, users, views, and DB objects required for the DB import.

◆ ORABUILD allows the resetting of an existing DB or will build the DB from scratch.

◆ ORABUILD Installation Files:

Log File: /tmp/install/R3INST.log

Parameter File: /tmp/install/orabuild.par

◆ Prerequisites:

Oracle must be installed - ORAINST, root.sh, and rootpre.sh (AIX & BOS/X)

ORASRV file must be correctly configured.

Execution is done by Oracle Admin user, ora<SID>.

Read access must be granted for its parameter file.

Read/Write access is needed for the init.ora file.

The Unix environment variables ORACLE_HOME and ORACLE_SID must be set.

All file systems must be large enough and mounted.

The Oracle redo log mirroring parameters must be consistent.

◆ The ORABUILD parameter file changes are limited to:

Relocating data tablespaces to other disks.

Increasing sizes of tablespaces.

Turning off the·Oracle default Redo Log mirroring if other means of mirroring will be used.

If the default Oracle mirroring is deactivated, the lines for the second LOG_GROUP entry for each log group should be removed/commented-out.

ORABUILD writes short messages to standard output as it is building the DB.

ORALOAD

The ORALOAD utility is another very useful Oracle database tool provided by SAP.

◆ It loads the empty DB built by ORABUILD using an Oracle DB dump delivered by SAP on the installation media or using the DB dump of a customer DB generated by the SAP tool ORAUNLOAD.

◆ It is integrated into the R3INST installation tool.

◆ It functions also as a standalone Unix program.

◆ ORALOAD allows resetting a previous run of ORALOAD.

◆ The import however, must be reset upon any errors encountered.

◆ Log File:

$ORACLE_HOME/sapreorg/oraload.log

$ORACLE_HOME/sapreorg/impfull.log

◆ Command line parameters:

-reset reset parameter

-l <logfile>   specifies the logfile to use.

-d <dumpdir> specifies Import dump directory.

◆ The ORACLE_HOME and ORACLE_SID must be set.

◆ ORALOAD Functions:

The user is prompted for passwords of Oracle dba users SYS and SYSTEM. These passwords are valid when ORALOAD is finished.

The DB parameter file is "tuned" to facilitate DB import.

The DB is restarted.

The DB import file is imported.

ORALOAD creates a log file and screens unneeded messages.

It re-activates the original Oracle parameters by DB restart.

When ORALOAD is finished the DB must be returned to Archive Log Mode.

ORAUNLOAD

◆ ORAUNLOAD dumps an existing DB generating a dumpfile suitable for a subsequent import with ORALOAD.

◆ It functions as a standalone program.

◆ Program Parameters:

-check	Appends size of the dump file, PSAPTEMP, and PSAPROLL to the logfile.
-l \<logfile\>	Specifies logfile. The DB dump file and all log files are written to this directory.

◆ Log file (default):

$ORACLE_HOME/sapreorg/oraunload.log expfull.log

◆ Prompts user for Oracle SYSTEM password.

◆ Deletes hardware dependent ABAP loads from the DB upon request. Generates a table of DB objects for checking purposes.

◆ Exports the DB contents.

ORABUILD_PRO

◆ Determines the space requirements of an existing DB and generates the template of an ORABUILD parameter file for copying an existing DB.

◆ Differentiates between:

Used Space	Minimum space needed by tablespaces.
Allocated Space	Currently allocated space.
Recommended Space	SAP size increase recommendations.

◆ Program Parameter:

   -full   Generates an additional file, minsize.tmpl, with all
            additional space per allocated and recommendations.

◆ Defaults to parameter file for a DB of the same size.

◆ Generated file: orabuild.par.tmpl

SAPINST

◆ SAPINST is an R/3 Instance Installation tool.

◆ Installation tasks may be split between root and R/3 users.

◆ It is called from R3INST.

◆ SAPINST may be executed as a standalone Unix shell program.

◆ The CHECKSAP program is used to determine which steps need to be
   done for SAPINST execution.

◆ Parameter File: CONFFILE

◆ Parameter file is created in directory where sapinst was called.

◆ Command line options:

   -l   List mode for root tasks

   -f   File name for conffile

   -s   Server name

   -i   Menu option

   -?   Help

◆ SAPINST installation may be reset by executing SAPCLEAN.

CONFFILE

◆ CONFFILE has the following uses:

   Defines file system structure.

   Specifies RAM requirements for the installation

   Defines system name

   Defines server names

◆ The initial installation uses no CONFFILE.

◆ SAPINST configures and starts the SAPOSCOL program.

Installing the Database Software

Some of the Oracle tools that are used during the Database Software installation are:

◆ orainst—Installs Oracle DB software and generates the root.sh script. Execution time: +/- 30 Min.

◆ root.sh—Executed by root user after ORAINST has installed the DB software.

◆ rootpre.sh—AIX and BOS/X specific configuration for installation of kernel extensions and activation asynchronous I/O.

Installation Example

1. Optimally, seven separate, one GB or larger, disks should be used for systems where there will be only one R/3 database on the computer.

    disk1:   /sapmnt

    disk2:   /oracle

    disk3:   /oracle/<SID>/sapreorg

    disk4:   /oracle/<SID>/sapdata1

    disk5:   /oracle/<SID>/sapdata2

    disk6:   /oracle/<SID>/sapdata3

    disk7:   /oracle/<SID>/sapdata4

 NOTE

In this example, if insufficient disk space exists on the physical disk where /usr/sap is located, then the /usr/sap/trans, /usr/sap/<SID>/DVEBMGS00/work, /usr/sap/<SID>/DVEBMGS00/data, and /usr/sap/<SID>/DVEBMGS00/log directories must be relocated via symbolic link to the /sapmnt/trans, /sapmnt/<SID>_DVEB-MGS00/work, /sapmnt/<SID>_DVEBMGS00/data, and /sapmnt/<SID>_DVEB-MGS00/log directories.

The /oracle/<SID>/sapreorg filesystem, approximately 800-900 MB, is needed for the DB import dump file. After the import is successfully finished, the two dump files may be deleted and the file system remounted as /oracle/<SID>/saparch.

→ not mount point for NFS

2. /usr/sap Directory Structure:

   - /usr/sap is a reserved directory name. It may not be used for anything other than R/3 System purposes.

   - /usr/sap is the fixed, logical R/3 directory structure.

   - /usr/sap may never be linked to another directory.

   - The default installation creates /usr/sap on the same partition as the /usr directory.

   - /usr/sap may be a local file system or directory on the /usr or /filesystems. It may never be an NFS mount point directory.

3. /sapmnt Directory Structure (default):

mount point for NFS

   - /sapmnt is the physical R/3 directory structure.

   - /sapmnt is the default installation directory for the R/3 executable files, profiles, and the global directory.

   - A customer may choose an installation directory with a name other than /sapmnt, i.e. /<customer> (excluded: /usr/sap, /usr/ora, /oracle/stage, and /oracle).

   - The default installation uses /sapmnt as a mount point directory on the Central DB Server.

   - /sapmnt should be mounted read-write per NFS on each Application Server.

   - /sapmnt should be mounted read-only per NFS on each Unix Presentation Frontend (default installation). Alternatively, the R/3 Frontend files may be physically copied to a Unix Frontend.

   - When /sapmnt is not mounted via NFS on external Application Servers or Unix Frontends the R/3 software must be manually distributed to update them.

4. /usr/sap/trans may be a mount point directory or a link to /sapmnt/trans. It should be exported from the DB Server and mounted, per NFS, on all DB and Application Servers where it may be shared for transport between R/3 Systems. The /usr/sap/trans directory requires at least 100 MB free file system space. Ownership of /usr/sap/trans as follows:

mount point for NFS

   User = <SID>adm

   Group = dba

5. Application Servers must have approximately 200 MB free disk space for the /usr/sap directory structures. The following directories may not be linked on Application Servers:

/usr/sap/<SID>/DVEBMGS00/work

/usr/sap/<SID>/DVEBMGS00/data

/usr/sap/<SID>/DVEBMGS00/log

[handwritten: message server central instance DB only, not on other application server]

- Only on Central Database Servers may these directories be linked as follows:

/usr/sap/<SID>/DVEBMGS00/work	/sapmnt/<SID>_DVEB MGS00/work
/usr/sap/<SID>/DVEBMGS00/data	/sapmnt/<SID>_DVEB MGS00/data
/usr/sap/<SID>/DVEBMGS00/log	/sapmnt/<SID>_DVEB MGS00/log

- If there is a minimum of 350 MB available in the Central Database Server /usr/sap file system, there is no need to link any of these directories.

- These directories must remain local on each Application and Database Server and may not be mounted via NFS on other Application Servers.

- Changes in R/3 profiles can affect disk space requirements for the Instance directories (i.e. change in size of the roll area).

6. The R/3 Administrator, <SID>adm, and the R/3 Database Administrator, ora<SID>, must have the same Unix UID (user ID) and GID (group ID) network-wide. These users must exist on all DB Servers and all Application Servers. The Unix UID for ora<SID> must be reserved network-wide so it does not get assigned to another Unix user (i.e. create a placeholder entry in /etc/passwd with no Unix login shell).

7. The following Oracle directories may never be located together on the same physical disks for data security reasons. They may not be mounted via NFS for performance purposes:

/oracle/<SID>/sapdata0—online-redo-log files may never be on the same disk as:

/oracle/<SID>/saparch—offline-redo-log files

may never be on the same disk as any of:

/oracle/<SID>/sapdata1 -|
/oracle/<SID>/sapdata2 -|-- DB tablespace data/index files
/oracle/<SID>/sapdata3 -|-- should not be on the same physical
/oracle/<SID>/sapdata4 -| disks.

Specifics:

/oracle/<SID>/sapdata0 may not be on the same physical disk as /oracle/<SID>/saparch or any of the disks holding the database (DB) tablespace data/index files.

/oracle/<SID>/saparch may not be on the same physical disk as /oracle/<SID>/sapdata0 or any of the disks holding the DB tablespace data/index files.

The DB tablespace data/index files should be on separate physical disks. They may however be on the same physical disk as long as /oracle/<SID>/sapdata0 and /oracle/<SID>/saparch are located on separate physical disks from them.

The SAPDATA DB tablespace data/index filesystems should be in separate file systems. These separate filesystems may however span physical disks.

When the DB tablespace data/index files (SAPDATA directories) are all on the same disk performance, degradation may occur due to disk i/o factors.

8. The Oracle database control files must be distributed over different physical disks. For example:

/oracle/<SID>/dbs/cntrl/cntrl.dbf
/oracle/<SID>/sapdata0/cntrl/cntrl.dbf
/oracle/<SID>/sapdata1/cntrl/cntrl.dbf
/oracle/<SID>/sapdata2/cntrl/cntrl.dbf
/oracle/<SID>/sapdata3/cntrl/cntrl.dbf

 NOTE

Depending on the physical disk configuration, control files should be distributed to insure that they are located on physically separate disks. Each file is approximately 50 KB and presents no space problem in distribution.

9. If available, a separate disk should be used for the offline-redo-log files, /oracle/<SID>/saparch.

10. If a separate disk for the /oracle/<SID>/saparch directory is not available it may be linked to another directory on a different disk. If the "saparch" directory must be linked it should be linked to:

   /sapmnt/oracle/<SID>/saparch.

11. Symbolic-links may not be used for database TABLESPACE MOUNT-POINT DIRECTORIES (/oracle/<SID>/sapdata[1,2,3,...N]).

12. Individual database tablespace files may never be linked.

13. Only in an *absolute emergency* may a single tablespace directory be symbolic-linked to another directory. The directory must exist in a Unix file system created using the required parameters for the Oracle database (blocksize=8K, fragmentsize=8K, long filenames).

   /oracle/<SID>/sapdata1/sourcei_2 may be linked to

   /sapmnt/oracle/<SID>/sourcei_2

 NOTE

This method is not recommended as a long-term solution for productive systems.

---

14. In those emergency cases in which tablespace directories are linked, the customer *must* be advised to make more hardware resources available for the R/3 database (i.e. buy more hardware).

   After more hardware is available the system should be brought back into compliance with the R/3 directory structure and file-naming conventions.

15. The SAP R/3 database utility SAPDBA should always be used for database administration actions. When tablespace extensions are added the file and directory naming convention must be strictly followed. All files belonging to a specific DB Tablespace should be on the same Unix filesystem to facilitate future tablespace reorganizations. For example:

   • /oracle/<SID>/sapdata[N,N+1,N+...] should be used as the directory name for additional file system mount point directories (i.e. /oracle/<SID>/sapdata5, /oracle/<SID>/sapdata6, ...).

*sapdata1
→ mount point
for LV. filesystem*

- /oracle/<SID>/sapdataN/sourcei_[N,N+1,N+...] should be used as the directory name for the tablespace file extension directory (i.e. /oracle/<SID>/sapdata5/sourcei_2, /oracle/<SID>/sapdata5/sourcei_3, ...).
- /oracle/<SID>/sapdataN/sourcei_2/sourcei.data2 should be used as the tablespace file name for the second data file added to the PSAPSOURCEI tablespace. The first data file for the PSAPSOURCEI tablespace is called /oracle/<SID>/sapdata1/sourcei_1/sourcei.data1.

16. The following directory name parameters in the /oracle/<SID>/dbs/init<SID>.sap file may not be changed to use other directory names: *for brbackup tool*

    backup_root_dir = (/oracle/<SID>/sapbackup)

    compress_dir = /oracle/<SID>/sapbackup

17. Two SWAP partitions are better to have than one big SWAP partition. Two SWAP partitions/areas should not be on the same physical disk.

18. The following parameters in /oracle/<SID>/dbs/init<SID>.ora may not be changed:

    oracle can not change R/3 value

db_name	(defined during R/3 DB creation)
db_block_size	----- |
user_dump_dest	|-- R/3 standard values must be used.
background_dump_dest	|
log_archive_dest	----- |

19. The following are reserved words and may not be used for a database SID names:

    SAP COM EPS MON OFF SET SGA SHO VAR DBA END LOG

    No SID's may begin with a numeric character.

20. File systems offering hardware or software "Mirroring" may be used or standard Unix file systems.

    Standard Unix file systems

    LVM - Logical Volume Manager

    AFS - Advanced File System (OSF/1)

    Online: DiskSuite (SUN)

    Disk Striping

    Disk Arrays

origloyn

The Database Online-Redo-Logs must be mirrored either via Oracle (sapdata0 and sapdata1 copies) or using, for instance, one of the previous mirroring techniques. *origlogR*

Raw disk partitions are not supported for R/3 using Oracle RDBMS. Separate hardware (i.e. SCSI) controllers may be used to increase system throughput for those disks with high i/o requirements (i.e. the disk containing the online-redo-log files, /oracle/<SID>/sapdata0).

21. TCP/IP Sockets: *origlogn*

    The TCP/IP port assignment sockets must be identical for all R/3 Central Database Servers, Application Servers, and all R/3 Frontends NETWORK-WIDE.

    SAP uses socket numbers 3200, 3300, and 3600 as default values. For example, the following /etc/services are created during a typical R/3 installation:

orasrv	1525/tcp	oracle
tcptlisrv	1527/tcp	oracle
sapdp00	3200/tcp	
sapgw00	3300/tcp	
sapms<SID>	3600/tcp	

22. Oracle Archive Log Mode:

    Production R/3 Systems must run in ARCHIVE LOG MODE. Test R/3 Systems should run in ARCHIVE LOG MODE. Data Security cannot be guaranteed for R/3 Systems not operating in ARCHIVE LOG MODE. Systems operating in ARCHIVE LOG MODE may be restored to a point current with system interruption/hardware failure.

Network Installation

The customer's R/3 System and their network gateway software and hardware must be correctly installed and configured before beginning.

1. Add SAP Walldorf entry to customer's /etc/hosts file(s):

   147.204.64.1   sapserv3   # SAP X.25 Server

2. Provide Customer IP Address and X.25 information to SAP Walldorf for R/3 Central DB Server and any gateways or routers necessary for X.25 access.

3. Test network connection by "PINGING" SAP.

4. Use R/3 Menu to start the SAPSERVR R/3 program:

    System

    Services

    X.25 Service

5. SAPSERVR establishes the initial X.25 link to Walldorf and registers the customer's installation for communications with SAP.

The Languages Your System Will Speak

When reading about languages in this chapter, keep in mind that this discussion is built around a system configured for English and Japanese. The concepts in general are still true for all other languages; you will have to change the values of the settings described in this section to fit the language(s) you are installing.

One of the great abilities of SAP is that one single system is able to communicate with many different people speaking many different languages (more than 30 languages). It is one thing to state a simple fact like this but it is quite another to configure the system to actually speak all these languages *correctly*. SAP has a globalization team that specializes in language installations. Any company installing a Multi Display/Multi Processing (MDMP) configuration would very strongly be advised to contact SAP during the initial installation of the system, especially when single and double byte code pages are mixed. That is English (single) together with Japanese (double). SAP discourages the use of an MDMP.

One of the most important installation steps is to decide which code page or code pages to use for the database and for the SAP system. Only these code pages will be supported by the system, and the system will only be able to manipulate characters associated with these preselected code pages.

The world today offers variety and choices. Many different companies require different language solutions. Some companies are located in a single city, others span countries on one continent, others may span continents, and to confuse the mix even more, some countries have a handful of different official languages. This means that the whole world demands unique solutions for each and every language combination possible.

SAP provides the following solutions:

◆ Native Language Support (NLS). Only one code page is used.

◆ Mixed Native Language Support (MNLS). Some combination of code pages is used. The new name for MNLS is MDMP (Multi Display/Multi Processing). The database has one code page whereas the application servers and front-end servers have different code pages.

◆ Multi Display/Single Processing (MDSP). Multiple different front-end servers with different code pages make use of an SAP constellation where the database and the application servers have the same code page.

◆ Blended Code Pages. Different code pages are merged to form a new code page.

◆ UNICODE. This is a new technology that enables applications to display any and all characters in all languages.

An SAP constellation consisting of a database server, application servers, front-end servers, and peripherals like printers and faxes requires these different types of code pages:

◆ System code pages

◆ Database code pages

◆ Front-end code pages

◆ Peripheral code pages

All these different environments need to communicate and to assimilate information. Code pages are the link that makes this interaction possible. Table 4-1 lists the standard code pages supported by SAP.

Language Installation Steps

1. Decide on the languages that you want to install.

2. Make sure that the combination of languages is supported by SAP.

3. Decide if you want to do NLS, MNLS, Blended Code Page, or UNICODE. Contact SAP to assist you with your language selection because not all language combinations are possible.

4. Install the locales for each language on all servers on the operating system level; that is, the database server and the application servers. You need to install the locales on a server even though you are not planning

Table 4-1 Standard Code Pages for SAP (©SAPAG)

Code Page	R/3 Code Pages			Keys		R/3 Language
	UNIX NT	AS400	WIN SAPGUI	3.x	4.x	
ISO8859-1	1100	0120	1100	D, E, F, I, K, N, O, P, S, U, V, 7	DE, EN, FR, IT, DA, NL, NO, PT, ES, FI, SV, MS	German, English, French, Italian, Danish, Dutch, Norwegian, Portuguese, Spanish, Finnish, Swedish, Malay
ISO8859-2	1401	0410	1404	C, D, E, H, L, Q, 4, 5, 6	CS, DE, EN, HU, RO, SL, HR	Czech, German, English, Hungarian, Polish, Slovak, Romanian, Slovene, Croatian
ISO8859-5	1500	0500	1504	E, R, W	EN, RU, BG	English, Russian, Bulgarian
ISO8859-7	1700	0700	1704	E, G	EN, EL	English, Greek
ISO8859-8	1800	0800	1800	E, B	EN, HE	English, Hebrew
ISO8859-9	1610	0610	1614	D, E, F, I, K, N, O, P, S, U, V, 7, T TR	DE, EN, FR, IT, DA, NL, NO, PT, ES, FI, SV, MS,	German, English, French, Italian, Danish, Dutch, Norwegian, Portuguese, Spanish, Finnish, Swedish, Malay Turkish
ShiftJIS	8000	—	8000	E, J	EN, JA	English, Japanese
GB2312-80	8400	—	8400	E, 1	EN, ZH	English, Chinese
Big5	8300	—	8300	E, M	EN, ZF	English, Taiwanese
KSC5601	8500	—	8500	E, 3	EN, KO	English, Korean
TIS620	8600	—	8600	E, 2	EN, TH	English, Thai

to use the language on that server. SAP will use that server without your knowing it.

5. Initialize the language tables: TCPOC, TCP0D, TCP09, TCPDB, and TCP0B. (TCP0B is used in SAP 30D and earlier.)

6. Initialize the SAP profile language parameters.

7. Create the CDP files using transaction SM59. Install them in the correct places and move them to the front-end server if required, setting all necessary environment variables.

8. Switch the buffer synchronization off.

9. Switch archiving off. (This step is optional.)

10. Classify languages that need to be imported in table T002C.

11. Import and/or supplement the languages required.

12. Switch buffer synchronization on.

13. Switch archiving on. (This step is optional.)

14. If you decided to switch archiving off, you have to make a backup of the system.

NLS—Native Language Support

An NLS system is a system with a single code page selected from Table 4-1. You will notice that some rows contain more than one language. The languages appearing in a single row make use of the same characters. This means that all the characters for these languages are encapsulated in one single code page.

MDSP—Multi Display/Single Processing

Single processing refers to the database and all the application servers making use of the same code page for processing. *Multi display* refers to the front end that is able to switch code pages dynamically on many front-end servers, each with a different code page.

Each user using a different code page will see the menu items, field names, and any GUI text in their native language.

The restriction with this implementation is that, although they see their own language, users can only enter characters that are allowed both by the application servers and the front end they are using. In other words, only characters that are in both code pages will function correctly. When a user enters a character on his or her GUI that is not allowed by the code pages of the application server and the database sever, these characters will be filtered out or replaced.

MDMP—Multi Display/Multi Processing

Due to the facts that the world is a multicultural society and UNICODE is not readily available yet, SAP developed a temporary language solution to enable customers to use multiple code pages on a single database. Although it will support an MDMP system, SAP strongly advises customers to either install an NLS or a blended code page system.

Say you have an MDMP system with English (ISO8859-1) and Japanese (ShiftJIS) code pages installed. People in the United States will enter characters belonging to ISO8859-1, and people in Japan will enter ShiftJIS characters into the system. An MDMP system works only if both of these groups keep to the code page assigned to them and they do not access data entered into the database by the other group. In short, strict data entering and manipulation rules must be in place.

Blended Code Pages

Blended code pages were developed by SAP to accommodate language combinations not supported by the standard ISO code pages. Table 4-2 lists the available blended code pages.

Table 4-2 Blended Code Pages (©SAPAG)

SAP Code Pages	SAP Supported Language Combinations	Release
Euro-Japan	Danish, Dutch, English, Finnish, French, German, Italian, Norwegian, Portuguese, Spanish, Swedish, Japanese	3.1H
Asian Unification C	Japanese, Simplified Chinese, English	3.1H
Asian Unification K	Japanese, Korean, English	3.1H
Asian Unification T	Japanese, Traditional Chinese, English	3.1H
Nagamasa	Japanese, Thai, English	3.1H

A blended code page is an SAP developed code page, which enables users to use multiple languages without the complexities and rules introduced by MDMP solutions. It is actually an NLS solution with nonstandard code pages. The disadvantage of this method is that, in order to accommodate additional languages in a single code page, some characters in all the languages combined were sacrificed. This means that special characters that are not frequently used are left out of the blended code page in order to accommodate the additional languages.

Again, you are required to involve SAP with the initial implementation of blended code pages, and eventually when SAP can support UNICODE, you need to contact SAP to migrate the blended code pages to UNICODE.

The code pages in Table 4-2 are easily migrated to UNICODE, but the code pages in Table 4-3 are not.

Table 4-3 Blended Code Pages with UNICODE Migration Difficulties (©SAPAG)

SAP Code Pages	SAP Supported Language Combinations	Release
Asian Unification	English, Japanese2, Chinese, Korean, Taiwanese	3.1H
Diocletian 3	German, English, French, Italian, Danish, Dutch, Finnish, Norwegian, Portuguese, Spanish, Swedish, Greek	3.1H
SAP Unification 4	German, English, French, Italian, Danish, Dutch, Finnish, Norwegian, Portuguese, Spanish, Swedish, Japanese1, Czech, Hungarian, Polish, Slovak, Romanian, Slovene, Croatian, Turkish, Greek	3.1H

UNICODE

UNICODE is the promised future where all characters for all languages are defined in a single code page. UNICODE is defined by the UNICODE consortium, which consists of world-leading companies in the IT industry, and is accepted as a world standard known as ISO/IEC 10646. SAP intends to implement UNICODE in Release 4.x and hopes that it will be available in the year 2002. Both the operating system and the database will have to support UNICODE in order for SAP to be able to utilize UNICODE. It is not enough that only SAP supports UNICODE.

The Language Installation

How does an administrator go about installing the language environment so carefully selected? Several areas need attention, as discussed in the following sections.

Operating System

Each operating system has its own peculiarities on how to install the different language locales. A *locale* is a set of rules defining how an application should perform text operations (e.g., case conversion, sorting the formatting of currency and date values) according to language and, in part, according to country-specific rules.

An SAP application adjusts its processing locale dynamically according to the system code page configured during installation and as specified by the user during the user logon process.

To see which locales are installed on a server, execute the command locale −a. This should result in a list of all the locales currently installed on the system.

Command:	locale −a
Listing:	en_US.iso88591
	fr_CA.iso88591
	fr_CA.roman8
	fr_FR.iso88591
	de_DE.iso88591
	de_DE.roman8
	is_IS.iso88591
	is_IS.roman8
	it_IT.iso88591
	it_IT.roman8
	ja_JP.SJIS
	ja_JP.eucJP

For each of the popular operating systems on which SAP runs, the following is the location where these locales reside.

ReliantUNIX	/usr/lib/locale/
AIX	/usr/lib/nls/loc/
OSF1	/usr/i18n/lib/nls/loc/

SINIX	usr/lib/locale/
HP-UX	/usr/lib/nls/loc/locales/
SunOS	/usr/lib/nls/loc/
Windows NT	\winnt\system32

With NT you need to install the NT Language Pack and the active locales are defined in the registry:

HKEY_LOCAL_MACHINE, SYSTEM, CurrentControlSet, Control, Nls, CodePage

On the UNIX systems, you only need to copy the required locales into the directories specified above.

Say the current SAP environment has a database server with a central instance and multiple application servers. You are installing an MDMP system mixing U.S.-English and Japanese, and you dedicate two of these application servers to the Japanese community. Where do you install the U.S.-English locales and where do you install the Japanese locales? You install them all on every server, English *and* Japanese alike! The reason for this is that the work processes switch locales depending on the job executing on the work process. For instance, if a Japanese user schedules a job to generate a Japanese report in the background and the job gets scheduled to run on one of the U.S.-English servers without a Japanese locale, you will get unpredictable results.

Language Tables

Following is a table listing all the language configuration tables. Some of these tables are very prominent in the configuration of the language environment. Only the prominent tables will be discussed further.

T002	Language keys
T002C	Customizing data for T002
T002P	HR language key
T002T	Texts for language key
TCP00	SAP character set catalog
TCP01	SAP character catalog
TCP02	Character set definitions (simple hex codes)
TCP03	Character set definitions (multiple hex codes)

TCP04	Translation table for uppercase letters
TCP05	Manufacturer identifications
TCP06	Character replacements
TCP07	Code page definitions (very long codes)
TCP08	Character description
TCP09	Correspondence between language and character set
TCP0A	Adjustment between language and character set
TCP0B	Mapping language to character set and setlocale()
TCP0C	Locale names for setting up C-libraries
TCP0D	Localizing the database
TCPA	Templates for characteristics management
TCPAT	Templates for characteristics
TCPBI	Batch input table for task lists
TCPDB	Code page used in this database

T002C

This table is used to classify the languages that should be imported into the system. Only the languages defined in T002C will be imported into the system. Use transaction SMLT, menu path Goto, Classify Language to define which languages should be imported. Select the language you want to maintain and select the display button. The screen displayed in Figure 4-1 will appear.

The screen is divided into four groups, namely, *Characteristics*, *Transport*, *Permitted functions*, and *Administration*.

Characteristics—Degree of translation allows you to select the degree to which the installed language is translated in SAP. Only English and German are translated completely and have a degree of translation of one. All other languages are a two, three, four, or zero. Zero is the lowest degree of translation. Zero is used for custom developed languages.

Characteristics—Specifics defines if a language is a single byte (English and most Western languages), double byte (Japanese, Chinese, and Korean), a combination of single- and double-byte (Thai), or a single byte inverse write direction language (Hebrew).

Transport—Install indicates that the language should be imported.

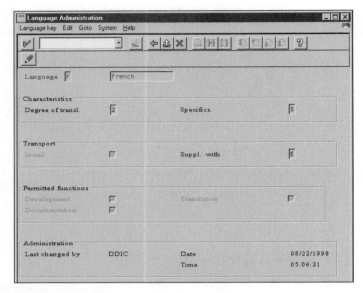

FIGURE 4-1 *Results of selecting the language you want to maintain and selecting the display button.*

Transport—Supplement with defines the language that should be used to supplement the language you are classifying. With the exception of German and English, most of the other languages do not have all their text items defined. Instead of having an empty text string, you can supplement the language with either German or English. This supplementation process will add English or German text into the text items that are empty.

Permitted functions—Development, Documentation, and *Translation* define the functions that users and developers are allowed to perform in this language. The Translation option indicates that a language is translated or supplemented in the system. If Translation is selected, you will not be allowed to supplement this language with any other language (you are only allowed to supplement with English or German).

TCB0B

TCP0B is an old table used in the SAP releases up to SAP 3.0C. Report RSCP0015 maintains table TCPDB.

TCP0C

The entries in this table are very important to the way SAP operates. The entries define the code page(s) and locales that have to be used depending on the user's login language. TCP0C replaces TCP0B as of SAP Release 3.0D. The entries listed in Table 4-4 are a very small subset of actual entries in this table. You typically only need the records that pertain to the platform that SAP is running on (i.e. OSF1 entries are required when SAP is running on a DEC machine).

If entries are missing or incorrect in table TCP0C, the administrator can correct these by changing or adding values with transaction SM31. Another method is to download the latest correct entries from sapservX. Execute a report RSCP0017. The initial screen of program RSCP0017 is displayed in Figure 4-2. This report allows you to import and manipulate the entries in table TCP0C. Before importing the new file, make a backup of the old entries. Another utility that reports on the current active TCP0C entries is RSCP0020.

Incorrect values in table TCP0C can cause the system to stop functioning. RFC connections might fail and you might get error messages pertaining to an invalid text environment.

Table 4-4 TCP0C

Platform	Language	Country	Modifier	Locale
AIX	E			en_US.ISO8859-1
AIX	E	JP		ja_JP.SJIS
AIX	J			ja_JP.SJIS
AIX	J	JP		ja_JP.SJIS
HP-UX_10	E			en_US.iso8859-1
HP-UX_10	E	JP		ja_JP.SJIS
HP-UX_10	J			ja_JP.SJIS
HP-UX_10	J	JP		ja_JP.SJIS
OSF1	E			en_US.ISO8859-1
OSF1	E	JP		ja_JP.SJIS
OSF1	J			ja_JP.SJIS
OSF1	J	JP		ja_JP.SJIS

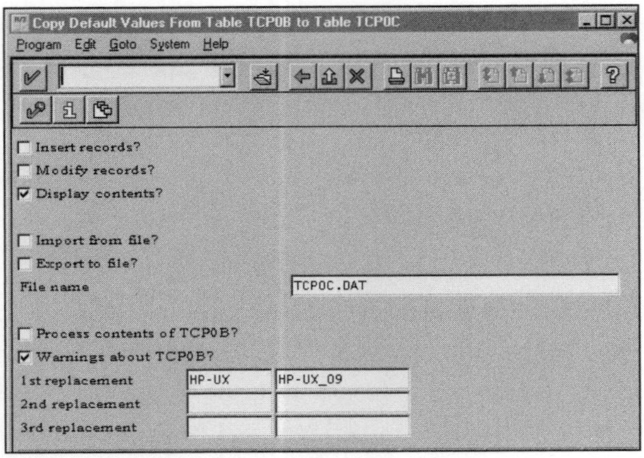

FIGURE 4-2 *RSCP0017 imports and manipulates the entries in table TCP0C*

TIP

If this ever happens, attempt to restart the system with the following profile parameters:

```
abap/set_text_env_at_new_mode  = 0
install/collate/active          = 0
```

If the above does not help, try:

```
rscp/TCP0B                        = TCP0B
```

Do not use the system productively while in this mode. Correct the entries in table TCP0C and remove the above-mentioned entries.

TCP0D

This is a small but potent little table. It localizes the database. For systems in the United States and Western Europe, the table should either be empty or contain a record with a space. This means that the code page belonging to each language installed on the system will be selected correctly based on table TCP0C (for example, ShiftJIS for Japanese, Latin2 for Polish, and Latin1 for English, German, French, Spanish, and so on).

If your company is Japanese and is located in Japan and you want English to be processed by the Japanese locale ShiftJIS, then you need to add the entry "JP" to table TCP0D. This will ensure that English is processed with ShiftJIS. This means that the special characters defined in the Latin1 code page will not be available in the system. The table has only one field called *country*. The entry in this table ties together with the country column in table TCP0C.

This table is not used with an MDMP system. It does not make sense because, on an MDMP system, all the languages are saved in their own code page format in the database. You will have both Latin1 and ShiftJIS characters in the database of a system where both code pages are used. Leave the table empty in an MDMP environment.

RSCP0020, displayed in Figure 4-3, will display the active TCP0C entries and, if selected, update the table TCP0D with an empty record or with a country code you select. The following minitable defines the different country codes and the associated country name.

Country Code	Country
' '	Western European languages
'JP'	Japan
'CN'	China (mainland)
'TH'	Thailand
'KR'	Korea

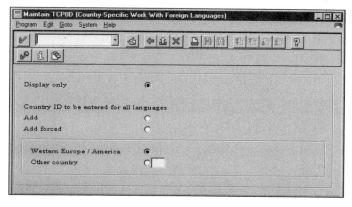

FIGURE 4-3 *RSCP0020—TCP0D maintenance program*

Country Code	Country
'IL'	Israel
'GR'	Greece
'TW'	Taiwan
'RU'	Russia
'TR'	Turkey
'CZ'	Czech Republic
'HU'	Hungary
'PL'	Poland
'SK'	Slovakia
'RO'	Romania
'SI'	Slovenia
'HR'	Croatia

TCPDB

This table defines the code pages used in the database. Under most circumstances, this table should only contain one entry. It contains more than one entry only if an MDMP system is configured. Table TCPDB consists of two fields as described in the minitable that follows.

Field	Description
CPTRANSFLD	SAP character set for transparent tables
CPPOOLCLUS	SAP character set for nontransparent tables

On an NLS system the table TCPDB will have only one entry. Following is an example of the contents of table TCPDB on a system with a Western European language. This is not the only value allowed in this table. If you are installing a Japanese system, you will use code page 8000 instead of 1100.

Code Page Transparent	Code Page Nontransparent
1100	1100

An MDMP system for Japanese and English will have the following entries:

Code Page Transparent	Code Page Nontransparent
1100	1100
8000	8000

Use the report RSCP0004 to display the entries in this table. This report can actually delete incorrect entries in table TCPDB, but it is much easier to use a SQL query directly on the database to delete all entries and to re-create the entries correctly. The following are the SQL commands you need to execute in order to remove and re-create the entries as per the example discussed.

```
Delete from sapr3.tcpdb;
Insert sapr3.tcpdb (CPTRANSFLD, CPPOOLCLUS) values (1100,1100);
Insert sapr3.tcpdb (CPTRANSFLD, CPPOOLCLUS) values (8000,8000);
Commit;
```

If TCPDB is left empty, the system will use the profile parameters *install/codepage/db/transp* and *install/codepage/db/non_transp*. It is better to have the entries defined in this table during installation because it directly controls the behavior of the SAP kernel.

TCP09

Table TCP09 contains all the possible code pages for a language that will be checked during the user login process. If needed entries are missing, use transaction SM31 to add the missing or incorrect entries. A useful report that validates TCP09 and inserts any missing records is RSCP0014. Each language installed in SAP requires entries defining the code page used for the specific language.

TCP09 consists of the following fields:

Field	Description
LANG	Language key
CPCODEPAGE	SAP character set identification

The following entries are required for an MDMP English-Japanese system:

Language Id	Language	Code	Locale Page
E	English	1100	SAP-intern, wie ISO8859-1
E	English	8000	ShiftJIS
J	Japanese	8000	ShiftJIS

Use the report RSCP0014, as portrayed in Figure 4-4, to display table contents with text descriptions.

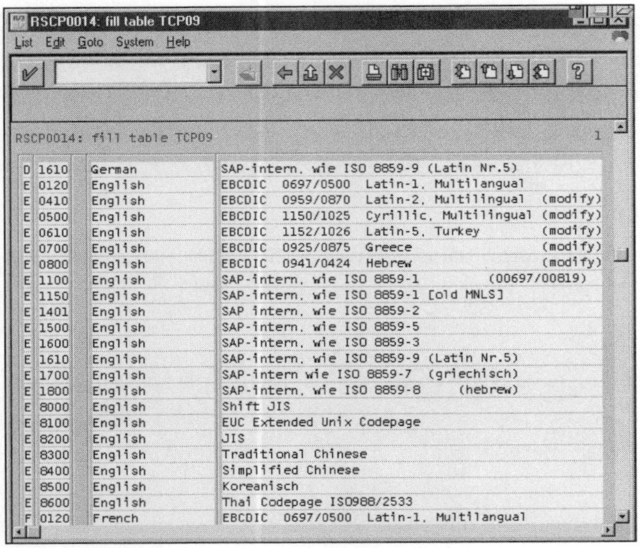

FIGURE 4-4 *RSCP0014 displays the contents of TCP09*

SAP Language Profile Parameters

A very important part of the language installation is the setting of the SAP profile parameters. You have parameters that you need to set in the default profile and parameters to set in the instance profile.

DEFAULT Profile

The parameters set in the default profile will be true for the entire SAP system. You will find below a description of each of the prominent language parameters that belong in the default profile. The values on the right of each of these parameters are examples as pertaining to a system with German, English, Japanese, Italian, and French installed.

◆ abap/set_text_env_at_new_mode   1

This parameter activates the new kernel language activities. Use this parameter when you are fixing language problems by setting it to zero.

◆ install/collate/active   1

This parameter activates ABAP locale commands. Use this parameter when you are fixing language problems by setting it to zero.

◆ rscp/TCP0B   TCP0C

This parameter defines the locale table that should be used. Up to SAP
Release 3.0C, table TCP0B was used for the locale definitions. Table
TCP0C is used with the later releases. Use this parameter when you are
fixing language problems by setting it to TCP0B.

◆ install/codepage/db/non_transp   Multi

This parameter defines the code page that should be used for nontrans-
parent tables in the database. NLS systems should have this value set to
some code page like 1100 for the Latin-1 code page. For MDMP systems, assign "Multi" to this parameter. If the table TCPDB is configured
correctly, it should not be necessary to set this parameter.

◆ install/codepage/db/transp   Multi

This parameter defines the code page that should be used for transparent
tables in the database. NLS systems should have this value set to some
code page like 1100 for the Latin-1 code page. For MDMP systems,
assign "Multi" to this parameter. If the table TCPDB is configured correctly, it should not be necessary to set this parameter.

◆ zcsa/installed_languages   DEFIJ

This is a language vector defining all the languages installed on the system. Only languages defined in this vector can be used during logon
time. This profile parameter will have a different value in the instance
profiles for each application server dedicated to a language.

◆ zcsa/system_language   E

This parameter defines the default system language. When a user logs
on, the language specified by this parameter will be used by default. In
an MDMP system, each application server dedicated to a specific language will have this parameter set to a different value.

Instance Profile Parameters (Western Instances)

The following parameters belong in the instance profiles defining the English or
Western instances. With the settings set as shown below only English, German,
French, and Italian users will be able to use this SAP instance.

◆ zcsa/system_language   E

This parameter defines the default system language. When a user logs
on, the language specified by this parameter will be used by default. In

an MDMP system, each application server dedicated to a specific language will have this parameter set to a different value.

◆ zcsa/installed_languages DEFI

This is a language vector defining all the languages installed on the system. Only languages defined in this vector can be used during logon time. This profile parameter will have a different value in the instance profiles for each application server dedicated to a language. Notice that one character is missing when you compare it with the same parameter in the DEFAULT profile. The "J" is missing; this means that Japanese users will not be able to log on to this server with Japanese as the logon language. Only German, English, French, and Italian users will be able to use this instance.

◆ abap/locale_ctype en_US.iso88591

This parameter defines the default locale for the particular SAP instance.

◆ install/codepage/appl_server 1100

This parameter defines the character code page that the work processes on this particular instance will use.

◆ saptemu/Codepage 1100

This parameter defines the character code page for the GUI. Notice that Codepage is written with an uppercase C.

Instance Profile Parameters (Japanese Instances)

The instance with the following parameters is a Japanese instance. Only users understanding Japanese and English will be able to use this instance.

◆ zcsa/system_language J

This parameter defines the default system language. When a user logs on, the language specified by this parameter will be used by default. In an MDMP system, each application server dedicated to a specific language will have this parameter set to a different value.

◆ zcsa/installed_languages EJ

This is a language vector defining all the languages installed on the system. Only languages defined in this vector can be used during logon time. This profile parameter will have a different value in the instance profiles for each application server dedicated to a language. Only English and Japanese users will be able to use this instance. The difference

for English users is that they are not using code page 1100 when logged
on to this instance but rather are using code page 8000.

◆ abap/locale_ctype   ja_JP.SJIS

This parameter defines the default locale for the particular SAP instance.

◆ install/codepage/appl_server   8000

This parameter defines the character code page that the work processes
on this particular instance will use.

◆ saptemu/Codepage   8000

This parameter defines the character code page for the GUI.

CDP Files

CDP files are code page conversion files. They are used to convert from one code
page to another. Each non-Latin1 code file requires at least two CDP files. For
example, if Japanese is installed on the system with Latin1, 11008000.CDP and
80001100.CDP are required.

You use transaction SM59 to create the CDP files. Following, you will find the
execution steps that will allow you to create the CDP files.

1. Execute transaction SM59.
2. Select RFC menu item.
3. Select Generate Conv. Tab.
4. Enter the following:

   Source - Code page   1100
   Target - Code page   8000
   Path for file   /usr/sap/SID/DVEBV00/data/

5. Press the Execute button.
6. Press the Back arrow on the next screen that appears.
7. Enter the following:

   Source - Code page   8000
   Target - Code page   1100
   Path for file   /usr/sap/SID/DVEBV00/data/

8. Press the Execute button.
9. Press the Back arrow on the next two screens that appear.

Full Language Import

Execute transaction SMLT, Schedule Import and complete the blank spaces as indicated by the SAP language documentation (see Figure 4-5). Complete the import and monitor the logs for any errors.

Supplementation

Not all languages are completely translated. Some text elements are missing, and these missing elements need to be supplemented with either English or German. Execute transaction SMLT, Language, Schedule Supplement to supplement all languages installed on the system. Only languages with the Translation option switched off in T002C will be supplemented.

An interesting language installation is to configure a language like Japanese in the system, but instead of importing the full Japanese language, supplement the complete Japanese language with English or German. This will cause the whole Japanese environment to be displayed in English or German. The Japanese users will be using code page 8000 although they see English text on the screen, plus they will be able to enter Japanese characters as well.

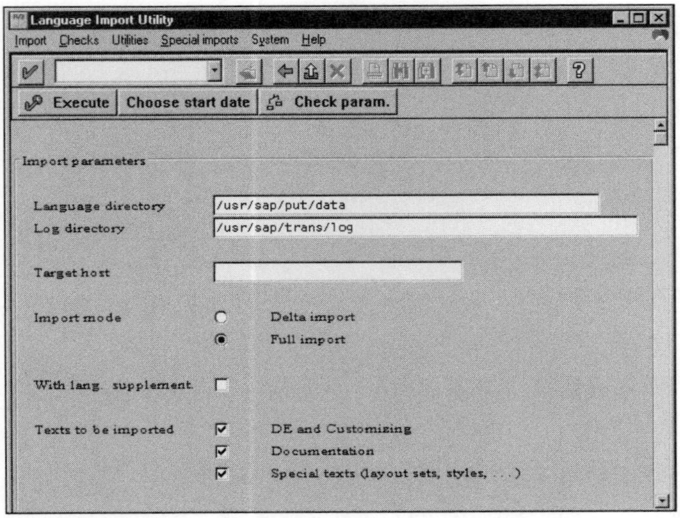

FIGURE 4-5 *Schedule Language Import*

TIP

It is possible to supplement a language completely with English or German, without importing the original language. When you do this, remember to change the status of the language to *installed*. Execute transaction SMLT, select the Language status button, select the language that you want to change, and press the Change status button.

RSCP* Utilities

SAP has a set of utilities that allow you to configure, monitor, and test the language environment. You will find a brief description of these programs below.

RSREFILL   Transport Translations between Clients

This program copies client-dependent language text from client 000 to client nnn if it does not exist in the target client.

RSCP0001   Use of SAP Code Pages

This program reports on the code page usage of an application server and any errors detected in the system. On an MDMP system, it reports errors that are not necessarily errors. This utility is developed for an NLS system. It checks table TCPDB to determine if it contains one single entry. When it detects more than one entry in this table it will report it as an error, and it is not an error.

RSCP0002   Generate Character Set Conversion Table

This program is the same utility as used in transaction SM59. It generates CDP files.

RSCP0004   Use of SAP Code Pages

This program displays the entries in table TCPDB and, with a little effort from the user, deletes incorrect TCPDB entries.

RSCP0010   List of the Applications
Servers and Languages

This program lists the languages and code pages used by each application server.

RSCP0013 Test Bytes on Front End

Use this program to test which characters are displayable on the SAPGUI when using different application servers with different languages installed. If you use a Latin1 GUI and you are logged on to a Japanese server, you will see that the special characters are #.

RSCP0014 Fills Table TCP09

This program populates table TCP09 with the correct data and reports on any incorrect or missing entries.

RSCP0015 Fills Table TCP0B

This program populates table TCP0B with the correct data and reports on any incorrect or missing entries.

RSCP0018 Check the Profiles for Language, Character Sets

This program does a complete test on the language environment and reports any errors. This is an excellent program to execute after a language configuration and installation.

RSCP0020 Maintain TCP0D (Country-Specific Work with Foreign Languages)

This program allows the user to maintain table TCP0D. It also reports the active locales on a specific application server.

Preparing the SAP Online System

The OSS system is the worldwide SAP support line for the thousands of customers who installed SAP software. The SAP online system offers the following services:

◆ Online Service System (OSS). The OSS system contains a wealth of solutions for problems and known bugs discovered in the SAP software. Clients depend on this system to get the latest up-to-date solutions for problems in their environment. Undocumented problems found by customers using the SAP system can be submitted to the SAP support personnel via the OSS system. These highly qualified individuals will then respond with suggestions and possible solutions.

◆ Early Watch Service. SAP has a group of specialized individuals who provide preventive maintenance support. Members of this group log on to your SAP environment to gather statistics. They use these statistics to determine the condition that SAP currently is in and, based on this, they make preventive suggestions.

◆ Online Correction Service (OCS). SAP bundles solutions together in Hot Packages. Instead of applying the thousands of individual OSS notes, SAP advises clients to install the Hot Packages. The OCS service provides not only SAP Hot Packages but also specialized Hot Package solutions for industry solutions, Legal patches, and the latest SAP Business Information Warehouse patches.

Configuration

Assume that the network and the SAP router are configured correctly. The only thing outstanding now is to configure the OSS system within SAP. Figure 4-6 displays the OSS Configuration screen. Within this screen, you define the host names and TCP/IP addresses of each SAP router host running on the customer's side of the network and the hosts running the SAP router and message service at SAP. When this screen is confirmed, the SAP system will define an RFC

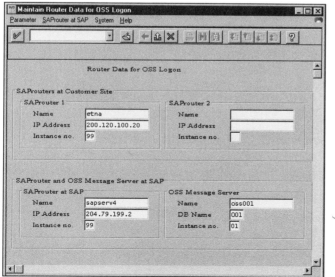

FIGURE 4-6 *SAP OSS Configuration screen*

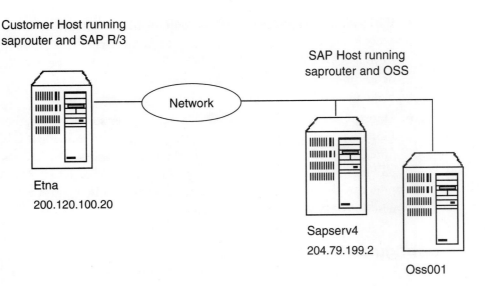

Customer Host running
saprouter and SAP R/3

SAP Host running
saprouter and OSS

Network

Etna
200.120.100.20

Sapserv4
204.79.199.2

Oss001

FIGURE 4-7 *Simple OSS constellation*

connection called SAPOSS. You can view this RFC connection with transaction
SM59. Figure 4-7 displays a simple OSS constellation as defined in Figure 4-6.
The host Enta, in this example, is also running SAP but it does not have to. The
SAP router can function independently from SAP.

SAP OSS Registration

Figure 4-8 displays the different registration functions defined in the OSS system.

Registration SSCR (Source Code Registration)

Register Developers

To be able to change objects within an SAP environment, you have to be registered as a developer. The system will prompt you for a name and it will return the
developer key after it accepts the developer name. Use this key when you develop
something for the first time on an SAP system.

Register Objects

Objects owned by SAP need to be registered in order for the developer to be able
to change standard SAP objects. You will require an object key when applying

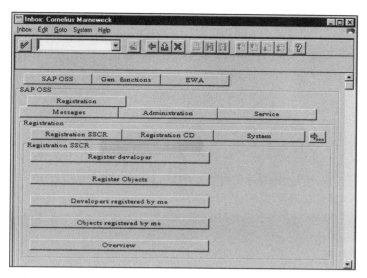

FIGURE 4-8 *OSS registration options*

OSS notes that instruct you to change certain SAP objects. SAP strongly advises customers to install Hot Packages rather than implementing single OSS notes. You also will require a key when you make custom changes to SAP objects. Making changes to SAP objects complicates future upgrades because all these changes have to be accounted for.

Registration CD

SAP developed a set of Knowledge CDs. These CDs have to be registered within SAP in order for you to use them. When installing the Knowledge CDs, the software will supply your registration information. Enter this information into OSS at this location and it will supply you with a key to register the CDs for legal use.

System

Register new SAP instances online. Enter the required information online and SAP will respond within three days with a license key It is not possible to remove licenses online. You have to send a license request to component "XX-SER-SWFL-LIC" and the appropriate form will be faxed to you. For legal reasons related to your license agreement, all information regarding deleted systems or systems planned for deletion must be submitted in writing.

SAP OSS Messages

The OSS system is an interactive system for reporting problems. SAP allows customers to report problems that they have in the OSS system. Depending on the priority, SAP will respond with possible solutions. Before opening a message with SAP, please exhaust the regular OSS notes first. Search for a solution within the SAP database; if you are unable to find a solution, only then should you contact SAP.

One of the fields that SAP requires is the component field. Fill this field out to the best of your knowledge. It helps with the routing of the ticket within SAP. Actually, all the information within the ticket is important. Be exact and give good descriptions of the problem—this just might assist SAP in solving your problem more quickly. Execute transaction BIBO, select the Create Button, and select the SAP instance that this new ticket will pertain to by double-clicking on it. This would open the screen displayed in Figure 4-9.

SAP OSS Administration

In order to be able to use the OSS system, you have to be a registered user. SAP allows customers to define new users, delete old users, and assign authorizations

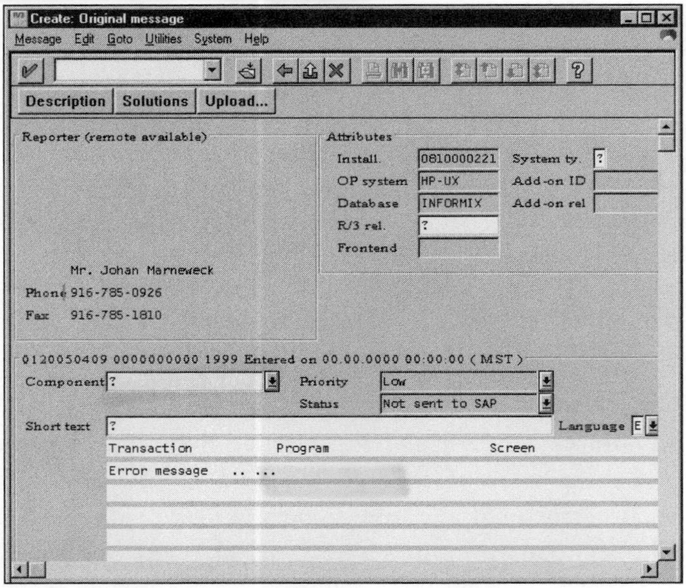

FIGURE 4-9 *OSS Message Entry screen*

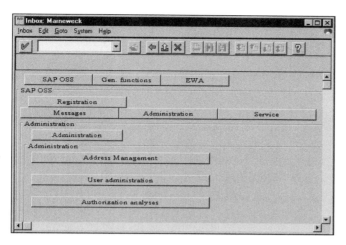

FIGURE 4-10 *OSS Administration screen*

to the different users using OSS. Execute transaction BIBO and select the Administration button; this will display the Administration screen in Figure 4-10.

SAP Service Connection

Every once in a while customers will require SAP to log on to their systems, be it to solve a difficult problem or for an Early Watch session. SAP cannot just connect to a customer's environment—the customer has to allow SAP to connect. The service connection functionality within OSS (as displayed in Figure 4-11) allows customers to open a service connection to their systems. Execute transaction BIBO, select the Service button and then select the Service connection button. The possible services are the following:

- ◆ R/3 Support
- ◆ Early Watch
- ◆ TCC Service Download
- ◆ Remote Consulting
- ◆ R/2 Connection
- ◆ Telnet Connection
- ◆ Netbios Connection
- ◆ PCanywhere

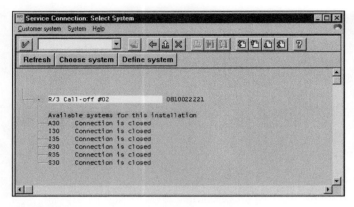

FIGURE 4-11 *OSS service connections*

◆ AS/400-5250 Connection

◆ BW RFC Connection

◆ BW GUI Connection

◆ Upgrade Assistant

General Functions

Notes

The OSS general functions are the door to a wealth of SAP related information. Figure 4-12 displays the initial General Function screen. From here, you can branch out to find OSS problem notes, release notes, upgrade notes, and so on. Execute transaction BIBO and select the Gen.Functions button.

Services

Within the services area, you can book SAP training courses, order upgrade and installation documentation, and enter the SAP system information. Figure 4-13 displays the relevant screen. You get to this screen by executing transaction BIBO, Gen.Functions button, and then select the Service button.

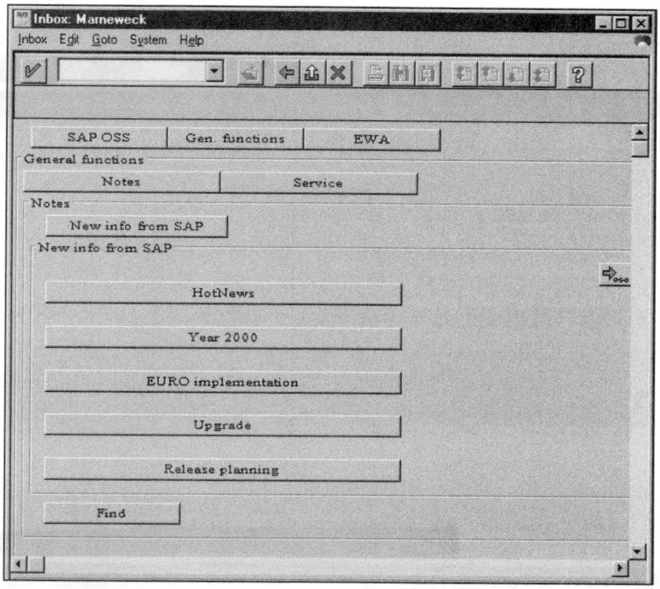

FIGURE 4-12 *Initial General Function screen*

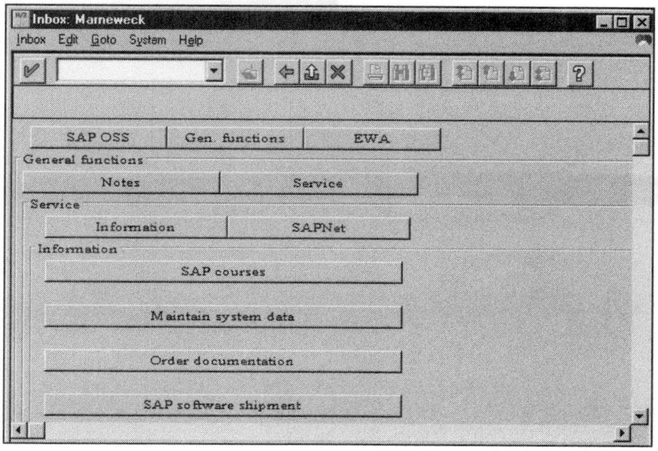

FIGURE 4-13 *Service Information screen*

Online Correction Support

The nice thing about an SAP installation is that you can apply all the SAP Hot Patches without the concern that you are overwriting custom changes to SAP objects—that is, if you did not develop anything before you applied the Hot Packages.

SAP provides the following online correction support:

◆ Hot Packages. A Hot Package is a bundle of corrections for severe SAP errors. Each of the fixes within a Hot Package has a related OSS note. It happens sometimes that you are unable to apply a Hot Package—the alternative then is to find the OSS note that solves the problem and to implement only that note.

The naming convention for Hot Packages is SAPKH<rel><No>, where <rel> is the SAP release that this specific patch pertains to and <No> is the patch sequence number. Hot Packages are SAP release specific; in other words, they have to be applied in sequence and you cannot skip a patch in the sequence.

Most of the Hot Packages can be downloaded from OSS, but some of them are too big. SAP will then ship these Hot Packages on a CD to customer sites.

◆ Conflict Resolution Transports (CRT). CRTs are transports for Industry Solutions. SAP works together with industry partners to develop specific industry solutions, also known as add-ons. These solutions change the standard SAP code, which means that special Hot Packages need to exist. SAP calls these Conflict Resolution Transports, or CRT for short. You apply a regular Hot Package and immediately after that the CRT.

◆ SPAM Updates. It is very important to make sure that you have the latest SPAM utility installed before attempting to install Hot Packages and CRTs. A SPAM update contains the latest enhancements and extensions to the SPAM utility.

◆ First Customer Shipment (FCS)—Final Delta Patches. SAP has a new release strategy, which is to release a first customer shipment (FCS) to selected customers. The FCS Final Delta patches (FFDP) take the FCS to its final state. The FFDP has to be installed before any of the other regular release-specific patches can be installed.

FCS→FFDP→ SPAM → Hot Packages → CRT
(SPDD, SPAU)

◆ LCP—HR Legal Patches. LCPs are Hot Packages for productive human resources systems. LCP replaces Hot Packages in these systems. The SPAM utility will reject any regular Hot Packages as soon as the first LCP is installed.

◆ Business Information Warehouse Patches (BWP). BWPs are the Hot Packages for warehouse systems. Only BWPs can be used on a Business Information Warehouse system.

SPAM—Utility

As of SAP Release 3.1H, the SPAM utility is able to apply more than one Hot Package at a time. The Hot Packages are loaded into a queue from which the Hot Packages are applied.

The SPAM utility enforces that Hot Packages are installed in sequence, and if CRTs are required, these will be implemented in the correct sequence as well.

As mentioned before, the SPAM utility will execute SPDD and SPAU to ensure that custom changes to the environment will not be overwritten. This is mostly true for upgrades but not for installations. Another advantage is that SPAM will make a backup of the objects being changed. This feature allows you to undo a Hot Package.

Steps for Installing Hot Packages

1. **Request Patches Form OSS.** Log on to OSS, select SAP OSS Services, and click on the button pertaining to the type of patches you want to download. You will notice that the add-ons are not listed on this screen. You have to select Hot Packages, Goto, View, Add-on Views. This will bring you to a screen where you can select add-on patches. Look for your current release, expand the list, and request the patches you require.

2. **Download Patches.** Log on to SAP, execute the transaction SPAM, and download the patches. Make sure that you download the SPAM patch first, implement it, and check OSS for any known problems associated with SPAM. Execute the transaction SPAM, then select Patch, Apply, SPAM Update, and then select Patch, Download to download the patches. The patches will be loaded into the queue, in the correct sequence, ready for installation.

TEST
STANDARD

3. **Define Patch Queue.** Press F4 to list the possible patch entries and select the patches to be installed.

4. **Settings.** The patch queue can be applied by following two different scenarios. One scenario is *Test* and the other is *Standard.* You select the scenario you want to follow by selecting the menu items Extras, Settings.

   You select the test scenario "T" when you want to determine if any modifications and adjustments are necessary in your environment before you actually apply the patches by confirming the changes at the end of the Hot Package installation. You are actually only using SPDD and SPAU to identify objects that were changed in the SAP system that conflict with changes in the Hot Packages.

   The standard scenario "S" applies the patch queue completely without the confirmation phase. Prior to release 3.1H this was the only option available.

5. **Apply Patch Queue.** The menu path Patch, Apply Queue does exactly what it says—it applies the patches in the SPAM queue. This is an iterative process. The SPAM utility will report any problems and conflicts with the SPDD and SPAU utilities. These problems need to be resolved in order to be able to confirm that the Hot Package was installed successfully.

6. **Review Logs.** The SPAM logs display any errors encountered during the installation process. The logs have to be checked before you can confirm the installation of the Hot Package. Typical errors would be conflicts with existing OSS Note changes in the system. It can happen that by applying an OSS note you changed a few objects in the system, the Hot Package changes the same objects but only a subset of what you changed. This could cause compilation and generation errors and you will not be able to confirm a patch with any issues outstanding.

7. **Confirm.** This indicates that the Hot Package was installed correctly; once a Hot Package is confirmed, it cannot be undone. You can opt for an undo for different reasons. There might be too many errors and you could have done a Hot Package installation only to identify any conflicts and adjustments during the SPDD and SPAU phases.

original version deleted
so, can not rollback

Distributing Patches

Patches are originally installed on the development systems. Before moving these patches to quality and production, please make sure that all the patches were applied correctly and that all conflicts (if there were any) have been resolved.

SAP implemented a few utilities that allow you to download the Hot Packages from the development system and upload it in the other systems in the environment. Use transaction SE38 to execute the following reports on the source and target systems, respectively.

- ◆ RSEPSDOL. Download patches from the source system.
- ◆ RSEPSUPL. Upload patches into the target system.
- ◆ SPAM, Patch, Upload in Release 4. As of Release 4.0A, the SPAM utility has an upload menu function to upload patches into the target system.

After downloading and uploading the patches, apply the patches to the target system as usual and transport any changes detected in the SPDD and SPAU phases to the target systems.

Summary

This chapter introduced you to the SAP installation process, the SAP language concepts, OSS, and Hot Packages. Knowing all this information and having a well-defined implementation plan should enable you to tackle any SAP installation with success.

PART IV

Configuration

5 Creating and Administrating Clients

6 Security Administration

7 Spool Administration

8 Correction and Transport System

9 SAP Performance Tuning

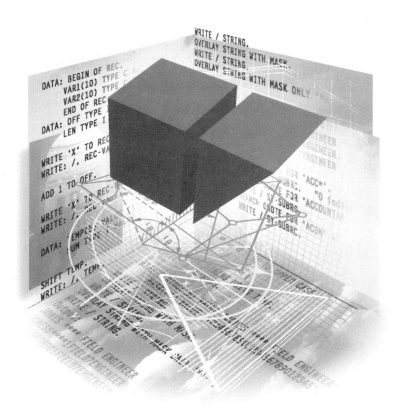

Chapter 5

Creating and Administrating Clients

In This Chapter

- ◆ The R/3 Client Concept
- ◆ Client Usage
- ◆ Client Creation Tools

The R/3 Client Concept

A client is an independent business or a legal unit within an SAP R/3 system. It could be different independent branches within a company. A client is the highest organizational unit. Data belonging to one client may not be shared or viewed by another client. After a successful installation of R/3, the system will have three clients: 000, 001, and 066.

Client 000 contains the client-independent data of the R/3 system and a test company with standard customizations and environment settings. The client-independent data in client 000 is accessible by all the other clients in the system. Special administrative tasks such as language supplementations are done in client 000 as user SAP* or DDIC. Language supplementations are executed in both client 000 and the customer defined clients. Language issues will be discussed in more detail in Chapter 4, An Administrator's Guide to Installing R/3.

Client 001 is a copy of client 000 with the difference being that the data is client-dependent. Data in this client will belong only to client 001. If you for instance do a language supplementation in this client, the language texts in this client alone will be updated. Client 001 is the candidate client to use for any new clients you create. Do not change any settings in client 001. It should remain standard, allowing you always to have a clean client with which to start over. Copy client 001 to any three-digit client number (except 000, 001, and 066) and make all the changes and configurations in the newly created client.

Client 066 is the SAP remote support client. Members of the Early Watch team use this client to log on to your system and to gather the statistics they need to write the preventative performance reports they send their appreciative customers.

Client Usage

The previous section discussed the three standard SAP clients and their usage. Now, how do customers use their remaining clients? Each of the systems defined in the Three-System Layout (see Figure 5-1) can have up to 996 different customer clients.

The following are typical clients defined by companies:

- **Customizing Master.** Master customizing data.
- **Primary Development.** Development and unit testing.
- **Sand Box.** Potential destructive testing.
- **Data load.** Test migration from legacy data to SAP.
- **User Master.** User authorization data.
- **Test.** Quality assurance testing before objects move to production.
- **Production.** Main production work client.

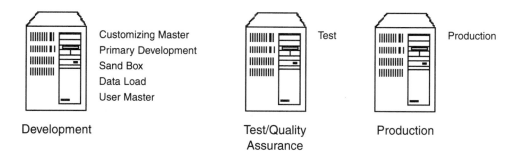

| Development | Test/Quality Assurance | Production |

Customizing Master
Primary Development
Sand Box
Data Load
User Master

Test

Production

FIGURE 5-1 *The three systems in a Three-System Layout are Development, Test/QA and Production.*

Chapter 3 discusses in much more detail the different clients and the strategies associated with each client.

Client Creation Tools

The first step after a successful SAP installation is to create the first customer client. Table T000 is the table that contains the client data. The reader can use transaction SM31 to maintain table T000 directly, or the reader can use transaction SCC4 to create the client. In both cases, the screen will look like the screen shown in Figure 5-2. The system in Figure 5-2 represents a development system. It has a sand box, a customizing master, and a primary development client. The screen is self-explanatory; it requires a descriptive name for the client, the city where the SAP system is located, and the standard currency that the client will use.

Clicking on the New Entries button results in the screen shown in Figure 5-3. The contents of this screen are discussed in detail in the following section.

Logical System *(ALE system)*

A client is a logical system. Information contained in SAP R/3 systems can be distributed to other systems all over the world, functioning independently from

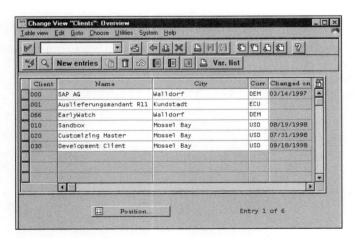

FIGURE 5-2 *Table T000 Client Configuration*

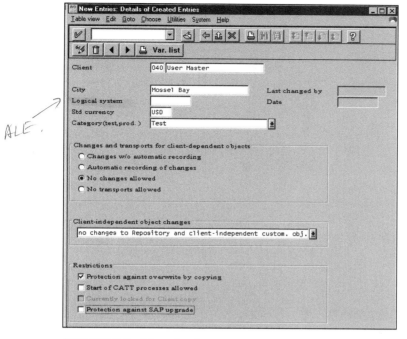

ALE

FIGURE 5-3 *Client Configuration*

each other. SAP developed a technology called ALE (Application Link Enabling) which allows these remote systems to communicate and exchange data as if they were one integrated (logical) system. This field pertains only to ALE systems and it should be left blank if ALE is not used. Once this field contains a value, it should not be changed. The logical system name is used to identify the different communication partners within the SAP R/3 ALE constellation. Intermediate documents (IDocs) are created in the system using this logical name, and if this name changed, the system will not be able to locate your data because it will assume that they were located in a different logical system. The logical system name is used to identify the different communication partners within the SAP R/3 ALE constellation. You can only have one logical system per client—that is, there exists a one-to-one relationship between a client and a logical system. It is beyond the scope of this book to address all the nuances of EDI and ALE.

Category

This field is mostly for documentation purposes. It describes the client role as one of the following:

◆ Production client *(protect against client copies from other)*

◆ Test client

◆ Training client

◆ Demo client

◆ Customizing client

◆ SAP reference client

The category field has one interesting feature though: If a client is a production client, this client will be protected against client copies from other clients. That is, you are unable to overwrite this client unless you change this setting to something else.

Changes and Transports for Client-Dependent Objects

SAP provides four options to record, allow, or disallow changes to the SAP customizing environment. It will depend on the type of client you define what option you choose. For instance, a sand box client should have the **No Transports Allowed** option and a production system should have **No Changes Allowed** selected.

◆ **Changes without Automatic Recording**

Any customizing changes are allowed in a client with this option selected. The changes will not be recorded in a transport request. This setting should only be selected for sand box or data load clients. Transport requests can manually be created to transport these customizing changes. The theory is that if you select this setting, no transports should be manually created, although it is possible.

◆ **Automatic Recording of Changes**

Changes to customizing data are automatically recorded in a transport request. This setting would make sense in the customizing master client on development. None of the other systems (test or production) should have this setting selected.

◆ **No Changes Allowed**

This option belongs to the test and production environment. Customizing is not allowed on clients having this option selected.

◆ **No Transports Allowed**

Changes to customizing are allowed but no transport request will be created (automatic or manual) to transport the changes from the system. Sand box, data load, and training clients should have this option selected.

Client-Independent Object Changes

This option pertains to SAP repository objects (reports, screens, dictionary objects, and so on) and client-independent customizing objects (factory calendar, definition of price list conditions, and printer controls).

development/

◆ **Changes to Repository and Client-independent Customizing Allowed.** Belongs only on a development system.

training sandbox/

◆ **No Changes to Client-independent Customizing Objects.** Pertains to training and sand box clients.

◆ **No Changes to Repository objects.** Pertains to training and sand box clients.

except development/

◆ **No Changes to Repository and Client-independent Customizing Objects.** Pertains to all clients (test, production, training, and the sand box) except development.

Restrictions

◆ **Protection against Overwrite by Copying**

This setting will allow or restrict client copy from replacing this client. Production and Customizing clients should have this setting set.

◆ **Start of CATT Processes Allowed**

Computer aided test tool, which usually should not be allowed on a production client.

◆ **Currently Locked for Client Copy**

This flag is set by the system to prevent users from logging in on the system while client copies are taking place.

◆ **Protection against SAP Upgrade**

Prevents the upgrade process from changing any data associated with the client. This is used in exceptional cases where the users want to use this client as a reference to merge upgrade customizing changes and the old customizing settings. If this option was selected during an upgrade and the settings were merged, this client should be deleted.

SAP distinguishes between two methods to duplicate a client:

◆ **Client Copy.** Takes place when a client is duplicated to the same system.
◆ **Client Transport.** Takes place when two different environments are involved.

Local or Remote Client Copy SCC0

As of release 3.1, this transaction is split into two transactions: SCCL and SCC9. The client copy documentation can be accessed through these transactions by pressing the information button ("I"). Refer to SCCL and SCC9 for more information on this transaction. SCC0 is absolute and not very user friendly; SAP advises not to use it because it will support only transaction SCCL. It still exists and you can use it.

Local Client Copy SCCL

Use this tool to copy one client to another within the same system. Data is duplicated in the system itself. No external files are needed. The Basis administrator needs only make sure that there is enough space in the database to duplicate a client. This involves specifying a profile, the data source client, and the user source client and then executing the copy in the background. With the *test run* option, the administrator can determine how big the client is and how much disk space will be required before the actual copy takes place. Figure 5-4 is the initial SCCL screen. With the fields populated as in Figure 5-4, the system will copy the user master data from client 40 to client 100.

Remote Client Copy SCC9 *(does not use transport dir. only main memory)*

SCC9 copies clients between two different systems. Data is copied from one system to another over the network using an RFC connection; no hard disk space is required. Both client-dependent and client-independent data can be copied by selecting the correct client copy profile settings.

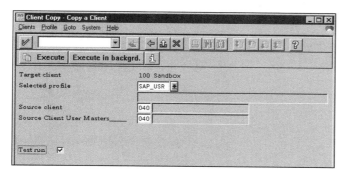

FIGURE 5-4 *Copy user master data from client 40 to client 100.*

Copying a Client per Transport Request SCC1 *(same system)*

Create a transport request that contains the tables that you want to transport to a different client within the same system. It is used to transport object lists between clients. Log onto the target client, execute transaction SCC1, specify the required parameters and transport name, and execute the transaction in the background. An example of this would be to copy variants from one client to another in the same system. You would create a transport request that contains the variant data and use transaction SCC1 to transport it to the target client.

 NOTE

The normal tp transport tools or transaction SCC6 can be used to transport it to a client in a different system.

Once you have used SCC1 to transport internally, the SCC3 overview screen can be used to view the client copy logs and internal transport logs.

Client Copy and Transport (Import and Export) SCC2

As of release 3.1, this transaction is split into two transactions: SCC7 and SCC8. Transactions SCC7 are used for importing clients and SCC8 for exporting clients. Transaction SCC2 is absolute and SAP advises not to use it because it will not be supported any longer. Once again, this functionality is still available and you can use it.

Client Export SCC8

Export a client by creating a transport. This transport requires physical hard disk space. It creates three files:

transport request {

DEVKO00011   client-independent data

cofiles {

DEVKT00011   client-dependent data

DEVKX00011   client-specific texts

Use transaction SCC7 (described in the following section) to import the client export. Use DEVKO00011 as the transport request name.

Client Import— Post-processing SCC7

Log onto the target system and target client and execute transaction SCC7 to import the client that has been exported with transaction SCC8.

Client Copy Log Analysis SCC3

This transaction monitors the progress and success of a client copy. The log contains the following information:

- ◆ The client for whom a copy was performed
- ◆ The time that the copy took place
- ◆ The type of client copy and the profile that was used for the copy
- ◆ The parameters used to perform the copy
- ◆ The name of the user who performed the copy
- ◆ The results of the copy

The progress of a client copy is recorded in a table called CCCFLOW. SAP defined a view on this table that can be viewed through transaction SM30. This table makes it possible to monitor client copies that are executed in the background. Another useful place to monitor a client copy is transaction SM50. Sometimes client copies just seem to hang, doing nothing for hours. With transaction SM50, the administrator can at least see if the client copy process is churning data. Figure 5-5 displays the initial SCC3 overview screen.

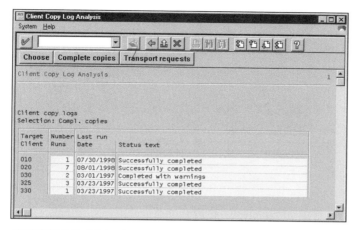

FIGURE 5-5 *SCC3 Client copy logs*

Deleting a Client SCC5 (or R3trans)

This transaction deletes the client in which this transaction is executed. If a target client is going to be replaced by a fresh copy from another client, it is highly advisable to delete the client before the client copy process is initiated. A client can be deleted using SCC5 or using R3trans at the operating system level. SAP suggests SCC5 because it will clean up the SAPscript and batch-input data. SCC5 also requires a smaller rollback segment. The main advantage of R3trans is that it deletes a client very fast.

Client Import per Transport Request SCC6

Import client-dependent or client-independent data into a new client using a transport request. If you have a transport that you created using SCC1, you can import it using this transaction.

Client Copy Profiles

Most of the previously mentioned client-copy tools make use of client-copy profiles. SAP distinguishes between different sets of data, namely user master, customizing, and application data. Figure 5-6 shows a profile SAP_ALL that can be used to copy a complete client form a source to a target client. You can select any of the different profiles available to suit your specific copy needs. Sometimes, you might want to copy only the user master data. You select SAP_USR to copy only user authorization data.

SAP defined the following default profiles:

SAP_ALL	All data of a client
SAP_APPL	Customizing, master and transaction data
SAP_CUST	Customizing data
SAP_UAPP	Customizing, master, and transaction data, and user masters
SAP_UCUS	Customizing data and user masters
SAP_USR/SAP_USER	Authorizations and user masters

Administrators can create their own client-copy profiles using a custom profile name (which must start with a Y or Z). Figure 5-6 shows the maintenance screen for client copy profiles. On each of the client-copy screens that require a profile, the menu bar has an option called Profiles. For instance, execute transaction

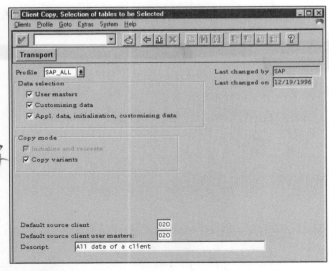

number range reset

Client transport only (

FIGURE 5-6 *Client Copy Profiles*

SCCL, then select the menu option profile. A list of profile maintenance options will appear. You have the option to create a new profile or to change an existing profile. The following is a discussion on the options displayed in Figure 5-6.

Choices Under Data Selection

- ◆ **User Masters**. Select or deselect if the user masters are copied.
- ◆ **Customizing Data**. Select or deselect if the customizing data is copied.
- ◆ **Application Data, Initialization Data**. Select or deselect if application data should be copied.

Choices Under Copy Mode

- ◆ **Initialize and Re-create**. This option is grayed out but can be activated by the menu path Extras, No Initialization. This option should always be selected unless you are sure that you do not want to initialize and re-create a client. The SAP documentation suggests that this option always should be selected, otherwise data inconsistencies might occur. The resetting of number ranges is also controlled from here—even if only customizing data is copied, there is no number range reset if the special function "Copy without initialization and re-creation" is selected.
- ◆ **Copy Variants**. Select or deselect if variants are copied.

Choices Under Transport Between Two Systems

- ◆ **Client-independent data**. Client-independent data can be copied from one client to another on a remote system. Be careful with this option because if client-independent data exists on the target client this data will be lost. This option is only available to transactions that do a client transport from one system to another. *(by client export only, not remote copy)*
- ◆ **Default Source Client**. The source client contains the data that needs to be copied.
- ◆ **Default Source Client User Master**. The source for the user masters. This source does not have to be the same as the data source.
- ◆ **Descript**. Briefly describes the functionality of the specific profile.

Client Copy Prerequisites

Access

An administrator or a user who wants to be able to do a client copy needs the following user authorizations:

- S_TABU_CLI for cross-client maintenance of tables
- S_TABU_DIS for the content maintenance of table CCCFLOW
- S_CLNT_IMP as of 4.5A

In order to be able to copy user master data, authorizations, and profiles, the client administrator also requires:

- S_USER_PRO for user profile
- S_USER_AUT for user master data

For cross-system client copies, the administrator requires transport authorizations. The SAP* user does have all the required authorizations. When a new client is created the default password for SAP* is "pass." Authorizations are discussed in Chapter 6, "Security Administration," in more detail.

Space

Always make sure that you have enough disk space. You have three options: Make a guess based on the total size of the source client, use transaction SCCL and do a test client copy, or write your own program to calculate the size of the client-dependent data of the source client. Just remember that the database does not save a row exactly the same size as that configured in the data definition. The database attempts not to waste space and will save only fields that contain data—empty fields will not be saved. For this reason, it will not work if you count the rows of the tables that contain a client field and multiply it by the actual row size. The *size* option is only available in SAP Releases 3.1 for Oracle Informix and ADABAS. A client without any data will require between 200MB and 250MB of disk space. Use transaction SCC3 to display the copy log and to determine the resource requirements.

Online

SAP suggests running a client copy in the background, but occasionally a client copy is so small that the administrator runs it online. Make sure that the maximum system runtime is long enough to accommodate your online client copy. The system profile parameter that controls this setting is *rdisp/max_wprun_time*. Real life examples of small client-copies are user-master copies and the copying of clients in SAP systems that do not contain huge amounts of transaction and customizing data.

TIP

A client being small does not mean that the client copy will be quick. The speed of a client copy depends on the number of clients you have and the amount of data in each of those clients. The data for all clients is contained in the same tables. Only the client field (mandt) distinguishes between data belonging to different clients. The client copy process has to go through all that data to capture all the data belonging to a particular client.

Background Process

Make sure RDDIMPDP is scheduled to run in the background as user DDIC. This job runs in client 000. Use transaction SM37 to verify that the job is running.

Variants

On SAP releases prior to 3.0F, variants cannot be copied with a client copy scheduled to run in the background. The reason for this is that the background processes require these variants to run, but the client copy deletes and replaces these variants. For old SAP releases, the Basis administrator has to use alternative methods to copy the variants. OSS Notes 41475 and 24427 describes alternative methods. In short, you can create a transport containing the table entries for the tables VARI, VARID, VARIT and TVARIT, create a R3trans control file selecting the data from these tables as described later in this chapter, or you can execute the program RGRVARIX.

Rollback Segments *(restriction for client transport)*

The largest table in a database needs to fit into the database rollback segment. SAP is constantly trying to reduce the dependence on large rollback segments. SAP release 3.1 requires big rollback segments when deleting clients or tables, during remote client copies, or while executing client transports. SAP release 4.0 and later has this restriction apply only to client transports. A big rollback segment is required for local client copies (SCCL) for SAP releases before 3.1G. As of release 3.1G, the client copy utility commits after every 512 records and therefore renders the big rollback segment requirement not unnecessary.

Client transport → large rollback segment, disk

Client copy → large memory, page memory

NOTE

Informix users should make sure your database has enough database locks for releases prior to 3.1G.

Paging Memory

Remote copy → RFC connection.
→ large paging memory, large rollback segment

Client copy

When doing client transports from one system to another using RFC connections, make sure that the page memory on the target and source systems can hold the largest table in your database. Also, make sure that your rollback segment is big enough, because when an RFC connection is used, the system can only do a *commit work* when the table is written in its entirety.

Target and Source Client Consistency Protection

While a client copy is taking place, users should not be using any of the source or target clients. Using a system while a client copy is taking place will cause inconsistencies in the data environment. SAP locks the target client when a client copy is initiated, but it doesn't lock the source client. A lock flag in table T000 is set to lock the target client. The administrator has to ensure that users stay out of the source client. One way to do this is to lock all non-administrative users using transaction SU01 or write a small ABAP program that locks all users. The lock flag cannot be used in the source client because it will prevent the client copy from logging on to this client in order to get the data.

option on source client: change / Currently locked Due to client copy

Client Copy Utilities

RSCLICOP

This is the program that gets executed when you use transaction SCC0. SAP suggests that administrators use SCCL instead of SCC0. This ABAP program contains the client copy documentation. Execute transaction SE38, select Documentation, and display. A window that contains the client copy documentation will appear.

RSCLIEXP

This ABAP program is used to transport a complete copy of a client to a different system than the source. It works together with the ABAP program

RSCLIIMP. SAP suggests that it is better to do a database copy to duplicate a client on a different system than to use this program. RSCLIEXP is useful when you have training clients that have to be refreshed frequently. The transport that contains the client data remains on the disk, and only RSCLIIMP is required to re-import it when needed.

RSCLIIMP

RSCLIIMP imports the export created by RSCLIEXP.

RSCLCCOP

RSCLCCOP is used to copy client-dependent tables from a client. The administrator defines a command list using transaction SC01 that contains the tables that need to be copied. This program can only be used to copy data between clients in the same system.

RSTXR3TR

Use this program to export and import SAPscripts, layout sets, texts, styles, and device types between clients and R/3 systems. A transport request that contains the objects needing to be transported is required.

The transport can contain any of the following entries:

- ◆ Layout sets

    R3TR FORM *name* (name is the name of the layout set)

- ◆ Styles

    R3TR STYL *name* (name is the name of the style)

- ◆ Texts

    R3TR TEXT *object*, *name*, *id*, *L*

    object stands for the text object (from table TTXOB)

    name stands for the text name

    id stands for the text ID (from table TTXID)

    L stands for the language key of the text.

- ◆ Device types

    R3TR PRIN *name* (name is the name of the device type)

RSCLTCOP

This ABAP program supplements RSCLICOP in the sense that it only copies individual tables from one client to another in a single system. This program can be used to copy User Masters from one client to another within a system.

RSAQR3TR

The report RSAQR3TR transports ABAP queries, functional areas and user groups.

Queries, functional areas, and user groups are stored in the table AQDB. This report can transport ABAP queries and everything associated with it to clients within the same system as well as to clients in a different system than the source. (ABAP queries are maintained with transaction SQ00.)

RSCCEXPT

With this report, you maintain a list of tables that you want to exclude from a client copy. It is sometimes useful to exclude tables that are giving you problems during the normal client copy process and then deal with these tables on an individual basis. You can exclude your own custom defined tables, but you should never use this program to permanently exclude SAP tables; contact SAP and consult with them if you want to exclude an SAP table permanently.

RSCLICHK

Check the tables on two different systems before a client transport between these two systems takes place.

RSCCPROT

RSCCPROT is used for client log analysis. This is transaction SCC3. Use this program to analyze the progress and success of a client copy.

A Client Copy in Action

Each client copy is different and requires different steps depending on the end goal with the new or refreshed client. The following table is a checklist of steps in a typical internal client copy. (The target and the source are in the same SAP system.) If you wanted to copy a client to a different system, you would need to export and import the client. Extra steps can be added or some can be left out. Each step takes a certain amount of time. If you document these durations, you can use it to calculate how long a subsequent client copies will take. The X column is a check box indicating that you completed a specific step. This is useful when you do more than one client copy at a time, and some of the steps do not have to be executed sequentially. Each of these steps and more are explained in Table 5-1.

Table 5-1 Client Copy Checklist

Steps	X	Duration
Notify Users	❏	20 Min
Check DB-Spaces	❏	5 Min
Check Disk Space	❏	5 Min
Set rec/client=OFF *(DEFAULT . PFL.)*	❏	5 Min
Toggle Archive Log Mode	❏	5 Min
Stop & Start SAP	❏	5 Min
Backup Users & Deleting Clients	❏	
Backup Users in Target Client	❏	5 Min
Print Users in Target Client	❏	5 Min
Lock Users in Target Client	❏	5 Min
Delete Target Client	❏	10 Hours
Client Copy		
Lock Users in Source Client	❏	5 Min
Copy Source to Target Client	❏	18 Hours
Restore Users from Backup	❏	5 Min
Import Variants from Source to Target Client	❏	10 Min
Import SAP script from Source to Target	❏	10 Min
Import Condition Tables from Source to Target	❏	30 Min
Import ABAP/4 Queries from Source to Target	❏	5 Min
Unlock Users in Source Client	❏	5 Min
Post Copy Activities	❏	
Set rec/client=ALL	❏	10 Min
Stop & Start SAP	❏	5 Min

Handwritten margin notes: "preparation", "Delete target client", "Client copy", "post"

Notify Users

Different companies have different methods of notifying users. Use transaction SM02 (System Messages) to send a system message to all users using the system. If the users have access to e-mail, send all of them an e-mail. You could also mention it in user-group meetings or send all users a voice mail message.

Check DB-Spaces

As a Basis administrator, you always have to monitor database space. Client copies introduce huge amounts of data into a SAP system. The database must have enough space to accommodate all this additional data. The following steps explain how to determine the size of a client and how to check if the database has enough space.

1. Log onto SAP
2. Execute transaction SCCL.
3. Select the required client copy profile.
4. Select the Test Copy option.
5. Execute the Client Copy in Background.
6. Use transaction SCC3 to view the log to see how much data will be copied.
7. Use transaction DB02, Current Sizes to see if enough space is available.
8. If not, use SAPDBA or contact your DBA to add additional space.

Check Disk Space

You also have to check the available disk space to accommodate the additional database space required. If you are using a tp transport to transport a client, you also have to make sure that the export will fit in the /usr/sap/trans file system.

1. Log onto UNIX.
2. Execute the UNIX command cd/usr/sap/trans
3. Execute bdf . to display the current size of the directory. There is a space between bdf and the period. The period indicates the current directory.
4. Check the space available against the size reported in the Test Client Copy Log.

5. If you discover a space shortage, find files to delete. Usually old co- and data files exist and can be deleted to make more space. Another option is to ask your UNIX administrators to add more disk space.

6. Execute 'bdf |grep sapdata'

7. Check to see if enough space is available for additional database files.

8. If you find that there is a space shortage, get the UNIX administrators to add more disk space to the file system.

Set rec/client = OFF / ALL

This step is only required if a customer uses this option to record changes to tables. Switching this option off will expedite the client copy process. To change the settings for this option, follow these steps:

1. Log onto SAP

2. Execute transaction RZ10.

3. Select the profile DEFAULT.PFL.

4. Select Extended Maintenance.

5. Select Change.

6. Look for the parameter rec/client and change its value from ALL to OFF at the beginning of the client copy and OFF to ALL at the end of the copy.

7. Select Copy and Back out.

8. Save and activate the changes to the profile.

If you do a client-independent client copy, you will have to use transaction RZ10, delete the old profiles, re-import the old profiles and then change the value of rec/client from OFF to ALL. Please remember to change the operation modes in CCMS after you have done the re-imports of the profiles.

Toggle Archive Log Mode Off/On

If the client that you are copying is very big, it is advisable to switch archive mode off. During this period, you should not do any productive work. After doing the client copy, you need to switch it on again and make an offline backup of the database. You can leave archive mode on. Make sure that you have enough archive space to accommodate all the client data and that your archiving system to backup tape is functioning correctly and is fast enough to be able to archive these logs off to tape quickly enough so as not to fill up the archive space.

1. Log onto UNIX as <SID>adm.
2. Execute stopsap R3.
3. Execute su ora<SID>.
4. Execute sapdba.
5. Select option f- Archive Mode.

   Select option a- Toggle database log mode.
6. Wait a few minutes for it to complete the task.
7. Select option x- Exit sapdba.
8. Execute startsap.

Delete Target Client

SAP suggests that you delete a client that exists before you replace it with a new copy from somewhere else. This will make the client copy faster and more secure. To delete a client, follow these steps:

1. Log onto SAP into the clients that you want to delete.
2. Execute transaction SCC5.
3. Select Delete in Background.
4. Select Schedule Job.
5. Select Immediate and save.
6. Set up the Print Background Parameters and then save.
7. Use transaction SCC3, SM50, SM30, and SM37 to monitor the client delete process.

> **NOTE**
>
> This option cleans up the SAPscript and batch-input data, but is very slow.

Another way you can delete a client is to do the following:

1. Log onto UNIX.
2. Execute the UNIX command cd /usr/sap/trans/cofiles.

3. Create a control file: cd<client>.ctl

   with contents: clientremove

                        client=nnn

                        select *

4. Execute:

   ```
   /sapmnt/<SID>/exe/R3trans -u 1 -w /usr/sap/trans/log/cd<client>.log
   /usr/sap/trans/cofiles/cd<client>.ctl &
   ```

5. Check the log file in the directory /usr/sap/trans/log with the command:

   ```
   tail /usr/sap/trans/log/ cd<client>.log
   ```

> **NOTE**
>
> This option is fast but requires a big rollback segment and it does not remove SAP-script or batch-input data.

Backup Users

The reason for backing up users is that you might not want to reconfigure from scratch the users currently using a client. It is easier to save them in a temporary place and restore them after the client copy has finished, as follows:

1. Log onto SAP into the clients that are going to be the user backup.
2. Execute transaction SCCL. *(local copy)*
3. Select profile SAP_USR.

   Default source client   xxx

   Default source client user masters   nnn
4. Select Execute in background.
5. Select Schedule Job.
6. Use transactions SCC3 and SM37 to monitor the user backup process.

Another method is to create an object list that contains the tables listed in the following steps. The Object list can then be exported form the R/3 system. This last mentioned method will not be described in this book, but rather yet another method. This method described in the following steps makes use of the R/3 utility called R3trans.

> **NOTE**
>
> The environment is constantly changing with each new SAP release. Make sure that you include all the user tables you need if you use the option described in the following steps.

1. Log onto UNIX
2. log in as <sid>adm.
3. Issue the UNIX command cd /usr/sap/trans/cofiles
4. Create a control file called 'usrbcknnn.ctl' with the following contents:

```
export
file='/usr/sap/trans/data/usrbcknnn.dat'
client = source -client-number (e.g. 131)
select * from USR01
select * from USR02
select * from USR03
select * from USR04
select * from USR05
select * from USR06
select * from USR07
select * from USR08
select * from USR09
select * from USR10
select * from USR11
select * from USR12
select * from USR13
select * from USR14
select * from USR15
select * from USR20
select * from USR30
select * from USR40
select * from USR41
select * from UST04
select * from UST10C
select * from UST10S
select * from UST12
select * from USTUD
select * from USGRP
select * from USGRPHD
```

5. Issue the UNIX command cd /usr/sap/trans/bin
6. Execute:

```
/usr/sap/<SID>/SYS/exe/run/R3trans -w /usr/sap/trans/log/usrbcknnn.log -u 1
/usr/sap/trans/cofiles/usrbcknnn.ctl
```

7. In a different UNIX session execute:

```
tail -f /usr/sap/trans/log/usrbcknnn.log
```

Print Users

Some companies want to be absolutely safe—they print all the user information so that if the worst happens, they will at least be able to type the user information back into the system. To do this:

1. Log onto SAP into the clients that are going to be replaced.
2. Print users using transaction SU01.
3. Select menu option Information, Overview, Users.
4. Select Profiles.
5. Select the List button.
6. Select the List, Print menu option.
7. Set up the print parameters and select the Printer button.

Copy Source to Target Client

The following procedure walks through the steps copying a client to another within the same SAP system. *(client dependant data only)*

1. Log onto SAP into the target clients.
2. Execute transaction SCCL.
3. Select profile SAP_UAPP
   Default source client   nnn
   Default source client user masters xxx
4. Select Action: Local Copy.
5. Select Execute in Background.
6. Select Schedule Job.
7. Select Immediate, and then save.

8. Set up the Print Background Parameters, and then save.

9. Use transaction SCC3 and SM37 to monitor the client copy process.

Lock Users

This option is required because the client copy process does not lock the users in the source system; it only locks the client in the target system.

1. Execute transaction SU01

2. Lock each user or write an ABAP program to lock them.

Unlock Users

You are strongly advised to write an ABAP program to lock and unlock users. It is extremely tedious to lock large groups of users, and when you are done you unlock them again. Another method you can consider is exporting the users in an unlocked state, lock the users, and then when the client copy complete, re-import the users you exported earlier.

1. Execute transaction /nsu01

2. Unlock each user or write ABAP code to unlock them.

Restore Users

Backing up users was explained in an earlier procedure ("Backup Users"). This procedure walks through the steps restoring the users you backed up earlier.

1. Log onto SAP into the new client.

2. Execute transaction SCCL.

3. Select profile SAP_USR

   Default source client   xxx

   Default source client user masters   nnn

4. Select Execute in background.

5. Select Schedule Job.

6. Use transaction SCC3 and SM37 to monitor the User Restore process.

7. Verify users using transaction SU01.

   Select menu option Information, Overview, Users. Then select Profiles and click on the List button.

NOTE

At the bottom of the list is the number of users; the backup should be the same as the source client and you can compare it with the user printouts you have.

Alternatively, you can do the following:

1. Log onto UNIX.

2. Issue the following UNIX command:

   ```
   cd /usr/sap/trans/cofiles
   ```

3. Create a control file called usrrstnnn.ctl with these contents:

   ```
   import
   file='/usr/sap/trans/data/usrbcknnn.dat'
   client = source-client-number
   ```

4. Issue the following:

   ```
   cd /usr/sap/trans/bin
   ```

5. Execute:

   ```
   /usr/sap/<SID>/SYS/exe/run/R3trans -w /usr/sap/trans/log/usrrstknnn.log -u 1
   /usr/sap/trans/cofiles/usrrstnnn.ctl
   ```

6. In a different UNIX session, execute:

   ```
   tail -f /usr/sap/trans/log/usrrstnnn.log
   ```

Export Client

You will have to create a custom profile to execute the client export because the client-independent option is not selected in any of the default SAP profiles. Follow these steps:

1. Log onto SAP into the client that will be exported.

2. Execute transaction SCC8.

3. Create the profile ZCUS_ALL.

   Data selection:

   X User masters

X Customizing data

X Appl. data, initialization, cust. data

Copy mode

X Initialize and recreate X Client-independent

X Copy variants

Default source client   xxx

Default source client user masters   nnn

4. Select Action: Export.

5. Select Execute in Background.

6. Select Schedule Job.

7. Select Immediate, and then save.

8. Set up the Print Background Parameters, and then save.

9. Use transactions SCC3 and SM37 to monitor the user backup process. Care should be taken when you monitor this export. SCC3 reports that the program was canceled, but after a few minutes it reports that it was successful. You will see in SM37 that it is running. You can use SE09 to monitor the creation of the client-copy transport. When you see this transport, you know that at least it is working.

10. At UNIX level execute `tail -f /usr/sap/trans/tmp/<SID>Etnnnnn.<SID>` where nnnnn is the transport number.

11. Find and remember the transport request number for the import into the target client.

Another option is to do the following:

1. Log onto SAP

2. Execute transaction SE38.

3. Type **RSCLIEXP** in to the program box provided.

4. Select variants.

5. Look for or create a variant called DEV_EXPORT with the following contents:

With master/transaction data   X

With user masters   X

With client-indep. tabs.   X

Target Sys. for client export   DEV

6. Back up to the initial SE38 screen.

7. Select Program, Execute, Execute with Variant.

8. Type the name of the variant you found or created in Step 5 (for example, DEV_EXPORT).

9. A screen with the variant attributes appears. They should look like those listed in Step 5.

10. Select Program, Exec. in Background.

11. Set up the Print Background Parameters, and then save.

12. Use transactions SCC3 and SM37 to monitor the user backup process. (You can use SE09 to monitor the creation of the client-copy transport. When you see this transport, you know that at least it is working.)

13. At UNIX level, execute:

    ```
    tail -f /usr/sap/trans/tmp/<SID>Etnnnnn.<SID> where nnnnn is the transport
    number.
    ```

14. Find and remember the transport request number for the import into the target.

Import Client

Exporting a client was discussed earlier in this chapter. The following procedures list the steps to import the client that was exported earlier.

1. Log on to SAP onto the client that will receive the new import.

2. Execute transaction SCC7.

3. Enter the number for the transport request that you created when you exported the client.

4. Execute in Background.

Alternatively, you can:

1. Log onto UNIX.

2. Issue the following UNIX command:

    ```
    cd /usr/sap/trans/bin
    ```

3. Execute:

    ```
    tp addtobuffer <SID>KT0nnnn.<SID>
    ```
    (Use SE09 to find the transport.)

4. Execute:

```
tp import <SID>KT0nnnn clientnnn <SID>
```

5. In a different UNIX session, execute:

```
tail -f /usr/sap/tranf/log/SLOGnnnn.<SID>
```

6. In a different UNIX session, execute:

```
tail -f /ust/sap/trans/tmp/<SID>IT0nnnn.<SID>
```

7. This process will run for a few hours. The logs mentioned above can be used to verify that the copy was successful or not.

Import Variants

Prior to Release 3.0F, variants were not copied when a client copy was scheduled in the background. In 3.0D pricing condition tables weren't copied either because it belonged to the $TMP development class. In later releases, this problem was fixed, but a procedure copying variants and tables are very useful even in the later versions of SAP.

Import Variants and Condition Tables (Cnnn and Annn Tables)

1. Get OSS note 39074

2. Log onto UNIX

3. Issue the following:

```
cd /usr/sap/trans/cofiles
```

4. Create a control file varcop.ctl with these contents:

```
clientcopy
source client = source -client-number
target client = target-client-number
select * from VARI
select * from VARID
select * from VARIT
select * from TVARIT
select * from C000
select * from C001
select * from C002
select * from C003
```

```
select * from C004
select * from C005
select * from C520
select * from C530
select * from C540
select * from C550
select * from A501
select * from A520
select * from A521
select * from A550
select * from A650
select * from A652
select * from A654
select * from A656
select * from A658
select * from A660
select * from A670
```

5. Issue the following UNIX command:

```
cd /usr/sap/trans/bin
```

6. Execute:

```
/usr/sap/<SID>/SYS/exe/run/R3trans -w /usr/sap/trans/log/variant_copy.log -u 1
/usr/sap/trans/cofiles/varcop.ctl
```

7. In a different UNIX session, execute:

```
tail -f /usr/sap/trans/log/variant_copy.log
```

ABAP Queries

To check if ABAP queries exist in the client you want to delete.

1. Execute transaction SQ00 or follow the menu path System, Services, ABAP Query.

If queries exist, do the following:

1. Execute transaction SE38.
2. Run the ABAP program RSAQR3TR.
3. Select the transport option Export.

4. Select Transport User Groups.

5. Deselect Test run when you are ready.

6. Select the Execute button.

7. Note the transport it created from the screen that appears.

8. Use the Back Out (green) Arrow to go one screen back.

9. Select Transport Functional Areas and Queries.

10. Select the Execute button.

11. Note the transport it created from the screen that appears.

You can import queries (to the same system) with the following steps:

1. Do not delete the client before you have imported the ABAP queries.

2. Log on to the client that will receive the ABAP queries from the old client.

3. Execute transaction SE38.

4. Run the ABAP program RSAQR3TR.

5. Select the transport option Import.

6. Deselect Test Run when you are ready.

7. Enter the transport number: *Transport request with imports: AnnK9nnnnnn.* First, import the transport with the user groups and then the transports with the function groups and queries.

8. Select the Execute button.

To import queries to different systems as well as the same system, follow these steps:

1. Execute transaction SE01.

2. Release and export the transport requests that you noted in Step 11 of export queries.

3. Use tp utility importing the transport with the user groups first and then the transports with the function groups and queries.

4. Use transaction SE01 or SE09 to analyze the transport logs for any errors.

Chapter 6

Security Administration

In This Chapter

- Methodology
- Authorizations
- Profile Generator
- Other Tools and Security Issues
- Security Roles and Responsibilities
- Audit Information System (AIS)
- Critical Authorizations Combinations

This chapter will assist the basis and security administrators with information for the overall implementation of authorizations and security for the SAP system and provide guidance for administrators on what auditors will be looking for and how to proactively avoid these pitfalls.

SAP creates an environment that is independent from the hardware and system software and allows adequate access to the configuration, master, and transaction data. Hence, the SAP login is independent of the login to the operating and database systems. In fact, the users log on to workstations that act as clients to the SAP servers (the user has no direct logon to the application or database servers) reducing the risk of unauthorized activity in the SAP environment.

The objective of implementing security and controls is to ensure that SAP authorizations will allow end users, project team members, and administrators to successfully execute transactions to which they have permissions and deny all other transaction access.

Security and control policies and procedures are in place to ensure that a company will be protected from data loss and corruption resulting from honest user mistakes or malicious intent.

Methodology

The process of defining the initial policies is a cyclical process that includes creating, reviewing, refreshing, and reapplying each policy. The three bullet points that follow can serve as a starting point for developing a security process and should be refined as SAP becomes more prevalent in your company.

- ◆ **SAP Project Scope and Assumptions**

  Number of users

  Number of roles/profiles

  Organization structure defined

  Timeline of overall project

  SAP system architecture defined and established

  Modules and functionality implemented

  Security for DEV/TST/PRD and training systems

  Application security

  Configuration security

  ABAP security

  Interface security (ALE/EDI/API)

  Basis security

- ◆ **Roles and Responsibilities**

  Change management team

  Security approval team

  Application/Basis security teamBusiness process owners

  Security audit team (outside firm)

- ◆ **Policies**

  Access change management policies and procedures

  Standards Naming conventions (users, authorizations, profiles, jobs, etc.)

For the three-system landscape of **DEV**elopment, **Q**uality **AS**surance and **PR**o**D**uction (DEV/QAS/PRD), you can set different levels of security depending on the types of users. For example, an application developer in the development will have different access than an application user in production.

Also, security may vary from company to company due to internal/external audits, ISO certification, or legal and regulatory requirements. For example, due to FDA regulations in the pharmaceutical industry, authorizations are applied as rigorously in the development system as in the production system to ensure that "unwelcomed" changes and programs are not transported in the production environment. However, in most other SAP implementations, the authorizations setup in the development system are typically broken down into the application area (FI, CO, MM, SD, etc.) and the technical area (Basis, ABAP, etc.) with the production system setup with full security setup.

The following list identifies the main areas within SAP that require security controls and standards implemented.

- ◆ SAP logon ID
- ◆ SAP user master data and defaults
- ◆ SAP authorizations/profile
- ◆ SAP transaction locking/unlocking
- ◆ SAP table security and logging
- ◆ SAP ABAP security and logging

As mentioned earlier in the chapter, you can set up different levels of security for the three different systems, as seen in the following:

- ◆ **DEV Environment**

    Application profiles

    Configuration/table profiles

    ABAP development profiles (interface profiles too)

    Basis profiles

    Security profiles

    Correction and transport profiles

    Operating system and database profiles

◆ **QAS Environment**

Test application user profiles

Basis profiles

End-user training profiles

◆ **PRD Environment**

End-user application profiles

Basis and security and audit profiles

Authorizations

Authorizations are the means by which access to the SAP system is granted. The complete process of setting up authorizations is a hierarchical procedure. The following section is a brief, step-by-step explanation of how to create each of the respective objects.

Authorization Classes and Objects

SAP custom authorization objects and fields are created only if you create your own Authority-Checks used in your ABAP code. SAP objects should not be deleted or modified because there are multiple links from fields or objects to other authorization objects.

Authorization Objects

Authorization objects are part of an object class and can be defined with a maximum of 10 fields. The object classes may be created or viewed via transaction code SU21 or choosing the menu path Tools, ABAP Workbench, Development, Other Tools, Authorization Objects, Objects.

Authorization Fields

The fields are given values that are checked during authorization checks. If they satisfy the conditions for each field authorization, then the task is executed. You may create your own fields for objects via transaction code SU21 or by selecting the menu path Tools, ABAP Workbench, Development, Other Tools, Authorization Objects, Fields.

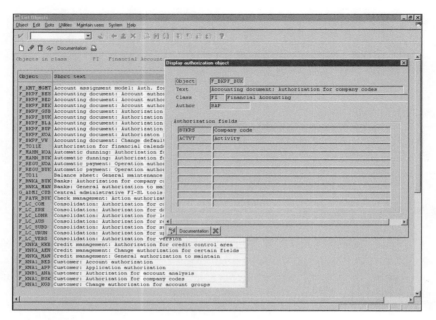

FIGURE 6-1 *Authorization fields for the F_BKPF_BUK object*

Authorizations

Authorizations allow you to execute a task based on the values set in the fields in the authorization object. The fields may contain as values one or more characters, a range of characters, or a wildcard (*) character. These authorizations are then used to create profiles, which are then added to the user master records. Any changes made to field values will affect authorization objects, profiles, and ultimately the end user immediately. Authorizations can be maintained manually or automatically using the profile generator (which will be explained later in the chapter). The authorizations are client-dependent but can be copied or transported from client to client or from SAP system to SAP system.

In Figure 6-2, an authorization will be created to restrict the use of the archiving transaction and the modules to which the user has archive access. To create the authorization, execute transaction SU03 or follow the menu path Tools, Administration, User Maintenance, Authorization. Then, Double-click on Basis: Administration (see Figure 6-3).

If you click on the Technical Names button, you will be presented with the same screen as before, but with the names of the authorization objects. This will assist

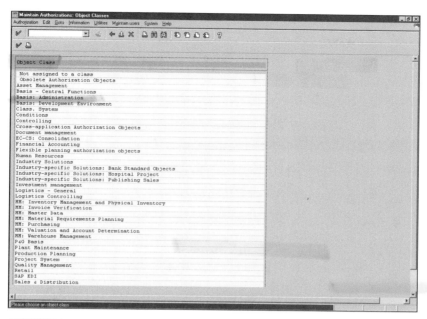

FIGURE 6-2 *Creation of an Authorization Step 1—Identifying the authorization object class*

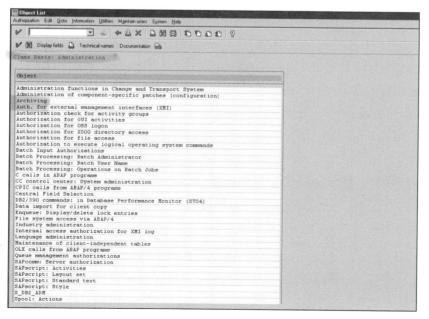

FIGURE 6-3 *Creation of an Authorization Step 2—Identifying the authorization object within a class*

in problem resolution when a user is unable to execute a transaction. Double-click on Archiving (see Figure 6-4).

Click on the Create button, and then type in an authorization name (ensure that it begins with the letter Y or Z—which is the customer name range) and a brief description (see Figure 6-5).

You are now presented with the maintaining field's screen, and you are required to double-click on each field name and insert values. In Figure 6-6, where the values for Activity are shown, select 03 and press Enter. (You may enter a range: Select 01 for From and 03 for To and this will insert a range 01-03, giving create, change, and display access.)

Repeat the process for Application Area and Archiving Object.

The final step is to activate the authorization, which is done by clicking on the Activate icon (see Figure 6-7). Clicking once on the Activate icon only creates a maintenance version (used when you create an authorization change but wish to implement at a later time or date, perhaps at the end of the day). When you click

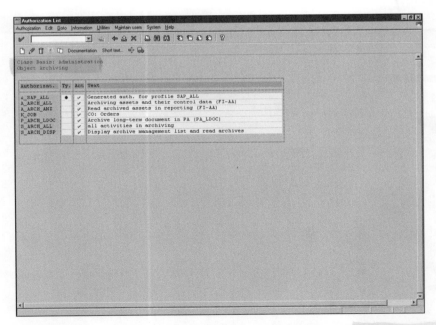

FIGURE 6-4 *Creation of an Authorization Step 3—Identifying the authorizations within a class and object*

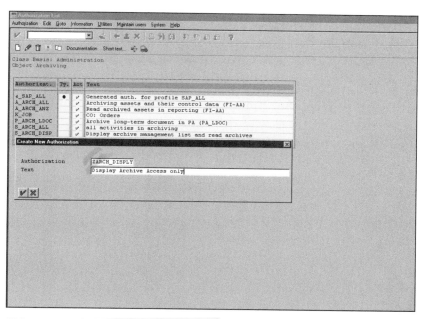

FIGURE 6-5 *Naming the authorization*

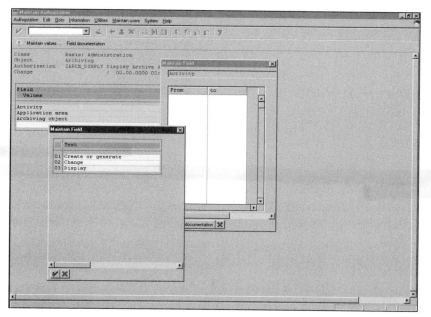

FIGURE 6-6 *Maintaining field values*

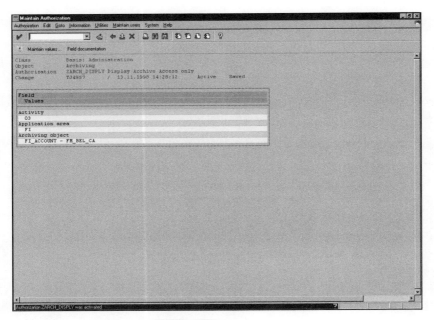

FIGURE 6-7 *Activating the authorization*

the Activate button the second time, the change is immediate and the new authorization is activated. When you press the green arrow to go one screen back, you will see the newly created authorization.

Authorization Profiles

As stated earlier, authorizations are not assigned to the user masters directly but are assigned to authorization profiles. Authorization profiles can be maintained manually or automatically using the profile generator. The profile generator creates single profiles, but manually created profiles can be made to generate composite profiles. The profile generator is the preferred method of creating profiles and will be discussed later in this chapter. The profiles can be maintained through transaction SU02 or by selecting the menu path Tools, Administration, User, Maintenance, Profiles.

Single profiles are a set of object names and corresponding authorization names and are assigned to the user master record. Changes to these profiles take effect the next time the user logs on. The authorization profiles are client-dependent but can be copied or transported from client to client or from SAP system to SAP system.

Composite profiles are a set of simple profiles grouped together and assigned to the user master record. Changes to these profiles take effect the next time the user logs on. The authorization profiles are client-dependent but can be copied or transported from client to client or from SAP system to SAP system.

To continue with your archiving example, execute transaction SU02 or follow the menu path Tools, Administration, User, Maintenance, Profiles.

Insert a customer names range name (starting with a Y or Z) and press the Enter key. Click the Create button and enter a new profile name (again starting with a Y or Z). Finally, press Enter to accept these values (see Figure 6-8).

The next step is to insert the newly created authorization from the previous step into the profile (see Figure 6-9).

Press the Insert Authorization button, and then double-click on the Basis: Administration line. Scroll down until you find the authorization—in the example it is ZARCH_DISPLY—and then double-click on the line. Now the object has been inserted. Click on the Activate button twice to immediately activate the profile.

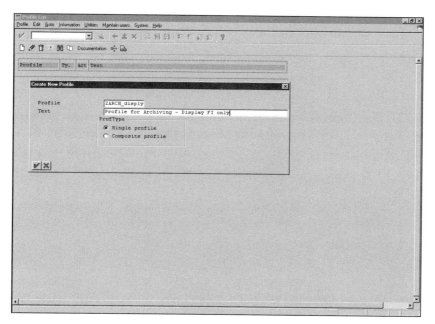

FIGURE 6-8   *Creating and naming a new profile*

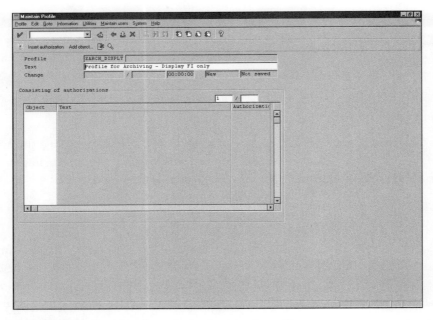

FIGURE 6-9 *Inserting the authorization into the profile*

User Master Records

User master records are allocated to each user and contain authorization profiles and other pertinent information, such as address, telephone number, parameters, activity groups, and so on.

The user master records can be maintained through transaction code SU01 or by selecting the menu path Tools, Administration, User Maintenance, User (see Figure 6-10).

Insert the user ID and click on either Create if it's a new user or Change if user has been previously defined.

Selecting the Profiles tab, you are able to insert a profile. In Figure 6-11, the ZARCH_DISPLY has been inserted and saved.

The user now has a logon ID with a password and access to the archive. (In this example, the user does not have access to execute transactions and will therefore require the S_TCODE authorization, the authorization check to execute a transaction, located in the cross application authorizations objects from transaction SU03.)

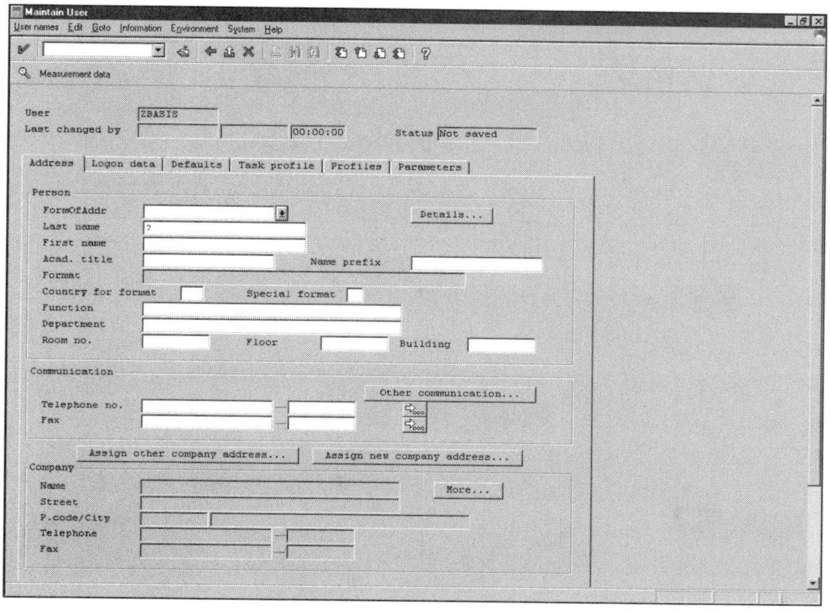

FIGURE 6-10 *User Master Record maintenance screen*

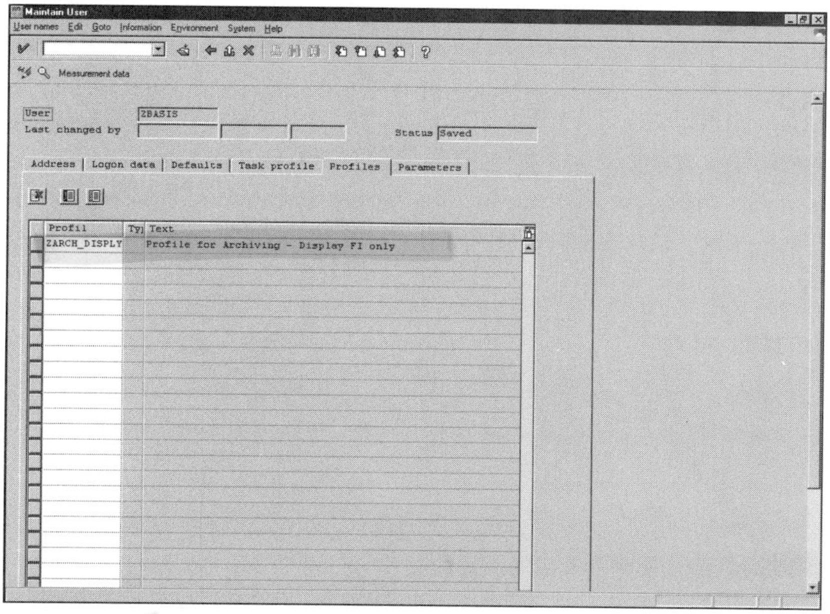

FIGURE 6-11 *User Master Record with a profile*

As seen in the Logon Data tab in the initial user master record screen, there are a number of types of users that can be defined (the default is dialog):

passord required

no passord required

- ◆ **Dialog.** A normal interactive user logging on to the SAP system and subject to password and authorization validation.
- ◆ **BDC (batch user).** A user type defined to process batch input sessions (a job that mimics a user on the keyboard inputting large numbers of data records with no interaction involved) and subject to authorization validation. Passwords are not required. However, you will not be able to use this method interactively.
- ◆ **Background.** A user type that processes jobs or reports using a background process, with no password required.
- ◆ **CPIC (interface user).** A user type that executes CPIC function calls and is not subject to password validation. But, a default password of ADMIN is used to connect to the SAP system. As with the BDC user type, you will not be able to use this method interactively.

default passord 'ADMID' →

Special User Accounts

Upon installation of the SAP system, there are a number of default clients, and within each client there are two users predefined.

Clients 000, 001, and 066 are created by default. Clients 000 and 001 are special data-populated clients, and client 066 is used for Early Watch. Within each client there are two predefined users: SAP* and DDIC. (Early Watch is a service that SAP provides pre- and post-production support to analyze SAP system performance and other SAP-related issues.)

> ▶ **TIP**
>
> Please reference OSS notes 40869 and 29276 for the Early Watch user and some useful reports to run.

SAP*—In clients 000 and 001, the default password is set to 06071992. It is best if the SAP* user is either deactivated (do not delete—it is used for various operations, such as client copies) or have its password changed. Then create a new superuser with the same profiles as SAP* and assigned to the Super user group.

TIP

To reset password for SAP, you can either write an ABAP:

```
Report ZSAPRESET.
Tables: USR02.
Delete from usr02 client specified
where mandt = '123'
    and bname = 'SAP*'.
Write: / 'Deleted password =' sy-subrc.
```

Or at the database level:

```
DELETE DEOM SAPR3.UTAB
                 WHERE TABNAME = 'USR02'
                 AND VARKEY = '123SAP*';
```

where 123 is the client number.

Please be aware that when a new client is created or copied, the default password of SAP* is set to PASS and has unlimited access. However, when the client copy is complete, the password will be set to the copied client's SAP* password.

DDIC—In clients 000 and 001, the default password is set to 19920706. This user has special privileges and must be secured by changing the password. Do not delete.

Passwords

A number of password restrictions are already programmed into the SAP system and several more may be configured to further enhance the security. The following are several of these system parameters:

 ◆ **login/ext_security**. Access control for the SAP system can be managed by external security tools, such as Kerberos and Secude.

 ◆ **login/fails_to_session_end**. Number of incorrect logins allowed before the login procedure is terminated.

 ◆ **login/fails_to_user_lock**. Number of incorrect logins allowed before login is locked for the user. The lock is released either by the system administrator or at midnight. An entry is also written to the system log.

- **login/min_password_lng.** Minimum length of the login password, with the default set to three characters. Ideally, you should change the setting so that a longer password needs to be entered.

- **login/no_automatic_user_sapstar.** When set to 1, the automatic use of the user master record of user SAP* will be deactivated. If set to 0 and SAP* is deleted, you can log on to the system again by using SAP* and the initial password PASS. SAP* now has the complete authorization, and the password PASS cannot be changed.

- **login/password_expiration_time.** A value of 0 means that users are not forced to change their passwords. A value greater than 0 specifies the number of days after which the user has to change the login password.

- **rdisp/gui_auto_logout.** If there is no activity or entry for defined seconds at the GUI, the SAPGUI automatically logs out. If the parameter has a value of 0, the SAPGUI will not automatically log out.

The USR40 table (see Figure 6-12) is another important area where you, as the Basis administrator, can increase security by excluding certain words that can be easily guessed by would-be hackers! For example, the words could be your company's

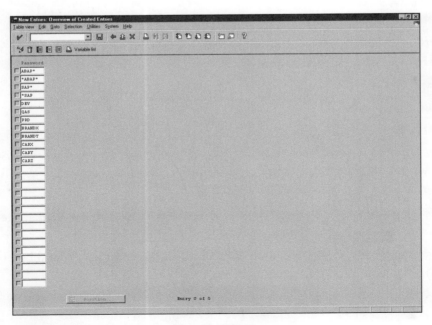

FIGURE 6-12 *Illegal passwords in table USR40*

product names, or SAP specific, such as SAP, ABAP, DEV, QAS, PRD. To maintain this table, use transaction code SM31, and type **USR40**, and click on the Maintain button. You may then enter the illegal passwords; wildcard characters are permitted (for example, ABAP* or *ABAP*).

For the majority of companies, SAP provides ample user security features and tools to implement a very strong security environment to ensure that the end users have adequate authorizations to perform their tasks, and that the SAP environment is not open to misuse.

Table Authorizations

Table security and logging is used by SAP and administrators to restrict access and log changes made to that table, by whom, and at what time. Configuration and system tables will log change when entries are inserted into the table or when the structure changes, whereas transaction tables will not log the entries, especially if there are thousands of entries made every day!

Table access restrictions may be instigated in a number of ways. One of the quickest methods is to secure access to the table authorization object S_TABU_DIS. This object restricts the tables that a user has access to and with what privileges. Use transaction code SU03 or the menu path Tools, Administration, User Maintenance, Authorizations, double-click on Basis: Administration and then double-click on Table Maintenance. This screen illustrates the standard SAP table authorization objects access (see Figure 6-13). If you double-click on one of these—for example, "C_A_ALL - PP: User, All Action"—the user given this authorization will have complete activity (denoted by the *), within the CA authorization group. In other words, when the user is given the C_A_ALL - PP: User, All Actions, the user will only be able to access tables that belong to the CA authorization group.

To create your own table authorizations, you are required to first create the authorization group (see Figure 6-14). Execute transaction code SM31 (table maintenance), enter **TDDAT** for the table's name, click the Maintain button, then click on the Authorization Group button.

Click on the New Entries button and add your customer authorization group. Please ensure that it begins with the letter Y or Z and has a maximum of four characters. (The tables can be classified as system, application, or customizing tables.)

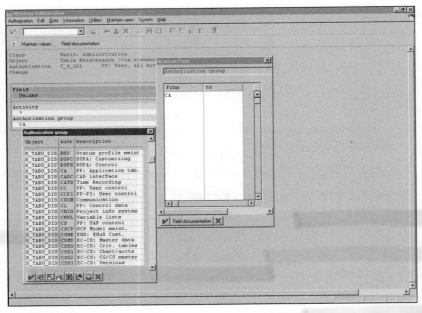

FIGURE 6-13 *Authorization fields values for object* S_TABU_DIS.

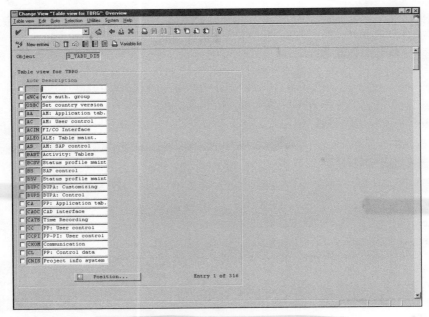

FIGURE 6-14 *Authorization Group Table maintenance transaction*

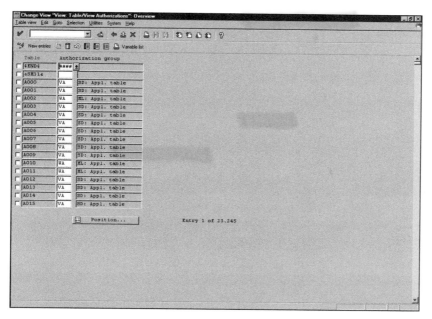

FIGURE 6-15 *Tables and views assigned to authorization groups*

If you click on the Assign Authorization Groups to Tables/Views button on the initial SM31/TDDAT screen, you are able to view or change the tables that are assigned to the authorization groups (see Figure 6-15).

After you have created your own table's authorization groups and assigned your tables to the groups, you can now assign the S_TABU_DIS object to the user as outlined earlier in the chapter.

To view tables that have log changes set, execute transaction code SE38, type in program **RSTBHIST**, and execute. Select Tables with History Management and click on List. You are then presented with a list of tables (and descriptions) that have table logging set.

To set a table to log changes:

1. Execute transaction code SE11.
2. Insert table name (e.g., T000) and click on Change.
3. Select Technical Settings.

4. Click on Log Data Changes (this change will create a repair/transport, which you may transport through your SAP landscape). The following figure is the screen for viewing the technical settings for table T000. Log Data Changes is the option setting circled in Figure 6-16.

Another method of viewing which tables have changes logged is through transaction code SE11, typing in **TPROT**, and clicking on the Display button. Follow the menu path Utilities, Table Contents, and then click on the Execute button. The output displays the tables, but the column PROTFLAG indicates whether the table has logging set, as seen in Figure 6-17.

TIP

To view online documentation regarding tables, execute SE38 and RSSDOCTB, then change or insert appropriate entries, and execute.

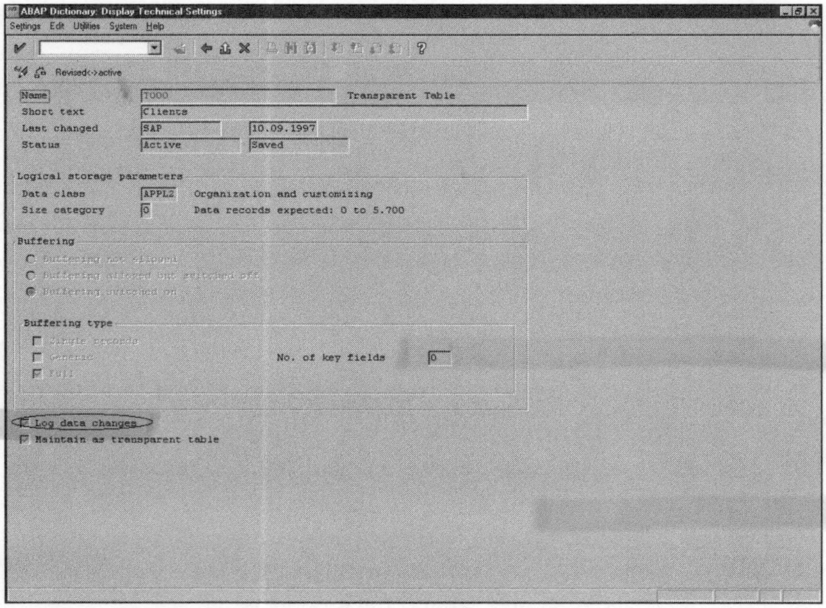

FIGURE 6-16 *Setting the Log data changes option for tables*

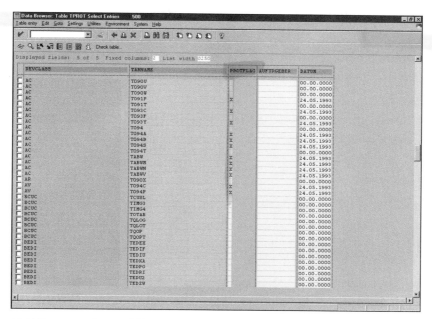

FIGURE 6-17 *View Tables that have table logging option set*

ABAP Authorization

ABAP authorizations are slightly more complicated than normal authorization access, as the transactions may require several authorizations privileges to execute successfully. The main authorizations required in executing, creating, or modifying ABAP programs are the following:

S_DEVELOP	ABAP workbench
S_PROGRAM	ABAP program run checks
S_QUERY	Authorization for ABAP query
S_C_FUNCT	C calls in ABAP programs
S_CPIC	CPIC calls from ABAP/4 programs
S_PATH	File system access via ABAP/4
S_ADMI_FCD	ABAP administration
S_ADMI_TRACE	Authorization for ABAP/4 trace

(handwritten, top margin)
① Create ABAP authorization group
② assign to program attribute
③ assign to authorization object

Several of these authorization objects contain fields that refer to an ABAP authorization group. These groups are used for authorization activities of which a large number have been created for you. However, you should always create your own either from scratch or by copying existing ones.

These ABAP authorization groups (similar to the table authorizations groups) are created by executing transaction SE16, typing in TPGP, and clicking the Execute button (see Figure 6-18).

If you then click on the Create button, you can enter new entries stating the application and the name (maximum of eight characters) of the group name.

These group names are then entered in the technical settings of the attributes of the program. Using transaction SE38, type in the program name, click the attributes radio button, click the change button, and then type in the authorization group name in its appropriate place.

The final step is to add the group or a range of groups to the authorization objects using transaction code SU03, then select the Authorization Class, then the Authorization Object, and then the Authorization. Double-click on Authorization Group ABAP Program field and then add the newly created group(s).

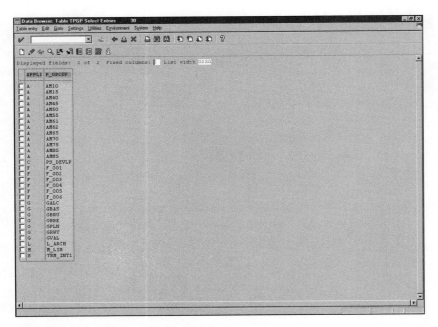

FIGURE 6-18 *Creating ABAP authorizations groups*

Authority-Checks

Authority to execute ABAP programs is triggered by the ABAP authority-check statement within the program source code when the transaction is executed. For example, when a programmer specifies the authorization field values in the program and the user executes the program, the authority-check will verify if the user has sufficient authority; if so, then the program will continue to execute or else it will give an error message. The objects, fields, and values are maintained through the menu path Tools, ABAP Workbench, Development, Other Tools, Authorization Objects, Fields and Objects.

An example of an Authority-Check:

```
AUTHORITY-CHECK OBJECT 'S_TRANSPRT'
           ID 'TTYPE' FIELD 'CLCP'
           ID 'ACTVT' FIELD '01'
IF SY-SUBRC EQ 0.
    'PERFORM A TASK'
ENDIF.
```

(handwritten: can depend on input value.)

This example illustrates that an authority-check will be performed in the client transport program only if the user has authorization with the field values CLCP and 01.

Profile Generator

The profile generator is a tool that is available from SAP R/3 Version 3.1G, which allows the creation and generation of profiles using a user-friendly tool, instead of the previous manual and tedious method. Transport patches from OSS are available to install the profile generator for earlier versions of SAP.

Several preliminary tasks need to be performed prior to using the profile generator.

- ◆ Set system parameter auth/no_check_in_some_cases = Y using transaction RZ11 or SE38 and typing RSPARAM.
- ◆ Define a development class for transport and executing transaction code SU25 work through the action steps in order from 1 to 3 (see Figure 6-19). *(handwritten: (installation of profile generator))*

You may edit these defaults at a later date using transaction SU24.

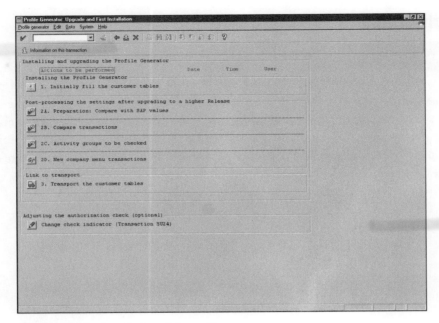

FIGURE 6-19 *Installation of the profile generator*

◆ Execute transaction SSM1, and generate the company menu. (Select the function modules you are implementing as this then becomes the basis for functions and transactions for an activity group.)

◆ Schedule report RHAUTUP1 to run daily, and the authorization profiles in the user master will be updated per the changes. (Use transaction SM37 to schedule this program)

Once the preliminary steps have been performed, you are then able to create authorizations using the profile generator.

Activity Group Creation and Assignment

1. From the profile generator menu (transaction PFCG), select Activity Groups. Click on the Create button and enter a name as the identification code and an appropriate description, and then save.

2. Click on the Menu button. The company menu generated earlier is displayed as a hierarchical structure.

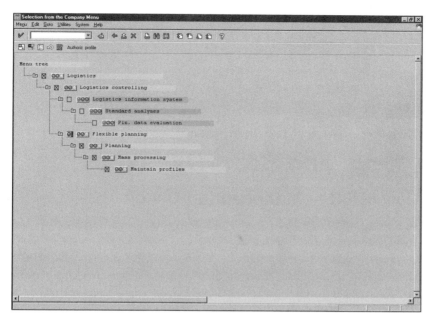

FIGURE 6-20 *Company menu tree selection using the profile generator*

3. Expand the appropriate functional areas and select the transactions you require, or select the complete functional area, such as logistics or flexible planning. In Figure 6-20, the company menu was generated with only Logistics controlling and Flexible planning in the main logistics functionality. Only the flexible planning will be permitted for this activity group. Selected areas will have their "stoplights" change to green. Save your selection.

4. Click on the Authorization Profile button to view that the authorization data is selected.

5. You are now required to maintain the organizational levels. Organizational levels are field values that relate to the company structure. You are only required to input them once in the Maintain Organizational Levels dialog box. Examples would include:

   • Company code

   • Warehouse number/complex

[handwritten margin notes: responsibility under activity group (optional) → derived activity group]

- Sales organization
- Distribution channel
- Plant identify

Save the activity group.

6. You now can assign the activity group to the user. *(by Agents button)*

Other Tools and Security Issues

Transaction SU53—Authorization Check

Transaction SU53 will assist in locating the authorization required to execute a transaction or particular field values. For example, a user is created with the authorization to only execute transactions (i.e. the S_TCODE authorization object). When a user tries to execute transaction code SU01 (create a new user), they receive the message "you are not authorized to create users". To track what authorizations are required, execute transaction SU53 and view the screen output.

Figure 6-21 illustrates the authorizations the user requires to perform the operation and what authorizations it checked—in the example it did not have any to check. Create an authorization with these field values and place them into a profile and add them to the user's master record and perform the task again (the user will be required to log off the system and log back into the system for these changes to take effect).

This whole process is an iterative one, as you will execute the operation, make changes, repeat operation, make more changes, and so on until the transaction is successfully executed.

Transaction ST01—Trace

To perform a trace for an authorization, execute transaction ST01 and click the Switch, Edit button. Now uncheck the trace types that are not required (all of them except the authorization check in our case). Next click the General filters button and select options for a particular process, user, authorization, or program to trace. In Figure 6-22, you can see that the trace will be performed for a particular transaction. Once you have selected an option, click on the Back button.

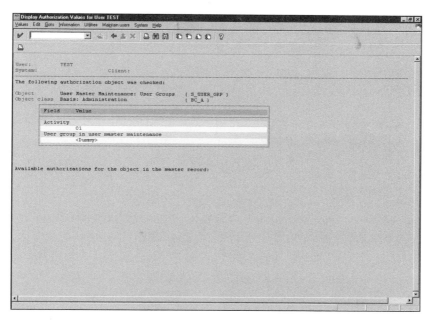

FIGURE 6-21 *Authorization values required to execute transaction SU01—create a user*

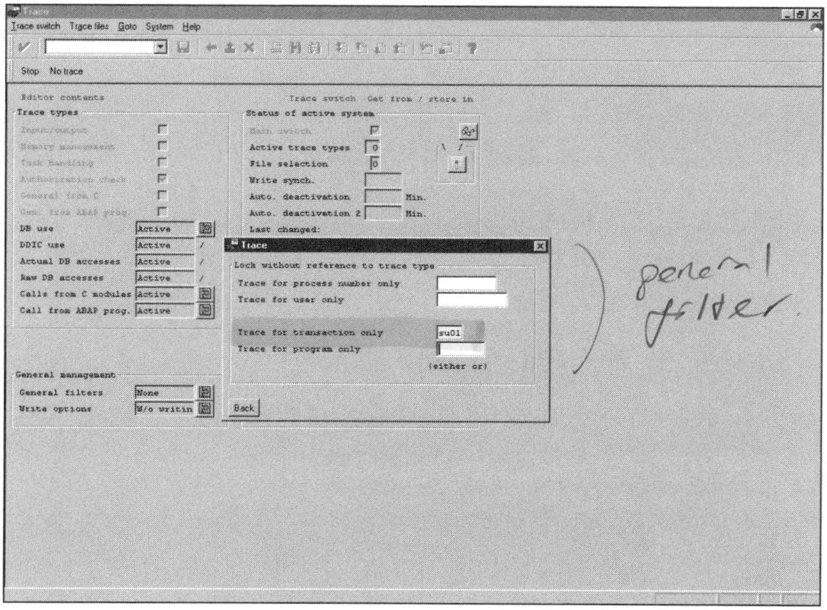

FIGURE 6-22 *System trace setup options*

The next step is to click the Write options button and select the Trace: Write to disk option and click the Back button. From the menu, select Trace Switch, Editor Save In, In Active System.

You are now able to perform the tasks that require the trace. In this example, transaction SU01 was performed. Once you have completed the required tasks, execute transaction ST01 again, and click the Switch, Edit button and then the stop button. The trace file has now been created. To view the file, from the menu, select Trace Files, Standard Options and only select the trace for authorization checks and click the accept button. Again from the menu, select Trace Files, Standard, and double-click the file to view the trace file.

The file, dependent upon your initial selection criteria, will show the traces for either the processes, users, authorization, or programs. You are now able to search the file for your transaction, and the objects you require to perform the transactions. In Figure 6-23, you can see that the SU01 transaction requires the S_USER_GRP and ACTVT objects.

```
                        SAP trace analysis                        21

  Terminal              Task Type  DO         PID        0000004415
  Time                  Date                  Trans/Rep. SU01
  user                  client                mode       1
  Host                  System

  +--------------+-----+
  | time         | ent |
  | with us      | t.  |
  +--------------+-----+

  15:46:48.526.824  AUT  0 <- S_TCODE:TCD=SU01
  15:46:48.527.196  AUT  0 <- S_USER_GRP:ACTVT=03,CLASS=
```

FIGURE 6-23 *System trace file*

Trace:
- set up trace ST01, filter select trace type, write option.
  start trace by menu/trace switch, editor save in
→ perform action for trace
→ ST01, stop trace by switch/editor/stop.
  trace file is created.
→ view file.

Transaction ST05—SQL Trace

Another method to see what authorizations are required to execute a transaction is to use the SQL trace tool within SAP, using transaction code ST05 or menu path System, Utilities, SQL Trace (see Figure 6-24).

Select the Trace On button and perform your problem transaction(s). Execute ST05 again, and click on Trace Off. You are now able to perform a trace on the problem transactions by clicking on the List Trace button. Figure 6-25 shows what tables and fields were acted upon for the transaction SU01 (display user TEST).

Additional information may be gathered by clicking on the optional buttons at the top of the screen.

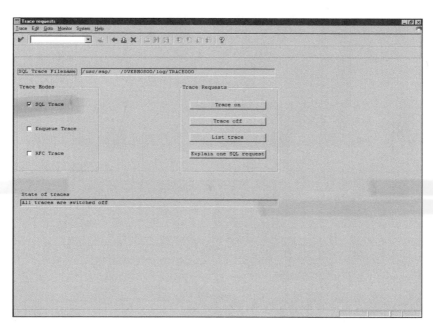

FIGURE 6-24 *Transaction ST05–SQL Trace*

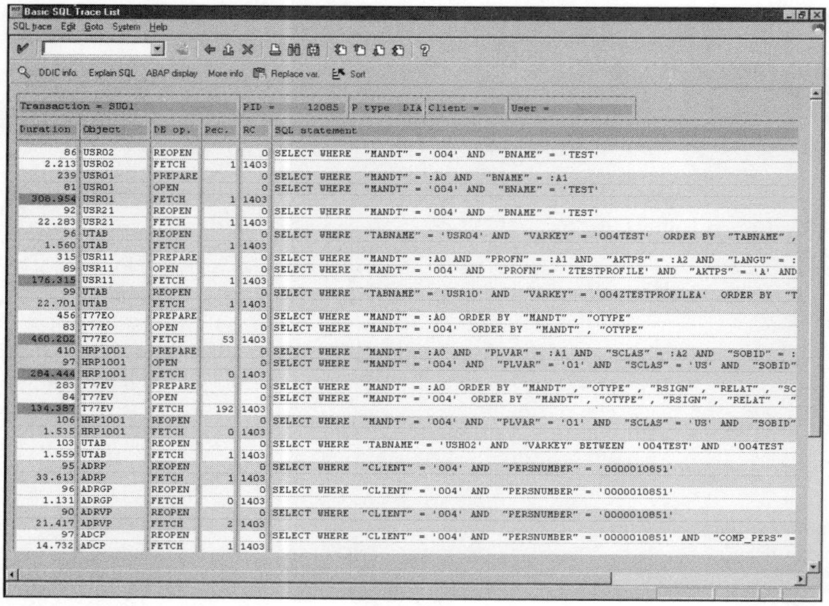

FIGURE 6-25 *Basic SQl trace list output*

Security Roles and Responsibilities

Before any authorizations can be created, the business process owners are required to define roles within each business unit. Each role should then identify transaction codes and field values (for example, F_BKPF_BUK has two fields: create/change/display and company code). The roles and responsibilities should then be documented and presented to the authorization administrator, preferably in a matrix form to accelerate the profile creation process, which should include naming conventions. (Remember that the authorization and profile names should begin with the letters Y or Z. The profile generator has its own authorization name/number scheme.)

For example, Table 6-1, Access to Customer Masters, depicts a typical matrix layout required to create authorizations.

The basis roles could effectively be broken down into three distinct roles; however, you could break down some of the activities even further, depending on the size of the company, your auditors' recommendations, and so on. However, the security administrator's role is reviewed in the following section.

Table 6.1 Access to Customer Masters

End-User Names	Tcode	Menu Path	Authorization Object	DefaultValues	APClerk	ARClerk	Payroll
Customer Master		Logistics->Sales and Distribution-> Master Data					
Create a sold-to Customer Master	V-03 (VD01)	Business partner-> Sold-toparty-> Create->Create	F_KNA1_APP	Activity: 01 Master Data:V	yes	no	no
Create a ship-to Customer Master	V-06 (VD01)	Business partner-> Ship-to party-> Create->Create	F_KNA1_APP	Activity: 01 Master Data:V	yes	no	no
Create a payer Customer Master	V-05 (VD01)	Business partner-> Payer->Create-> Create	F_KNA1_APP	Activity: 01 Master Data:V	yes	no	no

The SAP Security Administrator

The following courses are recommended for the SAP security administrator:

Course	Description
SAP020	SAP overview
SAP040	SAP architecture
CA010	SAP authorization concepts
BC310/14/17/60/61/70	Technical core competence
BC325	Workbench organization and transportation system

Role

The SAP security administrator's primary role is to assist in developing and managing SAP as well as overseeing the security of its components.

Skills

The SAP security administrator should have the following skills:

◆ Basic knowledge of the hardware (HP, Compaq, AS400, etc.)
◆ Basic knowledge of networking (TCP/IP, Novell, etc.)
◆ Knowledge of operating system (UNIX, Windows NT, AS400, etc.)
◆ SAP Basis knowledge
◆ SAP basic SAP system administration
◆ SAP basic SAP system monitoring
◆ SAP advanced SAP authorizations concepts

Responsibilities

The SAP security administrator will be responsible for the following:

◆ Documenting SAP security polices and procedures
◆ Creating and publishing forms and change documents
◆ Creating and maintaining operating system user policies

- Creating and maintaining network, dial-up, and Internet access policies
- Creating and maintaining database user policies
- Creating and maintaining SAP user policies
- Creating and maintaining SAP authorizations and profiles
- Creating and maintaining interface and data files policies and procedures
- Analyzing and resolving security issues

Audit Information System (AIS)

The Audit Information System is an auditing tool designed to improve the process of an internal or external audit by using a simple reporting tree. Depending on your version of SAP, you may need to import the AIS transport into your system (see OSSNote 77503 and 100609), but it is standard for Versions 3.1I and will be for 4.5B.

This tool is targeted for people in internal auditing, data protection, external auditing, controlling, and system auditing.

Auditors will require user master records in the SAP system in order to use the Audit Information System. Using SAP standard authorizations, set up DISPLAY access to execute the audit.

The audit report tree is accessed through transaction code SECR, as seen in Figure 6-26, and is broken down into two distinct groups: the system audit and the business audit.

System Audit and Business Audit

The AIS tool is one that can be used either by your auditors or SAP security administrators. It provides a step-by-step guide to the system configuration and business areas that you need to secure or document as a security administrator. The tool, in the form of a tree, is used to access certain information that can normally be accessed using other SAP transactions. For example, the auditor would check to see if the client is locked for any changes using SCC4—the auditor may click on the appropriate tree branch and view from this audit tree.

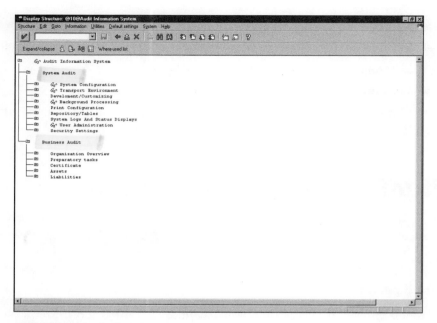

FIGURE 6-26 *Audit Information System*

The following lists the main areas for the system and business audits:

System Audit

System Configuration

Application

System

Communication

Parameters

Archiving

System Measurements

Clients

Operating System

Transport Environment

Transport System

Transport Control

Transport Management System

Configuration and Status

Monitoring Tools

Development/Customizing

ABAP Workbench: Tools

Naming Conventions

Coordination

Enhancement Concept

Transactions

ABAP Programs

Background Processing

Job Overview

Job Schedule Graphical

Batch Input Logs

Print Configuration

Printing Manual

Spool Administration

Spool Output Control

Spool Installation Check

Parameters

Repository/Tables

Data Modeler

Repository Information System

Table Information

Table Recordings

System Logs and Status Displays

Basis System Services

Upgrade History

Server States

System Log

Special Recordings

Application Link Enabling

Remote Function Call

Application Log

Terminations

Database Logs

User Administration

Users and Authorizations

Infosystem Authorizations and Users

Authorizations

Profile Generator

User Overview

Which User Is Allowed To...

Security Settings

System Parameters

Operating System Level

Database Level

External Communication

Business Audit

Organization Overview

Enterprise Structure (Graphic)

Account Assignment Elements

Reconciliation Accts (C/V)

Automatic Postings

R/3 Library >> Country-Specific Development

Preparatory Tasks

Change Settings

Customize Financial Information System

ABAP Query (Incl. Download)

Certificate

Planning

G/L Accounts

Completeness/Reconciliation

Year-End Closing

Assets

Tangible Assets

Financial Assets

Inventory Stocks

Receivables

Securities

Liquid Funds/Bank Payable

Accrual and Deferral

Exchange Rate Differences

Liabilities

Provisions

Bank Payables

Payables

Other Payables

Critical Authorizations Combinations

Critical authorization combinations are when a user may have authorizations that may put your system and your company at risk. For example, a user may have a combination where they are allowed to create a vendor and be able to pay that vendor—this would allow someone to create a fictional company and write checks to them, later emptying the vendor's bank account with your company's money. This may sound like an extreme scenario, but auditors do look for these types of scenarios.

The AIS tool locates these for critical authorizations combinations to enable you to be more proactive. The best approach is to check with specific business areas to discover what are considered to be critical combinations and restrict their use of such.

The business areas sometimes have legitimate reasons for a user to have critical combinations. For example, inadequate resources may mean that the user is a backup for someone else who may be out on vacation or sick.

A number of critical combinations will require your attention. A very small subset is shown below. You will be required to create your own critical combinations by checking with your business areas and SAP teams.

Posting Documents	and	Accounts Payable Master for Accounts Data Maintenance
Posting Documents	and	Accounts Receivable Master for Accounts Receivable Data Maintenance
Purchase Order	and	Accounts Payable Master Maintenance Data Maintenance
Purchase Order	and	Receiving Goods Maintenance
Purchase Order	and	Posting Supplier Invoices Maintenance
Receiving Goods	and	Posting Supplier Invoices

Several new transactions are available in SAP R/3 Version 4.x for auditing purposes. These include SM18/19 and SM20, each of which requires some configuration and manipulation. Please see online documentation for more details.

Summary

In this chapter, we have introduced the concepts of authorizations and how they may be created and grouped together to create a user profile. When these profiles are given to a user, that user is only allowed to perform these tasks within the profile.

The creation of the profiles is an iterative process, and we have introduced a number of ways to resolve additional authorizations requirements to perform certain tasks and transactions.

Auditors will be checking your system, whether it is from a government (Defense) or federal standpoint (FDA) or plain day-to-day business. It is your responsibility as the SAP security administrator to be more proactive and know what they will be looking for and enforcing any recommendations made by them.

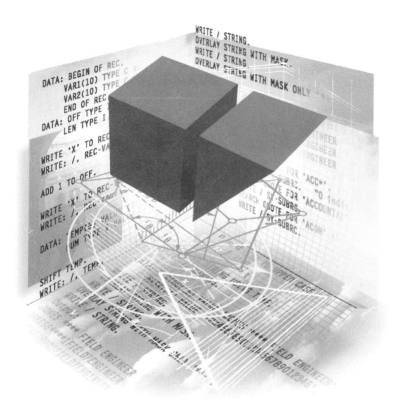

Chapter 7

**Spool
Administration**

In This Chapter

- ◆ Printer Installation
- ◆ Faxing Using Delrina/Winfax at the Workstation
- ◆ Faxing Using SAPcomm/TOPCALL at the Server
- ◆ Using SAPconnect

This chapter will introduce a strategy on setting up printers and printing in your SAP environment. This strategy will ask you questions about the type and quantity of printing your users will be performing; this will indicate the types of printers to use and how they should be configured.

As part of the printing process, SAPcomm and faxing have been introduced in this chapter and contain information regarding the configuration and usage of the technology. One further caveat, SAP has created a replacement for SAPcomm, known as SAPconnect, to provide a single interface to all communications to and from the SAP system. The basic concepts for SAPconnect are introduced in this chapter.

Printing

In order to set up printing within your SAP environment, you need to understand the type of printing activity your end users will be performing and also the type of output from the printing. For example, perhaps one of your end users will be printing job offer letters to prospective employees of your company and will therefore require a printer setup that would authorize only that person to print to that printer and to view the output requests within SAP. Another case might be that your company will require multiple copies of a bill of material (BOM) with SAPscript enhancements, for which you will need an impact/line printer supporting SAPscript.

Therefore it would be wise to develop a strategy whereby you use the printer definitions that are already defined within the SAP system and purchase the printers accordingly. (Most of the commonly used printers are defined in the SAP system and more are continually being developed and available on SAP's ftp server for download.)

Printers used for SAP can either be dedicated to SAP or shared by other workstation applications. However, there seems to be little advantage to using dedicated printers due to the evolving networking technologies and strategies, and also due to higher costs with regard to greater number of printers and their support.

Two general methods can be used for printing with SAP. The first is simply running a workstation daemon (Saplpd process, found in the /Sapgui/Saplpd directory) on the workstation where the printer is attached and configuring SAP to send print jobs to this printer. This method should only be used on a limited basis, as there are a number of networking issues involved, including the following:

◆ The SAP system emits an "are you alive" packet every five seconds to the Saplpd process over the network, where the saplpd in turn sends an acknowledgment packet back to SAP. If there is a large number of printers configured on workstations, then there is a chance that your network will become "flooded" with these packets and stop other more important network activities.

◆ Each workstation with an attached printer will require a dedicated IP address to be "hard-coded" into its configuration as SAP sends print requests to specifically assigned IP addresses.

◆ Beware that printers (with no hard disk or server connection) connected to the LAN directly and set up as an SAP print process will print the requests at the speed of the printer, thus slowing down print jobs.

Remote printing is the second method of printing for SAP. In remote printing, the print job is routed to a network file or print server that controls the printing. This method works well with printers that are shared by SAP and non-SAP applications.

Figure 7-1 illustrates the printer connectivity types used within the SAP environment, including printers attached to a workstation and printers connected directly to the network.

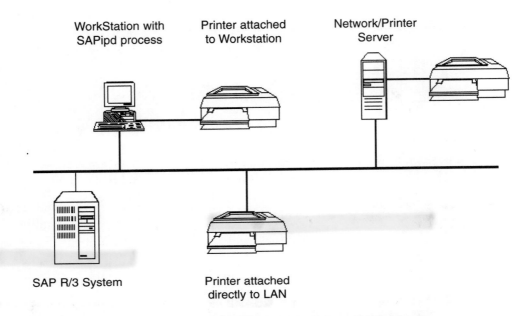

FIGURE 7-1 *How printers may be configured within an SAP environment*

There is one more thing to consider when setting up printing, and that is to understand the type of printing and printers required within your environment. Here's a quick look at a few common types:

◆ For mass printing (multiple copies of large sales and financial reports), you will require high-speed printers, which will be necessary to print the requests at off-peak hours to ensure system performance is not negatively affected.

◆ For time-critical printing (invoices, BOMs, delivery notes, contracts, etc.), you will require high-speed/quality printers to ensure that your business is not adversely affected. Also, some of these printers may be of the specific type to produce several copies at once, as normally required for BOMs.

◆ For confidential printing (checks, payroll, HR information, or other confidential material), you will require that the printers are secured in a closed environment or office and only specific users are able to print to the printer or see the output request within SAP.

Printer Installation

For a typical three-tiered SAP system (DEV, QAS and PRD), there are three components to setting up printing, each of which requires configuration. Ideally, you want to set up the printers identically in your SAP landscape: that is, with the same printer, print queue, and printer name defined in DEV, QAS, PRD. This type of setup will assist in the setup and support of printing throughout your SAP environment. The confidential printer may be the exception as you typically do not require that type of printer setup in the DEV and QAS environment!

The three components to setting up printing include:

- Starting the printer daemon (lpd for UNIX and lpdnt for Windows NT)
- Defining the printer at the operating system level (using SAM or SMIT for UNIX and the Start menu for Windows NT)
- Defining the printer at the SAP level

Adopting the strategy that you will set up all the printers identically throughout your SAP environment, you would only have to configure the UNIX and SAP configuration once and be able to copy the definitions from one system to the others. This would speed up the setup process in the short term and also assist in adding new printers in the future.

TIP

A number of companies have automated the printer definition and setup process using UNIX/Perl scripts that copy the directory trees /etc/lp and /var/spool/lp from one system to another and then copy the SAP definitions from the TSP* tables via R3trans and swapping out the host/SID specific values.

As mentioned earlier in this chapter, you are required to configure or start up three components to enable printing. These three are discussed in greater detail in the following sections.

Starting the Print Process at the Operating System

The print process at the OS level should automatically be created and started as part of the OS install. However, there are times when you may need to restart the process due to the processing errors or the process dying. For the HP-UX environment to check the process is running, login at the UNIX level as root and enter:

```
ps -ef | grep lp
```

and look for the entry:

```
lp 13300    1  0 08:47:51 ?        0:18 /usr/sbin/lpsched -v
```

This would show you that the process is running. To stop the process, enter:

```
lpshut
```

To restart the process again, enter:

```
lpsched -v
```

Finally, recheck that the process is running.

For Windows NT, the process is as defined in the Microsoft Windows NT Printer Installation section.

Setting Up the Printers at the Operating System

Once the processes have been started, you may begin the process of setting up the printers at the operating system level. In the examples that follow, the printer installation procedure is provided for the HP-UX and Windows NT environment.

HP-UX Printer Installation

Please refer to the HP Administrators' Guide for detailed information on configuring printers at the HP-UX level. However, for a brief step-by-step setup procedure:

1. Log on as 'root' to the SAP server where the SAP print process will run.
2. Startup SAM.
3. Select Printers and Plotters.
4. Select Printers/Plotters.
5. From the Actions menu, select Add Remote Printer/Plotter.
6. Enter the appropriate information for the following fields:
   - Printer Name
   - Remote System Name
   - Remote Printer Name

7. Save and Exit SAM

Microsoft Windows NT Printer Installation

Please refer to the Microsoft Windows NT Administrators' Guide for detailed information on configuring printers at the Windows operating system level. However, for a brief step-by-step setup procedure:

1. Log on to the SAP server where the SAP print process will run.
2. Select Start, Setting, Printers.
3. Double-click on Add Printer.
4. Select Local or Network Printer Connection.
5. Select the appropriate port (Lpt1, 2, 3, or 4).
6. Designate your printer manufacturer, printer type, and printer driver.
7. Enter the Printer Name
8. Print a test page.

Setting Up Printers at the SAP Level

Log on to the SAP system and execute the SPAD transaction, the spool administration transaction.

At the Spool Administration: Initial screen, you need to:

1. Click on the Change button.
2. Click on the Output Devices button.
3. From the menu, click on the Output device, create.

Enter the appropriate data into the relevant fields, using the Tab key to move from field to field. To see a list of available choices for a given field, click in the field and then click the Down arrow list button.

Table 7-1 tabulates the fields and their descriptions related to creating a new printer within SAP, and Figure 7-2 is an example of creating a printer in SAP.

TIP

If you click on the green arrow in the upper-left corner, as seen in Figure 7-3, you are presented with additional options for configuring the printers.

Table 7-1 Printer Setup Fields and Their Descriptions

Field	Description
Output device	SAP device name (not analyzed by R/3)
Short Name	SAP device short name
Device type	Printer device type (e.g., HPLJ4)
Spool Server	Automatically filled in by SAP - where the spool process runs
Host printer	UNIX printer name
Device class	Left blank for printer
Authorization Group	Authorizations enforced by S_SPO_DEV object
Access Method	L-print locally via LP/LPR with signal
Model	Model name (not analyzed by R/3)
Location	Description of the printer location
Message	Used to display a brief message regarding the device to end users
Lock Printer in R/3 System	Used to stop print jobs from being printed (uncheck the box to resume printing)
SAP Title Page	Printer will print a cover page with user and print job details

You may now save the printer setup and print a test page to check if you are able to print a request. If successful, you have correctly set up a printer for SAP. If not, please check that the spool process is running, and that the printer at the operating system and SAP are configured correctly.

Installing a Print Driver for a New Type of Printer

Print drivers are text files that contain the necessary escape sequences and printer instructions for a particular printer; each type of printer (sometimes even each model within the same family of printers) requires a separate print driver.

For printers that are not defined within the SAP system, you will need to obtain the print driver via FTP from SAP's SAPSERV3 or SAPSERV4 server, copy the file to an operating system directory on the platform where the SAP system resides, and then install it in SAP using the RSTXSCRP ABAP program.

Device type.
↔ print driver

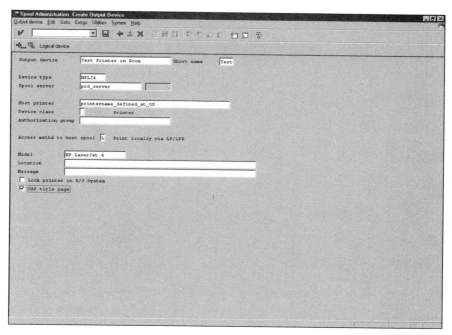

FIGURE 7-2 *Example of data input for setting up a printer*

The steps for installing an SAP print driver are as follows:

1. Use Ftp to download the printer driver file from SAPserv4 to /tmp on the database server of the R/3 system where you wish to install it. Ensure that the file has 775 UNIX permissions. If not, execute:

```
chmod 775 /tmp/<drivername>.pri
```

at the UNIX level to change its permission. For the Windows NT environment, ensure the file has read, write, and execute permissions.

2. Log on to the SAP R/3 application/database server, and execute the transaction SE38, ABAP execution.

3. In the Program field, enter **RSTXSCRP** and execute. Figure 7-3 illustrates the execution of the RSTXSCRP program and the required field inputs.

4. SAP now displays the contents of the print driver file.

   Scroll down the screen and ensure that the entry "Object Imported" is present. This indicates that the installation was successfully installed.

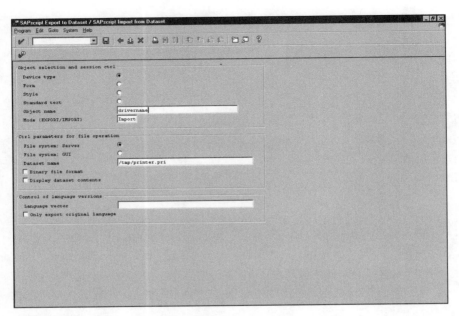

FIGURE 7-3 *Executing the RSTXSCRP program and input fields*

5. Execute the spool administration transaction, SPAD, and click on the Device Types box to display the list of device types installed in your system. Your newly installed device type should now be installed in the SAP R/3 system.

Printing Problem Troubleshooting

This section provides a guide for troubleshooting SAP printing problems. It is designed to isolate problems to one of the three print component levels and consists of the following three steps:

1. Test Printing from Your Windows Workstation

Attempt to print an application document (such as a Word or Excel document) from your Windows workstation. If the test is successful, proceed to the next test. If the test fails, the initial problem is not related to SAP but is likely to be a printer, network, or print server problem. Contact your system administration department to diagnose and resolve the problem. Repeat the test again to ensure the test functions correctly, and also repeat the print from SAP. If the Windows workstation test print works correctly, move onto Step 2.

2. Test Printing from the Operating System

Log on at the operating system as superuser root on your SAP system, and at the prompt, enter the following:

```
lpstat -a
```

The output will indicate the status of all the printers defined in your system. If the printer in question seems okay from the above output, perform a test print by entering the following command:

```
lp -d<printer_name> <filename>
```

where the `<printer_name>` is the name of the printer you are testing and `<filename>` is the name of a file to print—an example file could be the TPPA-RAM file located in the /usr/sap/trans/bin directory.

HP-UX will then attempt to print the file on the specified remote printer. If the test is successful, proceed to the next step; otherwise you have the problem related to the SAP system, or it is a configuration mismatch between SAP and HP-UX (i.e. the printer defined at the UNIX level is differently spelled in SAP).

Again at the HP-UX shell prompt, enter the following:

```
nslookup <remote_system_name>
```

The IP address resolution for the remote system is displayed either showing the address entries from the /etc/hosts file or the DNS. Ensure that the entry shown for the printer or print server is the correct IP address for that system and note the source of the IP address (i.e., /etc/hosts file or a particular DNS—you may need to make changes in either the host's file or DNS).

Again at the HP-UX shell prompt, enter the following:

```
/etc/ping <remote_system_name>
```

This HP-UX command pings the remote system—it sends a network packet to the remote system asking it to respond to the packet. If a response is found, then the ping was successful. Otherwise there is a networking error and you will need to diagnose your LAN/WAN network.

The previous procedure should show you that you may have a network LAN/WAN, router, bridge, or gateway.

3. Test Printing from the SAP R/3 Application

In order to test a print request, you need to generate a print file. Therefore, execute the Spool administration transaction, SPAD, and:

1. Select Output Device to display the Spool Administration: List of Output Types screen.

2. From the Output Device drop-down menu, select Print.

3. In the Output Device field, enter a device for the print this list.

4. In the Print Screen List, ensure that Print Immed., Delete after Print, and New Spool Request are checked and you select the printer in question as the Output device, as seen in Figure 7-4.

SAP forwards the print request to the specified printer. You therefore need to check the status of the spool request by executing the transaction SP01 to display the Spool: Request Screen. You may filter the print request you wish to observe by the current date, user, a specific printer, or the actual print request. Table 7-2 explains the Spool Request Output Status messages.

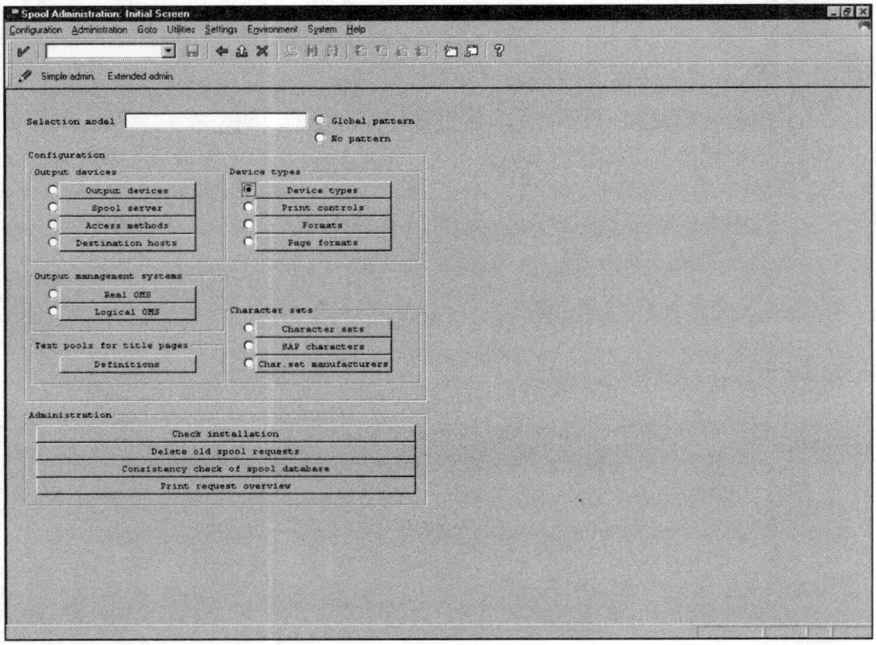

FIGURE 7-4 *Print Screen List options*

Table 7-2 Spool Request Output Status messages

Spool Request Output Status messages	Description and Diagnosis
complete	Spool request has been printed; **No further action is required** being sent to host spool
	Print request is at the OS queue and in the process of being sent to host. If a print request remains in this state for a significant amount of time, there is probably a problem in one of the areas: • OS Printer Name is disabled • Network configuration is incorrect • OS system and Network server • configuration error
-> SAP output device driver	This message indicates that there may be a problem either due to incorrect Host Name in the SAP output device configuration for the requested printer or SAP spooler process not running
waiting in host spool, pos. X	This message indicates that the print request has been successfully passed to the OS and possibly all the way to network print server. First check to see if the print deamon is running, then check if the print request has passed through the operating system, then check if the print server has served the print request. If a print request remains in this state for a significant amount of time, there is probably a problem, which may include printer is out of paper or printer is off-line.
Wait	Spool request(s) are waiting in SAP. **Check the Output Request Status for more information.**
Print	At least one spool request has not been completed. **Check the Output Request Status for more information.**
Error	Spool request has an error. **Display log generated to resolve the problem.**
Problem	SAP passed the Spool request to HP-UX but experienced a problem (e.g., non-printable character). **Check the Output Request Status for more information.**
(Blank)	No output requests exist for this spool request. Often caused by failing to select **Print Immed.** when generating the print request.

Viewing SAP Printing Errors

To view errors in the SPO work process, do the following:

1. Log on to SAP on the server where the spool process is active.

2. Execute transaction SM50, and note its work process number—the PID (the number to the immediate left) for the **SPO** work process (in the example shown in Figure 7-5, the process id is 16).

3. Execute transaction ST11, and double-click on the entry that has the format dev_wXX (where XX is the number of the work process noted above; in this example, dev_w16).

4. Scroll to the last page and look for any errors and scroll upward, because the most recent errors are appended to the end of the file.

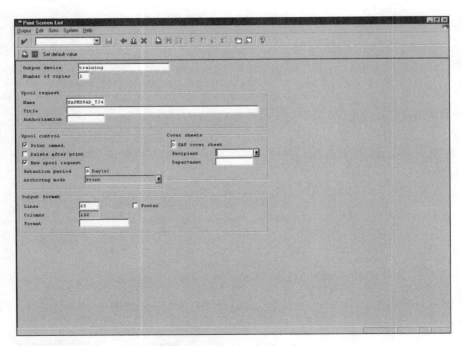

FIGURE 7-5 *Process number identification for the Spool process*

Resolving Typical SAP Printing Problems

A number of errors occur with printing in SAP. Several of the most common errors are explained in this section.

1. All SAP Printing Has Stopped

If all SAP printing is locked up and there are numerous error messages appearing in the log file for all print requests, it may be necessary to restart the spooler. This may be performed at any time and does not adversely affect the system. There is minimal possibility of causing further damage by attempting this procedure. To restart the spooler, follow these steps:

1. Execute transaction SM50 and locate the SPO work process. Check to see if the Time field is pink and over 1,000 seconds—this will indicate that there is a spooler error. (Another check is executing transaction SP01; you should observe print jobs backing up in the process state.)

2. Place your cursor on SPO, and from the menu select Process, Restart after Error, Yes.

3. If the Time field resets within a short time span, the problem has been rectified. Otherwise, from the menu select Process, Cancel without Core.

4. Return to transaction SP01 and confirm that jobs are now entering the Compl. stage. Repeat the restart process if necessary.

2. More than 150 Defined Printers

With the addition of new printers, new alerts are continually logged in the log file dev_wXX, explained earlier in this chapter. These alert logs entries usually indicate that there are not enough open print slots to allow printing to occur. The typical cause is that a maximum number of printers (for earlier versions of SAP) is by default set at 150. Any printers added after the 150th printer will not print. If the SAP system is stopped and started, the first 150 printers listed in transaction SPAD will be enabled, but the rest will not print.

To correct this error, add the following parameter into the instance profile of the SAP instance where the print process is defined, and then stop and start the system as defined in OSS note #19498:

```
rspo/global_shm/printer_list = <greater than 150>
```

Faxing

Faxing may be performed with the SAP system. However, it requires the third party faxing software to be configured to interface with the SAP system. There are two main methods in configuring the faxing software: either at the user's workstation or at the dedicated fax server.

Faxing Using Delrina/Winfax at the Workstation

This method of faxing should only be used for infrequent faxing from a local workstation or a print server. There are a number of steps that you will need to perform in order to configure the Winfax and SAP components.

At the workstation, do the following:

1. Install the Delrina Winfax software according to the manufacturer's instructions.

2. Ensure that the Winfax software starts up in the startup program of the workstation/server.

3. Copy saplpd.exe (also referred to as lpsdo.EXE) and sapfax.dll into a new directory. For example, C:\SAPAX\, and again ensure that SAPLPD or LPDSO starts up in the startup program of the workstation/server.

4. Configure the Com port for Winfax to be able to fax.

5. Set up user information in the user setup of Winfax.

At the SAP server, perform the following steps:

1. Execute the Spool Administration transaction SPAD and click on Output Devices.

2. Create a new output device, as shown in Figure 7-6.

3. Set up the telecommunications table using transaction SCOM and enter data for:
   - Location (see Figure 7-7)
   - Selection (see Figure 7-8)
   - Exceptions (see Figure 7-9)
   - Server Assignments (see Figure 7-10)

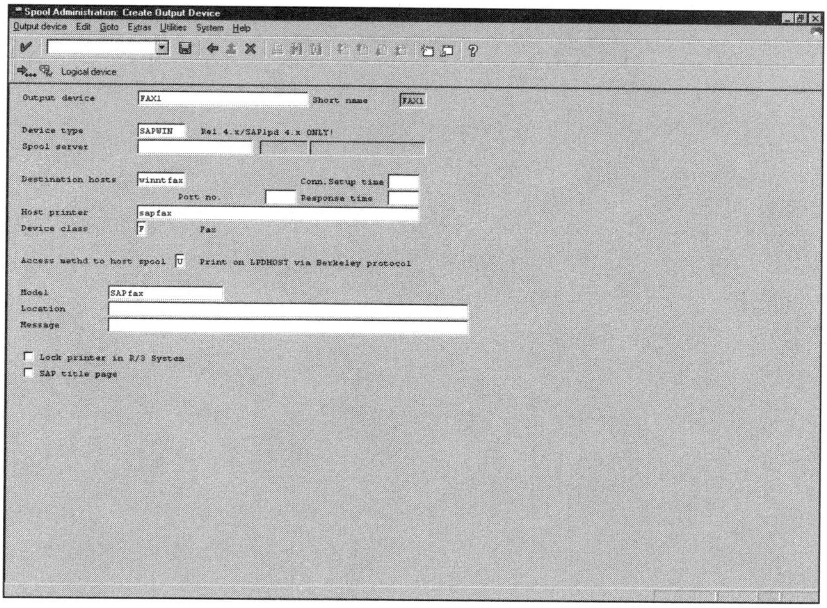

FIGURE 7-6 *Output Device setup for faxing within SAP*

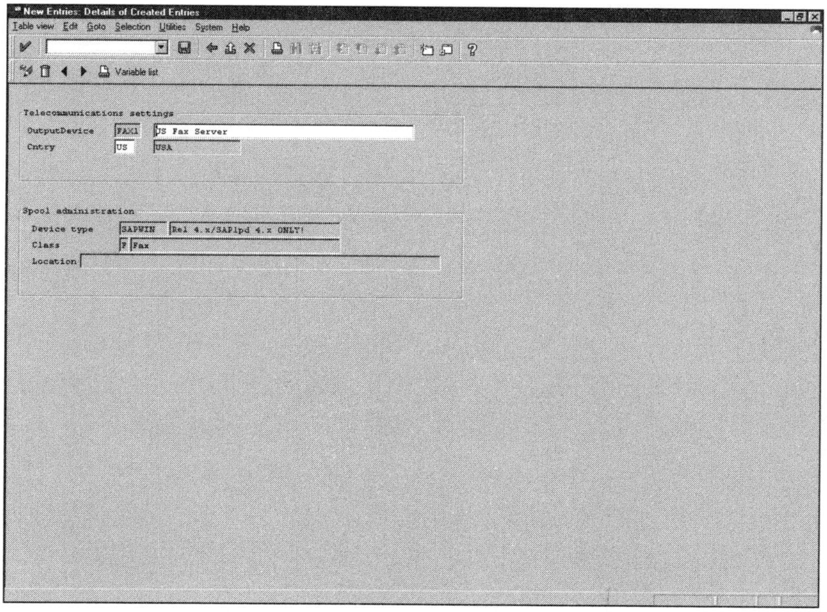

FIGURE 7-7 *Location data*

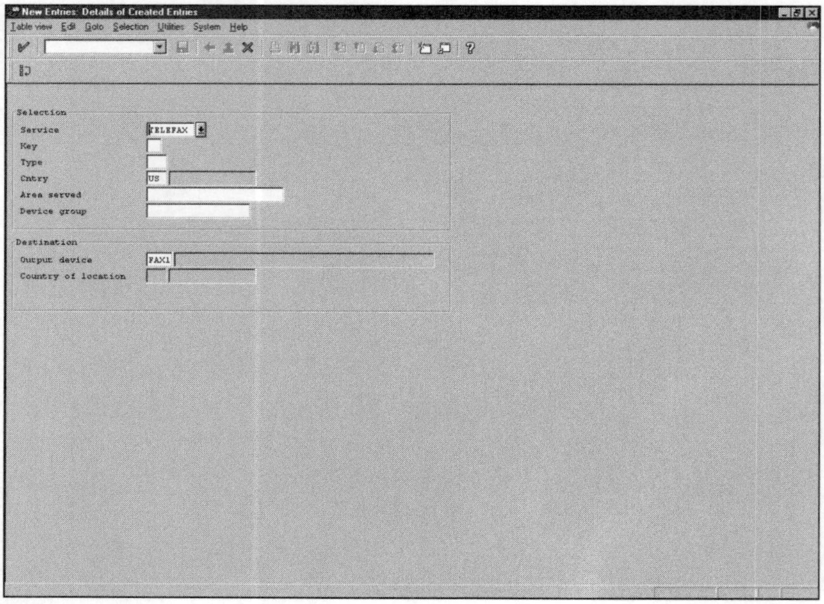

FIGURE 7-8 *Selection data*

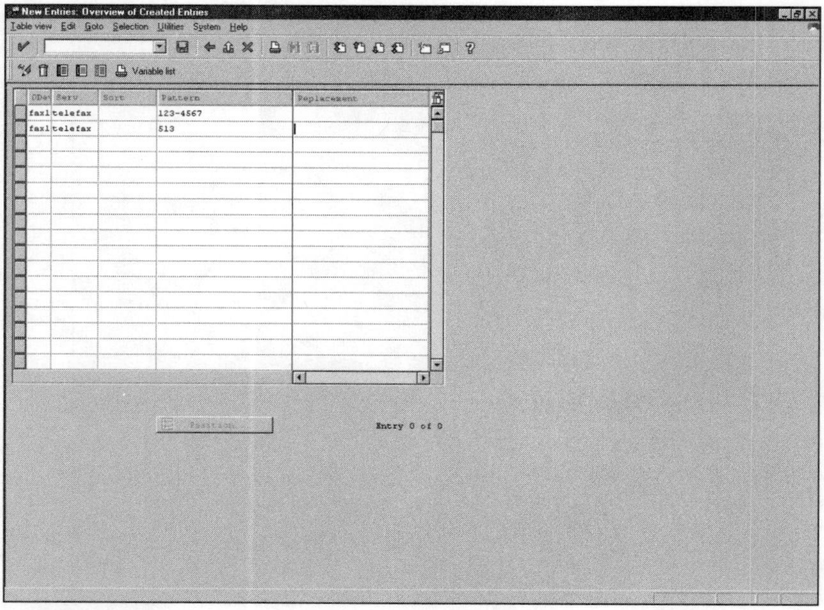

FIGURE 7-9 *Exception data*

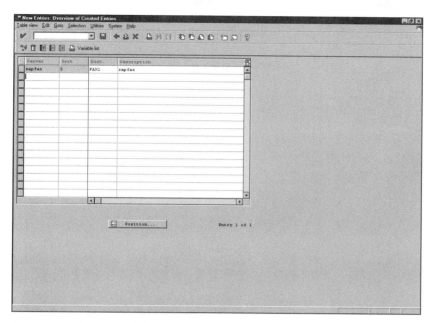

FIGURE 7-10 *Server Assignment data*

4. The next step is to check the configuration by clicking the Check button on the initial SAPcomm screen and then routing the Test button. These two checks ensure that the SAP system recognizes the parameters set up in the prior steps and is able to pass the document to the fax workstation or server.

5. Your final test is to send a multiple page document to a local fax machine to assist in viewing the output of the job.

Faxing Using SAPcomm/TOPCALL at the Server

Topcall is a very robust faxing solution for high-volume and large-document faxing. SAPcomm is the connectivity utility between the SAP system and the Topcall software and requires configuration, as described in the following section.

For each system and client that require SAP faxing, system- and client-specific configurations will be required in the SAP system and in configuration flat (ascii) files on the operating system running the SAPcomm utility (see Figure 7-11).

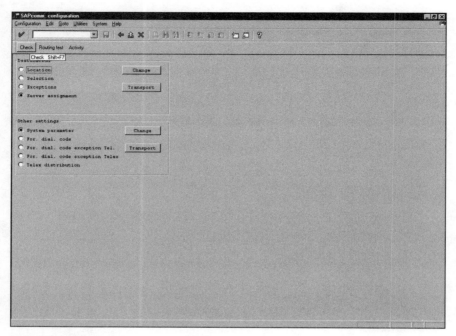

FIGURE 7-11 *SAPcomm initial screen*

There are three components required to install and set up the SAPcomm/TOP-CALL faxing solution:

◆ **TOPCALL application on a Windows NT system**

The Topcall system will only require setup once, usually by Topcall consultants, and will not require further modifications for additional SAP systems and clients.

◆ **SAPcomm user and fax spool device for each SAP system**

1. Using transaction SU01, create a user SAPcomm in the system and client as a CPIC user with adequate authorizations (typically SAP_ALL and SAP_NEW).

2. Using transaction SPAD, set up the output device as you would with a printer, except use F (Fax) as the Device Class and X (SAPcomm) as the Access Method.

◆ **Starting SAPcomm subsystem on host system**

1. Configure SAPcomm parameters. For the current example, set up the user sapcomm with the password **gateway1** at the HP UX OS level.

2. Edit the sideinfo and sapcomm.cfg files in the /usr/sap/com/SYS/profile directory. The following list shows an example of both files, where in the sideinfo file, the data between DEST= and CPIC_TRACE= constitute entries for each individual system and the values for PROTOCOL and CPIC_TRACE are static for all systems.

sideinfo file:

```
*@(#) sideinfo
DEST=<sid1>
LU=<host1>
GWHOST=<gatewayhost1>
GWSERV=sapgw00
TP=sapdp00
PROTOCOL=I
CPIC_TRACE=1
DEST=<sid2>
LU=<host2>
GWHOST=<gatewayhost2>
GWSERV=sapgw00
TP=sapdp01
PROTOCOL=I
CPIC_TRACE=1
DEST=<sid3>
LU=<host3>
GWHOST=<gatewayhost3>
GWSERV=sapgw00
TP=sapdp01
PROTOCOL=I
CPIC_TRACE=1
```

sapcomm.cfg file:

```
* @(#) sapcomm.cfg
PROGRAM SCB
    IGNORE_TIME_PLAN      OFF
    IGNORE_CC_ABORT       OFF
    LOGFILE_EXPIRATION  5
    ROUTING SAPCOMM
      SERVICE FAX
          TO-CHANNEL      <sid1>-360
      END-SERVICE
```

```
            SERVICE TLX
                TO-CHANNEL      <sid1>-360
            END-SERVICE
        END-ROUTING
        TRACE ON
            TRACE_ALL               OFF
            INIT                            OFF
            PGM_FLOW        OFF
            DATA_FLOW       OFF
            CS_RESPONSE             OFF
            FILES                   ON
            IPC                             OFF
            MEMORY                  OFF
            ROUTING                 ON
            QUEUE_MSG               OFF
            DEV_CTRL                OFF
            SCI_CALL                OFF
            SCI_PARAM               OFF
            SCI_ATTR                OFF
            SCI_PERF                OFF
        END-TRACE
    END-PROGRAM
* SAP: connection to SAP
PROGRAM SAP
    LOGFILE_EXPIRATION   5
    IDSAPCOMM            SCM<sid1>
    SIDE_INFO            /usr/sap/com/SYS/profile/sideinfo
    ARCHIVE                     OFF
    TRACE               ON
            TRACE_ALL   OFF
            INIT                OFF
            PGM_FLOW    OFF
            DATA_FLOW   OFF
            CS_RESPONSE ON
            FILES               ON
            IPC                 OFF
            MEMORY      OFF
            ROUTING     ON
            QUEUE_MSG   OFF
            DEV_CTRL    OFF
            SCI_CALL    OFF
```

```
                    SCI_PARAM       OFF
                    SCI_ATTR        OFF
                    SCI_PERF        OFF
                END-TRACE
    * SAP Destinations
    * <sid4> CLIENTS
        DESTINATION <sid4>-010
                SYSTEM   <sid4>
                CLIENT   010
                USER     SAPCOMM
                PASSWORD    GATEWAY
                LANGUAGE    E
                RELEASE     R3-30f
        END-DESTINATION
        DESTINATION <sid4>-020
                SYSTEM   <sid4>
                CLIENT   020
                USER     SAPCOMM
                PASSWORD    GATEWAY
                LANGUAGE    E
                RELEASE     R3-30f
        END-DESTINATION
    * SAP Selections
        SELECTION FAXES
                APPLICATION TELE
        END-SELECTION
    * SAP Periodics
    * <sid4> PERIODICS
        PERIODIC RCV<sid4>010
                INTERVAL 15
                FROM     00:30
                UNTIL    23:30
        END-PERIODIC
        PERIODIC SND<sid4>010
                INTERVAL 15
                FROM     00:35
                UNTIL    23:35
        END-PERIODIC
        PERIODIC RCV<sid4>020
                INTERVAL 15
                FROM     00:30
```

```
                    UNTIL     23:30
            END-PERIODIC
            PERIODIC SND<sid4>020
                    INTERVAL 15
                    FROM      00:35
                    UNTIL     23:35
            END-PERIODIC
    *  SAP Channels
    *  <sid4> CHANNELS
       CHANNEL     <sid4>-010
                DESTINATION <sid4>-010
                PERFORM   SEND
                    ACTION        SEND-SCHEDULE
                    PERIODIC      SND<sid4>010
                END-PERFORM
                PERFORM   SEND-NIGHT
                    ACTION        SEND-NIGHT
                    TIME          04:54
                END-PERFORM
                PERFORM   RECEIVE
                    ACTION        RECEIVE
                    PERIODIC      RCV<sid4>010
                    SELECTION     FAXES
                END-PERFORM
         END-CHANNEL
         CHANNEL     <sid4>-020
                DESTINATION <sid4>-020
                PERFORM   SEND
                    ACTION        SEND-SCHEDULE
                    PERIODIC      SND<sid4>020
                END-PERFORM
                PERFORM   SEND-NIGHT
                    ACTION        SEND-NIGHT
                    TIME          04:54
                END-PERFORM
                PERFORM   RECEIVE
                    ACTION        RECEIVE
                    PERIODIC      RCV<sid4>020
                    SELECTION     FAXES
                END-PERFORM
         END-CHANNEL
```

```
*   TST SAP test component
PROGRAM TST
    REQUEST_INTERVAL                15
    LOGFILE_EXPIRATION              5
    ARCHIVE                             OFF
    SAVE_RESPONSE_INFORMATION   OFF
    TRACE OFF
        TRACE_ALL         ON
        PGM_FLOW          ON
        DATA_FLOW         ON
        FILES             OFF
        ROUTING           ON
        QUEUE_MSG         OFF
        SCI_CALL          OFF
        SCI_PARAM         OFF
        SCI_ATTR          OFF
    END-TRACE
    CHANNEL   TST1
        SENDRC      0
*       RECEIVE     /usr/sap/com/SYS/ETC/receive.test
        PERFORM     TSTSEND
            ACTION      SEND-SCHEDULE
        END-PERFORM
        PERFORM     TSTRECEIVE
            ACTION      RECEIVE
        END-PERFORM
    END-CHANNEL
END-PROGRAM
*   APP : APPLI/COM, file API to TOPCALL
PROGRAM APP
    LOGFILE_EXPIRATION              5
    ARCHIVE                             OFF
    SENDREQUEST_BLOCKSIZE           1
    TRACE ON
        TRACE_ALL         OFF
        INIT              ON
        PGM_FLOW          OFF
        DATA_FLOW         ON
        CS_RESPONSE       ON
        FILES             ON
        IPC               OFF
```

```
                    MEMORY          OFF
                    ROUTING         ON
                    QUEUE_MSG       OFF
                    DEV_CTRL        OFF
                    SCI_CALL        OFF
                    SCI_PARAM       OFF
                    SCI_ATTR        OFF
                    SCI_PERF        OFF
           END-TRACE
           DESTINATION TOPCALL
                COM_OUT             /usr/sap/com/appli/out
                COM_IN                        /usr/sap/com/appli/in
                COM_JOB                        /usr/sap/com/appli/job
                COM_ACK             /usr/sap/com/appli/ack
                COM_ERR             /usr/sap/com/appli/err
                CONVERT_ID      PCL
           END-DESTINATION
           PERIODIC SNDTOP
                INTERVAL 5
                FROM      00:02
                UNTIL     23:57
            END-PERIODIC
           PERIODIC RCVTOP
                INTERVAL 5
                FROM      00:03
                UNTIL     23:58
            END-PERIODIC
           CHANNEL    <spool/fax device name>
               DESTINATION TOPCALL
               PERFORM    SEND
                  ACTION       SEND-SCHEDULE
                  PERIODIC SNDTOP
               END-PERFORM
               PERFORM    SEND-NIGHT
                  ACTION       SEND-NIGHT
                  TIME    03:02
               END-PERFORM
               PERFORM    RECEIVE
                  ACTION       RECEIVE
                  PERIODIC RCVTOP
```

```
                           END-PERFORM
                    END-CHANNEL
             END-PROGRAM
```

The last step is to ensure that all system-client identifiers in sapcomm.cfg have representative directories in usr/sap/com/sap/data as shown in the following example. You will want to ensure that ownership (sapcomm), group (sapsys), and permissions (777) match what is shown in the following:

```
drwxrwxrwx   3  sapcomm   sapsys     1024  mmm  dd  tt:tt  <sid1>-<010>
drwxrwxrwx   3  sapcomm   sapsys     1024  mmm  dd  tt:tt  <sid1>-<020>
drwxrwxrwx   3  sapcomm   sapsys     1024  mmm  dd  tt:tt  <sid2>-<010>
drwxrwxrwx   3  sapcomm   sapsys     1024  mmm  dd  tt:tt  <sid2>-<020>
drwxrwxrwx   3  sapcomm   sapsys     1024  mmm  dd  tt:tt  <sid3>-<010>
drwxrwxrwx   3  sapcomm   sapsys     1024  mmm  dd  tt:tt  <sid3>-<020>
```

Using SAPconnect (Replacing SAPcomm)

SAP has developed SAPconnect to replace the SAPcomm utility because it will provide a single common interface for all communications between SAP and other SAP systems, and also SAP and other application systems, which includes faxing, paging, SMTP, and SAPoffice. It performs this task via its application programming interface—the RFC interface.

As with the SAPcomm function, SAPconnect requires setup to be within each client for the SAP system and that the remote system specify those particular clients.

The transfer of data between SAP and the other systems occurs in the form of objects, defined in a similar manner to SAPoffice documents, i.e. SAPoffice mail or Internet mail.

The are two components to the SAPoffice document: the "main" document and the "attachments." These attachments may be of different formats, and it's the SAPconnect's responsibility to ensure that the conversion between SAP and the other systems' formats occurs with no errors. These documents may in turn be used by programs for further processing.

Two additional functions provided by SAPconnect include a scheduling function to pass objects to other systems at specific times, and the routing function to route the messages to the correct system.

SAPconnect further utilizes two function modules, SX_OBJECT_RECEIVE and SX_OBJECT_STATUS_RECEIVE, to move the objects and gather its status for both inbound and outbound transfers. These transfers can only be called in one of two ways:

◆ an application workstation triggering a function module execution on the SAP remotely

  OR

◆ via the SAP gateway (the remote server "registers" with the SAP gateway on its initial boot up and the SAP system setups corresponding RFC destination).

The RFC SDK software for workstation connectivity to the SAP system is found on the SAP Presentation CD (shipped with your SAP installation CDs). You should read and install the software per the instructions in the readme file, after which you are required to configure and set up certain tables and structures. These include:

◆ tables

  packing_list

  contents_txt

  contents_bin

  receivers

◆ structures

  receivers_info

  document_data

  system_data

Rather than duplicate examples, sample structures and table configuration examples are provided on the SAP Presentation CD when you install the RFC SDK software.

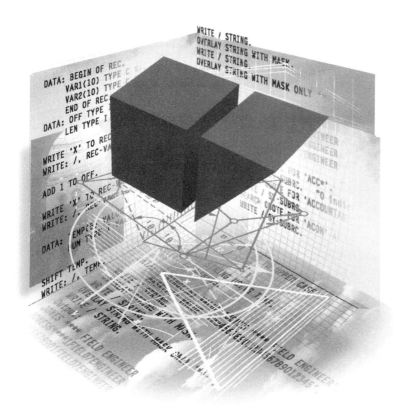

Chapter 8

**Correction
and Transport
System**

In This Chapter

◆ Terminology

◆ Transport Types

◆ Transport Management System

◆ Setting Up Correction and Transport System at UNIX Level

◆ CTS Initialization

◆ Maintenance of the CTS Environment

In this chapter we cover the Correction and Transport System. Let's first start with some basic terminology and principles.

Repairs *for SAP owned objects*

A *repair* is a change to an object that is not owned by the current system. Put in another way, it is a modification to objects that were not created or did not originate on the current system.

(Example: changes to SAP objects are repairs because these objects were originally created by German developers on a system named SAP <SID>, in Walldorf. A customer system name of SAP is forbidden, hence SAP objects will never be originals on a customer system.)

Typically, it does not make sense to perform a repair (also known as "open a repair") on a customer object. Repairs are normally only done on "SAP owned" objects (source code).

An Object Access Key from OSS is required to make repairs on SAP objects. An Object Access Key remains valid in the system until the repair is released.

Correction *for changes to customer objects. ZX, YA*

A *correction* is a change to an object that is owned by the current system. Put in another way, it is a modification to objects that were created or originated on the current system.

(Example: changes to customer objects, i.e. programs that start with either Z or Y.)

System Change Option

The *System Change Options* of a system also dictate whether or not a repair is permitted on that system.

1. No objects can be changed—production system (no repairs can be done).
2. Only original objects can be changed—development system (no repairs can be done).
3. Customer objects can be changed—development system (no repairs can be done). *↳ correction only*
4. All objects can be changed—development system (repairs can be done).

Transport Types

 NOTE

The Change Request (Transport Request) number is always created first before the TASK (Correction or Repair) number.

Use Type K to transport objects to a consolidation system. This request copies objects to the target system without change authorization, (similar to a T type).

In other words, the target system *would not* become the new owner of that object. Ownership would remain with the source system of the transport request.

transport to consolidation system → Type K (repairo)
transport to non consolidation — C. original, complete
T. repair

If the object being transported was originally created on the source system, further modifications to that object on the target system could only be done with a repair—*if* the system change settings allowed for repairs on the target system (all objects can be changed).

To transport to any system other than a consolidation system, you can use types C or T.

Use Type C transports to "check" the original of an object into or out of an integration system. For example, you would use type C transports to move a set of related objects from a central integration system to a development system where you could work on the objects in isolation.

Type C requests transport of the original of an object and *moves* the change authorization with the object to the target system. The target system then becomes the new owner of that object. You should therefore use type C requests only in the system that contains the original of an object.

Only complete objects can be transported with a C Type transport, such as R3TR, PROG, TABL, etc. That is to say, all associated objects with the object you are attempting to transport must be included. LIMU, REPS, DTED, etc., are pieces of objects that do not include the main object. Only complete objects may be transported as originals, or in other words, C typed.

TIP

Change the development object list names of LIMU & REPS to R3TR and PROG to accomplish a C type transport.

Use Type T requests to transport *repairs* of SAP objects between systems in your network. A Type T request transports a copy of the object without change authorization. This request copies objects to the target system without change authorization.

In other words, the target system *would not* become the new owner of that object. Ownership would remain with the source system of the transport request.

If the object being transported was originally created on the source system, further modifications to that object on the target system could only be done with a repair—*if* the system change settings allowed for repairs on the target system (all objects can be changed).

C Type *(move with authorization)*

INT—> DEV, object now owned by DEV. Further modification possible by opening a correction on DEV, but prevented on INT.

Further modification of the object on INT isn't possible by opening a REPAIR—because the system change settings on INT are set to prevent this (original objects only).

DEV—> INT, object now owned by INT. Further modification possible by opening a correction on INT, but prevented on DEV.

Further modification of the object on DEV could be possible by opening a REPAIR—the system change settings would allow this (all objects can be changed).

T Type *(move w/o authorization)*

INT—> DEV, object still owned by INT. Further modification possible by opening a correction on INT, but not on DEV.

Further modification of that object on DEV could be possible by opening a REPAIR—the system change settings would allow this (all objects can be changed).

DEV—> INT, object still owned by DEV. Further modification possible by opening a correction on DEV, but not on INT.

Further modification of that object on INT isn't possible by opening a REPAIR—because the system change settings on INT are set to prevent this (original objects only).

K Type *(consolidation)*

INT—> CON, object still owned by INT. Further modification possible by opening a correction on INT, but not on CON.

Further modification of that object on CON isn't possible by opening a REPAIR either—because the system change settings on CON are set to prevent this (no objects can be changed).

CON—> INT, object still owned by CON. Further modification isn't possible by opening a correction or REPAIR on CON or INT. This type of transport scenario would probably never exist.

Common Scenarios in a CTS Environment

No repairs of any kind should be done on the integration and consolidation systems. (The System Change Settings — "only original objects" should be set).

Repairs should always be done on development first, then transported to integration using a T or K type transport.

Integration should contain the originals of all objects. All customer objects should be mastered (developed) on the development system whenever possible. Risky and non-standard development should be done on the development system first, such as User Exits.

Only C and T type transports should be allowed between integration and development systems. K types should never really be done.

Transport Requests are referred to as Change Requests in 3.0 and 4.0, and Corrections and Repairs as Tasks.

Object Types Related to the Correction and Transport System

LIMU	Obj.	"Parts of development environment object"
R3TR	Obj.	"Object summaries, i.e. the entire development object"
R3TR	TABU	"Table Data"
R3TR	TABL	"Table Structure"
R3TR	TABD	"Table Data and Structure"
R3TR	TDAT	"Customizing Table Data"
R3TR	MSAG	"Message Class"
R3TR	BMVA	"Variant"
R3TR	DEVC	"Development Class"
R3TR	DOMA	"Domain with Documentation"
R3TR	DTEL	"Data Element with Documentation"
R3TR	DOCU	"Document"

R3TR	DYNP	"Dynpro"
R3TR	FUGR	"Function Group"
R3TR	MCID	"Matchcode Id"
R3TR	SUSO	"Authorization Object"
R3TR	TFRM	"Table entries for formulas and conditions"
R3TR	XPRA	"Program generation after transport"

Transport Management System (TMS)

You can perform and monitor transports between all SAP systems with the Transport Management System (TMS) with release 4.X

Operating system level access is no longer necessary, because all the necessary information and functions can be performed from within SAP. The Transport Management System can perform the following tasks:

◆ Configure the transport routes within SAP using a graphical editor display

◆ Display the import queues of all R/3 systems that are listed in the transport domain, which you have defined

◆ Start the import of all the requests in an import queue, without having to have OS level access

◆ Perform advance imports of pre-defined requests

◆ Transport between R/3 systems without a common transport directory

Transaction STMS is the transaction used to access the Transport Management System.

TMS Concepts

A transport administrator can now perform transports using the Transport Management System. The Workbench Organizer still supports the developer in the software development process until a change request has been released. The Transport Management System now can support the administrator when importing the request into the target system. TMS and the Workbench Organizer work very closely together.

A transport domain now contains all components of the R/3 systems that are to be administered together. The transport domain can contain system settings that are identical for all R/3 systems. Transport routes is an example of this. One R/3 system within the transport domain acts as a master and contains the main reference configuration. Copies of this reference configuration are contained within all of the other R/3 systems of the same transport domain. This master R/3 system containing the reference configuration is called the transport domain controller.

Typically, one common transport directory is shared by all R/3 systems in a transport domain. In some cases this is not possible. Reasons for this might be:

◆ A "slow" network connection to which an R/3 system is connected

◆ Hardware vendor limitations

◆ Security issues that will not allow for direct file access by other R/3 systems (for example, NFS mounted file systems in UNIX or NT shares)

R/3 systems with a common transport directory can each form a transport group. TMS can support several transport directories within a transport domain in that group.

Configuring TMS

TMS must be configured on all R/3 systems in your system landscape before you can begin working with the Transport Management System, just as was required in earlier releases of SAP with transaction SE06. The TMS configuration includes:

◆ **Configuring the transport domain:** You must define which R/3 systems in your system landscape should be grouped in a transport domain and which R/3 system is to be the transport domain controller.

◆ **Configuring transport routes:** The transport routes are used to define the target system in which you want to consolidate change requests and the R/3 systems to be given this information automatically.

◆ **Configuring the transport control program tp:** The transport control program needs information about the transport directory and the R/3 database for each R/3 system. This information is stored in a global parameter file.

Setting Up Correction and Transport System at UNIX Level

1. Verify the central transport directory, /usr/sap/trans.
2. Verify that transport directory /usr/sap/trans is accessible locally or mounted via NFS on all systems participating in the transport.
3. Review the subdirectories under the transport directory /usr/sap/trans.
4. In the transport directory (/usr/sap/trans), you must have the following subdirectories:

/usr/sap/trans/bin	Executables and scripts
/usr/sap/trans/buffer	Files with names: <SID>. Contents: Transport requests
/usr/sap/trans/cofiles	Information files
/usr/sap/trans/data	Data
/usr/sap/trans/log	Log files for the individual transport steps
/usr/sap/trans/sapnames	User of C&T. Contents: Information on C&T actions
/usr/sap/trans/tmp	Temporary files

5. Examine optional directories, if any.

   /usr/sap/trans/olddata: if "tp cleanup" is run regularly to remove old log and data files.

   /usr/sap/trans/backup: for backing up data with R3TRANS.

6. Verify the above on all application servers on which background work processes are installed, (since different transport steps can be processed by any background work process of the respective system).
7. Verify that the transport control program tp and the transport program R3TRANS are accessible by all systems participating in the transport.
8. Verify file-naming conventions and removal of unnecessary files in the above subdirectories.
9. Verify the file names in the /usr/sap/trans/buffer directory.

10. Verify the file names in the /usr/sap/trans/log directory.

    The name of a log file is built from the names of the transport request, the executed step, and the system in which the step was executed:

    ```
    <sourcesystem><action><6 digits>.<targetsystem>
    ```

    Where possible values for `<action>` are as follows:

    A: Dictionary activation
    C: C source transport
    D: Import of application defined objects
    E: R3TRANS import
    G: Report and dynpro generation
    H: R3TRANS dictionary import
    I: R3TRANS main import
    P: Test import
    R: Execution of reports after put (XPRA)
    T: R3TRANS table entries import
    X: Export of application defined objects.

11. Verify that data files get written in the data directory.

    The name of a data file is built from the names of the transport request and a key letter that distinguishes between R3TRANS data files and those generated by additional programs for additional development environment objects (ADOs), created for SAP applications:

    ```
    R<6digits>.<sourcesystem>  R3TRANS
    D<6digits>.<sourcesystem>  ADO programs
    ```

12. Verify that Transport Request Information File gets written to the cofiles directory.

    The transport request information file contains information on a transport request, including the transport type and the kinds of objects to be transported. It also contains information on the steps required for the transport request, including exit codes and time of execution. The name is also derived from the name of the transport request:

    ```
    K<6digits>.<sourcesystem>
    ```

13. Verify any special conditions and proper documentation of special conditions when R3TRANS is used.

Examining Unix Users, Groups, and Permissions

1. Verify that all UNIX users under which an SAP system is started (i.e., every <sid>adm), must have read, write, and execute (rwx) authorization for all subdirectories.

2. Verify all the <sid>adm accounts created are in the same group and rwx authorization must be assigned to owner and group.

3. Verify that all files under /usr/sap/trans are owned by a certain user (for example, <sys>adm). tp always runs under the same user.   *<sys>adm*

4. su — root ;

5. cd /usr/sap/trans

6. chown <sys>adm */*

7. Verify that permissions are set on all tp-related files (including logs, buffer-files, data-files, etc.)

Verify Control Tables and Parameter Files for CTS

1. Verify the existence and contents of Parameter file TPPARAM.

2. Verify the contents of Table TSYST.

3. Verify the contents of Table TASYS.

4. Verify TASYS and TSYST are replicated on all the participating SAP Systems.

5. Verify the entry for the system called SAP in TSYST.

Examine Control File TPPARAM

Examine the parameter file TPPARAM (in /usr/sap/trans/bin). Verify the following entries in TPPARAM:

◆ Global Entries 'transdir' and 'r3transpath'.

◆ transdir = /usr/sap/trans/

◆ r3transpath = /usr/sap/$(system)/SYS/exe/run/R3trans

Entries for each system participating in the transports:

◆ <SID>/dbname = <ORACLE-SID>

◆ <SID>/dbhost = <name of the DB server>

Additional Entries to be Verified

◆ **startsap:** shell script which is executed by TP to start the SAP system.

◆ **stopsap:** shell script which is executed by TP to stop the SAP System. (Verify that the scripts stop only the SAP System and not the database system as well. TP is connected to the database when this command is issued and will abort very urgently if the database is stopped.)

◆ **startdb:** shell script which is executed by TP to start the database.

◆ **stopdb:** shell script which is executed by TP to stop the database.

◆ **clientcascade:** Verify usage of R3TRANS imports with the client cascade option.

Verify any additional optional parameters' usage (if any).

Verify that the <sid>adm user can read the file with the commands:

◆ cd /usr/sap/trans/bin

◆ tp go <SID>

(The environment for the logon of the tp program to the system database <SYS> is output and can thus be checked. If implausible values are output here, the entries for the system <SID> must be checked in TPPARAM. In particular, pay attention to hidden blanks or special characters.)

Verify that the R3trans, which was entered for the target system in TPPARAM, with its complete path is accessible and usable by all the computers of the source system. (Thus, the directory /usr/sap/<target system>/SYS/exe/run must also be mounted on the application servers of the source system, if the path entered above is used. If this is not the case, the test import that is started directly after the export cannot be carried out.)

Verify entries in TPPARAM for event triggering:

```
<sid>/impdp_by_event = yes
<sid>/sapevtpath = /usr/sap/<sid>/SYS/exe/run/sapevt
```

Verify the existence of a dummy system and documentation procedures for special conditions to which to release transports (if needed).

Verify setup of the dummy system; for example, DUM. Make entries in table TSYST and set the corresponding parameters in /usr/sap/trans/bin/TPPARAM: DUM/dbhost = dum. Verify type of release transport request to DUM.

Examine Table TSYST

◆ Verify that all participating systems are listed in TSYST.

◆ Verify that TSYST is replicated on all participating systems.

Examine Table TASYS

◆ Verify the systems that receive automatic transports are listed in TASYS.

◆ Verify that TASYS is replicated on all participating systems.

Examine Table TDEVC

◆ Verify Customer Development classes, naming conventions, and transport routes in TDEVC.

◆ Verify that TDEVC is replicated on all participating systems.

CTS Initialization

The installation of the correction and transport system can be a somewhat confusing task as described in the R/3 system installation guide. The one task that is well documented is the installation of the UNIX file systems that are required, and these file systems must be present for the CTS to work correctly, so follow the instructions concerning their creation in the manual.

There is confusion, however, in tasks such as running the transaction SE06, how to edit the parameter file TPPARAM and the script T_EXP, and where RDDIMPDP should be running. The purpose of this chapter is not to go into specific details of the correction and transport system, but to give specific information that an installer of the R/3 system can use to verify that initialization of the correction and transport system has been properly carried out at a minimal level.

SE06

This is the program that actually initializes the transport and correction tables, i.e., TADIR and others, and specifically sets the correction number assignment of an installed system.

TPPARAM

This file resides in the file system /usr/sap/trans/bin and is the parameter file for the tp interface to R3trans. As supplied by SAP, this file contains entries for systems T11 and P11. Each system that you are installing must be described in this file.

TSYST

This table should have at least two entries in it. One entry should be SAP and the other should be for the system that you are installing. If the entries for your system(s) are there, you are successful thus far in setting up CTS. If there are three system entries in this table and the third entry is correct, then leave it there. But, if it's incorrect, simply delete it (see Figure 8-1).

TDEVC

Edit this table manually and put in an entry that looks like the following entry for Z001. Replace the entries for integration system as shown with the <SID> that you are installing. If you are installing a consolidation system, then that field should match that <SID>. The concern that you should have is that the two entries in these fields must be existing entries in the table TSYST. Another valid option is to leave both of these fields blank. The entries on the second line entry, however, must be completed like in Figure 8-2.

TASYS

A typical TASYS entry is shown in Figure 8-3.

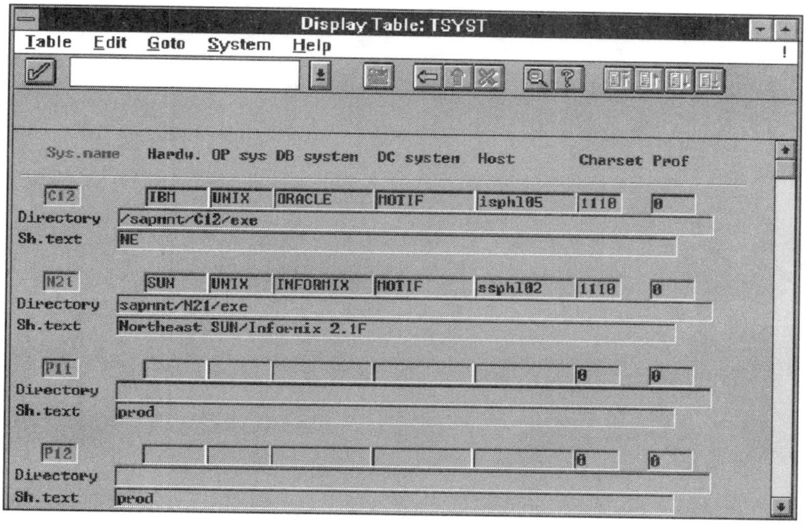

FIGURE 8-1 *Display Table: TSYST*

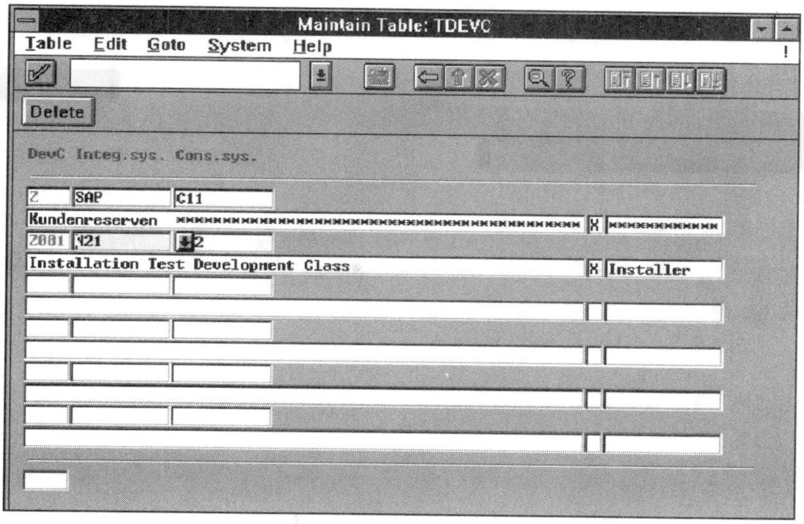

FIGURE 8-2 *Maintain Table: TDEVC*

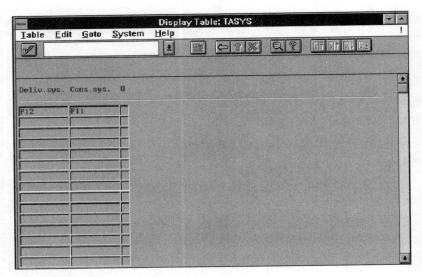

FIGURE 8-3 *Display Table: TASYS*

RDDIMPDP

This program is the CTS daemon, and contrary to popular belief, must be scheduled to run in batch in each system in the CTS configuration. This program must be scheduled as DDIC in client 0. Scheduling this job to run at five-minute intervals can be accomplished by executing the program RDDPUTPP.

At this point the CTS system should be initialized. An object can be created, and implicit insertion of a development class and creation of a correction number should occur. Once this happens, you can cancel out of the object creation because you have verified the correct installation of the Correction and Transport System.

Maintenance of the CTS Environment

1. Verify that job RDDIMPDP is scheduled.
2. Verify that the RDDIMPDP is scheduled for event triggering (via RDDNEWPP).
3. Verify transports mechanics (Type of Transports) between systems of different purposes.

4. Determine the procedures in place for keeping the control tables consistent across systems.

5. Verify the procedures currently in place to clean up the /usr/sap/trans directories.

6. Verify the status of each SAP system (whether set to No Change or All Change, etc.).

7. Examine the transport types between systems.

8. Examine the procedures that are in place to import the released transports to the target system.

9. Verify that the logs are checked to ensure that the test import completed.

10. Examine any special modes issued with tp to run imports.

11. Verify the procedures in place for ensuring the security of the CTS system (prevention of unauthorized use of the transport system).

12. Review the procedure in place for creating corrections, documenting the corrections, releasing the corrections to transports, reviewing the transports, releasing the transports, importing the transports, examining the success of the transports.

13. Review the procedure for handling Repairs (creation, release, and propagation and system consistency).

14. Review procedures for client specific transports (e.g. Client Cascading).

15. Review procedures for importing DD objects (e.g. creation at DB level on target system).

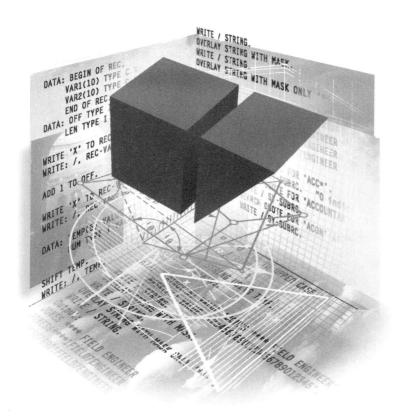

Chapter 9

SAP Performance Tuning

In This Chapter

In this chapter, you will find three sections, the first Planning Considerations, the second Database Performance Considerations, and last SAP Performance Considerations.

The first section will start off with a few definitions to get you familiar with the performance environment. Throughout the section, you will find suggestions on how to configure your initial SAP environment and how the operating system should be tuned.

The second section concentrates on the database. It defines some database concepts and makes suggestions on how to solve database related performance issues.

The third section concentrates on tuning the SAP environment as far as memory and buffers are concerned.

Planning Considerations

Administrators use two methods to do performance planning and tuning. The "ostrich method" is where the administrator hides his or her head in the sand, throwing hardware at problems, hoping the problems will go away—not a very effective way of dealing with the situation. The other method is to deal with problems directly and actually solve the performance issues for what they really are—problems in the environment that require tuning, not additional hardware.

Performance tuning starts the first day that you implement SAP. It is very important to start correctly because later, during the lifetime of the SAP system, you are bound to have to redo performance settings if they were not done right the first time. The initial performance considerations are the following:

- System layout, distribution, and network architecture
- Hardware architecture
- Storage devices and file systems
- Software and database layout

The next few sections explain each of the initial considerations for building a well-tuned system. Keep in mind that these are *initial* performance considerations. Throughout the lifetime of your R/3 system, you will revise and build upon this initial setup.

SAP Services

SAP is a highly configurable system and provides a set of specialized services that can be distributed to any of the available application servers defined in the environment. But before discussing the distribution of the SAP services, the different services need to be defined:

Dialog (Online)	Used for interactive online processing.
Batch (Background)	Used for jobs running in the background.
Update (V1)	Used for time-critical updates that need to happen immediately.
Update (V2)	Used for updates that are not critical, which are delayed until resources are available to process the updates.
Enqueue	The single "central lock management service" that controls the locking mechanism between the different application servers and the database.
Spool	Responsible for servicing print requests and for demanding the job statuses in the host spool systems and scanning the spool database for requests lost through queue overflows. As of Release 4.0, SAP allows more than one spool process per instance.
Message Server	Responsible for communication between the different application servers. It routes messages between the servers and is used for licensing. An SAP instance has only one message server.
Gateway	Used for transport of bigger amounts of data between application servers as well as external (non-SAP) systems that communicate with SAP.

small amount of data between application servers is done by Message Server

System Layout, Distribution, and Network Architecture

A typical SAP environment has development (integration), test (consolidation), and production systems. Each of these systems can have zero or more application servers associated with it. Referring to Figure 9-1, how do you connect these systems and how many of each do you need?

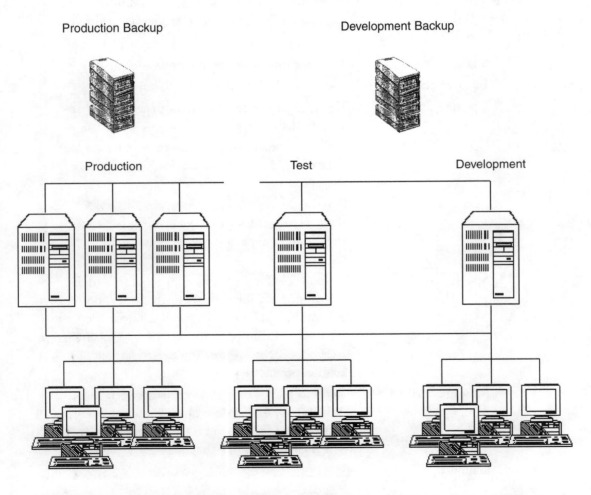

FIGURE 9-1 *A network layout displaying two separate inter–SAP networks and a single user–SAP network.*

An SAP system has two networks associated with it:

♦ **A network for inter-SAP communications.** The database and application servers use this network to exchange data and information.

♦ **A network for user-SAP communications.** All user interactions and communications with SAP are supported on this network.

It would be great to have both of these networks be dual FDDI rings, but alas, customers usually settle for a Dual FDDI Token Ring for inter-SAP communications and Fast Ethernet for user-SAP communications.

Split these two networks in order to ensure the best network performance between the database and its application servers. Data traffic between the database and application servers can be very high at times. For this reason, you will typically want to connect the database server and the application servers over the same LAN on the same segment and not over a WAN. Users also have a tendency sometimes to transfer huge files over the network, thereby slowing the network down.

Should development, test, and production share the same inter-SAP network? It depends on the activity on your system and your ability to purchase the required hardware. Some companies do have all their environments sharing the same network; others split them up between production (one network) and development and test (another network). The latter is the more advisable configuration for security and performance reasons.

Backup strategies also play a very important role in performance of an SAP environment. Given the fact that you require the best and fastest backup hardware, you also have to decide on the connectivity of the backup environment with the SAP environment.

Production needs a separate backup environment from development and testing. This will avoid many backup contention problems. You have the choice to connect the backup system on either one of the two networks or to the system itself. An excellent but expensive backup strategy is to mirror your disks threefold. When it is time to do backups, you stop the database, break one mirror disk from the set, start the system, back up your mirror disk, and, when the backup is done, add the disk back to the mirror set. This mirroring strategy does not require a network and thus reduces the load on the network. Backup strategies will be discussed in Chapter 12, "Database Administration." Keep in mind for now that backups introduce extra load on networks, and this extra load can introduce performance problems.

TIP

Remember this rule of thumb: A production environment should have one application server for every 100 users, a batch server depending on your batch load, and a definite database server.

Database Server

The database server can either host both the database and the central SAP instance or only the database. A server running both the database and central instance is called a *database server with central instance*. The only requirement for a server to be a database server is that the database be running on it.

Configure the central instance—if it is running on the database server—to be as small as possible (two dialog processes, no batch, the only enqueue, and more than one update process). Make use of load balancing and logon groups to ensure that users are unable to connect to this system.

Move the central instance from the database server when the database server is unable to cope with both the database and the central instance running on it. Keep in mind that when you do this you will have to include the database server and the central instance in the "high availability" strategy.

Central Instance

By definition, the *central instance* is the instance that hosts the enqueue service and the message server.

TIP

Use the central instance as an update server. Define most of the update processes on this server. This strategy will avoid network traffic between the update processes and the network.

The central instance can be installed on either the database server or its own application server. The advantage of installing both on the same server is that only one machine requires inclusion in the "high availability" strategy. The advantage of having the central instance on a separate server is improved performance for both the database and the central instance.

When the central instance is running on the database server, move all non-database-related services to the other application servers. The enqueue and update services are the services most closely related to the database. The minimum number of dialog processes is two on each server, but all the other services can move to different servers.

Application Server

in ∞ instances/application server

An *application server* is a server that hosts one or more SAP instances. An application server is synonymous with an SAP instance only if one SAP instance is running on the server. Application servers are used for different reasons. Two typical uses for application servers are as dialog servers or batch servers.

if dialog and batch use same server,
use operation mode. if different, no need
operation mode

Batch Instance

It is usually very difficult to determine what the batch load on your systems will be when you are installing SAP for the first time. There is always a trade-off between performance for dialog users and background jobs. In general, background jobs should be scheduled to run during low user-activity periods. SAP provides utilities like operation modes to assist administrators to define different modes for different processing periods. For use during the night when user activity is low, create a batch operation mode that will accommodate batch processing, and for daytime create a mode that will accommodate users. The problem with this is that the world is round—while it's day in one part of the world, it is night in another. How do you define operation modes around this problem? It is very difficult! If the batch load warrants an extra server, create a server that is dedicated only to batch processing. Another option is to spread the load between all the available application servers. Do this as long as user performance stays unaffected.

Dialog Instance

One hundred users per application server mean 10 dialog processes per server. This at least gives you an idea of how many servers to buy initially. Dialog application servers are the domains of the SAP users, and the number of application servers depends on the load these users introduce to the system.

The workload on the application servers can be distributed according to the different functional modules. Some modules require more resources than others do. Group the less resource-intensive modules together, and put the users using these modules on one server and the users using resource-intensive modules on their own servers. The sales and distribution (SD) module is known to put the highest load on a system, so dedicate some of the available application servers to SD and share the remaining servers between the remaining modules.

Load Balancing

It is easy to create logon groups, but it is more difficult assigning these logon groups to different application servers. Logon groups are usually associated with the functional modules in SAP. For instance, you can create a logon group called Finance for the functional module financial accounting (FI). Some of the functional modules that are closely related share data and code; try to group these related modules on the same application servers.

Transaction ST07 in Figure 9-2 is the application monitor, used to monitor the activity of the different functional modules in SAP. These statistics can be applied to the distribution of logon groups over the different application servers.

```
Application Monitor: User Distribution                              _ □ ×
User distribution  Edit  Goto  Environment  System  Help

▼  ◄ ⇐⇑✕  ▣▥▦  ▤▧▨▩  ?

Choose │ Sort │ R/3 buffers │ DB accesses │ DB memory │ Response time │ Quantity structure │ History

Database  Name    C01              R/3 Release    31H
          Server  sapc01           Time           12:04:39
          System  ORACLE           Date           11/02/1998

User              591              all clients
Number of servers   5              Work processes       90
```

Application	Number of users			Sess.per	Appl.
	loggedOn	active	in WP	Users	Server
Basis Components	11	3	1	1.55	4
Controlling	1	0	0	1.00	1
Financial Accounting	11	1	0	1.91	3
Materials Management	5	0	0	1.60	3
Project System	5	0	0	1.60	3
Sales and Distribution	6	1	0	1.67	2
Other	14	0	7	1.93	4
total	53	5	8	1.74	5

FIGURE 9-2 *ST07 application monitor assists with load balance statistics per functional module.*

Financial Applications

FI Financial Accounting

CO Controlling

EC Enterprise Controlling

IM Capital Investment Management

TR Treasury

Human Resources Applications

PA Personnel Administration

PD Personnel Development

Logistics Applications

LO General Logistics

MM Materials Management

PM Plant Maintenance

PP Production Planning

PS Project System

QM Quality Management

SD Sales and Distribution

The advantage of grouping related modules is that the use of the SAP data buffers is more efficient. When modules are mixed excessively, the buffers are constantly loaded and unloaded in order to accommodate requests for different unrelated data.

Each of the SAP modules has a different transaction workload, but when installing a system for the first time, this transaction workload is unknown. As mentioned before, SAP or any implementation partners should have statistics available based on experience. Another option is to guess by gathering statistics on the workload of the legacy systems in the company and then configure your system according to these findings. Let the system run for a month or two in normal production mode, gather new statistics from the production SAP environment itself, and then redo the load balancing for the system. Transactions ST07 and ST14 are valuable sources for transactional load statistics per functional module. Figure 9-3 displays transaction ST07, the response time per functional module.

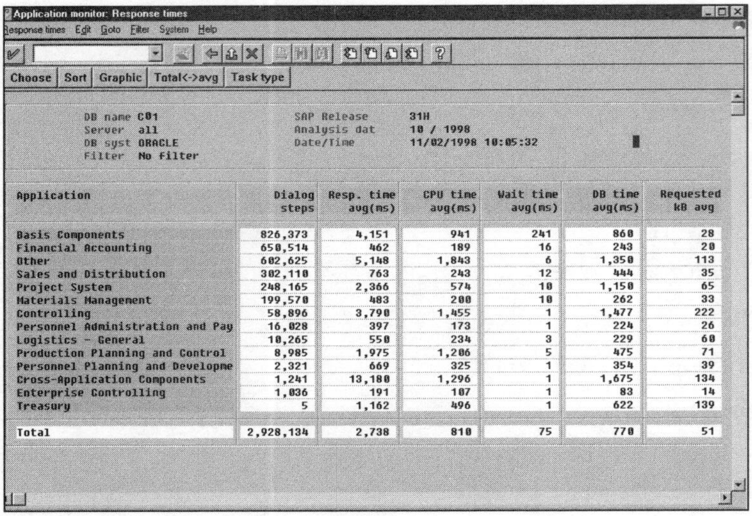

Application	Dialog steps	Resp. time avg(ms)	CPU time avg(ms)	Wait time avg(ms)	DB time avg(ms)	Requested kB avg
Basis Components	826,373	4,151	941	241	860	28
Financial Accounting	650,514	462	189	16	243	20
Other	602,625	5,148	1,843	6	1,350	113
Sales and Distribution	302,110	763	243	12	444	35
Project System	248,165	2,366	574	10	1,150	65
Materials Management	199,570	483	200	10	262	33
Controlling	58,896	3,790	1,455	1	1,477	222
Personnel Administration and Pay	16,028	397	173	1	224	26
Logistics - General	10,265	550	234	3	229	60
Production Planning and Control	8,985	1,975	1,206	5	475	71
Personnel Planning and Developme	2,321	669	325	1	354	39
Cross-Application Components	1,241	13,180	1,296	1	1,675	134
Enterprise Controlling	1,036	191	107	1	83	14
Treasury	5	1,162	496	1	622	139
Total	2,928,134	2,738	810	75	770	51

FIGURE 9-3 *Response time per module*

How should a system be configured based on Figure 9-3? Say you have a database server with a central instance and four application servers with a single SAP instance installed on each. The modules this company uses are as in Figure 9-3.

There could be many different answers. One possible layout is as follows:

Database instance:	No functional groups
Application server 1:	FI, CO, TR, EC, PS, and PD
Application server 2:	FI, CO, TR, EC, PS, PD, SD, MM, LO, PS, and PP
Application server 3:	SD, MM, LO, PS, and PP

FI, MM, and SD are the modules that introduce the highest workload. Try to separate these three modules for performance reasons; at the same time, keep the layout as redundant as possible and group related modules together. Application server 2 is over-committed, but that can be remedied by restricting the number of users allowed to use that instance. The next step is to monitor the system and tune it accordingly.

Hardware Architecture

An administrator's wish is always to have the biggest and fastest hardware with unlimited disk space and memory.

Yes, hardware is important! SAP is supported on many different hardware platforms, which allows SAP customers to plan their environment in order to get the best performance for the least amount of money. Even if money is not an issue, it is always advisable to carefully plan your environment.

The advantages of a well-planned environment are that:

- ◆ It is inexpensive to have a good solution (happy management).
- ◆ It assists in making maintenance and troubleshooting problems in the environment less complex (happy administrator).
- ◆ The result is good performance (happy users).

Initial performance considerations for a brand-new SAP installation are more difficult than performance-tuning efforts later, mainly due to a lack of performance information and statistics. You do not know how the system will react in your business environment.

SAP has more than 1,500 installations worldwide and has partnerships with many different hardware vendors. New customers can leverage this wealth of performance information to plan their initial system layout. All the hardware vendors have some tool to assist customers in guessing how to size their environment. The bottom line is to make your guess as good as possible, making sure that you have enough capacity for future growth. SAP provides a tool called QuickSizer, which can be located on SAPNet and is intended to estimate the size of the system necessary to run a particular workload.

Storage Devices and File Systems

Implementing an SAP production system goes hand in hand with implementing one of the RAID technologies on the market today. The advantages of a RAID set are as follows:

- ◆ **Redundancy.** Data is duplicated or can be reconstructed (depending on the RAID technology). This reduces the risk of data loss when a disk in a RAID set gets bad blocks.

◆ **Serviceability**. Some of the RAID technologies allow administrators to swap hot disks while the system is still up and running. The system then rebuilds the data on the new disk provided.

◆ **Performance**. RAID technology has the potential to improve performance if it is configured correctly. If you use it improperly, RAID can actually slow your system down.

◆ **Availability**. Depending on the technology, if one or two disks in the array go bad, the data stays available to the system.

Below you will find a list of the different RAID technologies and a brief description of each:

◆ RAID-0 striping

◆ RAID-1 mirroring

◆ RAID-0+1 mirroring and striping

◆ RAID-3 bit striping over multiple disks, one parity disk

◆ RAID-4 block striping over multiple disks, one parity disk

◆ RAID-5 block striping over multiple disks, with distributed parity

RAW Devices versus File Systems

A *raw device* (or *logical device*) is not formatted by the operating system to contain a file system. A file system has file pointers, and users are able to create files and directories within it. A raw device does not have file pointers, files, or directories.

A raw device improves performance for data files that have a very high I/O rate associated with them. If you have an interactive SAP environment (users doing a lot of interactive online transactions), a raw device will probably not improve your response time. On the other hand, if you have multiple I/O-intensive batch jobs, it probably will increase performance.

The reason for this performance increase is that file systems introduce file system management overhead. File systems have their own cache, which means that the DBMS first writes to the DBMS cache, then to the file system cache, and finally to disk. With raw devices, the DBMS writes directly from the database cache to the disk.

File systems have lock management that prevents multiple users from accessing the same file at a given time. In a striped environment, raw devices will improve the parallelism of disk access thanks to the absence of lock restrictions.

NOTE

With the high performance disks and disk arrays available today, think twice before you use raw devices. If you've thought twice about it and you really believe that a raw device will solve your problem, please do make use of it. Know your business environment and plan your solution based on how it functions.

An administrative advantage to file systems is that they're easy to resize, back up, add, and remove. Performance versus administration is the crux of the matter.

A combination of raw devices and file systems usually provides a very good solution. Put the data files that are I/O-intensive on raw devices and the rest of the data files on normal file systems.

Presume that you have a single tablespace per file system. That is, PSAPUSER1I is in sapdata1, PSAPPROTI is in sapdata2, PSAPROLL is in sapdata16, and so on for each of the 27 different tablespaces that exist in SAP.

You need to find the I/O activity of each of the tablespaces defined for SAP. You have two choices: get one of those database-tuning books and whip up a quick SQL script that reports the I/O per file system or use transaction **ST04**, menu path Detailed Analysis Menu, File System Requests, I/O per Path. Add the reads and writes together for each of the tablespaces. The tablespaces with the highest number of I/O requests are potential candidates for raw devices. The tablespaces with low I/O requests can remain on the file systems where they currently reside. Figure 9-4 displays the I/O distribution per data file.

Software and Database Layout

An SAP system consists of many different software applications and data files working together to provide an integrated solution. Figure 9-5 displays a typical SAP software distribution over different disks.

Distribution Rules

The distribution rules govern how you ultimately want to lay the system out. They reflect a wish list that is not always practical or affordable. A good distribution makes use of these rules but also optimizes the disk space usage, I/O performance, and ease of system administration. For the best performance, you will have each software component on its own disk. But this obviously wastes disk

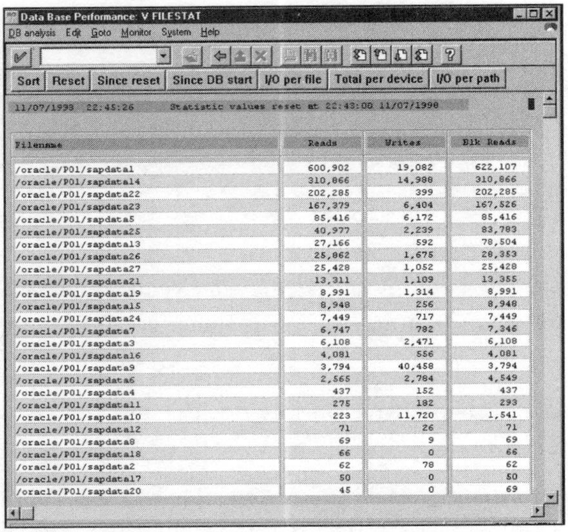

Filename	Reads	Writes	Blk Reads
/oracle/P01/sapdata1	600,902	19,082	622,107
/oracle/P01/sapdata14	310,866	14,988	310,866
/oracle/P01/sapdata22	202,285	399	202,285
/oracle/P01/sapdata23	167,379	6,404	167,526
/oracle/P01/sapdata5	85,416	6,172	85,416
/oracle/P01/sapdata25	40,977	2,239	83,783
/oracle/P01/sapdata13	27,166	592	78,504
/oracle/P01/sapdata26	25,862	1,675	28,353
/oracle/P01/sapdata27	25,428	1,052	25,428
/oracle/P01/sapdata21	13,311	1,109	13,355
/oracle/P01/sapdata19	8,991	1,314	8,991
/oracle/P01/sapdata15	8,948	256	8,948
/oracle/P01/sapdata24	7,449	717	7,449
/oracle/P01/sapdata7	6,747	782	7,346
/oracle/P01/sapdata3	6,108	2,471	6,108
/oracle/P01/sapdata16	4,081	556	4,081
/oracle/P01/sapdata9	3,794	40,458	3,794
/oracle/P01/sapdata6	2,565	2,784	4,549
/oracle/P01/sapdata4	437	152	437
/oracle/P01/sapdata11	275	182	293
/oracle/P01/sapdata10	223	11,720	1,541
/oracle/P01/sapdata12	71	26	71
/oracle/P01/sapdata8	69	9	69
/oracle/P01/sapdata18	66	0	66
/oracle/P01/sapdata2	62	78	62
/oracle/P01/sapdata17	50	0	50
/oracle/P01/sapdata20	45	0	69

FIGURE 9-4 *Transaction ST04 displaying the I/O distribution per data file*

space in abundance. If you put everything on one disk, your performance will be poor and administration will be very difficult. You have to strike a balance between growth, performance, and security:

- **Growth (size).** Tablespaces (like PSAPBATBD) that grow very fast and are very big compared to other SAP tablespaces need to be on their own disks to allow for growth and to avoid I/O contention with other tablespaces.
- **Performance.** Some files in the SAP environment—especially some tablespaces—have very high I/O rates. It is wise to put these highly active files on their own disks in order to avoid I/O contention. It also happens in SAP that certain tables cause I/O contention. These tables can be moved to their own tablespace, and this tablespace can then be located on its own disk or can be striped across multiple disks.
- **Data security.** Data security deals with the ability to reconstruct the SAP environment in a timely fashion after some kind of disaster, major or small. An administrator needs to minimize the impact that, for instance, a disk crash might have on a system. Say you have all the redo

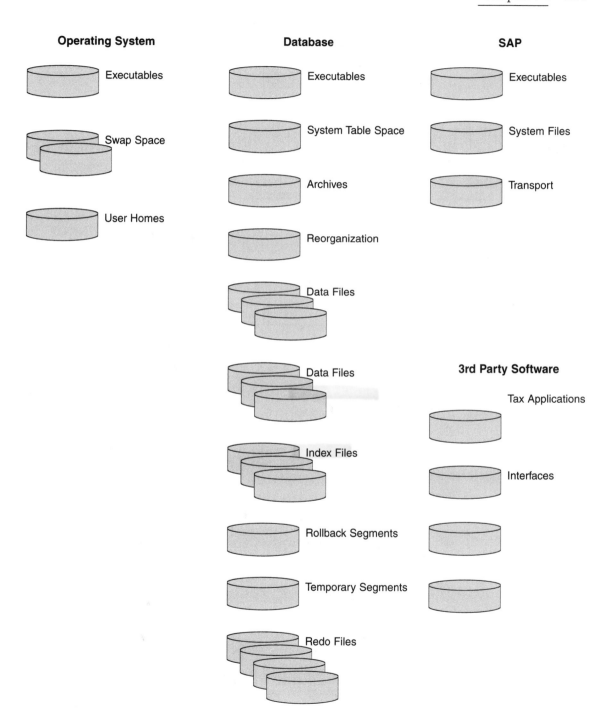

FIGURE 9-5 *SAP software distribution*

logs and the archiving files on one disk and this disk crashes; the only way you will be able to recover this database is from backup, and chances are that the backup might be days old. Some files just do not belong on the same disk.

The SAP environment consists of different layers of software. The following table shows how layout goals pertain to each component:

Table 9-1 SAP Environment with Different Layers of Software

Operating System	
Data Security	Put the operating system on its own disk.
Performance	Again, put the operating system on its own disk.
	Get dedicated disks for the operating system swap files.

Database	
Data Security	Put the database executables on their own disk.
	Put the system data files on a separate disk.
	The mirror redo logs should not be on the same disk as the accompanying redo log file. This heightens the probability that you will be able to recover your database if you lose the disk where the log files are located.
	Keep the archive files apart from the data files, index files, system files, rollback segments, and redo log files. This reduces the risk of losing your data and the means to recover your data at the same time. Archive files are just as active as redo log files, and by separating the archives from the other files, you avoid I/O contention.
Performance	Separate data files from their accompanying index files. Data files and index files are usually accessed at the same time. By placing them on different disks, you avoid I/O contention.
	Keep the rollback segments apart from the data files, index files, redo log files, and temporary segments. This is one performance rule that should not be violated. Rollback segments are very I/O-intensive, and by placing them on a different disk, you will definitely improve system performance.
	Keep temporary segments apart from any of the data files, index files and rollback segments. Temporary segments have the potential to be very active; this activity depends on the number of large sorts done by SAP.

Database *(Continued)*

	The redo logs (origlogA and origlogB) should not be located on a single disk. This avoids contention between the Oracle log writer and the archive processes.
	Keep the redo log files apart from the data files, index files, system files, rollback segments, and archive files. Redo log files are very active because every transaction that changes data in the database ends up in a redo log file. By separating the redo log files from the other files, you will avoid I/O contention.
	Put the reorganization area (export dump area) on its own disk to improve performance during database reorganizations.

SAP Application

Performance	Put the SAP binaries, the transport files, and the SAP system files each on its own disk.

Third-Party Software

Performance	Keep third-party software separate from the SAP environment.
Data Security	Follow performance and security rules specified for this software.

With this set of rules, you will get the layout pictured in Figure 9-5. The rules pertaining to performance and disk space are more flexible than the rules pertaining to data security.

Performance Guideline

Determine the I/O load on each data file. Keep the files with a high I/O load on their own disks and combine the files with low I/O activity.

Once again, make use of the transaction **ST04**, follow menu path Detailed Analysis Menu, File System Requests, I/O per Path. See Table 9-2 for a list of the different tablespaces sorted by I/O activity. Add the reads and writes together for each of the tablespaces. The tablespaces with the highest number of I/O requests should be located on their own disks. The other tablespaces can be balanced among the remaining available disks. Keep in mind that size and growth play a very important part in placing data files. Gather the I/O activity, the current sizes of the data files, and the growth rate into a spreadsheet.

Table 9-2 Database Growth and I/O Distribution

File System	Tablespace Name	DB Used Now (MB)	Growth per Month (MB)	I/O Activity
10	PSAPTEMP	0.01	0	0
2	PSAPUSER1I	0.43	0	8
18	PSAPLOADI	0.23	0	11
20	PSAPDOCUD	13.16	0	11
8	PSAPLOADD	0.23	9	14
17	PSAPDOCUI	5.65	0	15
12	PSAPUSER1D	0.59	0	17
4	PSAPSOURCEI	36.38	0	18
11	PSAPSOURCED	25.70	15	39
6	PSAPPROTD	402.59	48	236
9	PSAPROLL	800.79	0	236
15	PSAPCLUI	147.37	14	931
16	PSAPDDICI	122.25	0	1,444
24	PSAPEL31HI	14.72	2	1,461
7	PSAPDDICD	152.98	0	2,876
19	PSAPPOOLI	414.59	16	3,962
27	PSAPES31HI	900.83	6	4,678
26	PSAPES31HD	2,075.73	5	5,676
21	PSAPPOOLD	660.92	22	6,392
25	PSAPEL31HD	481.49	52	9,933
22	PSAPCLUD	1,383.44	153	11,013
5	PSAPSTABI	1,172.07	67	11,743
3	PSAPPROTI	193.95	24	27,096
23	PSAPSTABD	1,727.34	117	37,556

Table 9-2 Database Growth and I/O Distribution *(Continued)*

File System	Tablespace Name	DB Used Now (MB)	Growth per Month (MB)	I/O Activity
13	SYSTEM	93.80	3	45,353
14	PSAPBTABI	4,515.38	470	183,759
1	PSAPBTABD	8,805.24	943	403,498

 NOTE

This data was gathered not long after a database offline backup. This is not a good time to gather the statistics because users have not made use of the system yet and the data might not represent the actual load on the data files.

You see from this data that PSAPBTABD, PSAPBTABI, SYSTEM, and PSAP-STABD should be located on their own disks. The others should be balanced using the I/O activity, size, and growth over the remaining disks.

Operating System Tuning

The bulk of the operating system tuning happens during initial SAP installation and later with the redeployment of SAP. SAP continuously makes suggestions on how to improve SAP application performance by tuning the operating system, and different operating system vendors develop patches to fix bugs and improve performance.

Kernel Parameters

Each of the operating systems that SAP runs on has its own set of *kernel parameters*. The SAP installation and upgrade guides discuss these parameters in more detail. SAP might revise the values for the kernel parameters from time to time; such changes are usually reported in OSS notes related to upgrades and installations.

Memory Management

Memory is one of those resources that you never have enough of. Applications have a tendency to consume all that's available as soon as it is added. How much memory does SAP need? It depends on your environment, the SAP functionality you implement, number of users, memory requirements of individual ABAP programs, availability of finances to purchase the required memory, and performance constraints placed on the system. For the best performance, you need enough memory to execute SAP completely in memory without any OS paging and swapping.

Physical Memory

Physical memory is also known as *random access memory*. It is the temporary electronic memory installed on a computer. It is temporary because you can put as much information in physical memory as you like, but the information is lost as soon as the power is turned off. You need "enough" physical memory in order to improve performance.

A CPU can only access this physical memory, so a program needs to be in physical memory to execute. If it's not in memory, the operating system has to get it from disk and load it into physical memory. Every time the operating system goes to disk, you pay performance penalties. By installing enough physical memory, you avoid the operating system paging and are able to run bigger and more programs. A CPU that spends most of its time processing paging requests is *thrashing*. Thrashing brings a system virtually to a standstill.

Besides programs that require physical memory, the operating system requires memory in order to function correctly. HP-UNIX requires about 12MB of physical memory, so the rest can be used by user programs.

Use QuickSizer to make the initial guess on the amount of memory needed; thereafter, monitor the SAP system and tune and acquire memory as needed. QuickSizer is a tool developed by SAP and various hardware partners to assist clients with sizing their SAP environment. You supply it information pertaining to your business processes and users and QuickSizer will estimate a size for your environment.

Swap Space

Swap space is an extension to physical memory. It is the area on disk that the operating system uses to page information in and out. As mentioned before, the CPU can only access physical memory. If the system does not have enough memory, it starts paging information out to the swap space in order to make space in memory for the process information it requires. The ultimate goal is to avoid using swap space, although this is typically impossible.

SAP requires three times the main memory plus another 500MB for non-SAP-related processes for swap space. That is, if you have 512MB of physical memory, you require 3 * 512 + 500 = 2GB swap space.

Sizing swap space is a very controversial subject. Three times the available memory is sometimes too much and other times not enough. SAP suggests a minimum of 1GB of swap space. It is confusing. The bottom line is you do not want the system to run out of swap space. Remember always to configure enough swap space for extraordinary circumstances, not for the norm. Play it safe: For systems with less than 512MB memory install a minimum of 1GB swap space; use the *three-times-memory* formula for systems with memory up to 2GB, and for systems with more than 2GB it will mostly depend on the behavior of the application. Only add swap space if the system needs it and you are sure that the system will consume all the available swap space. A formula you can use for systems with more than 2GB memory is *Memory + 2GB*.

[handwritten annotations:]
RAM < 512 MB   1 GB
*512M < RAM < 2 G.   3 * ROM + 500.*
RAM > 2 G.   RAM + 2 GB

TIP

Swap tips:

◆   Keep all swap files the same size.

◆   Place different swap files on different disks or volume groups.

These days, with 64-bit operating systems that are capable of addressing huge amounts of main memory, you will need to get a different formula for the required swap space. If you have a system with, say, 8GB of main memory, it would mean that you require 24.5GB of swap space. This is obviously a waste of valuable disk space. A better formula would be main memory plus another 2GB. This would mean that the system with the 8GB of main memory will have 10GB of swap space.

Virtual Memory *(RAM + swap space)*

The total memory requirements of a process can be much bigger than the actual physical memory installed in a machine. A CPU can only access physical memory, which means that a process requiring more physical memory than is available will not be able to execute. This is true for one process, but what happens when you run more than one process?

Virtual memory is a system's memory that allows execution of a process that requires more memory than the physical memory installed. It is physical memory and swap space combined. The operating system pages information in memory out to swap when it is not needed and pages it back into memory as required. As an example, total virtual address space for a single process running on HP-UNIX (not HP-UNIX 11) is 4GB.

The ideal situation is zero paging. You can achieve this by installing more physical memory or you can tune the SAP environment to function within the given memory limits.

Buffer Cache   *I/O ↑ → buffer cache ↑ → process memory ↓*

A certain percentage of memory is allotted to *buffer cache*. AIX assigns 80 percent, DECUX 50 percent, and HP-UNIX 50 percent of its main memory to this buffer. The operating system places data read from some file system into this buffer in order to increase I/O performance. It is advisable to have this percentage high when the applications on a system are very I/O-intensive. (The buffer cache does not affect raw devices.)

When an application performs large amounts of I/O, the operating system will increase the size of the buffer cache to the maximum value allowed (that is, 80 percent and 50 percent as defined by default or by the operating system administrator).

The I/O environment and process environment are competing for the same memory. The operating system assigns the maximum amount of memory to the buffer cache, and as the processes require more memory, the operating system will shrink the buffer cache, freeing memory and assigning it to the processes requiring more memory. A problem arises when both the I/O and process memory requirements are very high. This situation causes the system to allocate and deallocate memory between buffer cache and process memory space, creating a large amount of overhead. There is also a good chance that the system is paging at this point, causing even more overhead.

The buffer cache should be set low for systems with low I/O activity and high process activity and should be set high for systems with high I/O activity and low process activity. A system that has both high I/O and process activity requires large amounts of physical memory.

SAP database servers qualify as systems that have low I/O activity and high process activity. This is a dangerous statement to make; databases typically have high I/O requirements. Databases usually implement their own cache. Why do you need the operating system to cache something that is already cached by the database? It only causes contention between the buffer cache and memory allocated to the processes.

SAP suggests the following UNIX kernel parameter settings for dedicated SAP servers:

↳ buffer cache 7 %

- Execute the command `vmtune -p <minimum> -P <maximum>` on AIX systems to reduce the buffer cache from 80 percent to 7 percent.
- Change the kernel parameter "dbc_max_pct" on HP systems to reduce the buffer cache from 50 percent to 7 percent.
- Change the kernel parameter "ubc-maxpercent" on DEC systems to reduce the default to 7 percent.

Systems with large amounts of physical memory installed also benefit by reducing the buffer cache to a lower value (say, 25 percent). Monitor the system after any changes to the buffer cache and tune accordingly.

Private and Shared Memory

Depending on the operating system and the methodology it uses to implement memory, most UNIX systems divide the virtual memory into four memory regions:

- The first region contains the process's text segment and sometimes some of the data.
- The second region contains the data segment (static data, stack, and heap). *(heap, private memory)*
- The third region contains shared library code, shared memory-mapped files, and sometimes shared memory.
- The fourth region contains shared memory segments, shared memory-mapped files, shared library code, and I/O space.

shared memory (interprocess communication)

The second region is the heap or private memory and the third and fourth regions are the shared memory as defined by SAP.

The process owning the private or local memory itself can only access private memory. An SAP dialog process using private memory is unable to partake in SAP context switching. Context switching is the ability that SAP has to swap user information (context) out of a work process, enabling another user context to be swapped in, thus allowing multiple users to share the limited dialog processes.

Shared memory can be accessed by multiple processes at the same time and is typically used for interprocess communications. SAP attempts to make extensive use of shared memory rather than private memory for users.

Disk I/O Monitoring

Disk I/O, memory, CPU, and network activities are factors that influence performance. Disk I/O plays a huge role in overall system performance. There are three actions that you can take to keep disk I/O low:

- Distribute I/O load across multiple disks.
- Use more than one swap file and place it on different disks.
- Enable asynchronous I/O if the operating system allows it.

This last option warrants further discussion.

Synchronous Disk I/O

Most operating systems use synchronous disk I/O when writing data to disk. When a program makes an I/O request, this program waits until the I/O request completes and control is passed back to the program.

Asynchronous Disk I/O

When an operating system writes to disk asynchronously, the program makes an I/O request; the request is scheduled to take place on its own time, and the program regains control immediately, without waiting for the I/O request to complete.

Asynchronous disk I/O improves performance for I/O bound processes but has the disadvantage that file system metadata and user data might get lost when the system crashes. Synchronous disk I/O is safe but does not offer the performance improvement. One way to reduce the risk of a system crash is to use a UPS (uninterruptible power supply). Most of the time, disastrous crashes are due to some kind of power failure.

Use transaction **ST06**, follow menu path Detail Analysis Menu, Disk (Snapshot Analysis). Figure 9-6 displays the snapshot values for the disks installed on the system.

The goal is to identify disks that have most of the I/O directed to them. Figure 9-6 shows that disk c1t0d0's utilization percentage is 62 percent. The value should be less than 15 percent on average. Although only a snapshot, Figure 9-6 is useful in identifying disks that have high utilization. Use transaction **ST06**, and follow menu path Detail Analysis Menu, Disk (Previous Hours) to analyze disk utilization over the previous hours to see if the disk in question is constantly being accessed at a utilization rate of 62 percent. In Figure 9-7, you see that this is not the situation.

Other utilities you can use include the UNIX commands *sar* and *ioscan*. There is third-party software on the market that monitors and gathers statistics on operating system activities. These usually include trending tools that can be of tremendous assistance to an administrator.

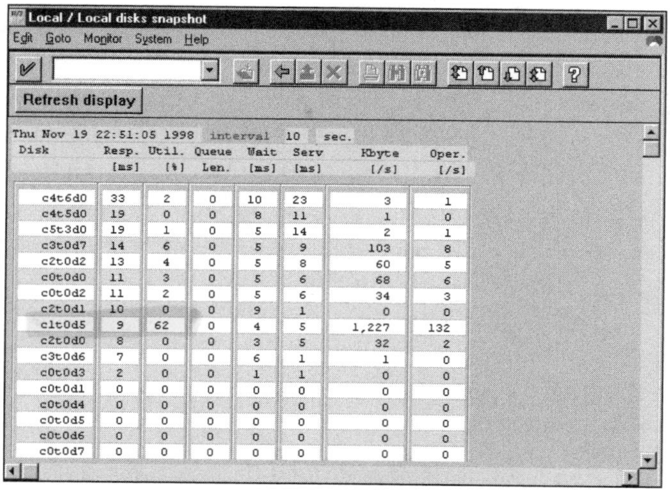

Disk	Resp. [ms]	Util. [%]	Queue Len.	Wait [ms]	Serv [ms]	Kbyte [/s]	Oper. [/s]
c4t6d0	33	2	0	10	23	3	1
c4t5d0	19	0	0	8	11	1	0
c5t3d0	19	1	0	5	14	2	1
c3t0d7	14	6	0	5	9	103	8
c2t0d2	13	4	0	5	8	60	5
c0t0d0	11	3	0	5	6	68	6
c0t0d2	11	2	0	5	6	34	3
c2t0d1	10	0	0	9	1	0	0
c1t0d5	9	62	0	4	5	1,227	132
c2t0d0	8	0	0	3	5	32	2
c3t0d6	7	0	0	6	1	1	0
c0t0d3	2	0	0	1	1	0	0
c0t0d1	0	0	0	0	0	0	0
c0t0d4	0	0	0	0	0	0	0
c0t0d5	0	0	0	0	0	0	0
c0t0d6	0	0	0	0	0	0	0
c0t0d7	0	0	0	0	0	0	0

FIGURE 9-6 *Disk activity*

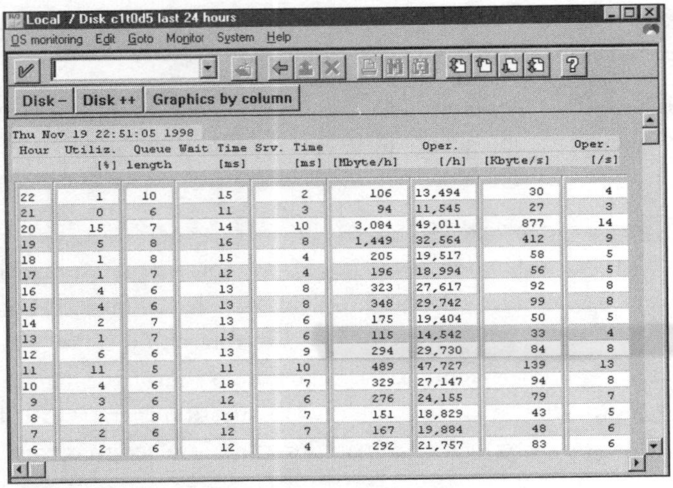

```
┌─────────────────────────────────────────────────────────────────┐
│ ▓ Local / Disk c1t0d5 last 24 hours                    _ □ X     │
│ OS monitoring  Edit  Goto  Monitor  System  Help                │
│ ┌───────────────────────────────────────────────────────────┐   │
│ │ ✓ │        ▼ │ ◄ │ ← ↑ X │ □ ▦ ▦ │ ♻ ▢ ▢ ▢ │ ? │          │
│ └───────────────────────────────────────────────────────────┘   │
│ ┌─────────┬────────┬────────────────────┐                        │
│ │ Disk –  │ Disk ++│ Graphics by column │                        │
│ └─────────┴────────┴────────────────────┘                        │
│ Thu Nov 19 22:51:05 1998                                        │
│ Hour  Utiliz.  Queue Wait Time Srv. Time        Oper.      Oper. │
│       [%]     length    [ms]    [ms] [Mbyte/h]   [/h] [Kbyte/s] [/s]│
│                                                                  │
│  22    1     10      15      2     106  13,494      30     4      │
│  21    0      6      11      3      94  11,545      27     3      │
│  20   15      7      14     10   3,084  49,011     877    14      │
│  19    5      8      16      8   1,449  32,564     412     9      │
│  18    1      8      15      4     205  19,517      58     5      │
│  17    1      7      12      4     196  18,994      56     5      │
│  16    4      6      13      8     323  27,617      92     8      │
│  15    4      6      13      8     348  29,742      99     8      │
│  14    2      7      13      6     175  19,404      50     5      │
│  13    1      7      13      6     115  14,542      33     4      │
│  12    6      6      13      9     294  29,730      84     8      │
│  11   11      5      11     10     489  47,727     139    13      │
│  10    4      6      18      7     329  27,147      94     8      │
│   9    3      6      12      6     276  24,155      79     7      │
│   8    2      8      14      7     151  18,829      43     5      │
│   7    2      6      12      7     167  19,884      48     6      │
│   6    2      6      12      4     292  21,757      83     6      │
└─────────────────────────────────────────────────────────────────┘
```

FIGURE 9-7 *Disk utilization over the previous hours*

Database Performance Considerations

Laying out the database was discussed earlier in the chapter, but databases are much more than a few files placed strategically on different disks. You need to look at memory, tables, indexes, locks, and latches, among other things. The best resource for Oracle tuning is a book that deals specifically with Oracle and its tuning peculiarities; the same holds for any other database used in the SAP environment. This section will address Oracle from an SAP viewpoint. In order to tune SAP using Oracle, you need to know the Oracle architecture and how it functions. Choosing Oracle as the database for discussion was not an easy task. SQL Server, Informix, ADABAS D, and DB2 are all excellent databases. Each database has its own features and tuning peculiarities and might have a chapter of its own if space were unlimited. Oracle wins out, though, because Oracle currently owns the largest portion of the database market.

The discussion about database performance considerations in this chapter will be based on Figure 9-8 and Figure 9-9. Figure 9-8 portrays the Oracle memory and process architecture, and Figure 9-9 displays the window SAP has on the database it is using. Both these figures are important in order to understand how certain aspects of the database and SAP are tuned.

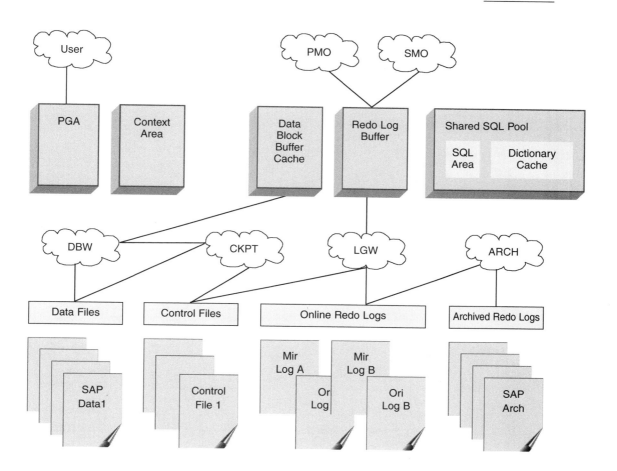

FIGURE 9-8 *Oracle architecture*

System Global Area (SGA)

The SGA is an area in memory set aside for the use of the database. It consists of data block buffers, redo log buffers, dictionary cache, and shared SQL pool.

Process Global Area (PGA)

The PGA contains the data and structures associated with one Oracle user or server process. The memory in the PGA belongs to a single user and cannot be shared among different users.

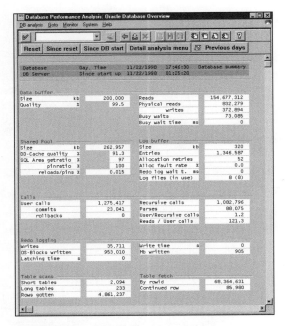

FIGURE 9-9 *CCMS database monitor*

The size of the PGA can be approximated by the following formula:

PGA = 2.5MB * (*NumberofShadowProcesses* + 10)

Data Block Buffer Cache

This buffer is a portion of the SGA set aside for data blocks read from the database files. The objective of this cache is to avoid unnecessary disk reads. The ideal situation would be to have all data in the data block buffer cache because this will ensure zero disk I/O and better performance. The data blocks in the cache are arranged from most-recently used to least-recently used. When the cache is full, the oldest block gets removed (written back to the data file if it has been changed) and the new block gets loaded.

Typically, what happens is that a user executes some select statement using an index. The data blocks read from this action get loaded into the data buffer cache. Any other user that requires the same data then gets the data from cache instead of reading it from disk.

In Figure 9-9, you will notice a heading Data Buffer. This heading refers to the data block buffer cache. SAP reports the size in kilobytes, but the actual Oracle parameter DB_BLOCK_BUFFERS specifies the size of this buffer cache in number of blocks. SAP suggests using the 8,196 byte block size. In other words, in "oraSID.ini" DB_BLOCK_BUFFERS will have a value of 25,000 (8K blocks) and SAP will report 200,000K.

Reads *(cache reads)*

This is the number of reads satisfied from the data block buffer cache without going to physical disk.

Physical Reads *(disk reads)*

Physical Reads are reads satisfied from reading the physical disk. The data was not buffered yet.

Physical Writes

This is the number of data blocks that have been physically written to disk.

You want the quality of this buffer to be 100 percent or very close to 100 percent. A value greater than 97 percent is acceptable. In order to get a buffer quality of 100 percent you need to make the buffer cache big enough to hold all data frequently used by all users. A data buffer cache that is too big will waste memory, and one that is too small will impede performance. The buffer quality is calculated by:

$$Quality = \frac{Reads}{Physical\ Reads + Reads} * 100$$

$$\frac{buffer\ reads}{total\ reads}$$

A suggestion would be to increase this buffer in steps improving the buffer quality and avoiding operating system paging. What advantage do you gain by avoiding disk I/O within the database when the operating starts paging, causing exactly the I/O you're trying to avoid?

Busy Waits

The Busy Wait statistic is a summary of transaction **ST04**, menu path Detail Analysis Menu, Wait Situations. An indication that "wait situations" should be analyzed more closely is when the total number of wait situations exceeds 5 percent of the total number of reads. A further indication of excessive contention is

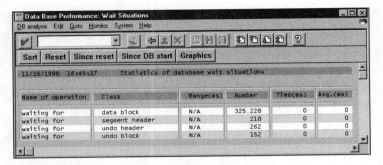

FIGURE 9-10 *Database wait situations*

when any of these classes exceeds 1 percent of the total number of reads (see Figure 9-10).

Undo Header and Block *(rollback segments?)*

Adding more rollback segments to the database can reduce waits on the undo header and undo block classes.

Data Blocks → *data buffer size ↑* *DBUR ↑ → Asyn I/O, DBUR I/O Slave*

Waits for data blocks may be due to the data buffer size not being large enough (check quality ratio above). Another reason might be that the database writer (DBWR) is unable to keep up writing changed data back to the data files. The solutions for this problem include enabling Operating System Asynchronous Writing or creating additional DBWR I/O slaves.

Segment Headers *(free lists?)*

Waits on segment headers often indicate contention for freelists. Oracle keeps information in memory for blocks that are available for creating new records (inserting new rows) in a table. This is referred to as the freelist for the table. When Oracle wants to insert a new record into a table it searches the table freelist for blocks that can accommodate the new record. If it is unable to find a block in memory, it has to go to disk in order to get more information. A problem usually arises when multiple transactions want to insert rows into a table. This leads to multiple processes searching the freelist at the same time, causing freelist contention.

A possible solution for freelist contention is increasing the freelist parameter on the insert and update intensive tables. Keep in mind that you will have to export the data from the table, delete and re-create the table with the new freelist setting, and reimport the data into the table.

Shared SQL Pool

[handwritten: ⟨ SQL area / data dic. cache ⟩]

The shared SQL pool consists of mainly two areas: the SQL area and the dictionary cache. These two areas cannot be individually changed; you have to change the entire shared SQL pool. Oracle calculates the sizes for the SQL area and the dictionary cache internally.

SQL Area

The SQL area contains all the SQL statements executed by users since the database was started. This improves performance by allowing users to share frequently executed SQL statements. To be more exact, the SQL area contains the binding information; run-time buffers, parse-tree, and execution plan for all SQL statements that currently fit into the available memory. (Refer to Figure 9-10.) You will notice a heading called Shared Pool. This is the shared SQL pool as defined in Oracle. Use transaction **ST04**, menu path Detail Analysis Menu, SQL Request to display more information on the SQL statements in the Shared SQL area as portrayed by Figure 9-11.

The information in this Figure 9-11 is useful for tuning individual select statements. You can either rewrite the SQL statement to be more selective or introduce a new secondary index on a table. The statistics on this page can also indicate that an index is fragmented or missing. The three important columns are Total Execution, Reads/Execution, and Gets/Execution.

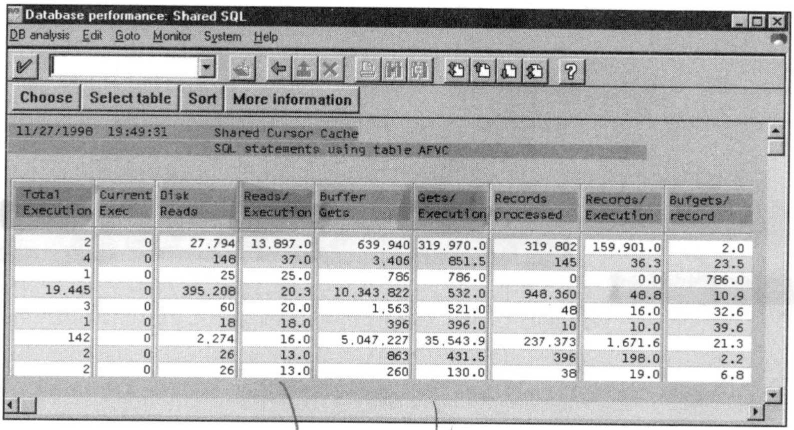

Total Execution	Current Exec	Disk Reads	Reads/ Execution	Buffer Gets	Gets/ Execution	Records processed	Records/ Execution	Bufgets/ record
2	0	27,794	13,897.0	639,940	319,970.0	319,802	159,901.0	2.0
4	0	148	37.0	3,406	851.5	145	36.3	23.5
1	0	25	25.0	786	786.0	0	0.0	786.0
19,445	0	395,208	20.3	10,343,822	532.0	948,360	48.8	10.9
3	0	60	20.0	1,563	521.0	48	16.0	32.6
1	0	18	18.0	396	396.0	10	10.0	39.6
142	0	2,274	16.0	5,047,227	35,543.9	237,373	1,671.6	21.3
2	0	26	13.0	863	431.5	396	198.0	2.2
2	0	26	13.0	260	130.0	38	19.0	6.8

FIGURE 9-11 *Shared SQL area*   *[handwritten: disk, buffer]*

- **Total Execution** is the number of times this statement was executed.
- **Reads/Execution** is the number of reads from disk performed when this statement was executed.
- **Get/Execution** is the number of buffer gets from memory performed when this statement was executed.

Large values in all three columns will indicate that a statement is executed frequently and reads massive amounts of data from disk or from memory. Statements that have these characteristics need to be analyzed and possibly tuned.

Dictionary Cache

The dictionary cache contains a subset of the Oracle data dictionary. The data dictionary is data about the tables, indexes, segments, users, privileges, extents, and data files. Oracle keeps this information in the system tables that live in the system tablespace. This dictionary data is loaded into the data dictionary cache to avoid repetitive I/O requests for the same information from disk.

Every time a user executes a transaction against some data dictionary object (e.g., a table) and the information about this object is not in the dictionary cache, Oracle issues a recursive call reading the required information from disk. Frequent recursive calls impose a significant performance impact.

Use transaction **ST04**, menu path Detail Analysis Menu, Dictionary Buffer to display more information on the different types of objects that are loaded into the data dictionary cache as portrayed by Figure 9-12. Oracle tunes this area internally. This information is useful only to see where possible contention is. The only practical action to alleviate contention is to increase the shared SQL pool size as explained in the following section.

Size

This is the total size of the shared SQL pool in memory. Set the parameter SHARED_POOL_SIZE in the initSID.ora file. The size of this pool should be large enough to maintain a high data dictionary cache quality, SQL area get ratio, and SQL area pin ratio. The bottom line in tuning the shared SQL pool is to increase the size of the pool until you are happy with the different qualities and ratios.

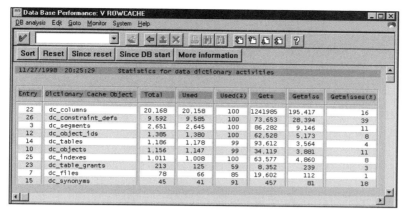

FIGURE 9-12 *Data dictionary*

The Data Dictionary Cache Quality

The value should be in the high 90-percentile group. It reflects how often data-dictionary data was retrieved from cache instead of disk.

SQL Area Get Ratio

This statistic reflects how often Oracle was able to access a SQL statement from the SQL area instead of reloading it. This ratio should also be in the high 90-percentile group.

SQL Area Pin Ratio

This ratio is how often SQL statements are re-executed. This ratio should also be in the high 90-percentile group.

Reloads/Pins

Reloads/pins is the ratio of how often Oracle had to reload SQL statements against the number of pins. This value should be very low. Multiply reloads/pins by 100 and the value should be very close to zero. A high value indicates that you have to increase the shared SQL pool.

Redo Log Buffer

Oracle records all changes in the redo log buffer before the data is written to the online redo log files. The data is written to file when the redo log buffer fills up or when a transaction issues a commit. It is the task of the log writer (LGWR) to write the data from the buffer cache to the online redo log files.

Size

The default size for the redo log buffer is 320K. The size of this buffer is controlled by the initSID.ora parameter LOG_BUFFER. If you have to increase this buffer, please make sure that the size is a multiple of DB_BLOCK_SIZE.

Entries

This is the number of redo entries since database startup.

Allocation Retries

redo log buffer ↑
redo log file ↑

This is the number of unsuccessful attempts made to allocate space in the redo buffer. This happens when the redo buffer fills up and LGWR has to wait for a redo log switch to occur in order to free up some space in the redo log buffer. Two possible solutions for excessive allocation retries are to increase the redo log buffer or to increase the redo log file sizes. Both will reduce the frequency of allocation retries.

Allocation Fault Rate

An allocation fault rate higher than 1 percent during normal SAP system usage should be investigated. This rate is the percentage of the allocation retries divided by the total number of redo entries since database startup.

redo allocation latch — LOG_SIMULTANEOUS_COPIES
redo copy latch — LOG_SMALL_ENTRY_MAX_SIZE

Redo Log Contention

Two latches regulate redo log activity. (A *latch* is the memory equivalent of a database lock.) These are the redo allocation latch and the redo copy latch. The redo allocation latch regulates the allocation of space in the redo log buffer in order to write information to the redo buffer, and the redo copy latch regulates the copy of information to the redo buffer.

The tuning objective is to minimize the wait conditions on the flow of redo entries to and from the redo log buffer. Execute transaction **ST04**, menu path Detail Analysis Menu, Display V$ Values, V$LATCH. The important latches in Figure 9-13 are latches 15 and 16. Make use of the values associated with the redo latches when making the following calculations.

Latch name	Latch number	Gets	Misses	Sleeps while wait	Immediate Gets number	Immediate Misses number
latch wait list	0	61,247	11	11	0	0
process allocation	1	2,005	0	0	2,005	0
session allocation	2	1,241,238	5	8	0	0
session switching	3	21,060	0	0	0	0
session idle bit	4	62,865,941	2,924	4,213	0	0
messages	5	2,721,980	271	306	0	0
enqueues	6	2,649,820	89	96	0	0
trace latch	7	0	0	0	0	0
cache buffers chains	8	47977,246,547	411,354	585,926	191,473,370	36,249
cache buffers lru chain	9	21,513,459	559,211	1,020,427	2268364,548	293,482,163
cache buffer handles	10	1,700,752	7	8	0	0
multiblock read objects	11	508,720	0	0	0	0
cache protection latch	12	0	0	0	0	0
system commit number	13	42,704,864	4,362	5,990	0	0
archive control	14	174,485	0	0	0	0
redo allocation	15	12,121,676	1,813	2,599	0	0
redo copy	16	127	109	128	2,242,359	212

FIGURE 9-13 *V$LATCH – redo allocation and redo copy*

If either of these values has a value greater than 1, then contention is occurring on the corresponding latch.

To alleviate redo copy latch contention, consider checking the initialization parameter LOG_SIMULTANEOUS_COPIES. It should be set to twice the number of CPUs installed on the system.

To alleviate redo copy latch contention, consider reducing the maximum size of a redo entry that can be copied using this latch. This should reduce the amount of time that a latch is held by a process. The initialization parameter is LOG_SMALL_ENTRY_MAX_SIZE.

Database Writer (DBWR)

The database writer (DBWR) background process writes modified, new, or deleted blocks from the data block buffer cache and data dictionary cache back to the data files.

Database Writer Contention

In order to avoid DBWR contention, a Basis administrator can do two things: increase the number of DBWR slaves or enable asynchronous writing if the operating system allows it. Use only one of these options. More than one DBWR works well on an operating system with synchronous writing enabled. You can destroy your data if you use asynchronous writing together with more than one DBWR slave.

On operating systems with asynchronous writing enabled, use only one DBWR. Using asynchronous writing has one possible risk: you might lose a small amount of data if a system crash occurs. Asynchronous writing enables a process to pass an I/O request to the operating system, and control is passed back to the process immediately. In the background, the operating system handles the I/O request passed to it by the user process. If a system crash happens to occur somewhere between giving control back to the user process and the operating system saving the data, your data will be lost. Depending on the situation, you might have to restore your database. Remember that system crashes do not happen very frequently and you can avoid crashes due to power failures by installing a UPS.

Another contention issue that was mentioned in the section dealing with data file layouts was how to avoid I/O contention between the LGWR and the DBWR. Try to avoid putting your redo logs on the same disks as your data files. If you have to put them on the same disk, please put them together with low activity data files.

Most of the time, one DBWR is more than efficient, but increase the number of database writers when you notice that your DBWR cannot keep up. A possible indication that the DBWRs are unable to keep up is if the *data block waits* are more than 1 percent of the total *reads* (see Database Wait Situations in Figure 9-10). The initialization parameter for additional DBWR slaves is DBWR_IO_SLAVES.

Log Writer (LGWR)

The log writer (LGWR) is the only background process that writes the contents of the redo log buffer to the online redo log files. As of Oracle 8, you are able to have log writer slaves. You can set the initialization parameter LGWR_IO_SLAVES to some value greater than 1 and this should improve LGWR performance.

Oracle has three background processes that write very actively to disk; namely, DBWR (writes randomly), LGWR (writes sequentially), and ARCH (writes sequentially). The performance objective is to avoid these processes contending with each other. It comes back to planning your data file layout. Keep data files away from the online redo logs and alternate redo logs on different disks. Put redo log group A on disk 1 and put redo log group B on disk 2. This means that while the log writer is writing the redo buffer cache to disk 1, the archive process writes redo log B to the offline redo log archive.

Checkpoint (CKPT)

The CKPT process is an extension of the log writer. Every time a redo log file fills up, the LGWR signals a commit. When activated, it assumes the task of signaling checkpoints from the log writer. The log writer has the sole responsibility of writing the redo log buffer cache to disk. This optional process is only required on high transaction load systems if this load causes delays during log switches.

Archive (ARCH)   *type*

When ARCHIVELOG mode is enabled, the ARCH process writes the online redo log files to an archive directory. The SAP administrator backs up these archived files to disk and then deletes them from disk. The fun usually starts when this archive directory fills up. The system will stop any and all processing until the administrator makes space available for new archive files. In other words, the LGWR writes redo entries from the redo buffer cache to the online redo log files in a cyclical manner, and as soon as a redo log file fills up, the ARCH process archives it to the archive directory, where it is backed up for possible future database restores. Oracle 8 will have an additional parameter called ARCH_IO_SLAVES, which will enable you to create more archive writers.

Calls

User Calls

This is the number of user calls to the Oracle kernel since the database was started. A user call is a parse, an execute, or a fetch.

Commit

This is the number of transaction commits since the database was started.

Rollbacks

This is the number of transactions that failed and rolled back since the database was started. This value should be zero. A transaction can roll back for various reasons—a user-aborted transaction, some logical error in the ABAP code, some internal Oracle error, deadlocks, or abnormal program terminations, to name only a few. If this value is high, please investigate. Look in the SAP system log (SM21), SAP dumps (ST22), Oracle user process trace files, and the Oracle alert file for error messages.

Recursive Calls

When a user executes a select statement specifying some tables and fields, the user process needs to retrieve information on these tables. This information can either come from the data dictionary cache or from somewhere in the SYSTEM table-space. When the user process retrieves it from the SYSTEM tablespace, it is called a recursive call. Recursive calls are bad for system performance and should be avoided as much as possible. The reason why it is bad is because it introduces extra disk I/O. Every time you read data you are also reading database meta-data from disk instead of reading it from memory. At initial database startup, this value should be very high compared to the number of user calls, but the ratio should go down as time goes by. A high number of recursive calls compared to the number of user calls is an indication that the data dictionary cache is too small.

Parses

Parsing a SQL statement means creating the actual executable statements that will be used to retrieve the data from the database.

These steps are involved in parsing a SQL statement:

1. Check the semantics and the syntax of the statement.
2. Check to see that the user executing the statement has the relevant permissions.
3. Allocate space in the private SQL area in order to save the statement.
4. Search the shared SQL area to find a copy of the SQL statement currently being parsed.
5. Save the parsed statement to the shared SQL area if it does not already exist there.

The objective with saving already parsed statements in the shared SQL area is to avoid continuous parsing of duplicate SQL statements and, in so doing, improve performance. A parse ratio higher than 25 percent might be an indication that your shared SQL pool is too small and you need to increase it. The formula used to calculate the Parse Ratio is as follows:

$$Parse\ Ratio = \frac{Parses}{User\ Calls} * 100$$

User/Recursive Calls

Recursive calls and user calls were discussed earlier. This is only the ratio of user calls to recursive calls, which should be greater than four.

$$\frac{UserCalls}{RecursiveCalls} > 4$$

Read/User Calls

Each user call to the Oracle kernel was satisfied X number reads from the data block data cache.

$$Ration\ ReadsPerUserCall = \frac{Reads}{UserCalls}$$

[handwritten annotation:] big ration → read-intensive → ABAP code ⟶ Small ration → buffer cache too Small

> ### TIP
>
> Each user call should read on average between 15 and 50 blocks from the data block buffer cache.
>
> $$15 < \frac{Reads}{UserCalls} < 50$$

A big ratio means that each user call is very read-intensive. You will need to find out why the application is read-intensive. The ABAP queries might be reading unnecessary data. A small value means that each user call does not read a lot of data from the data block buffer cache; one reason for this might be that the buffer cache is too small.

Redo Logging

Online Redo Log Files

It was already discussed where to place redo log files in order to avoid contention. Now you will examine how big a redo log file should be.

The Oracle log writer writes to the redo logs in a cyclical manner. When one redo log fills up, it needs to switch to a new redo log file in order to be able to continue to record transactions. This process is called a *log switch*. A log switch forces a database checkpoint, at which time Oracle must flush dirty blocks from the SGA to disk to ensure system integrity. The goal is to get log switches to occur less frequently. This entails more changes being applied to the same dirty blocks before the next (checkpoint) flush occurs. Once again, this results in less I/O.

Monitor V$LOGHIST for the frequency of redo log switches. Increase the size of your redo log files so log switches occur every 20 to 30 minutes.

During a standard SAP installation, the default size of the four redo log members is 20MB each. Changing the size of these logs has a direct impact on performance and data security. Tuning is a balance — you have to weigh the risks associated with enlarging the redo log files and settle for the best compromise.

Advantage of bigger log files:

◆ It holds a possible performance increase.

Disadvantages of bigger log files:

◆ When a big redo log file gets lost, more data gets lost—but with mirroring and backups, this risk is minimized.

◆ Recovering an instance might take a little longer.

◆ Starting the database will take a little longer.

Use the following steps to enlarge the Oracle redo log files:

1. For security reasons, force a log switch for each of the redo logs you have. By default, SAP systems will have four log files, so force four log switches.

2. Archive your offline redo log files.

3. As a precautionary measure, make a complete backup of the database.

4. Change the database mode to NOARCHIVELOG.

5. Start the database in restricted mode.

6. Drop the old redo log groups.

7. Delete the physical redo log files.

8. Create the new log members with the new size—or if required, at a new file location.

9. Change the database log mode to ARCHIVELOG.

10. Again, make a complete backup of the database because changes to the redo log files constitute a structural database change that is recorded in the control files.

A question you need to ask is: "When do you add more redo log files?" Under load conditions when the Oracle archiver is not fast enough to save the inactive redo log files before the log writer makes its round through the other log files returning to the log file the archiver is currently writing.

Refer to Figure 9-9 Log Buffer and Redo Log Wait Time. This value should be zero. Another place to look is transaction **ST04**, menu path Detail Analysis Menu, Display V$ Values. Select the view V$SYSSTAT. Look for:

◆ Redo log space requests   1
◆ Redo log space wait time   0

Both these numbers should ideally be zero or very close to zero. If this is not the case, the number of redo logs should be increased.

Redo Log Writes

This statistic represents the number of write operations that executed on the redo log. It is the task of the log writer to write to the redo log files.

OS-Blocks Written

This is the number of blocks written to the redo logs.

Table Scans

A full table scan happens when all the data within a table is sequentially read whether the data retrieved is relevant to the transaction or not.

Full table scans are unacceptable for online users. Batch jobs, on the other hand, can be more tolerant with full table scans.

A big disadvantage with full table scans is that data read from a full table scan is removed from the SGA very quickly. This means that the data read from full table scans is not shared between different users on the system and is frequently reread from disk.

A full table scan occurs in the following situations:

- ◆ The table used in the query does not have an index.
- ◆ The select statement does not have a where clause.
- ◆ The select statement's where clause does not contain the first column of any index defined on the table queried.
- ◆ The fields in the select statement are used in expressions or inequalities; for example, Cost > 500, MAX (Cost), or Cost is null.

Short Tables *(full table scan better than index)*

This is the number of full table scans on tables consisting of four or fewer Oracle data blocks (3.2MB). Full table scans are preferable for short tables instead of making use of indexes. Data read using a short table scan is placed in the least recently used (LRU) queue, which means that users will be able to share data accessed in this manner.

Long Tables *(make index)*

This is the number of full table scans on tables consisting of five or more Oracle data blocks (4MB and bigger). A large number of long table scans is an indication that indexes might be missing or that some tables are in desperate need of new indexes. Data read during long table scans is immediately marked as old and is removed from the buffer cache as soon as possible.

Rows Gotten

This is the number of rows retrieved when doing full table scans.

Blocks Gotten

This is the number of blocks retrieved when doing full table scans.

full table scan

Ratio Rows per Block

A ratio close to zero is an indication that a lot of empty space is contained within the scanned table. This is usually caused when huge amounts of data are deleted from a table without reorganizing the table.

$$Ratio = \frac{RowsGotten}{BlockGotten}$$

ratio ↓ → reorganize table

Table Fetch by Row ID

This is the cumulative number of rows read from the database by making use of a row ID. This is usually the result of a select statement making use of an index.

Table Fetch Continued Row

Every time an additional block is read, reading a single row, this statistic gets incremented. This occurs when the data in a row spans more than one block or when the data in a row is migrated to other blocks. A migrated row is a row of data which has been moved to a different block after an update caused it to expand to a size larger than the block it currently resides in.

$$Ratio = \frac{FetchedByRowID}{FetchedContinuedRow} > 1000$$

A number less than 1,000 is an indication that something is wrong and should be investigated. Tables with migrated rows need to be reorganized.

Sorts

Memory

This statistic represents the number of small enough sort operations that occurred completely in memory.

Disk

This statistic represents the number of sorts that require more memory than is currently available. The sort operation made use of temporary segments on disk.

$$SortRatio = \frac{DiskSorts}{MemorySort + DiskSorts} * 100 < 5\%$$

The sort ratio should be far less than 5 percent. A higher ratio might be an indication that you should increase the SORT_AREA_SIZE in order to get more sorts to occur in memory. Just be careful that you do not introduce operating system paging when you increase this initialization parameter.

Rows

This is the total number of rows sorted.

Process Monitor (PMON)

PMON is a background process that runs periodically to monitor user processes. When a user process aborts, for whatever reason, PMON will clean up after the aborted process. It rolls back all the transactions that have not been committed and releases all locks held by that process.

System Monitor (SMON)

SMON keeps the database "clean." (It looks after the well-being of the database.) It has the following functions:

◆ When Oracle starts up, SMON does an automatic instance recovery (as needed) using the redo log files.

◆ SMON releases temporary segments not used by user processes that created these segments in the first place.

◆ During periods when the database is idle, SMON coalesces fragmented free space extents into larger extents. It can only coalesce neighboring extents. That is, when two extents have a data extent between them, this process will not be able to combine them into one extent.

◆ When two processes are stuck in a deadlock situation waiting for each other to release mutually used locks, SMON will attempt to detect this situation. It will choose one of the processes and send an error message to the user using this chosen process.

SAP Performance Considerations

You configured the environment and tuned the operating system and the database for performance. Finally, you will look at the reason for all this initial planning, configuration, and tuning: SAP the application, the portion of the SAP iceberg that's visible above the water, the part seen and used by users and managers. If something goes wrong with this, you'll hear, "SAP is broken! SAP does not work! SAP does not perform! SAP is slow! SAP hangs!" It's worth an administrator's while to make sure this small portion above water is perceived to perform well.

Memory Management

SAP has three memory management schemes:

disk oriented, (batch oriented)

◆ The old paging scheme for SAP releases prior to 3.0.

◆ The memory scheme for SAP Releases 3.0A and 3.0B

◆ The new memory management scheme for SAP releases after 3.0B

memory oriented

For the purpose of this book, only the new memory management scheme will be looked at. It is still possible to use the old paging scheme, and some installations still do make use of the old scheme. These installations are typically batch-oriented and lack interactive users. The 3.0C+ scheme is the same as the 3.0A/B scheme but with a few minor changes. The advantages of the new memory management scheme are that it:

◆ Improves performance.

◆ Facilitates faster context switches.

◆ Provides faster access to internal tables and lists.

◆ Can use new complex ABAP data types. These types require direct access to the address space of a user context.

◆ Places less of a load on the CPU and the disks.

The reason for the above-mentioned advantages is that direct memory access is much faster than disk access. The old paging scheme is disk-oriented, whereas the new scheme tries to accommodate most of the memory requirements from primary memory.

Work processes draw memory from different memory structures in order to satisfy user memory requirements. Figure 9-14 displays the different memory areas. All the users and processes on a system have to share the available SAP memory. The total memory requirements for a single user are known as the *user context*. The user context consists of memory blocks allocated from roll, page, extended, and heap memory. Usually an SAP system accommodates hundreds to thousands of users on only a limited number of work processes. SAP implemented a concept known as *user context switching* to enable users to share the available work processes among themselves. Obviously, when a user context is switched out, this context must be saved (rolled) somewhere.

The discussion that follows will be around Figure 9-15: the roll, page, and extended memory buffers. Each of the parameters governing these areas will also be discussed. *user context - roll, page, extended, heap*

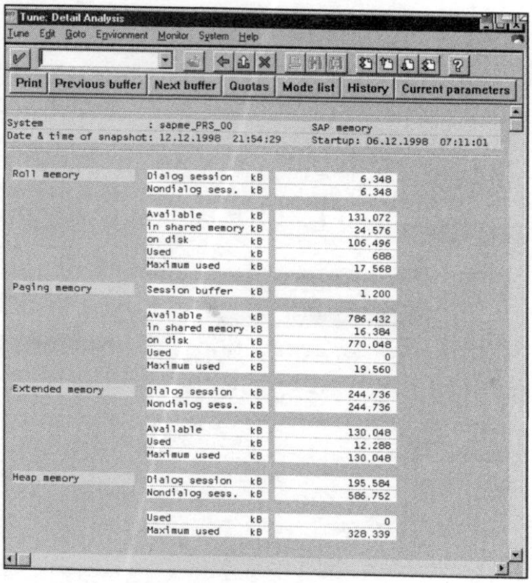

FIGURE 9-14 *SAP memory*

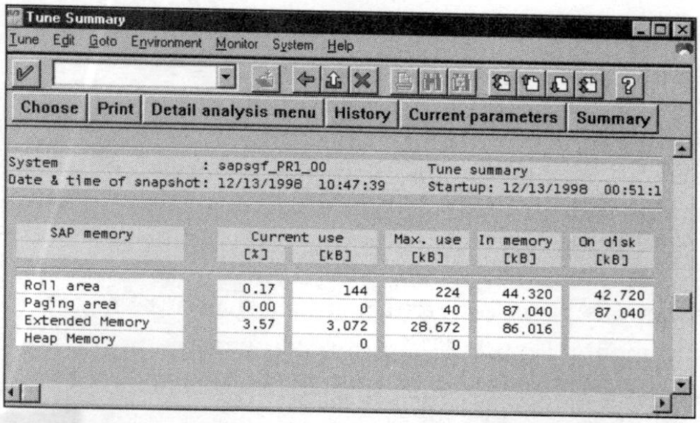

FIGURE 9-15 *ST02 roll, page, and extended memory buffers*

Roll Memory *– to save all roll areas from context switch*

Roll memory is set aside for user context switching. This memory area should be large enough to accommodate all users potentially being rolled out on the system.

Depending on the configuration of the SAP environment, the roll memory can be located completely on disk, completely in shared memory, or some combination of the two.

Placing it on disk implies that the system does not have enough memory and performance will not be so good. On a central instance with a database that is used very extensively, it could possibly introduce contention between the database buffers and the operating system cache buffers.

Placing everything in memory will be best for performance but will waste memory. It is very rare that all the available roll memory is constantly consumed. A combination using memory and disk is the best solution.

As administrator, you have to determine the daily working limit for the roll memory, put that portion in memory, and put a large chunk on disk for exceptions. Use transaction ST02 and monitor the history for the roll memory.

Knowledge of the sequence of memory allocation is very important for the process of SAP memory tuning. The sequence of memory allocation is different for dialog and non-dialog processes. Below you will find two lists indicating the sequence of memory allocation.

Non-dialog processes (typically batch processes):

1. **Roll area** until all the roll memory is exhausted.
2. **Process private memory** until all this memory is exhausted.
3. **Extended memory** until it is exhausted.
4. Process terminates.

Dialog processes (typically online user processes):

1. A portion of the **roll area**.
2. **Extended memory** until all this memory is exhausted.
3. **Roll area** until all this memory is exhausted.
4. **Process private memory** until all this memory is exhausted.
5. Process terminates.

Roll memory is configured using the following two parameters:

◆ **rdisp/ROLL_MAXFS.** This parameter defines the total amount of roll memory available on the system. It does not matter where the memory is located—on disk or in memory or a combination of the two—ROLL_MAXFS is the maximum. ROLL_MAXFS is measured in 8K blocks.

Suggested value:

$$ROLL\_MAXFS = NumberOfUsers\ ztta / roll\_area\ 8192$$

The roll area will be discussed later, but it is that portion of the user context that gets rolled out to make room for another user context. The value for this parameter usually ranges between 1MB and 8MB. As an example, say you have 50 users on the system and the roll area is defined as 8MB; then a good value for this parameter would be:

```
ROLL_MAXFS = 50 * 8 * 1024 * 1024 / (8 * 1024) = 51200
```

The SAP recommendation is 32,768 blocks for this parameter on a 50-user system.

A very large size will not have any adverse effects on the system. Just make sure that you have enough resources to accommodate the amount of memory that you set aside for the roll memory. This parameter can be tuned to represent the actual roll memory usage of the SAP system.

◆ **rdisp/ROLL_SHM.** This parameter defines the fraction of ROLL_MAXFS that will be located in shared memory. If this parameter is set to zero, all the roll memory will be located on disk; if set to ROLL_MAXFS, all the roll memory will be located in shared memory. A zero value introduces performance issues, and a value equal to ROLL_MAXFS wastes memory resources and will probably introduce OS paging (not only wasting memory but also degrading performance).

SAP suggests 4,096 blocks for a 50-user environment. My advice is to guess a value between 0 and 51,200 (4,096 is a good value) and tune this parameter to its optimal value. Make use of transaction ST02 and monitor the history for this specific buffer.

Earlier, ztta/roll_area was used in an equation, the sequence of memory allocation was mentioned, and the roll memory was described. Next, the roll area will be defined.

Roll Area

Each user logged on to the system gets allocated a portion of roll memory, known as the roll area. This area gets rolled out every time a context switch takes place. The bigger the roll area is, the slower the context switches are.

The roll area is once again governed by two parameters:

- **ztta/roll_first**. As of Release 3.0C, this is the initial portion of memory allocated for the user context. Initially, only this "roll first" area is rolled out. Remember the sequence of memory allocation: first a portion of the roll area, then shared memory, and then roll area again. Only the user context in the roll area gets rolled out, not the portion in shared memory.

    If the system has enough memory, make roll first 1 byte. The default value set by SAP is 1,000,000 bytes. This will improve roll performance because initially only 1 byte needs to be rolled, but it will also consume a lot of shared memory. Once the available shared memory is consumed completely, SAP will start allocating the remaining memory in the roll area. This means that users using a moderate amount of memory will initially have great performance, but if they start consuming huge amounts of memory, their performance will degrade due to slower context switches.

- **ztta/roll_area**. This parameter governs the maximum size of the roll area that can be allocated to one user. A large value will influence context-switching performance and will also require a larger roll memory allocation (ROLL_MAXFS).

Extended Memory (Shared Memory) *(not context switch, normally not used by batch, update)*

The user context extends into extended memory once the roll first memory is consumed. All users on the system share this memory, so a single user can consume all available memory, affecting the performance for all other users even if they're using only moderate amounts of memory. A memory hog can also cause other processes to starve due to the lack of memory, forcing the other processes into heap memory (PRIV mode) and eventually causing them to terminate. This memory does not partake in context switching. The data that can move between work processes stays in shared memory, while the roll area partakes in context switching. Once the available extended memory is consumed, SAP falls back to the roll area allocating that memory until it also is entirely consumed.

Batch and update processes typically do not use extended memory. As of 30C, non-dialog processes are also able to allocate extended memory as a last resort. It first uses the roll and heap, and when all of that is used, it uses extended memory.

- **ztta/roll_extension.** This parameter indicates the maximum extended memory a single user can consume. The objective with this parameter is to get as much user-context into shared memory as possible, avoiding heap memory usage and operating system paging. This is one of guess first, tune later parameters. SAP suggests 20MB for a 50-user system. The default is 250MB. Use transaction ST02 and extended memory history to fine-tune this parameter. To avoid having other users starve, do not make the value for this parameter too big. Another factor that makes it difficult to tune this parameter is the single not-so-frequently executed transactions that require huge amounts of memory.
- **em/initial_size_MB.** This parameter sets the upper limit of extended memory that all the users on the system can use. This parameter should be considerably larger than the roll extension because you typically want to fit more than one user's context into memory. The average user context is usually between 1MB and 20MB. A value of 5MB is a good estimate, or you can use transaction **ST03**, menu path Detail Analysis Menu, Global One Recent Period, Previous Months, Select a Month, press the Memory Profile button, and examine the average memory usage per user or transaction, as portrayed in Figure 9-16.

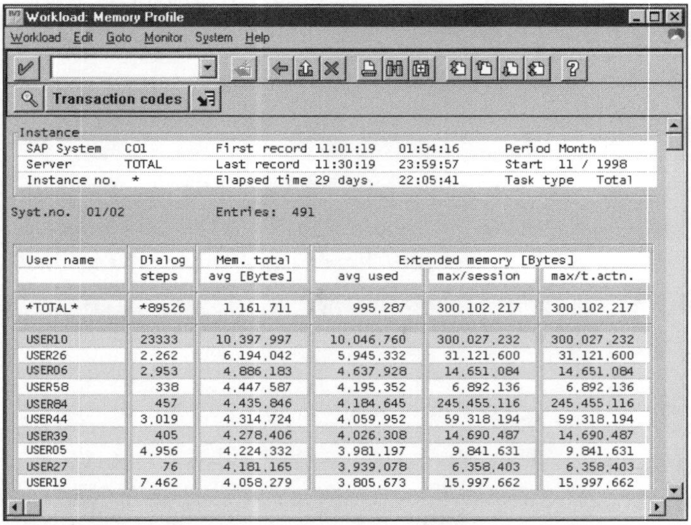

User name	Dialog steps	Mem. total avg [Bytes]	Extended memory [Bytes] avg used	max/session	max/t.actn.
TOTAL	*89526	1,161,711	995,287	300,102,217	300,102,217
USER10	23333	10,397,997	10,046,760	300,027,232	300,027,232
USER26	2,262	6,194,042	5,945,332	31,121,600	31,121,600
USER06	2,953	4,886,183	4,637,928	14,651,084	14,651,084
USER58	338	4,447,587	4,195,352	6,892,136	6,892,136
USER84	457	4,435,846	4,184,645	245,455,116	245,455,116
USER44	3,019	4,314,724	4,059,952	59,318,194	59,318,194
USER39	405	4,278,406	4,026,308	14,690,487	14,690,487
USER05	4,956	4,224,332	3,981,197	9,841,631	9,841,631
USER27	76	4,181,165	3,939,078	6,358,403	6,358,403
USER19	7,462	4,058,279	3,805,673	15,997,662	15,997,662

FIGURE 9-16 *Memory profile per user*

Page Memory *(ABAP data type)*

The ABAP processor for storing various types of data uses SAP paging.

This includes the following:

- Lists
- Hide information
- Internal tables
- Data extracts
- Data clusters
- Parameters for calling programs, dialog modules, and transactions
- Internally defined macros

Following you will find the profile parameters that controls the page memory.

- **rdisp/PG_MAXFS**. This parameter specifies the total amount of page memory available to a process in 8K blocks. SAP suggests a value of 2,048 blocks, but this parameter should be set high enough to accommodate the paging requirements of the SAP system. Monitor the page memory using transaction ST02.

- **rdisp/PG_SHM**. PG_SHM specifies the fraction of PG_MAXFS that resides in shared memory. If the system SAP is running on does not have enough main memory, consider making this parameter zero.

Process-Local Storage (Heap) — *process private memory*

The contents of the heap cannot be shared among the different work processes on a system. It's therefore called *private* memory. It is good for batch processes to make use of this memory, but dialog processes should not. Once a dialog process allocates heap memory, the process is unable to partake in context switching until the job on the specific work process either finishes or aborts. If too many dialog processes make use of heap memory, performance will degrade drastically.

- **abap/heap_limit**. Once a work process starts allocating heap memory, this memory is not returned to the operating system until that work process is terminated. This parameter specifies the limit at which the dialog process becomes eligible for a restart. The process does not stop and restart when it reaches this limit; instead, it completes whatever it is busy doing, and when it is done, the process will terminate and then restart. The default value is 40MB. If the system has a huge amount of memory and OS paging is not an issue, leave the value at 40MB. This value can be reduced to 20MB or even lower if the system is experiencing memory shortages.

◆ **abap/heap_area_dia.** This parameter specifies the maximum amount of heap memory a single dialog process can allocate before it terminates. The goal should be to keep dialog processes from allocating memory from the heap. If this goal is accomplished, the dialog heap area can be relatively small. The default value for this parameter is 80MB, which should be sufficient in most cases. Depending on the SAP environment and memory usage, this parameter can be increased to 200MB.

◆ **abap/heap_area_nondia.** This parameter defines the amount of heap a batch process may allocate. The value for this parameter should be substantially higher than the dialog heap memory. Depending on the environment, this value should be between 190MB and 900MB.

◆ **abap/heap_area_total.** This parameter sets the maximum amount of heap an application server can allocate. All the work processes together may not allocate more heap memory than is specified by this parameter. You might sometimes notice that a process terminates due to a memory shortage and that this process did not even start to allocate the amount allotted to it by the heap_area_dia or heap_area_non_dia. The reason for this termination is the overall lack of heap memory. This means that heap_area_total is set too small or that you are allowing too many processes to allocate too much heap memory.

◆ **rdisp/wppriv_max_no.** This is the maximum number of processes allowed to be in private mode at any given time.

◆ **rdisp/max_priv_time.** This is the maximum amount of time a process is allowed to stay in private mode.

Table 9-3 is a summary of possible values for the SAP memory and process parameters pertaining to a server running the central instance and application servers.

Table 9-3 Typical Memory Parameter Values

Parameter	Unit	Central with Update	Application
Main Memory	GB	2	2
Swap Space	GB	6.5	6.5
Active Users	Count	< 10	100
Work Processes	Count	17	25
Rdisp/wp_no_dia	Count	2	12
Rdisp/wp_no_vb	Count	10	4
Rdisp/wp_no_vb2	Count	4	2
Rdisp/wp_no_enq	Count	1	0
Rdisp/wp_no_btc	Count	0	6
Rdisp/wp_no_spo	Count	0	1
Ztta/roll_first	Bytes	1	1–1,000,000
Ztta/roll_area	Bytes	6,500,000	6,000,000–8,000,000
Ztta/roll_extension	Bytes	60,000,000	200,000,000
Em/initial_size_MB	MB	60	500–2,000
Abap/heaplimit	Bytes	20,000,000	20,000,000
Abap/heap_area_dia	Bytes	80,000,000	200,000,000
Abap/heap_area_nondia	Bytes	200,000,000	200,000,000–900,000,000
Abap/heap_area_total	Bytes	600,000,000	600,000,000–2,000,000,000
Rdisp/PG_SHM	8KB	0	# Users*200KB/8KB
Rdisp/PG_MAXFS	8KB	16,384	64,000
Rdisp/ROLL_SHM	8KB	0	# Users*1024KB /8KB
Rdisp/ROLL_MAXFS	8KB	8,192	32,000

(handwritten annotation in left margin: "individual user" bracketing Ztta/roll_first, Ztta/roll_area, Ztta/roll_extension; bracket grouping Abap/heaplimit through Abap/heap_area_total)

Memory Management Tools

Many different books, OSS notes, and SAP performance-tuning professionals will make suggestions on what the initial SAP memory parameters should be. The initial parameter settings should not be a big concern. Almost any preliminary guess is good as long as you play by the "parameter rules" and make sure to tune the SAP memory environment afterward. The goal with memory tuning is to keep the application running in memory—extended (shared) memory in particular—and to keep processes from using the swap and page memory on disk.

SAP is rich in utilities that allow you to monitor and tune the environment. These are discussed in the following sections.

RSMEMORY *(individual memory area)*

This program allows you to define both the size and the sequence of the individual memory areas in the SAP memory. Use this utility only for testing purposes. It is well advised to use transaction RZ10 and to modify memory parameter settings instead of using an editor.

A very useful menu option in this utility is Goto, EM/HEAP Areas. It displays the memory usage per user and the remaining available memory in the system, as portrayed in Figure 9-17.

A	User	EM	HEAP	Mode 0	Mode 1	Mode 2	Mode 3
001	USER01	503711	0	503711	0	0	0
002	USER01	422665	0	422665	0	0	0
003	USER01	1171719	0	1171719	0	0	0
004	USER01	1419014	0	1419014	0	0	0
X	USER02	0	398496	0	0	0	0
006	SAP*	458548	0	458548	0	0	0
X	JMARNEWECK	629803	0	282269	347534	0	0

```
Free space in EM area [MB]:              422
Free space in heap area [MB]:            880
```

FIGURE 9-17 *RSMEMORY EM/HEAP AREAS*

ESMON   *(share memory)*

esmon -b -c300 pf=C10_DVEBMGS00_etna displays a text bar graph reporting the current extended memory usage every five minutes. In order to see more options, execute **esmon** on its own. This utility should help you to identify excessive extended memory usage. One way to reduce extended memory usage is to reduce the page (PG_SHM) and roll (ROLL_SHM) buffers.

Fundamentally, there are two extended memory consumption concerns:

◆ The available memory is consumed by too many users. Solutions would be to increase the available memory or buy additional application servers. What it comes down to is that you have to increase em/initial_size_MB if possible.

◆ The available memory is consumed by only a few users. This is usually caused by misbehaving ABAP programs. Another reason might be that memory parameter values are set too low or are incorrect. The parameter ztta/roll_extension might be too big in relation to em/initial_size_MB. Consider reducing the first-mentioned parameter and allow memory-hungry ABAP programs to use heap memory instead. Be careful, though, because you do not want online (dialog) ABAP programs to use heap as a *rule*—it has to be an *exception*. Having programs execute in heap memory as a rule introduces other performance issues. The best solutions for memory-hungry programs are to change them to use less memory and to execute them in batch.

SAPPFPAR *(check environment after change memory param)*

SAPPFPAR is a very important utility. When you change any or all memory parameters, run this utility to check the environment. Make it a rule because if the SAP memory environment is configured incorrectly, you will not be able to start SAP. The best time to run this utility is with SAP stopped. You can run it with SAP up and running but take the error messages with a grain of salt. It sometimes reports that the shared memory segment size is too small when actually it is not. Use it only to calculate shared memory pool sizes when you execute it with SAP running. Another piece of advice is to remove any orphaned shared memory segments after you've stopped SAP and before running this utility. Removing orphaned shared memory segments will be discussed later in this chapter.

The following is sappfpar check pf=C10_DVEBMGS00_etna:

```
================================================================================
== Checking profile: C10_DVEBMGS00_etna
================================================================================
Shared memory disposition overview
================================================================================
Shared memory pools
  Key:   10  Pool
                  Size configured.....:   330000000 ( 314.7 MB)
                  Size min. estimated.:   326577102 ( 311.4 MB)
                  Advised Size........:   330000000 ( 314.7 MB)
Shared memories inside of pool 10
  Key:      1  Size:      2000 (    0.0 MB) System administration
  Key:      2  Size:   1633872 (    1.6 MB) Disp. administration tables
  Key:      3  Size:  32193000 (   30.7 MB) Disp. communication areas
  Key:      6  Size: 104448000 (   99.6 MB) ABAP program buffer
  Key:      7  Size:     14838 (    0.0 MB) Update task administration
  Key:      8  Size:  89129060 (   85.0 MB) Paging buffer
  Key:      9  Size:  45383780 (   43.3 MB) Roll buffer
  Key:     11  Size:    500000 (    0.5 MB) Factory calender buffer
  Key:     12  Size:    120000 (    0.1 MB) TemSe Char-Code convert Buf.
  Key:     13  Size:    500000 (    0.5 MB) Alert Area
  Key:     14  Size:   4400000 (    4.2 MB) Presentation buffer
  Key:     16  Size:     22400 (    0.0 MB) Semaphore activity monitoring
  Key:     17  Size:    348260 (    0.3 MB) Roll administration
  Key:     18  Size:    696420 (    0.7 MB) Paging adminitration
  Key:     19  Size:  10000100 (    9.5 MB) Table-buffer
  Key:     31  Size:   4206000 (    4.0 MB) Dispatcher request queue
  Key:     33  Size:   5120100 (    4.9 MB) Table buffer, part.buffering
  Key:     34  Size:   4096000 (    3.9 MB) Enqueue table
  Key:     41  Size:   6010000 (    5.7 MB) DB statistics buffer
  Key:     42  Size:    796432 (    0.8 MB) DB TTAB buffer
  Key:     43  Size:   3981216 (    3.8 MB) DB FTAB buffer
  Key:     44  Size:   1933216 (    1.8 MB) DB IREC buffer
  Key:     45  Size:   1421216 (    1.4 MB) DB short nametab buffer
  Key:     46  Size:     20480 (    0.0 MB) DB sync table
```

```
Key:        47  Size:      3072000  (   2.9 MB) DB CUA buffer
Key:        48  Size:       300000  (   0.3 MB) Number range buffer
Key:        49  Size:      3000000  (   2.9 MB) Spool admin (SpoolWP+DiaWP)
Key:        51  Size:      3200000  (   3.1 MB) Extended memory admin.
Key:        52  Size:        20000  (   0.0 MB) Message Server buffer
Shared memories outside of pools
Key:         4  Size:       100000  (   0.1 MB) statistic area
Key:        54  Size:        16384  (   0.0 MB) Export/Import buffer
Key:      1002  Size:       400000  (   0.4 MB) Performance monitoring V01.0
Key: 58900100  Size:         4096  (   0.0 MB) SCSA area
No. of operating system shared memory segments: 5
Shared memory resource requirements estimated
================================================================
Total No. of shared segments required.....:          5
System-imposed number of shared memories.:          120
Shared memory segment size required min..:  330000000 ( 314.7 MB)
System-imposed maximum segment size......:  738197504 ( 704.0 MB)
Swap space requirements estimated
================================================================
Shared memory....................:   632.4 MB
..in pool 10   311.4 MB,    98% used
..not in pool    0.5 MB
Processes........................:   127.0 MB
Extended Memory .................:    85.0 MB
- - - - - - - - - - - - - - - - - - - - - - - - - - - - - - - - .
Total, minimum requirement.......:   844.4 MB
Process local heaps, worst case..:   762.9 MB
Total, worst case requirement....:  1607.3 MB
Errors detected..................:     0
Warnings detected................:     0
```

The important values in the previous are as follows:

- Shared memory pool sizes (advised size)
- Shared memory resource requirements estimated (only with SAP not running)
- Swap space requirements estimated (worst case)

MEMLIMITS *determine max. shared memory, swap size*

This utility should also be executed while SAP is not running.

The following is the output generated by the memlimits utility:

```
SAP R/3 address space configuration test tool V3.2 (96/03/20)
============================================================================
Check the maximum data size per process (malloc)
Check the available swap space (malloc in several processes)
Process 15131 allocating   ... Size =   640MB   Total:   640MB
Process 15132 allocating   ... Size =   640MB   Total:  1280MB
Process 15133 allocating   ... Size =   640MB   Total:  1920MB
Process 15134 allocating   ... Size =   424MB   Total:  2344MB
Process 15137 allocating   ... Size =     4MB   Total:  2348MB
Process 15138 allocating   ... Size =     0MB   Total:  2348MB
Total available swap space = 2348MB
Check the maximum size of mapped file (mmap anonymous, dev/zero)
Check protection operations on this area (protect)
Trying to mmap       512MB ...    successful
Trying to mmap       768MB ...    failed
Trying to mmap       640MB ...    successful
Trying to mmap       704MB ...    successful
Trying to mmap       736MB ...    failed
Trying to mmap       720MB ...    failed
Trying to mmap       712MB ...    failed
Trying to mmap       708MB ...    successful
Trying to mprotect   708MB ...    successful
Maximum mapped file size: 708MB
Maximum mprotect size:    708MB
R/3 parameter em/initial_size_MB up to 708 permitted
Check the maximum address space per process usable
both by process local memory and mapped file
Maximum address space ( mmap(708 MB)+ malloc(512MB) ): 1220MB
+----------------------------------------------+
|                     Result                   |
+----------------------------------------------+
Maximum heap size per process........:   640 MB
```

```
Maximum mapped file size (mmap)......:   708 MB
    this value is probably limited by swap space
Maximum protectable size (mprotect)..:   708 MB
    em/initial_size_MB > 708 MB will not work
Maximum address space per process....:  1220 MB
    this value is probably limited by swap space
Total available swap space...........:  2348 MB
    main memory size x 3 recommended , minimum 1 GB
```

The results are quite self-explanatory. The utility attempts to allocate as much memory as possible in order to determine the maximum shared memory size and maximum swap space per process. These values are a very good indication of the maximum values for some memory parameters. It is also very important to clear all orphaned shared memory segments.

CLEANIPC, IPCS, and IPCRM *(remove shared memory segments)*

In the previous section, the need to remove orphaned shared memory segments was mentioned. How do you do this? SAP developed a utility called **cleanipc,** which removes shared memory segments. SAP has to be stopped before you can execute this utility because SAP will crash if it is not stopped.

The syntax for this utility is:

```
cleanipc <Inst. No.> remove
```

Sometimes it happens that **cleanipc** does not remove the shared memory segments. Then you need to fall back on UNIX commands to remove these segments (namely **ipcs** and **ipcrm**).

The syntax for **ipcs** is **ipcs −ma** to display the memory segments and **ipcs −sa** to display the associated semaphores. An identification number is associated with each segment and semaphore. You need to execute **ipcrm −m <*ID*>** to remove the memory segment and **ipcrm −s <ID>** to remove the semaphore.

CAUTION

Do not remove any segments or semaphores of running programs or programs that do not belong to <SID>adm or ora<SID>. Make sure that SAP is stopped, **saposcol** does not run, **saprouter** is stopped, and the database is not running. Once this is done, it is safe to execute these utilities.

/$ST

This transaction toggles the display of the current executing transaction's memory consumption on the bottom status bar of the SAPGUI window. As an alternative you can use the following menu path to accomplish the same effect: System, Utilities, Resource Usage.

RZ10 and RZ11

RZ10 and RZ11 are not so much tuning transactions as maintenance transactions. RZ10 allows you to change profile parameters, and RZ11 contains useful information about parameters. Another method to maintain profile parameters is to make use of an external text editor such as the vi editor in UNIX. For data integrity and security reasons, it is always better to make use of the SAP profile editor to change parameter values. Figure 9-18 displays the Profile Basic Memory Management screen.

When SAP is initially installed or after a database copy, the SAP administrator needs to import the profiles at the OS level into SAP.

To import all the profiles of the current active servers, execute transaction **RZ10**, menu path Utilities, Import Profiles, Of Active Servers, as portrayed in Figure 9-19. This will load the profile data into table TPFET. Once the data is loaded into SAP, you can select any of the profiles from the Profile Selection List and maintain the administration, basic, or extended profile data.

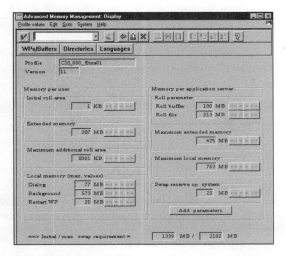

FIGURE 9-18 *RZ10 basic maintenance for memory management*

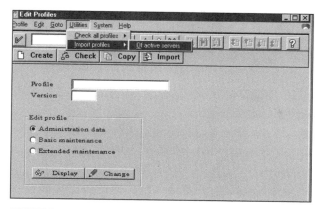

FIGURE 9-19 *RZ10 profile maintenance – import profiles for active servers*

Since Release 3.0E, SAP has the ability to switch a few parameters dynamically. These parameters are ztta/roll_first, ztta/roll_extension, ztta/roll_area, abap/heap_area_dia, abap/heap_area_nondia, abap/heap_area_total, em/stat_log_size_MB, and em/stat_log_timeout. Maintain the parameters as you normally do with transaction RZ10. Once the changes are saved, you can use transaction **ST10**, follow menu path Profile, Dyn. Switching, Display Parameters, or Execute to switch to the new values.

Operation Modes and Profile Maintenance

SAP distinguishes between different kinds of work processes—dialog, batch, spool, and update processes. During a monitoring effort, suppose you notice that the wait time is extremely high. You execute transaction SM50 on each application server and notice that all the batch processes are being used and jobs are waiting for batch processes to become available. You also notice that you have dialog processes to spare (some dialog processes are never used). This situation can be rectified online by making use of operational modes, which allow you to redistribute work processes. You would do the following:

1. **Load SAP profiles (RZ10).** Import profiles from the operating system into SAP. Use RZ10 to maintain the profile settings for security reasons and because RZ10 generates an automatic audit trail.

2. **Configure operational modes (RZ04).** Create the operational modes and give them meaningful names like "Daily Online" or "Nightly Batch." Define the productive instances and their process distribution. Assign

the operational modes to each of the instances and define new process distributions for each operational mode. The "Nightly Batch" operational mode will have more batch processes than dialog processes and "Daily Online" will have more online processes.

3. **Set timetable (SM63).** Each of these operational modes has to be assigned to a timetable indicating the period during the day that each should be active. The timetable is cyclic and repeats every day. There is also a timetable for exceptional operations. This last-mentioned timetable is not cyclic and will set the SAP system in a specific mode only once.

4. **Control operational modes (RZ03).** When changes are made to an operational mode, these changes do not take effect immediately. With transaction RZ03, you can force operational mode switches. RZ03 will also alert you if the profiles and the operational modes are inconsistent.

SM66, SM51, and SM50

It is sometimes necessary to monitor individual processes for memory usage. SM66 and SM51 are not memory-monitoring transactions but rather "locator" transactions in the sense that you use them to locate where a particular batch or long-running dialog job might be running. SM66 tells you on which application server it is running, and SM51 allows you to switch to SM50 on the specific application server indicated by SM66.

Execute transaction SM50, select the work process running the program you want to monitor, and select the Detail Info button. From here, you can monitor the process's memory usage. The process being monitored in Figure 9-20 is a batch process. Notice that mostly private memory is being used.

ST06 or OS06

ST06 is the window SAP has on the operating system it is running on. Figure 9-21 displays the ST06 Operating System Monitor.

Together with transaction ST04, this transaction provides a wealth of interesting facts about the environment SAP is running in. This transaction provides a snapshot of the system at any given time. It reports the physical memory installed on the system, the amount of memory that is currently available, and the paging information.

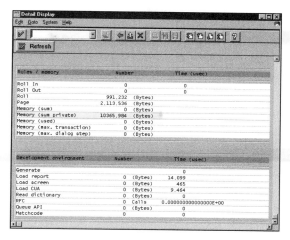

FIGURE 9-20 *SM50 detail information*

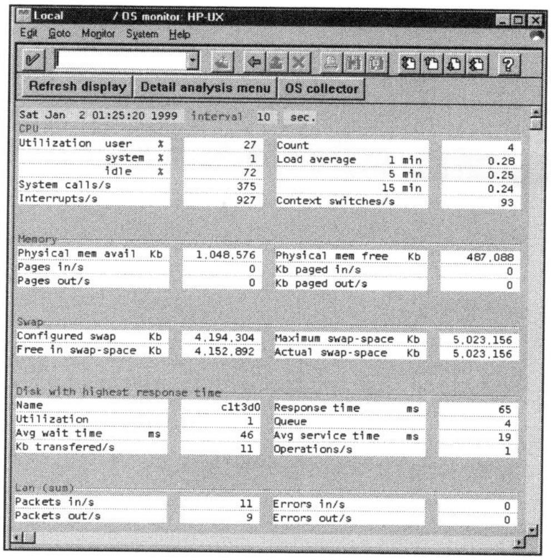

FIGURE 9-21 *ST06 operating system monitor*

For history on memory usage, select Detail Analysis Menu. The window that appears allows you to display the memory, swap, and paging information for the last 24 hours. It also allows you to list the average memory usage for the last few days. (The number of days depends on how the system was configured.) The paging information is usually an indicator that some program is consuming too much memory. Paging in is usually not a problem but paging out is. The system should always page information it requires into memory. Paging out means that the system ran out of memory and has to make space for new information in memory. It pages the oldest pages out to disk to make room for the new pages it will load. Ideally, the page out value should be zero or very close to it. It is also acceptable to have paging occasionally high, especially when database backups are taking place.

When the operating system pages, it is using CPU and I/O resources. This becomes a potential problem when the user processes (programs) suffer. An indication of this situation is that the processing time for a particular user program is much greater than the time actually spent on the CPU. Use transaction **ST03**, follow menu path Workload Analysis, Detail Analysis Menu, Today's Workload, Dialog to investigate if this situation is taking place. In order to calculate the processing time use the following formula: *Response Time – Load Time – Wait time – DB Request Time*. See Figure 9-22.

ST03

Use transaction **ST03**, follow menu path Detail Analysis Menu, Workload, Memory Profile to pinpoint transactions and users consuming large amounts of memory. Figure 9-22 shows the initial workload overview.

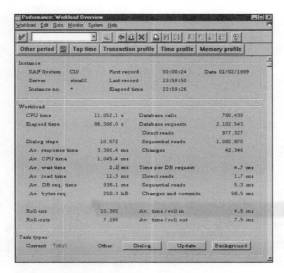

FIGURE 9-22 *Performace workload overview*

You can display the memory consumption for the last few minutes, today, past days, past weeks, and past months for each of the work process groups (dialog, background, and update). Transactions consuming unacceptably high amounts of memory should be investigated. Look for OSS notes that might remedy the memory usage issue for a particular transaction. Check with the functional business analyst to see if a specific program can be executed with different criteria to accomplish the same task. (This could be done perhaps by running multiple instances of the same program, specifying different parameters. For example, split a report accumulating data for a complete year into 12 reports, thereby getting the same information but without using huge amounts of memory.) Custom programs and transactions have a tendency to consume large amounts of memory because the code is not optimized for memory usage. Code should not only be tested for syntax and logical errors before it is moved to production but it should also be tested for memory usage and performance. Get the developers to revisit code that is not optimally coded.

SM04

SM04, menu path Goto, Memory (see Figure 9-23) allows you to monitor the memory usage of users currently logged on to an application server. You will typically use SM04 while troubleshooting memory-related issues such as finding users and transactions causing excessive memory consumption.

Cl.	User	Tcode	Key	Roll	Page	Mem(Total)	Mem(Private)
020	USER02	SART	1917	458,752	172,032	3,165,610	0
020	USER24	VL01	1894	311,296	32,768	6,834,382	0
020	USER12	SART	1924	253,952	40,960	2,010,515	0
020	JMARNEWECK	SM04	1915	253,952	24,576	4,507,563	0
020	USER03	SART	1960	253,952	40,960	2,010,867	0
020	USER32	VA42	1956	245,760	32,768	4,854,991	0
020	USER40	CJ2B	1968	212,992	155,648	7,071,734	0
020	USER15	VA02	1937	147,456	16,384	4,995,961	0
020	USER01	ME21	1954	139,264	0	576,147	0
020	USER53	FBL5	1944	131,072	16,384	944,946	0
020	USER57	VL02	1958	131,072	16,384	1,676,671	0
020	JMARNEWECK		1972	122,880	0	0	0

FIGURE 9-23 *SM04, Goto, Memory*

RZ03

Transaction **RZ03**, menu path Edit, Other Views, Memory Management reports a snapshot comparison between the current active application servers.

ST02

ST02 is another very informative transaction. It reports the current statistics on the SAP buffers. Please refer to the section "Buffer Management" for more information on this transaction.

STAT *(use statistics file on application server)*

This transaction retrieves statistics for transactions and programs executed from the statistics file located in the data directory. Each application server has its own statistics file. Therefore, you need to know which application server a program ran on in order to get statistics on it. Among many useful statistics, this transaction reports on the memory usage of a program.

Use this transaction to analyze the overall memory usage and performance of a program.

Buffer Management

Buffers help to reduce network traffic and direct database accesses, thus improving performance.

SAP has buffers in two memory locations:

◆ Shared memory *(extended)*
◆ Process memory *(heap) private*

Some of the SAP buffers are grouped in pools. Each buffer not in a pool usually consumes one shared memory segment for itself. For this reason, the pool concept was introduced in order to group buffers together and to place them into a single shared memory segment for improved performance and memory usage.

Tuning buffers is usually a trade-off between four things: optimal performance, paging, wasted memory, and the amount of physical memory available on the system. Remember that a larger buffer size consumes more memory. It might happen that the system does not have enough memory for you to increase buffer sizes. If extensive paging is a problem on the system, the only two options available to

paging↑ → buffer size ↓
↘ RAM ↑
↘ prioritize # buffers.

an administrator to reduce paging are to reduce the buffer sizes or to purchase more physical memory. Something else you can do is to prioritize the different buffers. Allow swapping to take place for less important buffers by reducing their sizes and giving this additional memory to buffers that are more important.

The following list is a priority list indicating the importance of each buffer (1 is the highest and 6 the lowest). If you want to allow some buffers to swap the GUI and Page file buffers will have the smallest impact on the performance of the system.

1. R/3 dictionary buffers/nametab buffers
2. Table buffers
3. Program buffer
4. Roll file buffer
5. Page file buffer
6. GUI buffers

buffer profile < size of buffer
< number of entries.

Most of the buffers are governed by two profile parameters, one for the size of the buffer and one for the number of entries allowed into a buffer. Swapping occurs when either of these parameters is too small.

The best time for tuning buffers is when the SAP system has been running for a while. During system startup, the buffers are loaded, which means that the buffer quality is bad. After a few days of extensive system usage, the buffer quality should increase to values greater than 90 percent. If the quality is bad, you should investigate.

Start with some value and tune the buffers according to the available memory you have and the swapping taking place. If a buffer is too big, it wastes memory; if too small, performance degenerates due to swapping.

Buffer Synchronization and Data Consistency *(multi server)*

An SAP installation consisting of one server does not have any buffer synchronization problems, but as soon as you introduce one extra application server, the buffers of these two servers need to be kept in synchronization. All the application servers should always be aware of changes to tables being buffered. If application server A introduces a change to a buffered table and application server B does not know this, serious data inconsistencies will occur. For this reason, mostly read-only tables are buffered.

Imagine that you have a database server and two application servers (1 and 2) and that these three servers have the following interaction:

1. The database server has a buffered table T123A with three records (A, B, and C).

2. Server 1 reads table T123A and buffers A, B, and C.

3. Server 2 reads table T123A and buffers A, B, and C.

4. Server 1 adds a record D to table T123A and updates its own buffer with A, B, C, and D.

5. Buffer synchronization does not take place.

6. Server 2 reads table T123a but gets the information from its own buffers (A, B, and C). D is missing!

SAP implemented a synchronization solution to resolve this data inconsistency problem. A central table called DDLOG is updated with a synchronization telegram every time a buffer changes. All the application servers periodically read this table and synchronize all the different buffers in the environment. The default period for this synchronization is every 60 seconds. There is still a very good possibility that during this 60 seconds data inconsistencies might arise. The trade-off is between performance and the buffers being up to date. A short synchronization means that the buffers are refreshed frequently, causing performance concerns. Making the period too long means that the data in the database and in the buffers might be inconsistent. Therefore, never buffer tables that contain volatile business data. To analyze the DDLOG and buffer synchronization, execute transaction **ST02**, follow menu path Detail Analysis Menu, Buffer Synchronization, select Synchronization Classes, and read the DDLOG.

The parameters that control buffer synchronization are as follows:

◆ rdisp/bufrefmode   sendon,exeauto
◆ rdisp/bufreftime   60

To switch synchronization completely off:

◆ rdisp/bufrefmode   sendoff,exeoff

sendon/sendoff

This setting controls whether or not an application server writes synchronization records.

exeoff/exeauto

This setting controls whether or not an application server reacts on synchronization records.

SAP Buffers

Table 9-4 lists each of the different SAP buffers, the key for each buffer, and the tuning parameters for buffers that can be tuned. Notice that some of the buffers are grouped in pools; this increases performance and reduces memory wastage. Instead of each buffer consuming a memory segment, a group of them share a single segment. The table also lists the profile parameters that control each buffer or pool.

Table 9-4 SAP Buffers

Segment Name	Key	Parameter
Application server administration	1	
Dispatcher administration tables	2	
Dispatcher communication areas	3	
IMS & MPE system state area	4	
ABAP program buffer	6	abap/buffersize
Update administration	7	
Shared paging buffer	8	rdisp/PG_SHM
Shared roll buffer	9	rdisp/ROLL_SHM
Pool 10	10	ipc/shm_psize10
Factory calendar buffer	11	zcsa/calendar_area
TemSe char-code conversion buffer	12	rsts/ccc/cachesize
Alert area	13	
Presentation buffer	14	zcsa/presentation_buffer_area
Semaphore activity monitoring	16	ipc/sem_mon_rec
Roll administration	17	rdisp/ROLL_MAXFS
Paging administration	18	rdisp/PG_MAXFS

Table 9-4 SAP Buffers *(Continued)*

Segment Name	Key	Parameter
Table buffer (generic key)	19	zcsa/table_buffer_area
Dispatcher request queue	31	rdisp/elem_per_queue
Table buffer (single key)	33	rtbb/buffer_length
Enqueue table	34	enque/table_size
Pool 40 (database buffers)	40	ipc/shm_psize40
DB statistics buffer	41	
DB TTAB buffer	42	rsdb/ntab/entrycount
DB FTAB buffer	43	rsdb/ntab/ftabsize
DB IREC buffer	44	rsdb/ntab/irbdsize
DB short nametab buffer	45	rsdb/ntab/sntabsize
DB sync table	46	
DB CUA buffer	47	rsdb/cua/buffersize
Number range buffer	48	
Spool administration	49	
Extended memory administration	51	
Message server result list buffer	52	
Message server result list buffer	54	
Performance monitoring	1002	

Tuning SAP buffers is not that difficult. Figure 9-24 displays the SAP buffer monitor, transaction ST02. SAP and many other experts on tuning make suggestions on the values that should be used for the different buffers based on application module groupings and the number of users. Use these suggestions initially but also tune the buffers according to your own unique SAP environment. Each of the buffers reported in transaction ST02 has history associated with it. Drill down by clicking on each buffer, display the history, and determine if you should add more memory to the buffer or remove some memory. The goal is to avoid

FIGURE 9-24 *ST02 buffer summary*

swapping and to have good buffer quality. Allocating too much memory to a buffer is a waste. Buffers with too much memory assigned to them should be reduced.

SAP Cursor Cache *(ABAP program)*

Occasionally the SAP system reports problems with the cursor cache (ORA-1023). SAP and Oracle suggest that when this happens you should rewrite your ABAP program, making use of fewer cursors—or you may also consider stopping and restarting the work process in question. **ST02**, menu path Detail Analysis Menu, SAP Cursor Cache IDs/Statements reports on the SAP cursor cache, and the parameter that controls the cursor cache is dbs/ora/stmt_cache_size.

CAUTION

Do not fiddle with this parameter unless SAP or some expert directs you to do so.

Shared Memory Buffers

As you are aware by now, SAP has many different buffers. Most of these buffers can and should be tuned. Use transaction ST02 to display the buffer performance statistics and use transaction RZ10 to maintain the buffer parameters.

TIP

A general rule of thumb is to start with a given value and tune your system according to the memory you have and the swapping that's taking place. If a buffer is too big, it wastes memory; if it is too small, performance degenerates due to swapping.

NOTE

Swapping does not always take place just because of lack of memory for user data; it also can occur because of lack of entries. The buffer size and number of entries need to be tuned for the buffer. The entry count parameter indicates the number of entries allowed in the buffer.

Table Monitoring (Buffering)

Buffering Hints

- Transparent and pooled tables are managed the same by the different buffers.
- Views are not buffered. A view accesses data directly, bypassing the buffers. If you need to buffer the data associated with a view, instead buffer the individual tables and access the data with more than one query.
- Buffers do not make use of indexes. A full scan is performed on a buffer when a buffered table is queried.
- Large tables should be indexed.
- Small tables should be buffered.
- Only select statements that use order by primary key make use of the buffers. Select statements that use only order by bypass the buffers.
- Tables that are changed frequently should not be buffered.
- Tables containing highly volatile data should not be buffered.

Transaction ST10 reports on the buffer efficiency for each of the tables being buffered using any of the buffering methods. Execute transaction ST10, select the buffering method you want to analyze, display the list of tables buffered, and double-click on any of the tables to view the buffer efficiency for the particular table. You can use this transaction to determine if tables that are not buffered should be buffered. Figure 9-25 is the initial ST10 table call statistics screen. Figures 9-26 and 9-27 are follow-up screens, displaying table call statistics based upon the options selected on the initial screen. Figure 9-26 displays a list of tables and the method used to buffer each table. Figure 9-27 displays detailed information on a specific selected table (accessed by double-clicking on a table row in Figure 9-26).

Checking Partial Buffering

If the percentage of updates, deletions, or insertions is greater than 20 percent of the total number of table accesses, do not buffer the table.

If a partially buffered table is frequently accessed using index range scans and the quality is poor, check to see if a generic key exists among the different select statements and make use of generic buffering.

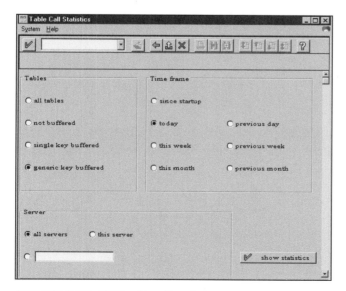

table buffer
single key buffered
generic key buffered
partial
Resident
generic with respective
number of keyfields

FIGURE 9-25 *ST10 table call statistics*

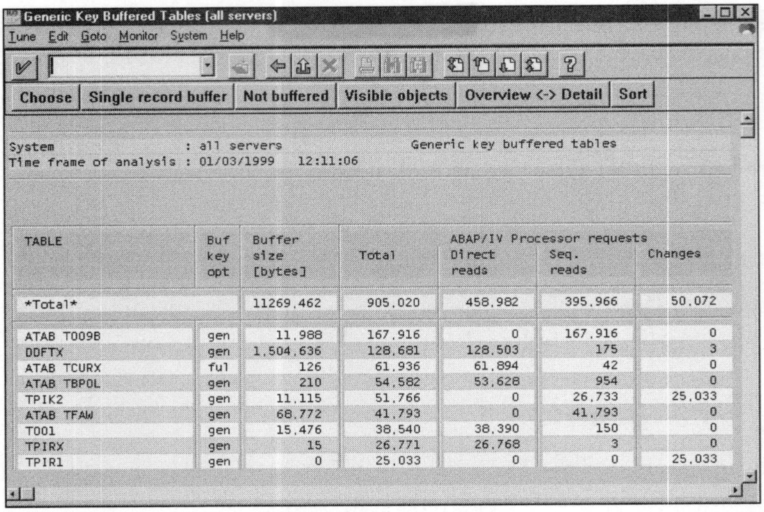

FIGURE 9-26 *List of generic buffered tables*

FIGURE 9-27 *Buffer efficiency for a single table*

Checking Resident Buffering

Very large tables should not be buffered using resident buffering. Typically, the maximum size of a table should be less than 100KB to qualify for this type of buffering. A very large table that is buffered will prevent smaller tables, which actually need to be buffered, from being buffered.

If the number of changes is greater than 5 percent of the total number of table accesses, the table should not be buffered.

A very large table that is accessed infrequently—and that, when accessed, uses a SELECT SINGLE statement—should be partially buffered.

A table should be buffered generically when the number of accesses to the table is less than 50 percent of the total number of records in the table. Another factor that should be considered for generic buffering is the table; it should be queried primarily by using range and select single statements.

Generic Buffering

Tables that are changed frequently should not be buffered.

A large table being buffered generically where the buffer quality is less than 70 percent should perhaps not be buffered at all, although the chance exists that the generic key is incorrect. An invalid generic key should be adjusted and the buffer re-evaluated.

Figure 9-28 displays a decision tree of the steps that should be followed to determine what type of buffering (if any) should be used on a table.

Summary

This chapter introduced you to initial performance planning and pointed out some useful hints you can use when tuning the OS, the database, and SAP. The performance on an SAP system is a seamless integrated entity. You have to tune the whole environment together, which is why you should have a good understanding of all the components in a SAP system.

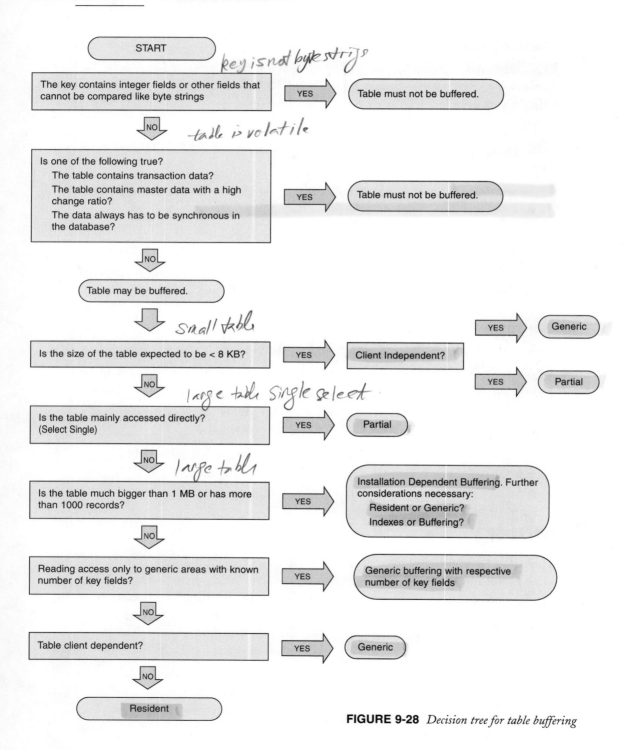

FIGURE 9-28 *Decision tree for table buffering*

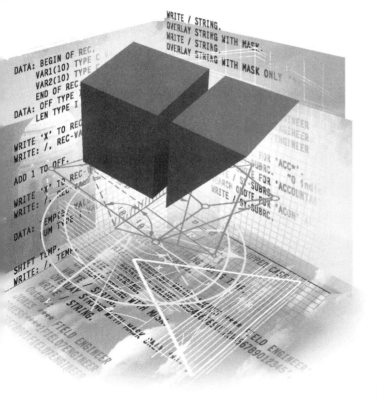

PART V

Administration

10 System Monitoring and Administration

11 Performance Monitoring and Administration

12 Database Administration

13 SAP Data Archiving for Administrators

14 An Administrator's Troubleshooting Guide

15 The Internet and SAP

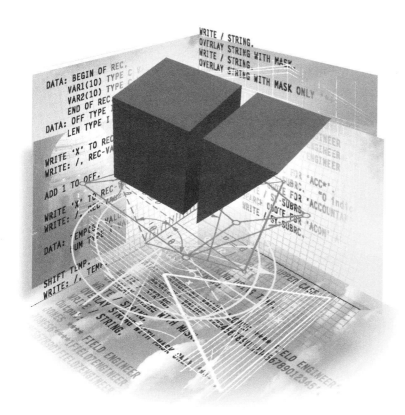

Chapter 10

**System
Monitoring and
Administration**

BMC Patrol to monitor systems

Maestro to monitor batch jobs

HP LanProbe network monitor

Autosys, DAZEL, Crossworlds, FTP

In This Chapter

◆ Monitoring SAP R/3

◆ Alert Monitor

Most of the chapters in this book discuss finite projects or activities, which are activities that have a definite beginning and end, such as installing SAP. Monitoring, administration, and troubleshooting (discussed in Chapter 14) are continuous efforts that last throughout the lifetime of the SAP system.

You need to monitor the network, hardware, operating system, database, and most importantly, SAP. This chapter will concern itself with monitoring SAP, the database, and the operating system.

Monitoring SAP R/3

This might sound trivial, but the most important thing to monitor is: Is SAP up and running? You might say that you will know immediately when SAP is not running because someone within your user community will complain. Not all SAP systems have users on them 24 hours a day, and some SAP constellations consist of multiple application servers of which some might be used, and others for the single purpose of running batch jobs. You need some method to determine that each of these servers is up and running. Some companies have scripts monitoring for the absence of SAP processes, others have operators watching the systems, and others implement third party tools like BMC Patrol to monitor the systems. Not only is this to detect if it is up and running but also to detect anything else that might go wrong on an SAP system.

Transactions RZ02 (SAP Startup Monitor depicted in Figure 10-1) and RZ03 or RZ08 (Control Panel depicted in Figure 10-2) are the center point of monitoring SAP. RZ03 and RZ08 are graphical monitoring tools that make use of different colors and patterns to indicate the status of the environment. RZ03 is the "text"

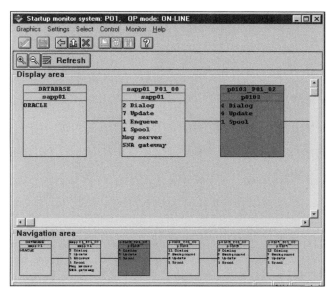

FIGURE 10-1 *RZ02 SAP R/3 Startup Monitor*

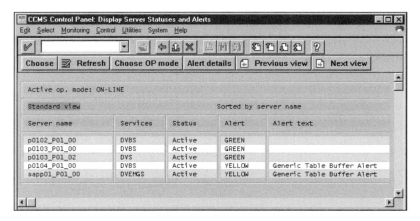

FIGURE 10-2 *RZ03 Control Panel*

version of RZ08. RZ08 is actually contained within RZ02 through one of the menu paths. The SAP system operators use these transactions to monitor SAP seven days a week, 24 hours a day.

This chapter will discuss monitoring the SAP system around these transactions, because these tools summarize the well-being of the SAP system.

RZ03 reports on the status of each application server:

Active, Configured	Green
Active, Not Configured	Green with diagonal lines
Inactive	Red
Unexpected Status	No color

Figure 10-2 lists all the different servers and displays the latest alert messages. In order to view the details of the alert, select one or more of the servers and click on the Alert Details button. The screen displayed in Figure 10-3 will appear. This screen lists the main alert categories of all the alerts. This chapter will discuss monitoring the system around these categories.

Lock Manager (Enqueue) (SM12)

The SAP system has only one lock manager, and it is located on the central instance. All the application servers make use of the central enqueue server to reserve locks on objects. The transaction you use to monitor the SAP locks is SM12. Troubleshooting the lock manager is discussed in Chapter 14.

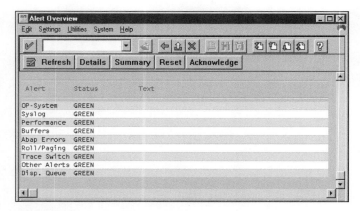

FIGURE 10-3 *RZ03, Alert Details*

You should be on the lookout for old locks. A lock should not be held very long. Ideally, a lock should be held for a few seconds. If a job has a lock for more than 30 minutes, you should be concerned. User sessions that terminate abnormally and updates that do not complete or fail completely can cause old locks to exist. Another cause can be an ABAP program that does not release locks as soon as it is finished with it.

CAUTION

Never delete a lock entry without verifying that by deleting the lock you will not cause data inconsistencies.

Occasionally, you will notice in transaction SM50 that a process has the status *Stopped ENQ*. An overflow in the lock table can cause this situation to occur. The profile parameter that governs the size of the lock table is **enque/table_size**. The default value for this parameter is 500 KB, which allows you about 2000 locks. The value of this parameter will depend on how lock-hungry your SAP jobs are. If the default value is too small, a better value would be something like 2000 or 4000 KB.

If you are experiencing lock problems, you can use transaction **SM12, Statistics** or **Diagnostics** or **Diagnostics in Update** to identify any potential problems and configuration inconsistencies.

You need to check transactions SM12 and SM13 (discussed later) two or three times per day.

The SAP R/3 System Log (SM21)

This transaction is discussed in the troubleshooting chapter (Chapter 14) in detail, but it needs to be reviewed from a monitoring perspective. RZ03 and RZ08 report critical system log entries to the operator or to whoever is watching. These critical system log entries should be monitored 24 hours a day. Not all these alerts are serious and most of them do not warrant attention, but occasionally serious errors do occur. As updates are being deactivated, these problems have to be resolved immediately. SAP realized that some messages will be informational and others will be serious. They included the functionality for you to filter the alerts and only display the alerts you deem serious. Transaction RZ06 allows you to define alert thresholds (among which system log thresholds are included) for all the SAP servers.

Performance (ST03)

Performance is discussed in Chapter 9 and performance monitoring is discussed in Chapter 11. Very briefly, the response time for dialog processes should not be higher than two seconds. Ideally, you want the response time for dialog requests below one second, and for update requests even less. Transaction **ST03**, **Detail Analysis Menu, Workload** reports on the average response time for the day. If the response time is unreasonably high, you will have to identify the bottleneck, be it the network, CPU, memory, the database, or even the ABAP code.

The performance of the system should be checked once or twice daily, and maybe once a week or once a month you should do history analysis of the performance of the SAP system. Use this information you gather to tune the system and possibly to buy additional hardware. The best time to do performance analysis is during high activity periods like during month-end, quarter-end, or year-end.

Buffers (ST02)

This is probably one of the most important monitoring tools. Once again, transaction ST02 is described in Chapter 9. Briefly, you do not want your buffers to swap, be it for the lack of memory or the lack of directory entries. Transaction RZ03 reports on the buffer hit ratio. The hit ratio for each buffer should always be higher than 95 percent except for the single key table buffer, for which the hit ratio should be higher than 75 percent. Table 10-1 lists the default SAP suggested alert and space thresholds.

You should use the History function that this transaction provides in order to do your buffer analysis over a period. You need to do this at least once a month or once a week initially, but as you notice the buffers are becoming more stable, you can monitor it less frequently. Tune your buffers to eliminate swapping and as available memory allows.

ABAP Errors (ST22)

Chapter 14 explains the functionality of the ABAP dumps (transaction ST22) in detail. ABAP programs can terminate for many different reasons. Terminations

Table 10-1 Buffer Alert and Space Thresholds

Buffer Type	Hit Ratio% Yellow	Red	Directory Used%	Space Used%
Nametab (NTAB)				
Table Definition	95	85	95	95
Field Description	95	85	95	95
Short NTAB	95	85	95	95
Initial Records	95	85	95	95
Program	95	85	95	95
CUA	95	85	95	95
Screen	95	85	95	95
Tables				
Generic Key	95	85	95	95
Single Record	75	50	95	95

range from simple TIME OUTS to complex logical errors in the ABAP code (RAISED EXCEPTIONS). TIME OUTS are easy to solve. Run long running reports in the background or increase the parameter **rdisp/max_wprun_time** with caution. These alerts usually mean that some business transaction is failing and the impact can be serious. For this reason, dumps should be monitored very closely. Make use of OSS to solve most of the SAP ABAP dump problems. Usually, after an installation or upgrade, the system will be quite unstable and you will get frequent ABAP dumps, but as time continues it will become fewer as you fix the problems.

Roll and Paging (ST02)

SAP has two memory areas: the roll area and the page area. The roll and page memory areas are discussed in Chapter 9 in much more detail.

The roll area contains the context information of all the users that are rolled out. There are only a limited number of processes and to give every user a chance to process their transactions on a work process SAP implemented context switching.

The roll area should be big enough to hold all the roll areas of all the users logged onto the system at a given time.

The page area is a memory management feature that tagged along from the old SAP release 2, memory management strategy. The page area contains lists and internal tables to name only two.

Each of these two memory areas makes use of shared memory and disk space as memory sources. The ideal is to configure the system so that the roll and page areas are in shared memory. This obviously will ensure the best performance.

Use transaction ST02 to monitor the roll and page areas. You will also have to make use of the history analysis provided in transaction ST02 to analyze it over a period. If possible, configure SAP to use shared memory for both.

It does not hurt to make the size of the disk portion of the roll and page areas' memory big because it will allocate the space as required. Just make sure that you have enough disk space to accommodate the maximum size that these two areas can grow to. The SAP page and roll file are located in */usr/sap/<SID>/D*/data*.

The best time to tune the roll and page areas is during high activity periods, which was mentioned in the performance section. Other than that, it should be monitored continuously to ensure that the SAP system does not run out of page and roll memory.

Trace Switch (ST05)

Having a trace switched on is not a problem in itself. It will only hamper performance and possibly fill an operating system file system. The monitoring tool RZ03 warns you that the system and developer trace levels are not set to the default. Trace what you need to and return the trace level to the default values once you are done. SAP issues a yellow alert when a SQL Trace is activated. You activate and deactivate a SQL trace using transaction ST05. Activate or deactivate developer traces by executing transaction **SM50**, **Process**, **Trace**, and **Components**.

Batch Jobs (SM37 or SM39)

The monitoring functionality within SAP for batch jobs is not very sophisticated. You typically want to know if a job started on time, executed successfully, and completed timely. If it happens that a job fails, you want the system to notify somebody responsible for the specific job. SAP does not have the functionality;

you will have to make use of third party software such as Maestro to monitor batch jobs to that extent.

SAP does have a transaction that you can use to manually monitor jobs—transaction SM37. Typically, you can get the business to identify the critical batch jobs, their start time, and approximated end time. Use transaction SM37 to monitor at least these jobs. Transaction SM37 has an option that you can use to filter and display only the failed jobs for a given period. Use this option to monitor for jobs that failed, possibly once or twice a day.

Another transaction you can use to monitor batch jobs is transaction SM39. It reports the status, the start time, the duration, and the amount of time the job was delayed before starting. If the delay times for your batch jobs get very high, there is something wrong in your environment. Use transaction SM50 to check if the number of batch processes are enough and use either transaction SM37 or SM58 to check if the dispatcher is not swamped with failing ARFC (Asynchronous Remote Function Call) jobs.

If background jobs are not acting right or the batch scheduler doesn't appear to be working properly, enter the following menu path: **SM65, Goto, Additional tests,** check all the check boxes, and press the Execute button. One of the options in transaction SM65 is a consistency test with an additional option to remove inconsistencies. It happens occasionally that the batch tables become inconsistent. Selecting these options in transaction SM65 will remove these inconsistencies.

Another easy test is to verify the time setting on all of the application servers, as one might be set incorrectly.

Updates (SM13) — *list recent update failure.*

The alert monitors will detect any update failures immediately and will report it in the system log and in the alert monitors. All update failures should be addressed as expediently as possible. You can use transaction SM13 to list all the recent update failures. Listing and resolving update errors should be done at least twice or three times a day, that is if you do not resolve them as they occur.

Processes (SM50)

From a monitoring point of view, you occasionally check the CPU usage of the work processes on each application server. The goal should be to have at least one work process per process type with its accumulated CPU time equal to zero. In other words, one of the dialog work processes should have its accumulated CPU time equal to zero.

If you are unable to connect to the SAP system, another way to monitor the work processes on an application server is the executable at operating system level called **dpmon**. The problem usually causing users not to be able to log on while a select few users are logged on is the shortage of dialog work processes. One or two of the users currently logged on to the system has a bunch of long running jobs that they execute online can cause this to happen.

Load Balancing (SMLG)

You want all the application servers in the SAP environment to work equally hard. Use transaction **SMLG, Goto, Load distribution** to monitor the user load on each application server. The load is usually skewed when users are not using logon groups to connect to SAP; they are using direct connections. The only way to remedy this is to configure their SAPGUI installations correctly.

The load balancing process is not very sophisticated. It is based on the average response time on an application server and the number of users on the server. The weight for response time is higher than the weight for the number of users. The weight is 5 to 1, respectively. You can change this ratio by changing the relevant ABAP code.

Occasionally it happens that this average response time gets skewed by a user running a long running job in the foreground instead of where it should be run—the background. When this happens, one application server might have only a few users, where the others have hundreds. Then again, something might be wrong with the specific application server. You will have to identify any bottlenecks and rectify them.

Active and All Logged on Users (AL08)

A question SAP will ask you in its certification exam: "What transaction do you use to display all the users on an SAP system?" The answer is: AL08. This transaction will show you where each user is logged on as well as the user distribution over all the application servers.

Another transaction you can use to display the same information is **SMLG, Goto, User list**.

Transaction SM04 displays a list of users currently using a specific application server. With this transaction you can see the different user sessions for each user and it allows you to terminate any user session you select.

Gateway (SMGW)

Occasionally, SAP might experience problems with the gateway process, be it for bugs in the SAP system or heavy system load. Use transaction SMGW to monitor the gateway process. The gateway has an associated developer trace file called *dev_rd*. You can view this file from within SMGW, and you can increase the level of information gathered by increasing the trace level. (Level 3 for massive information on the gateway process, level 1 for minimum info, 2 for medium, and 0 to turn it off.)

CAUTION

Do not leave the trace level for the gateway at level 3 or any trace level for that matter because additional trace information hampers performance.

You can also monitor the gateway process from the operating system. You have to execute the program *gwmon* and follow the menu options it displays.

Hot Package and Kernel Patch Level

Hot and kernel patches are not something that you monitor constantly. Occasionally, it happens that you want to upgrade to a newer patch level or you discover an OSS note that indicates that a problem is fixed in a specific patch. This is when you use this functionality to identify your current patch level and if SAP requires any additional patches to be installed.

The hot package level is displayed using the **System, Status** menu options. Look for the Hot Packages group; the Package number indicates the hot package level that is currently installed on the system.

To display what R/3 kernel version, issue the following command from UNIX:

```
disp+work -V
```

Another method you can use to display the kernel version is to execute transaction SM51 and select the Release Notes Button.

Both methods will display the SAP kernel level with a list of fixes and the OSS note numbers pertaining to each fix.

Operating System *(HA failure, HD failure)*

The important Operating System components that need to be monitored are CPU, memory, swap-space, and the file systems. You also need to know when the system crashes or, in a high-availability environment, when the systems fails to the standby equipment. Hard-disk failure is another important aspect for which to monitor.

SAP provides the CCMS environment as a monitoring tool to monitor, among other components, the OS. Other options you have: Write your own in-house monitoring scripts that you schedule to run frequently, or you can purchase third party products like BMC-Patrol to monitor your operating system.

CPU Load

The CPU Load should not constantly be in the high 90 percentiles. If it is, your CPU is overloaded, or some program (SAP or non-SAP) has a problem and is consuming all the available CPU cycles. If the CPUs are overloaded with normal work and you are unable to optimize the ABAP code any further, you will have to purchase additional CPUs or a more powerful server.

Occasionally a process misbehaves (be it an SAP process, a database process, or some other external process). To identify the SAP job that is causing the problem, execute transaction **ST06, Detail analysis menu, Top CPU processes**. This will list the top CPU consuming processes for the particular server that you are monitoring. You then need to tie this misbehaving process to an SAP user or batch job, the database, or some other process. If the process that is causing the problem belongs to SAP or the database, you need to optimize the ABAP code as far as possible. If the process is external to SAP and the database, you need to investigate the reason for the CPU consumption of this process. SAP typically suggests that you should not run other applications together with SAP.

Memory or Paging

For the best performance, you want the SAP system to never page out. Paging out is usually the cause for bad performance, especially on HP Unix machines. Always try to keep paging out to a minimum. The default alert values for paging out are 50 and 100 pages out per second, which is quite high. A page is 4KB, which entails that 50 pages are 200KB per second (or 720,000 KB per hour), and 100 pages is double that size. As mentioned before, the ideal is 0 pages per second. Ten pages per second (140MB per hour) should be a concern.

File Systems

File systems are probably the most important aspect of the operating system to monitor. You have to monitor file systems for space, and the fact that the file systems are mounted. Table 10-2 shows important file systems to monitor.

Table 10-2

File Systems to Monitor
SAP Administrator's Home directory
The transport directory
The physical SAP mount directory
The oracle home directory
The oracle log and trace directories
The archive directory
The SAP data directories
The interface directories
The SAP log and trace directories

The file systems that you should keep a close eye on are the file systems containing the SAP roll and page files, the SAP trace files, the SAP Job logs, the archive files, and the interface files. Bottom line, you do not want any file system to fill up. It can cause SAP, at a minimum, to loose some functionality, or worse, all functionality. A full archive file system has the tendency to suspend all activity until space is made available for normal processing to continue.

The transport directories should also be monitored and cleaned up frequently. With the commands **tp check all** and **tp clearold all**, you should be able to keep the transport directories clean. The TPPARAM parameters that govern the transport directory clean up effort are:

◆ datalifetime   = 90
◆ loglifetime   = 150
◆ olddatalifetime   = 150

The above-mentioned parameters will keep transport around for 90 days. After 90 days, transport is moved to the *olddata* directory where it is kept for an additional 60 days. The total lifetime for a transport in the system is 150 days.

Operating System Logs

The Operating System log is a text file containing any errors and warnings associated with the Operating System. Use transaction **ST06, Detail analysis menu, Operating system log** to display the OS log belonging to the host on which you executed ST06. You can write scripts to monitor this log file for specific errors or errors in general, or you can use third-party tools to monitor for any error entries.

The OS log file is actually a very important trouble-shooting tool. Do not forget about it just because you do not work with it frequently.

Database

The database is an integral part of SAP and you will find various tools that will assist you in keeping the database healthy. Table 10-3 lists the database specific transactions, and in Chapter 9, transaction ST04 is discussed in detail. The important transactions for monitoring are DB01 for exclusive locks, DB02 for space analysis, DB12 for backup logs, and DB14 for SAPDBA logs. If you are making use of the DB-optimizer, you will also have to verify that the statistic gathering utilities run frequently, because if it does not run, the SAP performance will degenerate.

Table 10-3 Database Monitoring Transactions

Transaction	Short Description
DB01	Analyze exclusive lock waits
DB02	Analyze tables and indexes
DB03	Parameter changes in database
DB05	Analysis of a table or index
DB07	ADABAS D: Diagnostic monitor
DB11	Early-Watch profile maintenance
DB12	Overview of backup logs
DB13	Database administration calendar
DB14	Show SAPDBA action logs
DB16	Trigger/browse infcfgcheck protocols
DB17	SQL check maintenance for CHECKTOOL
DB20	Gather DB Statistics for the DB-optimizer

Database File Systems

File systems are already addressed in the Operating System section, but from a database point of view, you constantly have to monitor the data and archive file systems. That is the /oracle/<SID>/sapdata and /oracle/<SID>/saparch directories. Never allow these file systems or any of the other file systems to fill up.

The Database Logs

In the ../saptrace directory, you will find two sub-directories called *background* and *usertrace*. The background directory contains the alert log for the database. This log file should be closely monitored for database errors. Make use of scripts or other third-party tools to report any errors as soon as they appear. You also need to monitor the usertrace directory for any new trace dumps. You want to react to errors reported within these trace files as soon as possible.

Backup and Archive Logs

Every time a backup or an archive occurs, you need to monitor for any failures. Backups and archives have to occur frequently; your ability to recover your database will largely depend on how successful you monitor your backups and archives. The backup logs reside in /oracle/<SID>/sapbackup, and the archive log files reside in /oracle/<SID>/saparch. You can also monitor these logs from within SAP using transaction DB12.

Database Consistency

SAP has its own data dictionary, and this data dictionary has to be consistent with the database data dictionary. Transaction DB02 reports when any tables or indexes do not exist in both locations. Transaction RZ03 will raise an alert when it detects missing indexes. Missing indexes can cause serious performance degradation. Luckily, indexes do not just disappear. In an environment where development is taking place, it is always possible that some transport deleted an index, or after an upgrade or installation, it is possible that some indexes or tables were not created. The worst possibility is that someone deleted the index.

Free Space and Extents

Free space and extents are the most important aspects of the database to monitor. Occasionally, users load huge amounts of data into the SAP system. All this new data has to go into existing tables that have already been optimized for normal growth. In other words, the max extent and next extent sizes of the tables and indexes are set low. When these huge amounts of data are loaded into the system, the tables and indexes reach max extent within a few minutes. You need to monitor for this kind of activity, namely fast extending tables and indexes, and tables and indexes with their number of extents close to the maximum allowed extents.

Transaction DB02 reports on *space critical objects*. Space critical objects are objects with a next extent size that will not fit in the available free space in a table space. Either the next extent size for these objects needs to decrease, or you need to add additional space. Always make sure that you have enough space in the database to accommodate the SAP system's space requirements.

TIP

If it ever befalls you that some table or index reached max extents due to a huge data load, remember to change all the next and max extent sizes for all the related indexes and tables. If a table reached max extents, then its indexes are bound to reach max extents soon.

You have a few choices on how to monitor for these aspects of SAP: manually, third-party monitoring tools, your own in-house scripts, or run **sapdba–check** frequently. **sapdba–check** can be resource-intensive. For this reason, one of the other options might be more feasible. Use transaction **DB14** to view the different check logs. The logs are located in the /oracle/<SID>/sapcheck directory.

Alert Monitor

The *alert monitor* is a graphical-monitoring tool. It allows the Basis administrator to monitor the SAP system in its entirety (global) or just the local instance or a remote instance. Execute transaction **STUN**. The first menu option is **Alerts**. Select this menu item to choose the environment that you want to monitor.

Global (AL01 – SAP System & AL02 - Database)

Figure 10-4 displays a typical graphical monitor with alert bar and light indicators. An example of a *light alert indicator* is "Database indices OK," and an example of a *bar alert indicator* is "User calls."

Light Alert Indicators

A green light indicates that everything is less than or equal to the defined threshold (OK).

A yellow light indicates that the threshold was exceeded by a relatively small amount. The system is still functioning fine, and nothing critical has happened yet that prevents users from using the system, but you might need to give it some attention.

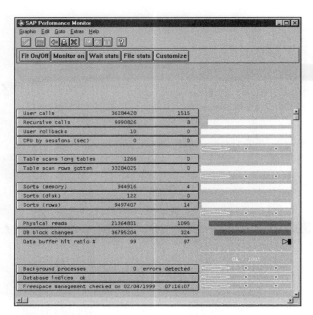

FIGURE 10-4 *Global Database Alert Monitor (AL02)*

A red light indicates that something critically wrong has occurred on the system. Users might not be able to use the system as intended. You have to resolve the problem immediately.

Bar Alert Indicators *(User calls monitor)*

The bar can be yellow, green-yellow, green, green-red, or red. The threshold for user calls is 1,500 per monitor interval of 10 seconds. The value monitored during the last 10-second interval was 1,515 user calls. The value is very close to the threshold of 1,500, which is why the bar will be completely green. If the number of user calls increases, the bar will become red; if it decreases, the bar will become yellow.

The other two global alert monitors are the SAP system and network monitors. The *SAP system monitor* is equivalent to the monitor associated with transaction RZ03. It displays alerts pertaining to the general SAP system health. The *network monitor* only works if the LanProbe hardware and software (a third-party product developed by HP) are installed on the network and if the required network monitor is configured.

Thresholds (RZ06)

The threshold values can either be set in the global monitor (using the Customize button you saw in Figure 10-4) or in transaction **RZ03, Monitoring, All Threshold Values** (RZ06). Select the set of thresholds you want to change and press the Change button (see Figure 10-5).

report again   *no report*

Resetting and Acknowledging Alerts

Acknowledge indicates that you are aware of the problem and that you are analyzing and possibly fixing it. The SAP system will not display any similar messages until you reset the alert.

The alert is *reset* to its initial state ready to report any alerts if a potential error situation occurs in the system.

Another option you have is to disable a particular alert: **RZ03**, select a server, **Alert Details**, select an alert group, **Details**, select an alert, **Settings, Disable**. In Figure 10-6 the DB-Logs alert is disabled.

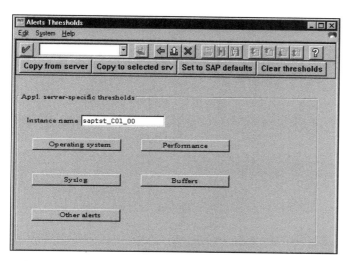

FIGURE 10-5 *The Alerts Thresholds screen allows you to set threshold values.*

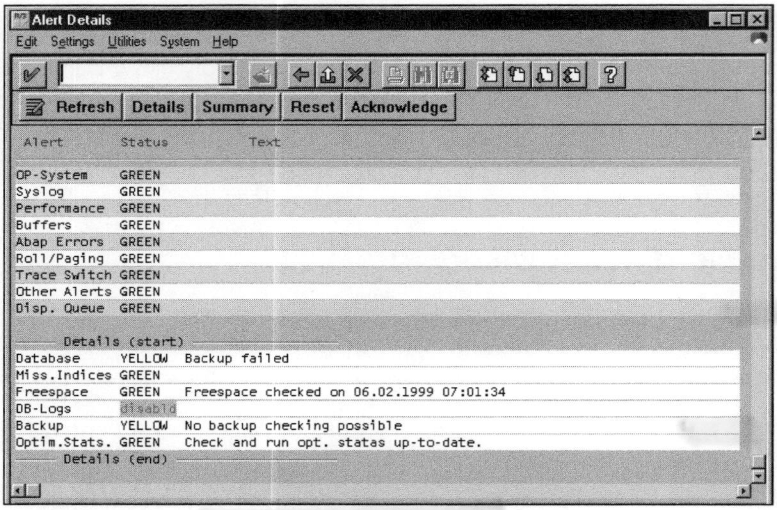

FIGURE 10-6 *Control Panel (RZ03) Alerts—Reset vs. Acknowledge*

Control Panel (RZ03)

Transaction RZ03 is a very powerful transaction, and it should be well protected. It not only displays alerts and a summary of the current health of the system, but it also allows you to switch operation modes and stop and start SAP instances.

Transaction RZ03 has many different views on the system. Each of these views report different statistics that should be monitored frequently in order to ensure a stable SAP system. RZ03 views include the following:

- Standard View
- Alert View
- Server Status
- Performance
- Buffer Quality
- Buffer Directory
- Buffer Memory
- Dispatcher Queues
- System Logs

Alert Transactions

Table 10-4 was generated using transaction **SE93**, listing all transactions starting with the characters **AL. AL** is supposed to be associated with alert monitoring, but there are a few of these transactions that start with AL and have nothing to do with alerts; for example, the transaction ALDB. Transaction ALDB is associated with logical databases. You will notice that transaction AL14 is missing. The reason for this it that it does not exist.

Table 10-4 SAP Alert Transactions

AL01	SAP Alert Monitor
AL02	Database Alert Monitor
AL03	Operating System Alert Monitor
AL04	Monitor Call Distribution
AL05	Monitor Current Workload
AL06	Performance: Upload/Download
AL07	Early Watch Report
AL08	Users Logged On
AL09	Data for Database Expertise
AL10	Download to Early Watch
AL11	Display SAP Directories
AL12	Display Table Buffer (Expert Session)
AL13	Display Shared Memory (Expert Mode)
AL15	Customize SAPOSCOL destination
AL16	Alert Monitor for Local Operating System
AL17	Alert Monitor for Remote Operating System
AL18	Local File System Monitor
AL19	Remote File System Monitor
AL20	Early Watch Data Collector List

Chapter 11

Performance Monitoring and Administration

In This Chapter

◆ CCMS Monitoring Transactions

◆ Determining Performance Goals

◆ ABAP Runtime Analysis

Chapter 9 discussed performance tuning and methods a Basis administrator can use to set up the environment for performance. Now that all the preparation and initial configuration is done, the goal is a well-tuned and excellently performing SAP system.

Chapter 10 digressed on monitoring in general: What, when, and how often. This chapter focuses specifically on performance monitoring and the tools required for performance monitoring. The chapter will start off with the monitoring transactions within CCMS, make a few suggestions on how to monitor for performance, and will finish off with the ABAP Runtime Analyzer. Before we start, CCMS stands for Computer Center Management Tools, and it does exactly that. CCMS is a set of tools that you as administrator will use to tune and manage your SAP environment.

CCMS Monitoring Transactions

The transaction STUN displays the main performance-monitoring window as depicted in Figure 11-1. From this window, you can navigate to all the main monitoring areas in the SAP environment—the system workload, the SAP buffers, the operating system, and other user and miscellaneous monitoring transactions. You will notice that Figure 11-1 starts off with a menu item called Alerts. The options under Alerts do not pertain to performance specifically but to monitoring the system in general. Let's address performance monitoring specifically first.

FIGURE 11-1 *Performance Monitoring (STUN)*

Monitoring Transactions

The menu headings in Figure 11-1 are self-explanatory and most of these menu items are addressed in Chapter 9. Transaction ST03 will be the focus for this discussion. The list of transactions below is the main performance monitoring and tuning transactions. Each of these transactions is very useful in monitoring, tuning, and troubleshooting performance problems. Transaction ST14 is a later addition to monitoring transactions and, it allows you to gather statistics on the different application modules. This information allows the functional groups to optimize the different application modules.

ST01	System Trace for Troubleshooting and Tuning
ST02	Set Up and Tune SAP Buffers
ST03	Performance, Statistics, and Workload Monitoring
ST04	Database Activity Monitoring and Tuning
ST05	SQL Trace for Troubleshooting and Tuning
ST06	Operating System Monitor
ST07	Monitor User Distribution over SAP Modules
ST10	Table Call Statistics for Table Buffer Tuning
ST11	Display Developer Traces
ST14	Application Analysis
ST22	ABAP Run-time Error Analysis
STAT	Local Transaction Statistics for troubleshooting and Tuning

Determining Performance Goals

The Basis team is delivering a service to the business community. The business community has specific requirements that certain transaction throughput has to be achieved per day, that batch jobs have to complete by certain times, and that users should have excellent response times.

In order for SAP to provide an expectable service to the business community, the following questions have to be answered and the answers should be accepted by the business community as well as the Basis team who commits to provide this level of service.

◆ What is desirable?

◆ What is possible?

◆ What is acceptable?

Every business uses different SAP functionality; they add different customizations to the SAP standard code. The business needs to identify each of their core transactions and business critical batch jobs. Once this is done, you need to define performance goals for each of these transactions. The list below defines an example of goals that you can set for your environment.

◆ **Average global dialog response time less than one second.** Another way to state this is that more than 80 percent of all transactions should complete within one second.

◆ **Certain transactions should complete within a specified amount of time.** The transactions that are used most in the system should be tuned. Users will perceive the most significant effect on overall performance when these transactions are tuned.

Typical SAP transaction execution times

Create Sales Order	VA01 < 1.5 seconds
Change Sales Order	VA02 < 1.5 seconds
Display Sales Order	VA03 < 1 second
Create a Delivery	VL01 < 2 seconds
Create Material	MM01 < 0.7 second
Post Account Document	FB01 < 0.6 second
Change Account Document	FB01 < 0.5 second

Display Account Document   FB01 < 0.4 second
Create Billing Document   VF01 < 1.5 seconds

◆ **Batch jobs have to complete within a given period.** A typical SAP system has a finite set of batch processes; these processes share a finite amount of memory and CPU resources. All the batch jobs in an SAP system have to share these resources. Some companies have batch jobs that have to complete within a strict amount of time in order to keep up with all the work to be performed. A batch schedule needs to be compiled to keep track of when each job should start and end. Another example would be a daily report that takes two days to complete. Jobs like these need to be tuned for optimal performance in order to keep a company competitive.

To achieve these goals you will have to tune the network, hardware, operating system, the database, and each of the ABAP programs involved. SAP also has OSS notes pertaining to performance in their troubleshooting knowledge base.

NOTE

Apply these performance notes before contacting SAP.

User Response Time

User response time is one of the most important factors determining if an SAP system is perceived to perform well or not. This type of response time is visible to the user community. If the system is performing well, but one user perceives the performance to be bad, the user community will say that SAP is not performing.

What is user response time? A typical user initiates a request on the SAP front end. This request is sent via a network to the SAP system where it enters the dispatcher queue. SAP services this request and sends it back to the user's front end. Response time is the elapsed time from the moment the initial request enters the dispatcher queue until the answer leaves the SAP system. Network transfer time is not taken into account. In long-distance or low-performance networks, this can lead to considerably longer, subjective response times.

User response time = Response time + Network transfer time

Response time is divided into wait time and dispatch time. The dispatch time consists of processing time, load time, roll in/out time, and database request time. The network time between the application servers and the database server is combined with the database request time. In other words, the database request performed on an application server will take longer than the time taken when the same request is performed on the database server. If the difference in database request time on the application server and database server is significant, you will have to consider that a network bottleneck exists.

Wait time is the time a user request waits for a work process to become available. The wait time starts accumulating as soon as a user request enters the dispatcher queue and stops when it leaves the dispatcher queue to be processed.

Dispatch time is the amount of time a user request occupies a work process. Dispatch time consists of the following:

◆ **Process time.** The time a work process spends processing in order to service a user request. Processing includes time spent on the CPU plus any other environmental overhead, like operating system paging, disk I/O, and networking.

◆ **Load time.** The time required for loading and generating objects like ABAP code as well as CUA and dynpro information obtained from the database.

◆ **Roll-in/out time.** The time required for loading and unloading user context data to and from a work process.

Figure 11-2 displays the navigational screen to all the different views on time distribution and other useful statistic screens. The screen in Figure 11-3 is usually the starting point for identifying performance bottlenecks.

Identifying Performance Bottlenecks

Performance troubleshooting starts with transaction ST03. This tool allows you to monitor anywhere from a month's worth of data down to a few minutes' worth of data. In Figure 11-3, a day's worth of data is analyzed.

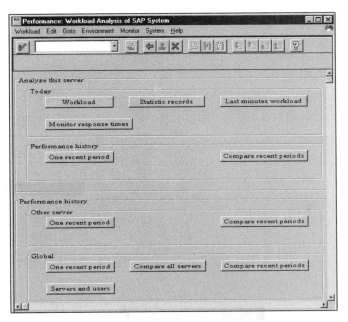

FIGURE 11-2 *ST03, Detail Analysis Menu*

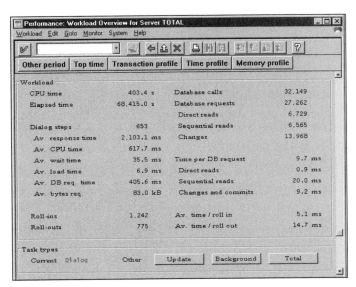

FIGURE 11-3 *ST03, Detail Analysis Menu, Workload*

Performance Is Bad for All Users

Execute transaction ST03, Detail Analysis Menu, Workload and analyze the response time. Ask yourself: "Which of the different time components are unacceptable?" Discussed below, you will find rules to assist you in identifying potential problems.

CPU Time Greater than 40 Percent of Response Time

Is the time that a request spends on the CPU unacceptably high?

If it is, then the only way to possibly improve performance is to analyze the ABAP code with ABAP traces. Analyze each statement for efficiency and recode the program. Use transaction SE30 to analyze the ABAP code.

CPU Time Far Less than Processing Time

Is the time spent on the CPU far less than the processing time?

This phenomenon is created by factors external to SAP, such as I/O bottlenecks, network problems, CPU bottlenecks, or memory bottlenecks. A frequent problem that causes this situation is operating system paging. Here are possible actions you can take to remedy the situation:

◆ Use transaction ST06 to analyze the operating system.

◆ Make use of a third-party network-monitoring tool to monitor the network.

◆ Use transaction ST06 to monitor the CPU load. If the load average is greater than three per specified period or if the percentage idle time is 0 percent, consider tuning the ABAP programs or buying more (and faster) CPUs.

◆ Use transaction ST06 to monitor the top CPU-consuming processes since external programs might also be the cause for CPU problems.

◆ Use transaction ST06 to check if paging is taking place. If no paging is taking place and some memory is still available, optimize SAP to run in the available memory. Use transaction ST02 to identify buffers that are swapping and require additional memory.

◆ If paging is taking place, use transaction ST02 to check the extended memory allocations for SAP buffers, database buffers, and roll and page buffers. Optimize these buffers to use less memory if possible; if not, buy more memory.

Wait Time Greater than 1 Percent of Response Time

Long wait times can only mean that for some reason, such as those following, not enough work processes are available:

◆ **Not enough work processes are configured.** Define more processes or make use of operational modes. Transaction SM50 and the CPU statistics within this transaction give valuable information on process usage. Ideally, one process of each type should always be free. In other words, one work process should have its accumulated CPU time equal to zero.

◆ **Processes are held up by long-running jobs or dialog programs making use of private memory.** Once a process makes use of private memory, it does not partake in user context switching anymore. SM50 is once again the transaction required to monitor these issues. A long-running program will have very long run times associated with it, and dialog processes in private mode will have a status PRIV associated with them.

◆ When you are monitoring a process (using transaction SM50) and you notice that the process is continuously stuck on semaphore 6 (roll administration semaphore), investigate for any resource conflict situations.

Load Time Greater than 10 Percent of Response Time

The SAP program buffer is probably configured incorrectly. Use transaction ST02 to analyze the program buffer situation. If the amount of free space and gaps are the same, the buffer needs attention. In most cases, the program buffer requires more memory.

Another indication that the program buffer is a bottleneck is transaction SM50. Analyze the action column for the action Load Report. If it occurs frequently, then the program buffer requires attention.

It happens frequently that the program buffer swaps extensively, although enough memory is available. As of SAP kernel release 3.1I patch level, the program buffer is divided into two sections. The 2048 program buffer entries are dedicated to large programs, and the entries after 2048 are assigned to small and medium-sized programs. A parameter named abap/buffersize_part1 defines the portion of memory within the program buffer assigned to the large programs. The delta is assigned to the small programs. How well you select the value for this parameter will determine how frequently the program buffer swaps.

Database Request Time Greater than 40 Percent of Response Time

◆ Check the database health with transaction ST04. Look at the buffer quality. It should be at least 95 percent. Check the reads per user calls (between 15 and 45) and make sure user calls per recursive calls is greater than 4.

◆ Use transaction ST02 to check the SAP table buffer qualities. The buffer qualities should be in the high 90 percentiles.

◆ Use transaction ST10 to identify tables that should be buffered and buffer them.

◆ Check for missing indexes using transaction DB02.

◆ Analyze individual database-intensive transactions. Transactions ST03 and STAT are very useful in analyzing transactions. Also, make use of transaction ST05 (SQL trace) to trace misbehaving programs and transactions. Tune any select statement that has potential and introduce additional indexes where required.

◆ Use transaction DB01 to identify any database lock-wait situations.

Tuning Rules of Thumb

There is a constant contest between developers and administrators on who should tune for performance. Administrators should identify all blatant performance bottlenecks and resolve them. As seen below, the most performance gain to be made is by writing optimal ABAP code. The SAP database and application should be tuned in the order that provides the highest performance gains:

◆ Application and SQL tuning—70 percent

◆ Memory—15 percent

◆ Disk—10 percent

◆ Memory contention—5 percent

ABAP Runtime Analysis

The objective with the ABAP Runtime Analyzer is to allow developers to analyze their ABAP code for unacceptable resource consumption. It can do the following:

◆ Assist in the detection of unnecessary database accesses

◆ Assist in the detection of CPU-intensive programming functions

◆ Assist in the detection of unnecessary calls to subroutines and function modules

◆ Assist in the detection of user-developed functions that replace existing SAP functions

The Tips and Tricks option contains a wealth of information on alternative coding choices to improve statement performance and allows you to compare the run time of different ABAP statements. Three parameters govern the ABAP Analyzer trace file at the operating system level:

    abap/atradir

    abap/atrapath

    abap/atrasizequota

Make sure that the directory that will contain the trace file has enough space to accommodate at least the default 10MB atrasizequota. This 10MB is usually not enough; you will probably have to increase the trace file size in order to accommodate all the trace information for long-running programs.

Execute transaction SE30; the screen in Figure 11-4 will be displayed. Enter the transaction or program that you want to analyze.

With Subroutines

With this option selected, the ABAP Analyzer will record the performance data of perform statements in the ABAP code.

With Internal Tables

With this option selected, the ABAP Analyzer will record the performance data for expensive READ, APPEND, COLLECTOR, and SORT statements. If

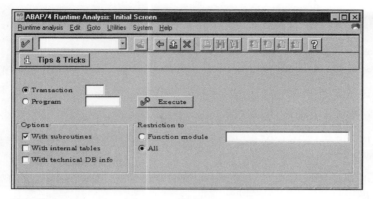

FIGURE 11-4 *ABAP Runtime Analysis: Initial Screen*

these statements are executed frequently within a report, this option should be selected in order to analyze the performance of these statements.

With Technical Database Information

With this option selected, the ABAP Analyzer will keep trace information on database and buffer operations.

Figure 11-5 displays a performance overview of the program that you are analyzing. The execution time is evaluated in microseconds. If a section of the execution time exceeds 50 percent of the total execution time, it is colored red—that section should be analyzed for possible performance improvements. In this case, it would be the database section. If the percentage execution time is less than 50 percent of the total execution time, the bar is colored green.

The statistics at the bottom of the screen specify the number of times a specific action or conversion took place.

Display Filter

Once you have analyzed the program in question, you can filter the results to display only what you deem necessary. In the initial ABAP Analyzer screen, select the menu items Edit, Display Filter. Select all the different categories that you want displayed. When you use the Hit List option of the ABAP Analyzer you will

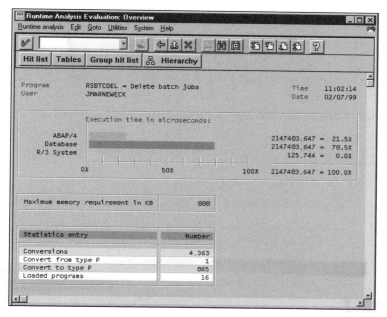

FIGURE 11-5 *Runtime Analysis Evaluation: Overview*

notice that only the options you selected are displayed. Table 11-1 lists the different filter options available and Figure 11-5 displays the results of the filtering process. The column on the right displays the Hit List Identifier.

Table 11-1 Filter Groups

Display Filter Group	Statement Hit List Identifier
Application Program	None
System Program	S
Database Interface (Open SQL)	OpenS
Database Interface (Native SQL)	NatSQ
Match Code Processing	MC
Screen System Processing Steps	Dy
Memory and Program Run Time Management	M

Hit List

The Hit List (Figure 11-6) displays the most expensive statements sorted by gross time and filtered according to the display filter. The analyzer allows the programmer to drill down to the actual source code. One of the columns (No.) is the number of times a statement was executed. Statements that are called frequently and that are relatively slow should be tuned first in order to make the most significant performance improvement. Each statement is associated with a statement type:

ABAP statements	" "
Database statements	"DB"
R/3 systems statements	"Syst"

Tables

This function lists all the tables accessed during the execution of the program. It also indicates the number of times it was accessed, the type of table, and the buffering method. With these statistics, you can determine if a small, frequently accessed table should be buffered (see Figure 11-7).

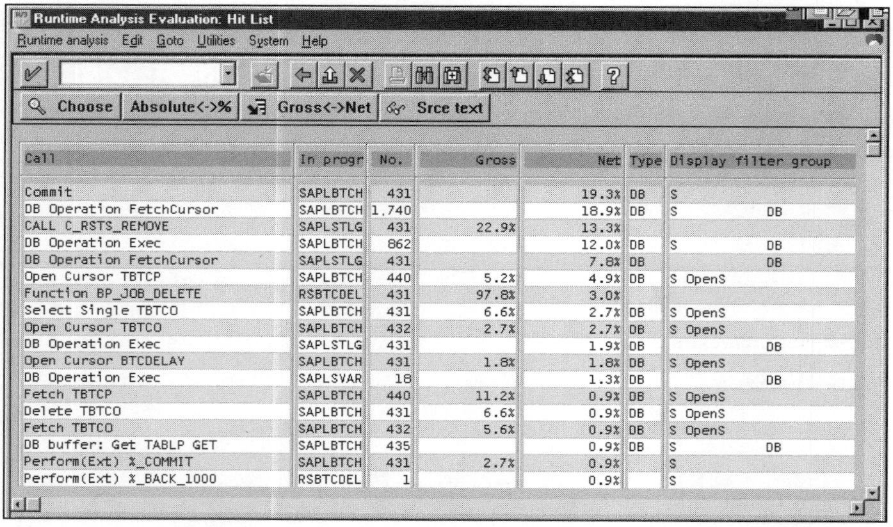

Call	In progr	No.	Gross	Net	Type	Display filter group
Commit	SAPLBTCH	431		19.3%	DB	S
DB Operation FetchCursor	SAPLBTCH	1.740		18.9%	DB	S DB
CALL C_RSTS_REMOVE	SAPLSTLG	431	22.9%	13.3%		
DB Operation Exec	SAPLBTCH	862		12.0%	DB	S DB
DB Operation FetchCursor	SAPLSTLG	431		7.8%	DB	DB
Open Cursor TBTCP	SAPLBTCH	440	5.2%	4.9%	DB	S OpenS
Function BP_JOB_DELETE	RSBTCDEL	431	97.8%	3.0%		
Select Single TBTCO	SAPLBTCH	431	6.6%	2.7%	DB	S OpenS
Open Cursor TBTCO	SAPLBTCH	432	2.7%	2.7%	DB	S OpenS
DB Operation Exec	SAPLSTLG	431		1.9%	DB	DB
Open Cursor BTCDELAY	SAPLBTCH	431	1.8%	1.8%	DB	S OpenS
DB Operation Exec	SAPLSVAR	18		1.3%	DB	DB
Fetch TBTCP	SAPLBTCH	440	11.2%	0.9%	DB	S OpenS
Delete TBTCO	SAPLBTCH	431	6.6%	0.9%	DB	S OpenS
Fetch TBTCO	SAPLBTCH	432	5.6%	0.9%	DB	S OpenS
DB buffer: Get TABLP GET	SAPLBTCH	435		0.9%	DB	S DB
Perform(Ext) %_COMMIT	SAPLBTCH	431	2.7%	0.9%		S
Perform(Ext) %_BACK_1000	RSBTCDEL	1		0.9%		S

FIGURE 11-6 *Hit List*

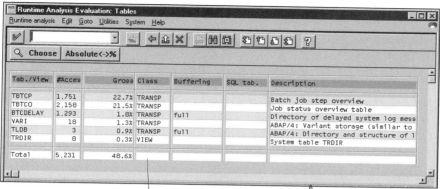

FIGURE 11-7 *Runtime Analysis: Tables* → type of table

Group Hit List

The group hit list classifies statements into the following listed categories:

- ◆ PERFORM
- ◆ CALL FUNCTION
- ◆ MODULE
- ◆ Open SQL
- ◆ Native SQL
- ◆ Database operations
- ◆ Buffering operations
- ◆ EXPORT/IMPORT,...
- ◆ Dataset
- ◆ Internal tables
- ◆ Generation
- ◆ Various

Hierarchy

The Hierarchy display option lists all the statements in chronological order. The Lv column indicates the call depth of each statement (see Figure 11-8).

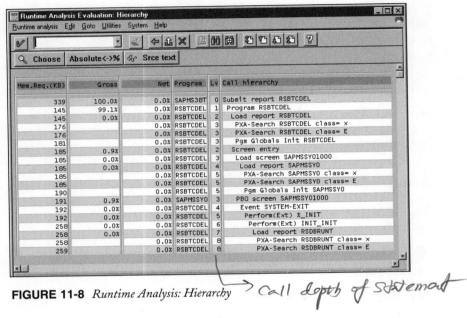

FIGURE 11-8 *Runtime Analysis: Hierarchy* → Call depth of statement

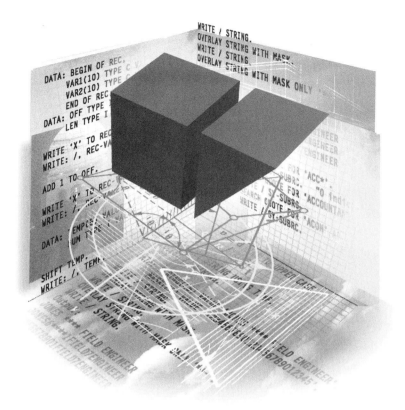

Chapter 12

**Database
Administration**

In This Chapter

As a Basis administrator, you assume the role of DBA (database administrator) as well. The different roles and responsibilities are discussed in the "Identifying Personnel Roles" section of Chapter 2. SAP runs on many different database platforms, such as Oracle, Informix Online, DB2 for AIX, MS SQL Server, and ADABAS. SAP defines a multitude of tools in CCMS to assist the Basis administrator with administering, tuning, and monitoring the database. SAP also attempts to define a single interface to all these different platforms in order to enable Basis administrators to move from one platform to another, making use of the same tools. SAP succeeds quite well, but all these database platforms still provide different functionality, and for this reason you will see differences in the tools. Where the database platforms intersect, the SAP tools are consistent.

This chapter addresses database administration from an Oracle point of view, but the SAP truths within this chapter will pertain to most databases. You have to secure your database by changing the default passwords, you have to develop a backup strategy, and you will have to maintain your database. The procedures within this are Oracle centric, but as a Basis administrator knowing the specifics of your database, you should not find it difficult to compile procedures specific to your environment. At the end of the chapter, you will find a procedure for a database copy. This procedure includes both the steps for Oracle and the steps that you need to execute within SAP in order to complete a successful database copy.

Roles and Responsibilities of a Basis Administrator as DBA

A Basis administrator cannot manage an SAP system without some DBA experience. The database is an integral part of the SAP system—someone needs to assume responsibility for it. The Basis administrator as DBA should be the gatekeeper of the database, handling the following:

- ◆ Installing and upgrading the database
- ◆ Assisting and managing the development process

- Database monitoring and tuning
- Database security
- Backup and recovery strategies
- Scheduled database maintenance

Installing and Upgrading the Database

Chapters 2, 4, and 16 discuss this topic in detail. Here's a brief summary of a few DBA tasks:

- Plan the physical and logical database layouts in order to improve performance and to minimize resource consumption.
- Execute the installation and upgrade utilities.
- Configure the database environment and parameters for optimal performance.

Assisting and Managing the Development Process

Traditionally, the DBA plays a very important role in the development process. The resources that you require for a development project are business and functional analysts, database administrators (analyst), developers, and testers.

The database is the responsibility of the Basis administrator. You have to keep it healthy because developers and business analysts will not. You as the Basis administrator will make sure that the database stays manageable. The development role of Basis administrators is not very prominent because most companies do not partake in development projects. Then again, companies do introduce some level of custom-developed tables and indexes, and these need to be managed.

Any custom-developed SAP table or index goes to the PSAPUSERx tablespaces. Because all of the custom-developed database objects go there, serious performance manageability and resource problems can arise. If you do not watch the developers, they will create tables and indexes within the other SAP standard tablespaces, which is also unacceptable. A well-defined custom database development plan will have a place for each table and index, optimizing the environment for performance and manageability.

The responsibilities of a Basis administrator as DBA in the development process are to:

- Define entity diagrams

◆ Define physical table layout diagrams

◆ Determine space requirements

◆ Establish performance requirements

◆ Generate execution plans

It is not the intention of this book to explain the development effort. A brief summary of the above-mentioned activities should suffice.

Define Entity Diagrams

Tables in a database are related to each other. The relationships are one-to-one, one-to-many, and many-to-many. The DBA's task also involves the normalization of the database. The new custom-developed database should have all these relationships defined and optimized.

Define Physical Table Layout Diagrams

The entity diagrams are converted into diagrams containing the physical table layouts with the fields and field attributes.

Determine Space Requirements

The new tables will introduce additional disk space consumption. Each of these tables should be analyzed and the immediate and long-term space requirements should be calculated. These statistics should assist you in placing the tables in the correct database space and disk.

Establish Performance Requirements

Some tables will contain master data; others will contain transaction data. Master data is usually read-intensive. Transaction data is quite dynamic and change-intensive. Tables should be placed very carefully in order to avoid contention between them; in other words, keep any two very active tables separated from each other. Execute transaction **ST03**, follow menu path Detail analysis menu, Workload, Goto, Profiles, Table profile to display a list of tables sorted in descending order according to the activity of each table. If the tables at the top of the list cause performance bottlenecks and disk contention, you can place each of these tables in its own tablespace and then distribute the tablespaces over multiple different disks.

Generate Execution Plans

Queries against the tables should also be optimized. All of the database technologies provide tools that assist you in explaining the execution plan of SQL statements. The SQL statements should be analyzed for performance and index usage.

Database Monitoring and Tuning

Chapter 9 explained tuning the SAP R/3 system, including the database. To briefly recap, you must plan the initial database layout well, resolve contention between existing tables, keep fragmentation low, if possible reorganize tables frequently, tune the database buffers, manage the rollback segments, manage the redo files, manage the database processes, and so on.

Database Security

[handwritten: SAPR3 — sap   SYSTEM
OPS$ <SID>ADM   SYS]

In the SAP environment, *database security* is not the same as in a regular database application environment. SAP manages the user security, although SAP does have a few users at the database level. Incredible as it may sound, these users need to be secured. Oracle has two users—SAPR3 and OPS$<SID>ADM—depending on the operating system platform. The default password for SAPR3 is sap. Bad news—the default password is now known to everyone reading this book, so if your password is still sap, then anybody who knows SAP can access your data.

One of the first tasks in installing the database is to secure it. In the Oracle realm, this means that you have to secure the users SAPR3, SYSTEM, and SYS.

Changing the SAPR3 Password in Oracle

Replace "<SID>" with the corresponding <SID> of your system, and replace the word "password" with anything except "password" or "sap". With the following three steps you effectively change the password for SAPR3. The user OPS$<SID>ADM owns a table called SAPUSER. When SAP starts up it will access this table as user OS user <SID>adm, read this table, and retrieve the password for SAPR3. SAP then uses this retrieved password to log on to Oracle. All the steps below are SQL commands that need to be executed in the **sqlplus** utility.

1. `sqlplus system/<password>`
2. `update OPS$<SID>ADM.SAPUSER` *(handwritten: table has password for SAPR3)*

   `set passwd = 'password' where userid = 'SAPR3';`
   (handwritten: new password)

3. `alter user SAPR3 identified by password;`

If OPS$<SID>ADM does not exist, complete the following steps:

1. `create user OPS$<SID>ADM identified externally`

    `default tablespace PSAPUSER1D`

    `temporary tablespace PSAPTEMP;`

2. `grant dba, connect, resource to OPS$<SID>ADM with admin option;`

3. `create table OPS$<SID>ADM.SAPUSER`

    `(USERID varchar2(256), PASSWD varchar2(256));`

4. `insert into OPS$<SID>ADM.SAPUSER values ('SAPR3', 'password')`

The OPS$User is functionality that Oracle provides, which allows a user to be validated using OS security. The word *User* in OPS$User represents the OS user that you want to allow to log on to Oracle without a password.

OS user 'User' can login to oracle as
$ sqlplus /

<table>
<tr><td>▶</td><td>TIP</td></tr>
</table>

When you are creating a user in Oracle, you can use an alternative clause `identified by password` instead of `identified externally`. Do not make the password for OPS$<SID>ADM the default password, *sap*. It defeats the purpose of having OPS$<SID>ADM functionality. Make the password something obscure that nobody can guess.

(no need password)

When SAP starts up, it uses OPS$<SIDADM> to log on to the Oracle database, reads the table SAPUSER, retrieves the secret password from the table, and uses the password to log on as SAPR3.

sapdata b (brtools)
is w Ith os
user ora<sid)
not<SID>adm

With the above-mentioned steps, you secure the user SAPR3, but when you secure the SYSTEM and SYS users, the **brtools** start requesting a password for the SYSTEM user. It becomes a problem when you use these tools in scripts. To get around this problem you need to create an OPS$ORA<SID> user as follows:

```
create user OPS$ORA<SID> identified externally
      default tablespace PSAPUSER1D
      temporary tablespace PSAPTEMP;
grant dba, connect, resource to OPS$ORA<SID> with admin option;
```

> **TIP**
>
> The **brtools** can then be used with the **–u /** option, which allows you to use it within scripts without specifying a username and password.

Backup and Recovery Strategies

Companies can go bankrupt for the very simple reason that they lack an established backup and restore strategy. Imagine a company that does backups every day for years and is very lucky; the company's database with all the financial data never crashes. When the company's luck eventually runs out and the database crashes, the first thing that company does is to recall the backups it has so diligently made. Alas, the company had never tested a restore! The company ends up filing for bankruptcy because it's lost all of its debtor and creditor information. This company was not running SAP. The following sections describe the capabilities that will help you avoid this same fate.

Physical Backups

The physical data blocks of the database are copied from disk to some kind of backup media. In other words, the data files are copied from disk to backup tape. *Physical backups* involve two backup strategies: offline (cold) and online (hot) backups. Either of these can be executed having ARCHIVELOG mode on or off. An online backup with ARCHIVELOG mode on allows for production uptime for seven days a week, 24 hours a day.

Logical Backups

Logical backups are defined as a copy of the data from within the database to backup media. A logical backup does not record the physical location of the retrieved data. Oracle tools that will accomplish logical backups are the import and export utilities. The utility R3load can also be used to load and unload data to and from the database. Logical backups work well on small databases, which is usually not the situation with SAP systems. **sapdba** has an option (option Export/Import on the initial screen) to export and import. *Exporting* the database is making a logical backup, and *importing* it is restoring the database. Another term for this is *reorganizing* the database, but reorganizing and backing up a database are completely different functions. Reorganizing the database will be discussed later in this chapter in the section called "Database Reorganization."

Online Backup (Hot Backup) *(must be in ARCHIVELOG)*

During an online backup, the database is open and operating in ARCHIVELOG mode. The users are logged in to SAP executing their transactions and may perhaps notice small performance degradations while the backup is taking place. An *online backup* should run during periods of low user and data change activity. In other words, do not run the online backup during periods in which write-intensive batch programs are running. The following is an overview of the steps that should be in place for a full online backup:

1. ARCHIVELOG mode must be on.
2. Make a full backup of all the data files.
3. Make a backup of all the archive log files immediately after the online backup. *(online redo log is not necessary)*
4. Make a backup of one of the control files.

If these steps are in place, then offline and online backups are equivalent. When you use the standard SAP tool **brbackup**, these steps are already in place. Online backups should run at least daily on a production system. On test and development systems, depending on the data activity, you might consider doing backups less often.

Offline Backup (Cold Backup)

An *offline backup* is the opposite of the online backup—SAP and the database are stopped. The following is an overview of the steps that should be in place for a full offline backup:

1. SAP and the database must be stopped.
2. Make a full backup of all the data files, control files, and the online redo log files.

SAP has the functionality that allows you to execute an offline backup while SAP is running. *SAP running* does not mean that users can use SAP during the time that the offline backup is taking place. SAP only provides functionality that allows application servers to be up and running while an offline backup is taking place. The goal with this technology is to allow the SAP buffers to retain their information, thus avoiding the performance loss caused by reloading the buffers. SAP has OSS notes that describe this technology in detail. The crux of the matter is that the work processes on the application servers wait until the database is open, and then they reconnect themselves on request to the database.

The parameters that define this technology are the following:

```
rsdb/reco_sosw_for_db = OFF
rsdb/reco_trials      = 3
rsdb/reco_sleep_time  = 5
```

Database Backup

In order to be able to restore the database, you must follow a few important rules:

- Maintain multiple copies of the control file. SAP enforces this by having three copies of the control file. Two of these reside in the directory sapdata1 and sapdata2 file systems, and one resides in the /oracle/<SID>/dbs directory on a UNIX system. These control files should be located on physically different devices, mounted on different device controllers. The initSID.ora file contains the location information for the control files. The entry in initSID.ora appears as follows:

  ```
  control_files = ( /oracle/SID/sapdata1/cntrl/cntrlSID.dbf,
  /oracle/SID/sapdata2/cntrl/cntrlSID.dbf, /oracle/SID/dbs/cntrlSID.dbf )
  ```

  To add another control file:

  1. Shut down SAP and the database.
  2. Copy one of the current control files to a new location.
  3. Add the new location to the control_files parameter in the initSID.ora file.
  4. Start the database.

- The online redo log files should be multiplexed or mirrored. Either the OS or Oracle should take care of the redo log mirrors. If Oracle is doing the mirroring, make sure that the mirror copy in each redo log group is on a different disk. In SAP terms make sure origlogA and mirrlogA are on different disks and controllers; the same is true for origlogB and mirrlogB. The redo log file information is displayed using the V$_LOGFILE view. To create additional log files, execute the following commands:

  1. Execute **svrmgrl**.
  2. Issue the command: **connect internal;**
  3. Issue the command: **alter database add logfile group 15**
     ('/oracle/<SID>/origlogA/log_g15m1.dbf',
     /oracle/<SID>/mirrlogB/log_g15m1.dbf') size 20M;

◆ Always keep two copies of the archive redo log files on different backup media. In the SAP environment, the ARCH process writes the online redo log files that reached the full capacity of 20M as in the example above, to the /oracle/<SID>/saparch file system. **brarchive** backs up these offline archives to tape. Make sure that you back up these archived logs to two different tapes.

◆ Make sure that your archive log files are mirrored. You need these files to be able to restore to any given point in time. If the archive log files are destroyed and you do not have a mirror copy, be advised that you will have to do an incomplete restore, probably losing production data in the process.

◆ Whenever the database structure is changed by adding, moving, or dropping a data file, make a backup of the control file. **sapdba** will prompt you to make a backup after you have added a data file.

The Oracle command to back up the control file is:

```
alter database backup controlfile to 'file specification';
```

◆ Run the database in ARCHIVELOG mode. **sapdba** has an option to toggle ARCHIVELOG mode. Make sure SAP is not running when you do this. Execute **sapdba**, select **Archive Mode**, and **Toggle Database Log Mode**. This will shut down the database and restart it depending on your input.

sapdba has another option: Toggle Automatic Archival. When this option is set to automatic, the ARCH process archives all the online archive logs to the archive file system. When this option is set to do manual archiving, you as administrator will choose the time when archiving should be done. Every time the command archive log all is executed, Oracle will archive the log files.

Full Backup vs. Tablespace (Partial) Backup

We already touched on the definition of a *full database backup*. It is an image backup of all the data files, control files, and redo files, online or offline.

When a few highly active tablespaces are selectively backed up, this is called a *partial backup.* This strategy comes into play when databases become too big (100GB and bigger) and there is not enough time in a day to back up the full database. Making partial backups is a good solution, but it is still wise to make a full backup of the whole database at least once a week.

Complete vs. Incomplete Recovery

During any recovery process the first thing that should be established before any restore effort is initiated is: Will the restore effort recover all the data or just a portion of the data? A recovery effort with no data loss is known as a *complete recovery*. An *incomplete recovery* then is a recovery attempt in which only a portion of the data is recovered. An incomplete recovery is usually necessary when an archive file or online redo log file gets lost. It is important to determine if data will be lost because that determines the recovery strategy. An incomplete data recovery has an additional requirement: After the incomplete recovery is done, the database must be opened with the reset logs option. The following is the Oracle command that accomplishes this:

after incomplete recovery

```
alter database open resetlogs;
```
→ *DB open with reset logs option*

Please note that this command must be executed after the restore. If you do it before the restore, you will not be able to restore the database.

sapdba Full/Partial and Complete/Incomplete Recoveries

The following four figures pertain to the **sapdba** recovery strategies. Options a, b, and c in Figure 12-1 are associated with Figures 12-2, 12-3, and 12-4, respectively.

Option a, **Partial Restore and Complete Recovery**, in Figure 12-1, allows for partial complete recoveries. Partial means that only a selected few data files will be restored, and complete means that all the data will be recovered. You will notice that the redo logs and the control files are prerequisites. The reason is that a complete recovery can only be performed with these files available. If, say, two of the control files are missing, you can copy the remaining control file to the locations where the other two should have been.

incomplete

Option b, **Full Restore and Recovery**, allows for full restores and incomplete recoveries. Based on an administrator-supplied time, the database will be recovered up to that point. If all the redo logs were destroyed, a time should be selected that falls within the last time an online redo log file was archived. (Check the database logs.)

Option c, **Reset the Database**, is a last resort. With this option, you can restore a database without any roll forward recovery, although one of the sub-options allows you to recover manually. This manual option requires Oracle recovery knowledge.

Figure 12-2 displays the manual and automatic recovery options for **sapdba**. Always attempt automatic recovery first. If automatic recovery fails, you should

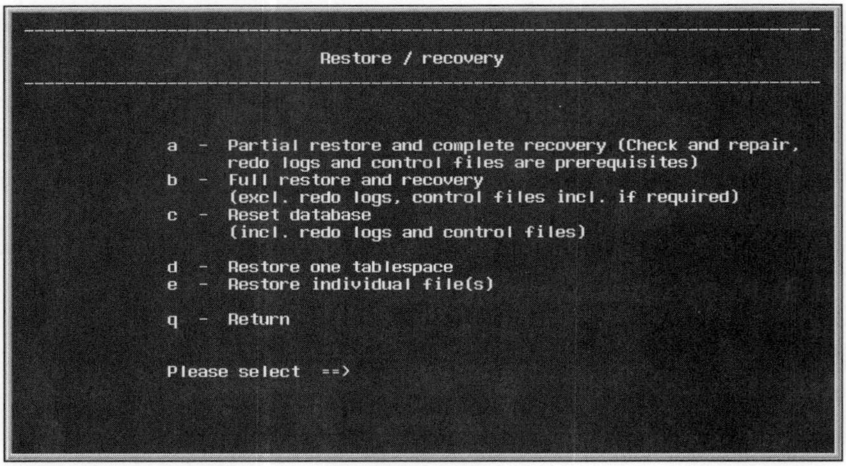

```
-------------------------------------------------------------------
                        Restore / recovery
-------------------------------------------------------------------


    a  -  Partial restore and complete recovery (Check and repair,
          redo logs and control files are prerequisites)
    b  -  Full restore and recovery
          (excl. redo logs, control files incl. if required)
    c  -  Reset database
          (incl. redo logs and control files)

    d  -  Restore one tablespace
    e  -  Restore individual file(s)

    q  -  Return


    Please select  ==>
```

FIGURE 12-1 *Full, partial, and complete restore capabilities of sapdba Version 40B*

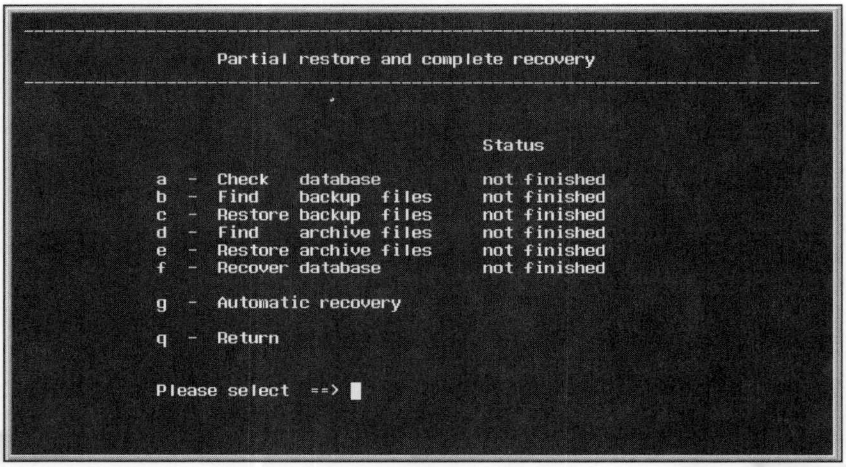

```
-------------------------------------------------------------------
             Partial restore and complete recovery
-------------------------------------------------------------------


                                          Status
    a  -  Check    database               not finished
    b  -  Find     backup   files         not finished
    c  -  Restore backup   files          not finished
    d  -  Find     archive files          not finished
    e  -  Restore archive files           not finished
    f  -  Recover database                not finished

    g  -  Automatic recovery

    q  -  Return


    Please select  ==> ■
```

FIGURE 12-2 *Partial Restore and Complete Recovery (sapdba Version 40B)*

manually follow options a through f. For these recovery options to be successful make sure your control files and redo log files exist.

Figure 12-3 displays the **sapdba** options that allow for an incomplete recovery. It does a full restore of all the data files and rolls through the redo logs up to the time specified with option b.

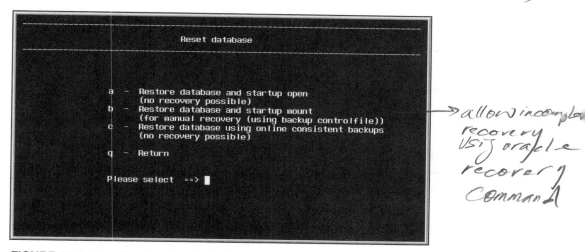

```
------------------------------------------------------------
                    Full Restore and Recovery
------------------------------------------------------------


    DATABASE STATE    : open
    RESTORE / RECOVER: disallowed (see status)

                                            Current setting

    A - Select a full online/offline backup
    b - Recover until                         now
    c - Show status
    D - Restore and recover

    q - Return


    Please select  ==>  ▮
```

FIGURE 12-3 *Full Restore and Recovery (sapdba Version 40B)*   *(incomplete recovery)*

```
------------------------------------------------------------
                         Reset database
------------------------------------------------------------



        a   -   Restore database and startup open
                (no recovery possible)
        b   -   Restore database and startup mount
                (for manual recovery (using backup controlfile))
        c   -   Restore database using online consistent backups
                (no recovery possible)

        q   -   Return

        Please select  ==>  ▮
```

→ allow incomplete
recovery
using oracle
recovery
command

FIGURE 12-4 *Reset Database (sapdba Version 40B)*

Option a in Figure 12-4 restores the full database and opens the database as soon
as the restore is complete. If the database is opened without the recover command
being invoked, the database will not be recovered any further and it will not be
possible to continue with the restore process. At this point, the database is consistent and ready for use; you obviously have lost all the roll forward information.

Option b in Figure 12-4 allows for incomplete recoveries. Once again, if a database is restored incompletely, you have to execute the RESETLOGS command in Oracle once the restore process is complete. This option leaves the database in a database mount state. This allows the administrator to intervene manually and to restore the database manually using the Oracle recover commands.

Now you can use the **svrmgrl** utility to proceed with the recovery as follows:

1. Execute **svrmgrl**
2. Issue the command `connect internal;`
3. You have three restore options, depending on the situation, from which you can choose:

   a. `recover database until cancel;`
   b. `recover database until time 'YYYY-MM-DD:HH:MM:SS';`
   c. `recover database until cancel using backup controlfile;`

   These options are discussed below.
4. Issue the command `alter database open resetlogs;`

Restoring the Database Until Cancel or Until Time

Until cancel allows you to recover one archive log file at a time. After a log file was applied, Oracle will give you the option to cancel. You will need this strategy if one or more of your archive logs are bad and you are unable to recover it.

Until time is used to do a recovery to a point in time that you know the database is consistent and correct. You will need to use this type of recovery when users introduce data into the system that causes the data to loose its integrity.

Restoring the Database Using a Backup Control File

With recovery option `recover database until cancel using backup controlfile;` you have two choices: you can either restore one of the backup control files that you have made so diligently after every database structure change or you can create a new control file if the database is consistent.

The steps to create a control file and to recover are as follows:

1. Before attempting this recovery method, make sure you have a backup of all the available redo log files, data files, and control files.
2. Execute **svrmgrl**

3. Issue the command **connect internal;**
4. Issue the command **startup nomount;**
5. Issue the create controlfile command. (See the Oracle documentation.)
6. Perform any recovery if needed.
7. Issue the command **alter database open [no]resetlogs;**
8. Issue the command **shutdown normal;**
9. Make a full backup of the database.

In order to use a backup control file in the recovery process, you have to restore the backup control file and copy it into the directories where the control files should reside. If you do a complete recovery, it is not necessary to execute the RESETLOGS option.

Summary of Backup Strategies and Alternative Strategies

You as Basis administrator will have to compile a sound backup strategy best suited for your environment. Below are a few strategy considerations that will assist you in compiling your own:

1. Make an offline backup once a week and online backups every day. Archive the offline redo log files to two different locations. Back up the archives after every online backup. Before the archive backup is executed, execute the Oracle command **alter system switch logfile;** once for each log file group defined in the database. The disadvantage is that production is affected during the offline backup. The advantage is that you have a consistent backup at least one a week.

2. Make only online backups every day of the week. Archive the offline redo log files to two different locations. Back up the archives after every online backup. Before the archive backup is executed, execute the Oracle command **alter system switch logfile;** once for each log file group defined in the database. There is no difference between this online backup and the previously discussed offline backup.

3. For big databases (larger than 100GB), consider making backups of only the highly active tables. A full online or offline backup should be executed at least once a week.

4. Copy the database to different backup disks or a different computer system and run an offline backup from that location. The advantages of this are fast backups and having a backup readily available on disk for immediate restore. The disadvantage is that it requires additional disk space or hardware.

5. On the market today are technologies that implement disk arrays with three-disk mirror sets. The objective is to break the third mirror from the set, make a backup, and join the disk back to the set. The advantage of this is minimal production downtime during the backup, but these solutions are typically very expensive.

brbackup, brarchive, and brrestore

These three executables are the tools SAP uses to back up and restore the database. These utilities can be used interactively or through the **sapdba** utility.

init<DBSID>.sap *(brtool set)*

The init<DBSID>.sap file contains the initialization parameters for the **brtool** set. It defines how the backup and restore process will function. It includes backup types, compression methods, backup volume names, and so on. This file is located in the /oracle/<SID>/dbs directory.

Init<DBSID>.dba *(sapdba)*

This profile configures the **sapdba** utility. This profile defines how **sapdba** will react when used. It contains default values for certain actions and questions **sapdba** asks of the Basis administrator. This file is located in the /oracle/<SID>/dbs directory.

Scheduled Database Maintenance and Support

An SAP database is a very dynamic entity. Data is constantly being changed, deleted, or added. Today the growth might seem constant; tomorrow the business may implement another SAP module, and the growth may double. The typical database also goes through different stages of activity—during any period end, database activity usually increases.

An ever-changing SAP environment should be monitored and managed accordingly, as summarized in the following:

- Always be on the lookout for performance issues (ST04).
- Monitor the memory and buffer qualities (ST04).
- Monitor the growth of the database and disk space consumption (DB02).
- Monitor for disastrous database error messages (ST04).
- Manage the database extents (sapdba).
- Monitor for exclusive locks (DB01).
- Monitor free space and free space fragmentation (DB02).
- Monitor the archive disk space (OS).
- Verify the integrity of the database (Oracle DBV).

Capacity Planning

[handwritten: DB growth → free space in DB → free space in FS, volume group]

Database capacity planning is an integral part of the Basis administrator's responsibilities. You constantly have to add new data files to accommodate the growth within the database. **sapdba** has the functionality to add new data files to the database. In order to prevent a disk space shortage, the database growth should be trended and compared against the current available space in the file systems. Transaction DB02 is a valuable tool for capacity planning (see Figure 12-5).

It is not enough to evaluate the database growth only against the available free space within the database. You also have to evaluate it against the space available in the different file systems and the volume groups.

Changing Storage Parameters

A few methods exist to change table storage parameters: by manually setting the Oracle *pctincrease* parameter or by implementing the **sapdba –next** functionality.

The next extent size for tables and indexes should be chosen wisely. The objectives should be the following:

- The block size of each segment should be a multiple of five. Oracle does automatic rounding up to a multiple of five blocks. For instance, if you select a size 32KB with the block size set to 8KB, Oracle rounds it to 40KB, which is five 8KB blocks.
- The different next extent sizes you use should be multiples of each other. In other words, define small next extent sizes for tables with low activity and large values for tables with high activity; these small values should

	Tablespace history											
History System Help												

02/17/1999 22:50:39   History of Tablespaces

Interval: 03/01/1998 - 02/01/1999   Measurements: 12   Scale: Month

Scale: Month	Size (Kbyte)		Free(Kbyte)	Used (Kbyte)		%-Used		Tables/Indices		Extents	
Tablespace	Total	Chg/month	Total	Total	Chg/month	Total	Chg	Total	Chg/month	Total	Chg/month
PSAPBTABD	11,771,904	376,087	1,213,136	10,558,768	501,961	89	4	1,951	13	2,356	50
PSAPBTABI	7,770,112	366,778	2,229,384	5,540,728	261,255	71	4	2,656	18	3,559	110
PSAPSTABD	2,719,744	93,091	742,408	1,977,336	60,276	72	2	2,144	26	2,480	59
PSAPCLUD	2,764,800	93,091	1,204,800	1,560,000	59,812	56	2	32	0	64	2
PSAPSTABI	1,572,864	0	239,328	1,333,536	36,276	84	2	2,893	32	3,465	86
PSAPPROTD	465,920	9,775	48,552	417,368	18,696	89	4	94	1	118	3
PSAPEL31HD	774,144	43,691	263,176	510,968	16,241	66	2	11	0	50	4
PSAPTEMP	1,048,576	0	1,019,448	29,128	15,316	2	1	2	1	14	7
PSAPPOOLD	1,048,576	0	353,048	695,528	10,695	66	1	4,241	62	4,544	90
PSAPPOOLI	527,392	9,309	81,064	446,328	9,426	84	1	4,320	64	4,772	104
PSAPPROTI	307,200	9,309	108,592	198,608	8,660	64	3	98	1	130	4
PSAPCLUI	262,144	0	90,080	172,064	7,338	65	3	32	0	58	2
PSAPES30DD	1,835,008	0	1,049,304	785,704	5,120	42	0	129	0	159	0
PSAPLOADD	1,294,336	0	1,294,104	232	3,724	0	0	6	0	6	0
PSAPROLL	1,945,600	0	1,125,592	820,008	2,982	42	0	20	0	40	0
PSAPES30DI	1,036,288	0	465,360	570,928	2,560	55	0	176	0	477	1
PSAPES31HD	2,560,000	0	431,728	2,128,272	1,787	83	0	160	0	547	1
PSAPES31HI	1,228,800	0	305,712	923,088	1,720	75	0	221	0	1,042	2
SYSTEM	262,144	0	166,096	96,048	761	36	0	144	0	439	1
PSAPEL31HI	61,440	0	46,288	15,152	573	24	1	12	0	22	1
PSAPDOCUD	24,992	0	8,640	16,352	262	65	1	98	1	112	2
PSAPDDICI	262,144	0	136,920	125,224	135	47	0	180	1	244	2
PSAPUSER1D	9,992	0	9,384	608	90	6	1	24	0	24	1
PSAPDOCUI	14,992	0	9,048	5,944	15	39	0	106	1	113	2
PSAPSOURCEI	149,992	0	112,744	37,248	7	24	0	55	0	56	0
PSAPDDICD	262,144	0	105,448	156,696	4	59	0	168	2	194	1
PSAPUSER1I	4,992	0	4,552	440	1	8	0	23	0	23	0

FIGURE 12-5 *Transaction DB02*

divide exactly into the bigger values. This strategy ensures that when segments are dropped, other new segments will be able to reuse that space and in doing so reduce the fragmentation of the database.

Changing Storage Parameters Manually

Execute **sapdba**, reorganization, Alter/Show table and index storage parameters, select a table or index, and alter/show the parameters. Figure 12-6 shows the sapdba screen for changing extent sizes. It will suggest a value that you may elect to use or not. Maintaining the next extent sizes manually is not always practical, especially if you want to change extent sizes consistently and you have thousands of tables to maintain and more than one Basis administrator changing them.

Pctincrease

The default value for this parameter is zero. With the value set to zero, the database will grow linearly, but any value above zero will cause geometrically high growth over time. Keep this value zero and choose the values for the initial and next extent sizes with care.

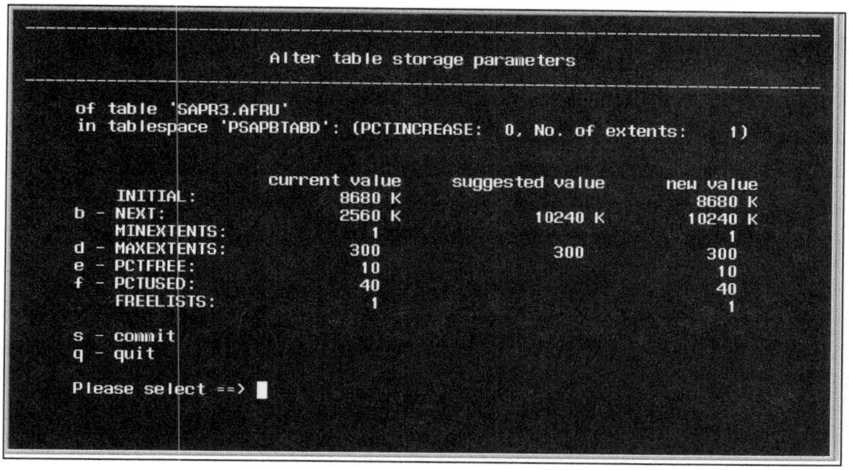

```
                    Alter table storage parameters
-----------------------------------------------------------------
of table 'SAPR3.AFRU'
in tablespace 'PSAPBTABD': (PCTINCREASE:  0, No. of extents:    1)

                        current value      suggested value      new value
        INITIAL:           8680 K                                8680 K
 b - NEXT:                 2560 K             10240 K           10240 K
     MINEXTENTS:              1                                     1
 d - MAXEXTENTS:            300                 300               300
 e - PCTFREE:               10                                    10
 f - PCTUSED:               40                                    40
     FREELISTS:              1                                     1

 s - commit
 q - quit

 Please select ==>
```

FIGURE 12-6 *Changing storage parameters manually using sapdba*

sapdba –next/-nextb <tablespace(s)>

This functionality is SAP's attempt to manage the growth of next extent sizes. It is very important to choose the category for custom-defined tables within SAP very carefully because this category is used in the calculation of the next extent size for each table.

sapdba -next does the following to determine the next extent size for a table or index:

◆ For the first value, it retrieves the current next extent size.

◆ For the second value, it calculates 10 percent of the total space allocated to the database object. If the object does not exist, it would use 10 percent of the initial extent size.

◆ For the third value, it uses the category definition for each table and index in the table DD09L to look up a potential next extent size from tables TGORA and IGORA as seen in Table 12-1.

The system attempts to use the maximum of these three values. If the maximum value is the last value looked up from TGORA or IGORA (the third value above), this value will be used, without any changes. When either of the other two values (the first and second values) is the greatest, the system has to do some calculation because this value is not necessarily contained in tables TGORA and IGORA.

The system will retrieve the value from one of these two tables that is just smaller than the maximum value (the first and second values) it has just calculated. If the retrieved value is less than five blocks of the calculated maximum value, the retrieved value will be used; otherwise, the next greater value in these tables will be used. If the value is greater than the largest value from TGORA or IGORA, this value is maintained except for when it does not deviate more than five Oracle blocks from the largest value.

Table 12-1 The Next Extent Sizes for Tables and Indexes as Used by sapdba

Table	Index	Next Extent Size in KB
0	0	16
	1	80
1	2	160
2	3	640
3	4	2560
	5	5120
4	6	10240
5	7	20480
6	8	40960
7	9	81920
8	10	163840
9	11	327680
10	12	655360
11	13	1310720
12	14	2621440
13		5242880
14		10485760
15		20971520

TIP

Always round the next extent sizes to five Oracle blocks.

As an example, presume the system determined the following two maximum values for two different tables:

Maximum value A	40,990
Maximum value B	41,960

Refer back to Table 12-1. For maximum value A, the system will choose 40,960 for the next extent size. For maximum value B, the system will choose 81,920 for the next extent size.

The **–nextb** option ignores the existing next extent size. With this option, **sapdba** uses only the other two methods to calculate the maximum size for the next extent value. This is useful in setting initial next extent values for all tables. Do this if you do not know the current state of your extent sizes.

Database Reorganizations

Reorganizing a complete database is a slow, time-consuming task. SAP databases are becoming so big that a complete reorganization of the database is usually impractical. Organizing the complete database is luckily not the only method of reorganizing a database. The different methods are to:

◆ Reorganize the entire database. This method is not practical for large databases, especially if production downtime should be minimized.

◆ Reorganize a tablespace with all its tables.

◆ Reorganize a single table or index or a list of tables and indexes.

◆ Move a data file from one location to another.

Figure 12-7 displays the different reorganization options **sapdba** provides.

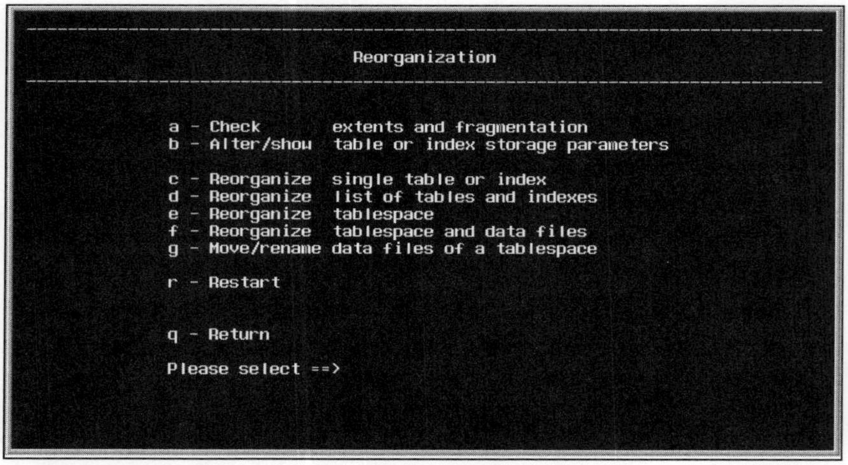

FIGURE 12-7 *The different reorganization options sapdba offers*

Reasons for Reorganization

As mentioned before, database reorganizations are slow and time-consuming; you do not reorganize a database on a whim, but you may need to do so for one of the following reasons:

◆ To better performance

◆ To reduce data and free space fragmentation

◆ Space and extent limitations

Reorganize to Better Performance

The following are a few things you can do to improve performance:

◆ Merge data for a single object into one extent. As data is added to tables, it fills up existing extents and new extents are created. After a while, the table will consist of multiple extents. You have to reorganize a table in order to combine these extents into a single extent. Theoretically, it should not be necessary to reorganize tables and indexes for extents, but practical experience does show that after reorganization the performance does improve. It depends on how you select your next extent sizes. If you use the sizes as listed in Table 12-1, performance should be fine. A problem usually arises when you choose next extent sizes randomly.

update / *add*

◆ Reduce record chaining and migration. Row chaining occurs when SAP updates records and the additional data causes the size of the data to be bigger than the physical block size. Oracle attempts to save the data within the block the data currently resides in. If Oracle is unable to find space in the same physical block, the data will be saved in one or more other blocks. Row migration occurs when new data is added; Oracle then attempts to find a free block that it can save the entire updated row in. When Oracle locates this free block it moves the row with the updated information from its old location to the new location. Both chaining and migration reduces I/O performance because it causes multiple reads at different locations on disk instead of only one.

◆ Distribute the data evenly among the individual blocks. You have to identify your read-intensive, and write-intensive objects (tables and indexes). For read-intensive objects, you will reduce the percentage free space per block, and for write-intensive you might increase the free space per block. To put the changes you made into effect, you need to reorganize the objects you changed. When you reorganize read-intensive objects for which you've decreased the percentage of free space, you will fill the data blocks with more data based on the percentage free value and vice-versa for write-intensive objects. *read-intensive → pctfree ↓* / *write-intensive → pctfree ↑*

◆ Sort the data within a table in a different order. When a table is frequently accessed using a specific index, it would be advisable to sort the table in the same order as that index.

Reorganize to Reduce Data and Free Space Fragmentation

◆ Defragment free space within objects.

◆ Merge data from a tablespace into one or more data files.

TIP

Always back up the database before attempting database reorganizations. Either an offline or an online backup will suffice, but an offline backup is preferred. The reason why the offline backup is preferred is because you know you have a consistent backup and you are not dependent on archive log files to restore to the state before the reorganizations took place.

Reorganize to Return within Physical Space and Extent Limitations

◆ A table or index has reached the maximum extents allowed.

◆ The maximum number of data files has been reached. This limit is determined by the OS and Oracle.

An Example Table-Sort-Order Reorganization

Sometimes it is necessary to change the order of the rows in a table. This is known as *clustering.* If an index is frequently used to access data within a table, it might improve performance if the data within that table is sorted in the same order as the index. In short, all the data is then clustered together, allowing the database to read as much data as possible in one read attempt instead of requiring multiple read attempts from different locations on disk.

You have to execute the following steps to create a script that will allow you to sort a table in a different order:

1. Log on as ora<SID>
2. Execute **exp sapr3/<password> rows=no tables = <table name>**. This command will export the table information to a dump file called expdat.dmp
3. Copy expdat.dmp to reorg_arfu.sql
4. Edit (vi on UNIX) a file called reorg_afru.sql so that it reads like the following example:

 NOTE

AFRU is the SAP table used in the example below. # is just a character to designate a different name than the original table. Most of the information required to sort the table is already contained in the reorg_AFRU.sql file. You only need to make it more readable and add a few extra lines.

```
rename AFRU to AFRU#;
create table AFRU
    pctfree 10
    pctused 40
    initrans 1
    maxtrans 255
```

```
        storage (initial 153616k
                 next 20480k
                 minextents 1
                 maxextents 100
                 pctincrease 0
                 freelists 1
                 freelist
                 groups 1)
    tablespace PSAPBTABD
    as select /*+ index (AFRU# AFRU_____0) */ *
        from AFRU#
        where MANDT = '200';
```

TIP

The where clause is very important. This example uses **MANDT** = **'200'**;. You need a strong where clause in order to get the optimizer to select the index you want to use. In this situation, all the records in the table belonged to client 200. If the table did not have records belonging only to client 200, you would need to use a different where clause. Do not use >=, <=, <, >, or any other range selecting operators.

```
    alter table AFRU# drop primary key;
    drop index AFRU_____1;
    drop index AFRU_____2;
    create unique index SAPR3.AFRU_____0
                ON SAPR3.AFRU (MANDT, RUECK, RMZHL)
                tablespace PSAPBTABI
                pctfree      10
                initrans      2
                maxtrans    255
                storage (initial    17936k
                         next        2560k
                         pctincrease    0
                    /* used space 17936k */
                         minextents     1
                         maxextents   100);
    create index SAPR3.AFRU_____2
                on SAPR3.AFRU (MANDT, AUFNR)
                tablespace PSAPBTABI
                pctfree      10
```

```
                    initrans    2
                    maxtrans  255
                    storage (initial      12816k
                            next          2560k
                            pctincrease      0
                        /* used space   12816k */
                            minextents       1
                            maxextents     100);

create index SAPR3.AFRU_____1
            on SAPR3.AFRU (MANDT, PDSNR)
            tablespace PSAPBTABI
            pctfree   10
                    initrans    2
                    maxtrans  255
            storage (initial      10256k
                    next          2560k
                    pctincrease      0
                /* used space   10256k */
                    minextents   1
                    maxextents 100);
analyze table AFRU compute statistics;
```

5. Execute **sqlplus sapr3/<password> @reorg_AFRU.sql**

6. Depending on the table size, this script can run a while.

Database Copy

Copying the SAP database from one host to another is an activity that a Basis administrator has to complete frequently. The database is copied from the production environment to the QA or test environment. This allows developers and business analysts to do integration testing on real production data. A typical copy procedure pertaining to a UNIX environment will be described in this section.

Copy Preparation Tasks

1. Check to see if the source database will fit on the target host's file systems.

   On the source host execute:

   bdf | grep sapdata > list_1.lst

On the target host execute:

```
bdf | grep sapdata > list_2.lst
```

Make sure that the values in the used column of list_1 are less than the corresponding values in the allocated column of list_2.

If the target system does not have enough space, contact the platform administrator (UNIX administrator) to either add more disks or extend the file systems.

2. Export any instance-specific data from the SAP system on the target system. This is not required most of the time, but if target-specific data exists that can be exported and imported, do so because it makes the configuration process easier. Below you will find a list of instance-specific data that can be exported and re-imported. The information in parentheses is the transaction or the program that you need to execute in order to export or import the relevant data.

   - User masters (transaction SCC2)
   - Interface customizations (SE01—build an object list)
   - Target-specific device types for printers (RSTXSCRP)
   - Target-specific code pages (RSTXCPAG)
   - ABAP queries (RSAQR3TR)
   - Export any other target-specific data you can identify in your environment

3. Make screen dumps of all target host-specific configuration screens in order to be able to reconfigure the target settings after the database copy. Below, you will find a list of screens that you might consider capturing before you do the database copy.

   - Operational modes (RZ04)
   - Logon groups (SMLG)
   - RFC destinations (SM59)
   - Transport system configuration (SE06)
   - TXCOM (SM54)
   - THOST (SM55)
   - The SAP license on the target host (**saplicense –show**)
   - Any other configuration screens you have in your environment

Database Copy Tasks

1. On the target system, stop SAP, the OS Collector, the SAP Router, Oracle, and the Oracle Listener.

   a. Execute: **stopsap** (stops SAP and Oracle)

   b. Execute: **saposcol −k** (stops the OS Collector)

   c. Execute: **saprouter −s** (stops the SAP Router)

   d. Execute: **lsnrctl stop** (stops the Oracle Listener)

2. Delete all the data files on the target system by executing the following commands:

   a. **cd /oracle/<SID>**

   b. **rm -rf sapdata*/*_*** (removes data files)

   c. **rm -rf sapdata*/cntrl** (removes control files)

   d. **rm −f dbs/cntrl<SID>.dbf** (removes the control file)

   e. **rm −rf /oracle/<SID>/sapreorg/***

   f. **rm −rf /oracle/<SID>saparch/***

   g. Remove any other control files the database might have.

   h. Depending on the restore utilities that you are using, you might need to create all the subdirectories in the sapdata file systems. If the restore utility is able to create the directories, you can skip this step. Make a listing of all the data file directories on the source system and re-create them on the target system.

   i. It might also be necessary to re-create the cntrl directories in sapdata1 and sapdata2. Execute the following commands:

   ```
   mkdir sapdata1/cntrl
   mkdir sapdata2/cntrl
   ```

3. Create a symbolic link on the target system in order to let the system think it is restoring the database on the original system. Execute the following commands:

   ```
   cd /oracle
   ls -s <target SID> <source SID>
   ```

   original control files has location of data file in <source SID> only

4. Get a very recent backup of the source system.

5. Restore this backup on the target system.

6. The file ownership of the data files should now be incorrect on the target system. The files and directories will be owned by a user defined on the source system. You will need to switch user to *root* in order to be able to change the ownership of the files and directories. Assign a new owner called **ora<SID>** who belongs to a group **dba** to all **sapdata** files and directories. Execute the following commands in sequence:

```
su root
cd /oracle/<SID>
chown -R ora<SID>:dba sapdata*/*_*
```

7. The following step is very important. You need to re-create the control files on the target system, and the method to use is to generate a control trace file on the source system. Copy this trace file to the target system and make the necessary adjustments. This trace file should represent the database that was backed up and that will be used in this database copy effort. If it does not, you will have to modify the trace file to reflect the correct database settings.

   a. On the source system, log on as ora<SID>

   b. Execute: **svrmgrl**

   c. Issue the command: **connect internal;**

   d. Issue: **alter database backup controlfile to trace;**

   e. Issue: **exit;**

   f. Execute: **cd /oracle/<SID>/saptrace/usertrace**

   g. Execute: **ls −lt**

   h. Find the latest ora_xxxxx.trc file. The x's will be substituted with a sequence number. Copy this file to the target host. Call it <SID>_cntrl.sql.

8. Modify the control file to represent the following:

```
startup nomount
create controlfile set database "<TARGET SID>" resetlogs
        maxlogfiles 255
        maxlogmembers 3
        maxdatafiles 254
        maxinstances 50
        maxloghistory 1000
```

```
logfile
    group 11 (
        '/oracle/<TARGET SID>/origlogA/log_g11m1.dbf',
        '/oracle/<TARGET SID>/mirrlogA/log_g11m2.dbf'
    ) size 20M,
    group 12 (
        '/oracle/<TARGET SID>/origlogB/log_g12m1.dbf',
        '/oracle/<TARGET SID>/mirrlogB/log_g12m2.dbf'
    ) size 20M,
    group 13 (
        '/oracle/<TARGET SID>/origlogA/log_g13m1.dbf',
        '/oracle/<TARGET SID>/mirrlogA/log_g13m2.dbf'
    ) size 20M,
    group 14 (
        '/oracle/<TARGET SID>/origlogB/log_g14m1.dbf',
        '/oracle/<TARGET SID>/mirrlogB/log_g14m2.dbf'
    ) size 20M
datafile
    '/oracle/<TARGET SID>/sapdata1/btabd_1/btabd.data1',
    '/oracle/<TARGET SID>/sapdata2/user1i_1/user1i.data1',
    '/oracle/<TARGET SID>/sapdata3/proti_1/proti.data1',
    '/oracle/<TARGET SID>/sapdata4/sourcei_1/sourcei.data1',
    '/oracle/<TARGET SID>/sapdata5/stabi_1/stabi.data1',
    '/oracle/<TARGET SID>/sapdata6/protd_1/protd.data1',
    '/oracle/<TARGET SID>/sapdata7/ddicd_1/ddicd.data1',
    '/oracle/<TARGET SID>/sapdata8/loadd_1/loadd.data1',
    '/oracle/<TARGET SID>/sapdata9/roll_1/roll.data1',
    '/oracle/<TARGET SID>/sapdata10/temp_1/temp.data1',
    '/oracle/<TARGET SID>/sapdata11/sourced_1/sourced.data1',
    '/oracle/<TARGET SID>/sapdata12/user1d_1/user1d.data1',
    '/oracle/<TARGET SID>/sapdata13/system_1/system.data1',
    '/oracle/<TARGET SID>/sapdata14/btabi_1/btabi.data1',
    '/oracle/<TARGET SID>/sapdata15/clui_1/clui.data1',
    '/oracle/<TARGET SID>/sapdata16/ddici_1/ddici.data1',
    '/oracle/<TARGET SID>/sapdata17/docui_1/docui.data1',
    '/oracle/<TARGET SID>/sapdata18/loadi_1/loadi.data1',
```

```
    '/oracle/<TARGET SID>/sapdata19/pooli_1/pooli.data1',
    '/oracle/<TARGET SID>/sapdata20/docud_1/docud.data1',
    '/oracle/<TARGET SID>/sapdata21/poold_1/poold.data1',
    '/oracle/<TARGET SID>/sapdata22/clud_1/clud.data1',
    '/oracle/<TARGET SID>/sapdata23/stabd_1/stabd.data1',
    '/oracle/<TARGET SID>/sapdata24/el31hi_1/el31hi.data1',
      '/oracle/<TARGET SID>/sapdata25/el31hd_1/el31hd.data1',
      '/oracle/<TARGET SID>/sapdata26/es31hd_1/es31hd.data1',
      '/oracle/<TARGET SID>/sapdata27/es31hi_1/es31hi.data1'
# Set the Database in archive log mode.
   alter database archivelog;
# database can now be opened normally.
   alter database open resetlogs;
```

9. Execute the script listed above on the target system in order to rebuild the database.

   Execute: **svrmgrl**

   Issue the command: **connect internal**

   Run the script: **@<SID>_cntrl.sql**

10. Reset the SAPR3 and OPS$<SID>ADM user passwords by issuing the Oracle commands below:

   a. `drop user OPS$<source SID>ADM cascade;`

   b. `alter user SAPR3 identified by <password>;`

   c. `create user OPS$<target SID>ADM`

      `identified by <Secret>`

      `default tablespace psapuser1d`

      `temporary tablespace psaptemp;`

   d. `grant connect, resource to OPS$<SID>ADM;`

   e. `create table OPS$<SID>ADM.SAPUSER`

      `(USERID varchar2(256), PASSWD varchar2(256));`

   f. `insert into OPS$<SID>ADM.sapuser values ('SAPR3', 'password')`

   g. `Exit`

Post-Database Copy Tasks

1. Install the SAP license for the target system. Execute the following commands in sequence:

   a. **saplicense –show**

   b. **saplicense –delete** (remove the source system's license)

   c. **saplicense –install** (install the license as captured in the copy preparation tasks)

2. Remove all entries from table DDLOG in order to ensure that buffer synchronization continues to take place (see OSS note 25380).

   a. **sqlplus system/manager**

   b. **truncate table sapr3.ddlog;**

   c. **commit;**

3. Remove all the **brbackup** and **brarchive** history from within CCMS.

   a. **sqlplus system/manager**

   b. **truncate table sapr3.sdbah;**

   c. **truncate table sapr3.sdbad;**

   d. **commit;**

4. Remove all monitor and parameter history data.

   a. **sqlplus system/manager**

   b. **truncate table sapr3.pahi;**

   c. **truncate table sapr3.moni;**

   d. **truncate table sapr3.dbsnp;**

   e. **commit;**

5. Start the Oracle Listener.

   a. Log on as ora<SID>

   b. **lsnrctl start**

6. Make sure that no batch jobs will execute when SAP starts up.

   a. Log on as <SID>adm.

   b. Execute: **cdpro** (change directory the profile directory)

   c. Edit (vi) the central instance profile.

d. Comment out the parameter *rdisp/wp_no_btc* by placing a # in front of it.

e. Add a new parameter and value *rdisp/wp_no_btc = 0*.

7. Start SAP.

8. Use transaction SM37 and set all batch jobs in schedule status.

9. Release the standard SAP cleanup jobs and make sure RDDIMPDP is released.

10. Reconfigure the transport system using the screen dump from the copy preparation tasks. Use transaction SE06.

11. Stop SAP.

12. Make sure that the batch jobs will execute when SAP starts up.

a. Log on as <SID>adm

b. Execute the alias **cdpro** to change to the profile directory

c. Edit (vi) the central instance profile.

d. Remove the comment from the parameter *rdisp/wp_no_btc*.

e. Remove the line *rdisp/wp_no_btc = 0* that you added.

13. Start SAP.

14. Use transaction SM59 to configure the RFC destinations.

15. Use transaction SPAD to change the formatting server for all output devices.

16. Re-import all the configuration settings exported during the copy preparation tasks.

17. Use transaction RZ10 to re-import the SAP instance profiles.

18. Use transaction RZ04 to reconfigure the operational modes.

19. Use transaction SMLG to reconfigure the logon groups.

20. Use transaction SM12 to remove any old SAP locks.

21. Use transaction SM13 to remove any old update requests.

22. Use transaction SM61 to remove all foreign entries that do not belong in table BTCCTL.

23. Use transaction SP12 to reorganize the TemSe database.

24. Use program RSBTCDEL to delete all finished/canceled batch job logs.

25. Use transactions AL15 and SM59 to reconfigure the SAP OS
    COLLECTOR destinations.

26. Reconfigure SAP Office if necessary.

Summary

This chapter discussed database administration using Oracle as the database of
choice, but the concepts are just as true for any other database. SAP depends on
a well-tuned, smoothly operating database. This chapter touched briefly on what
you have to do on a day-to-day basis to keep the SAP database healthy. You
started off with planning your database development, continued with the database
security, backup, and restore strategies, and finished off with scheduled database
maintenance.

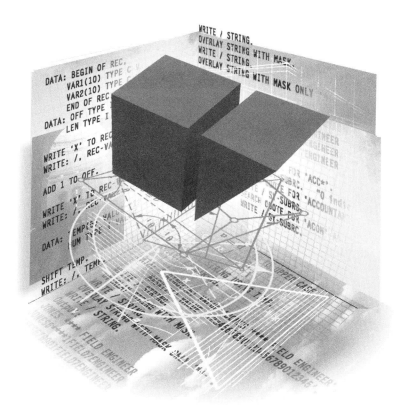

Chapter 13

Data Archiving
for Administrators

In This Chapter

◆ Archiving Concepts

◆ Developing an Archiving Strategy

◆ Archiving Authorizations

◆ Identifying the Archive Objects

◆ Performing the Archive

◆ Data Retention Tool (DART)

What is data archiving? Why would you want to archive SAP data? When would you do it? Who would be involved? How do you perform SAP data archiving? What, if any, are the legal and regulatory implications? This chapter will try to answer all of these questions.

Also, SAP has developed a new tool, known as DART, or data retention tool. This chapter will introduce the basic concepts of the tool and how it functions.

Over the course of time, several thousand transactions have been executed on a production system, and a significant amount of transactional data has been generated. As the data is stored and the database grows, reporting, querying, and performing any data manipulation becomes unwieldy. Performance is impacted, data storage costs increase, and additional database administration resources are required to maintain the database.

In the ideal situation, you need to have the most relevant and current information available online with the least accessed and most obsolete information on another form of media (for example, on a WORM CD: write once, read many CD), where reporting tools may be used to perform queries off-line.

Archiving is the method whereby you can achieve this goal of improving performance and saving database space. This chapter will introduce the concepts of archiving, what you may and may not archive, how to perform the archive and how often, and just as important, how to read archived files. Also, provided is a working example for the archiving of accounting documents.

When you archive, ensure you keep the following in mind:

- ◆ **Hardware independence.** The files you create should be readable by other makes of hardware. For example, if the archive file is created within an HP-UX system, this file may need to be imported to a Compaq-NT box and read with the appropriate application(s).

- ● **Data access and retention.** In the United States and many other countries, data must be archived so that it can be accessed later for tax-related purposes by other computer systems and kept for a certain period of time.

- ◆ **Release dependence.** Because the data structures may depend on the version of SAP you are using, record structure and field definition information must also be archived.

- ◆ **Data dependence.** Many data objects are dependent upon other objects; therefore you must determine whether archiving one particular data object requires that other objects be archived too.

- ◆ **Enterprise and business structure.** Certain data only makes sense if you know something about how the organization is structured (for example sales areas). Your archiving procedure must ensure that this information is also archived.

Archiving Concepts

The archiving process requires a familiarity with the SAP data dictionary and the relationships within and is based on the Archive Development Kit (ADK). The ADK provides the technical basis for the archiving transaction (SARA), accessed using menu path **System Administration, Administration, Archiving** from the main SAP menu or from the respective application components. If archive management is performed within the application component, then the application-specific settings (such as programs and archiving objects) are automatically activated. Otherwise, you are required to enter them into the relevant data fields for the SARA transaction.

The actual archiving is a two-step process, with a third optional process to recover the database space and increase database performance.

Step 1. Using predefined archived objects within SAP, known as *archive objects,* (which will be explained in greater detail later in this chapter) the archive process is performed, and the archive files (containing the archived data) are created at the operating system level.

Each archiving session is assigned a unique archiving session number. The archive files created in each session are then accessed using these numbers.

These archiving files can then be passed on to complimentary software providers' (CSPs) archive systems for storage and off-line access.

Step 2. Delete programs are used to purge the archived data. This step is the removal of the data from your SAP system database.

Step 3 - Optional. This optional step is executed to regain the emptied database space and therefore increase system performance by performing a reorganization of the tables or tablespaces and their respective indices using the SAP sapdba tool.

Developing an Archiving Strategy

Data archiving (not database archiving) is driven by business application areas whose data archiving strategy is governed by online data requirements. In other words, how much of the data is required online, and how much can be archived and placed on secondary storage units.

The Basis technical team should work closely with the business application area teams to define the data archiving strategy by identifying the business data, date periods, and methods by which the archived data may be read from the secondary storage system. (The most popular SAP complimentary software vendors for data archiving are IXOS, PBS, and Documentum).

Archiving Authorizations

In order to perform any kind of the archiving, the key business areas and appropriate personnel are required to have the correct authorizations to perform these tasks. The authorization object S_ARCHIVE is required with the field values as shown in Table 13-1. The authorizations are set up to allow the user to create, change, or display particular objects in their respective application areas.

Table 13-1 Authorization Object S_ARCHIVE with Examples of Field Values

Field	Value	Significance
Activity	01	Create or generate
	02	Change
	03	Display
Application area	AM	Asset management
	BC	Basis system
	CO	Controlling
Archive object	AM_ASSET	Asset-master data, values and movements
	BC_ARCHIVE	Archiving of archive management data
	COPA1_S001	Costing-Based CO-PA, Operating Concern S001

Identifying the Archive Objects

In order to archive data, the application experts will need to determine what objects relate to that particular data; for example, when you execute transaction SARA and click on the drop-down arrow, you will be presented with all the archive objects within the SAP environment. (See Table 13-2 for a complete list of objects.) If now you wish to archive sales documents, then you will need to perform the archive on the SD_VBAK object.

Table 13-2 Data Archiving Objects and Descriptions

Archive object	Description of data to be archived
AM_ASSET	Asset master data, values, and movements
AM_STEUER	Asset tax tables
BC_ARCHIVE	Archiving of archive management dat
BC_DBLOGS	Archiving customizing table changes
CATPROARCH	CATT - log/procedure
CA_KBL	Intern. RW docs. (funds reserv./fixed price/...)
COPA1_S001	Costing-based CO-PA, operating concern S001

Table 13-2 Data Archiving Objects and Descriptions *(Continued)*

Archive object	Description of data to be archived
COPA2_S001	Account-based CO-PA, operating concern S001
CO_ALLO_ST	Completely cancelled documents contrib., val.,...
CO_BASEOBJ	COPC: Base planning object
CO_CCTR_EP	Cost center - line item
CO_CCTR_ID	Cost center - actual data
CO_CCTR_PL	Cost center - planning data
CO_CEL_RCL	Reconciliation ledger: totals and line items
CO_COPC	Archiving product costing data
CO_COSTCTR	Cost center - all data (incl. center master)
CO_ITEM	CO line items
CO_KABR	Settlement documents
CO_KSTRG	Cost object with master and transaction data
CO_ML_BEL	Material ledger docs (MLHD/IT/PP/PPF/CR/CRF/CRP)
CO_ML_DAT	Material ledger records (CKMLPP, CKMLCR)
CO_ML_IDX	Index entries material document: material ledger
CO_ML_ML1	Material ledger period records (CKML1)
CO_ORDER	Orders with transaction data
CO_TEST	Test only
CS_BOM	PP object lists
CV_DVS	Document management system
DATAFDLOG	TR-TM: record all accesses to the data feed
EIS_CF001	Archive object for aspect CF001
EIS_CF705	Archive object for aspect CF705
EIS_CF779	Archive object for aspect CF779
EIS_CF850	Archive object for aspect CF850
EIS_CF900	Archive object for aspect CF900
EIS_CF922	Archive object for aspect CF922
EXAMPLE	Sample object
EXAMPLE_CL	Example object with archiving class
FI_ACCOUNT	G/L account master data

Table 13-2 **Data Archiving Objects and Descriptions** *(Continued)*

Archive object	Description of data to be archived
FI_ACCPAYB	Vendor master data
FI_ACCRECV	Customer master data
FI_BANKS	Bank master data
FI_DOCUMNT	Financial accounting documents
FI_MONTHLY	Sales figures A/P, A/R, G/L
FI_PAYRQ	Payment requests
FI_SCHECK	Prenumbered checks
FI_SL_DATA	Totals and line items in FI-SL
FLC_OBJECT	Totals records and line items in FI-LC
FM_BELEG	Act.commit. line item - finance budget management
FM_BEL_CA	Act.commitment line item - cash budget management
GLX-OBJEKT	Summary records and line items in FI-SL
IDOC	IDoc - intermediate document
J_1BN	Notas fiscais
LO_CHANGEM	Engineering change management
MC_S802	Info structure: S802, DB table: S802
MC_S805	Info structure: S805, DB table: S805
MC_S850	Info structure: S850, DB table: S850
MC_SELVS	LIS: stored selection versions
MM_ACCTIT	MM - accounting interface posting data
MM_ASMD	Service master
MM_CHVW	Batch where-used data
MM_EBAN	Purchase requisition
MM_EINA	Purchasing info. records
MM_EKKO	Purchasing documents
MM_INVBEL	Materials management: inventory documents
MM_MATBEL	Materials management: material documents
MM_MATNR	MM: material master
MM_REBEL	Material documents
MM_SPSTOCK	MM: special stock

Table 13-2 Data Archiving Objects and Descriptions *(Continued)*

Archive object	Description of data to be archived
PA_CALC	HR: payroll accounting results
PA_LDOC	PA: long-term documents
PA_TIME	PA: time data - results of analysis
PA_TRAVEL	PA: travel
PCA_OBJECT	Totals records and line items in EC-PCA
PI_PLAN	Master recipe
PM_EQUI	Equipment master data
PM_IFLOT	Functional location master data
PM_IMRG	PM measurement documents
PM_ORDER	PM/SM order
PM_PLAN	PM routings
PM_QMEL	PM messages
PP_BKFLUSH	Document log
PP_ORDER	Production order
PP_PLAN	Work plans
PP_WKC	Work centers
PR_ORDER	Process order
PS_PLAN	Standard network
PS_PROJECT	Project system: operative structures
QM_CHARACT	QM master inspection characteristics
QM_CONTROL	Q check transaction data
QM_METHOD	QM inspection methods
QM_PLAN	Inspection plans
QM_QMEL	Quality notification
RE_FLOW_DT	IS-RE real estate: rental contract transaction
RE_OFFER	IS-RE real estate: quotation
RE_REQUEST	IS-RE real estate: application
RE_RNTL_AG	IS-RE real estate: rental contract
RL_LINKP	MM-WM:warehouse mgmnt: system inventory records
RL_LINV	MM-WM:warehouse mgmnt: invent.count recs. history

Table 13-2 **Data Archiving Objects and Descriptions** *(Continued)*

Archive object	Description of data to be archived
RL_LUBU	MM-WM:warehouse mgmnt: posting change notices
RL_TA	MM-WM:warehouse management: transfer orders
RL_TB	MM-WM:warehouse management: transfer requirements
RV_LIKP	Deliveries
SD_AGREEM	Agreements and conditions
SD_COND	Pricing condition records
SD_VBAK	Sales documents
SD_VBKA	Sales activities
SD_VBRK	Billing documents
SD_VTTK	SD transport
SM_QMEL	Service notification
TESTOBJECT	Generated
TRTM_TRANS	TR archiving object
US_AUTH	User master change documents: authorizations
US_PASS	Change documents: user (other data)
US_PROF	User master change documents: authoriz. profiles
US_USER	User master change documents: user authorizations
WORKITEM	Work items from workflow system
WS_ACSITE	Retail: site master record
W_KALK	Pricing: pricing documents
W_SOR	Object for listing condition + modules

Typically, the archive procedure is similar to any other change introduced within the SAP environment. The archiving is first performed in the development environment on a very small subset of production data. Once the business areas have identified that the data archived is correct and that they understand the mechanics and implications of archiving, the process is repeated in the QA environment with a larger subset of production data and then finally in production. Prior to the archive in the production system, a complete backup of the system is performed just in case the archive procedure does not perform as it should have.

TIP

Be aware of certain operating system limitations—for example, archive files and their indexes should not be larger than 2GB for certain UNIX systems. Also, if no index is created, single record access will not be possible either.

Performing the Archive

Once the business area experts have identified what data requires archiving and the archive object that will be used to perform the archive, then you are ready to begin the task.

A number of logical steps are taken to perform the archive.

Step 1: Parameters Setup

A number of parameters are required to be set up so that the SAP system places the archive file in the correct system directory and adheres to your company's file-naming convention.

Setting Up the Global Archive Path *(Client-independent)*

In order to set up the file directory where the archive files will be created, you must do the following:

- Execute transaction code **SARA** and select **Customizing** from the Icon toolbar. The customizing box appears, as seen in Figure 13-1.

NOTE

For SAP version 3.x, execute transaction code **SPRO** to enter the IMG and follow the path, Implementation Guide for R/3 Customizing, Basis Components, General, Platform Independent assignment of file names.

- Execute the **Client-independent file names/paths** option, and then acknowledge the warning box indicating that the table is client-independent and you will be at the setting up the logical file path screen, as in Figure 13-2.

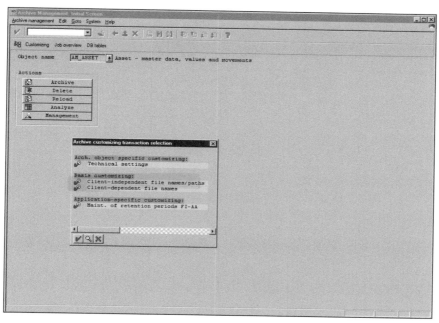

FIGURE 13-1 *Customizing selection for archiving*

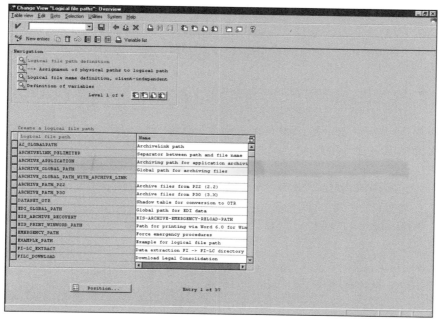

FIGURE 13-2 *Setting up the logical file path*

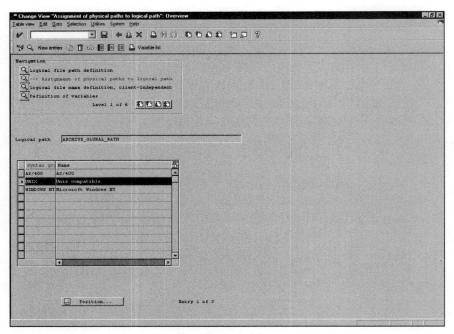

FIGURE 13-3 *Assigning the logical to physical file path*

◆ Click on the box beside the Archive_Global_Path, and then click on the magnifying glass beside Assignment of Logical to Physical Files Paths. See Figure 13-3.

◆ Click on the box beside the operating system of your choice, and then from the menu, select Selection, All Selected Entries. See Figure 13-4.

◆ Enter the global path where the files will be stored and then save the configuration change. The Directory /usr/sap/<SYSID>/SYS/global/<FILENAME>.ARCHIVE is set as the default, where <FILENAME>.ARCHIVE will be set up in the next step.

◆ Create the directories at the operating system if you are using other directories and sub-directory names.

Setting Up Archive File Name (Client dependent)

In the previous section, you created and set up the directory path where the archive files will be created. You will now set up the file name of the archive file.

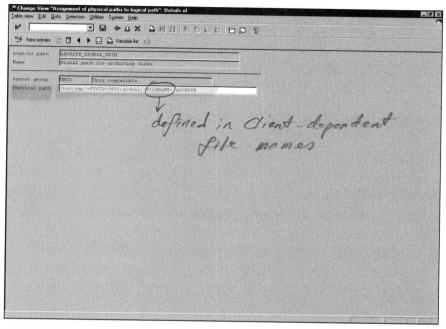

FIGURE 13-4 *Defining the physical file path*

◆ Execute transaction code **SARA** and select **Customizing** from the Icon toolbar and execute the Client-dependent file names option (see Figure 13-5).

◆ Click on the box next to **Archive_Data_File,** and then select new entries.

◆ Using the down arrow for the Logical File, select the Archive_Data_File option, and by default, the other fields are populated. You can now change these default values according to your company standards and needs of the business (see Figure 13-6).

 NOTE

For SAP version 3.x, execute transaction code **SPRO** to enter the IMG and follow the path **Implementation Guide for R/3 Customizing, Basis Components, General, Platform Independent** assignment of file names. Then execute the Additional client-dependent file name maintenance option.

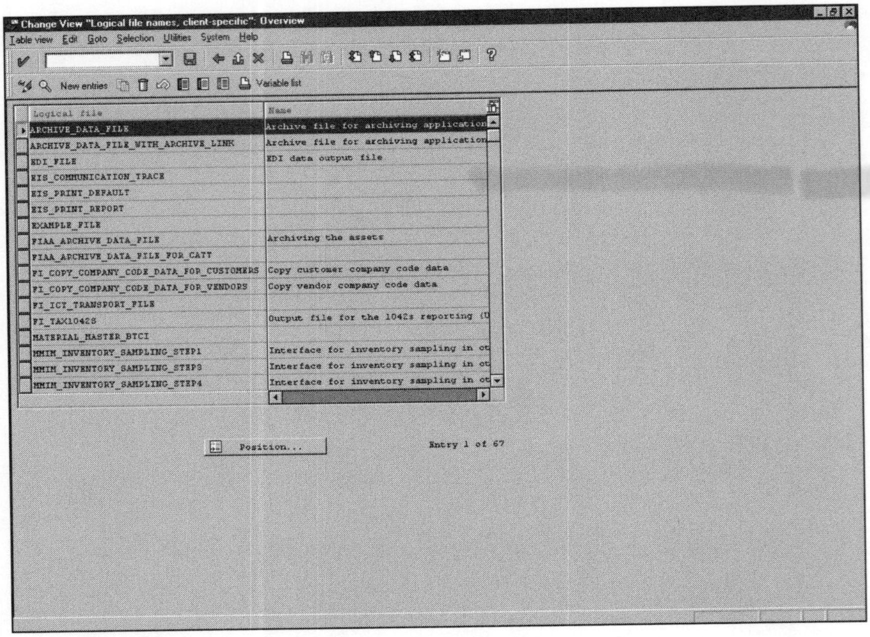

FIGURE 13-5 *Client dependent file name customizing*

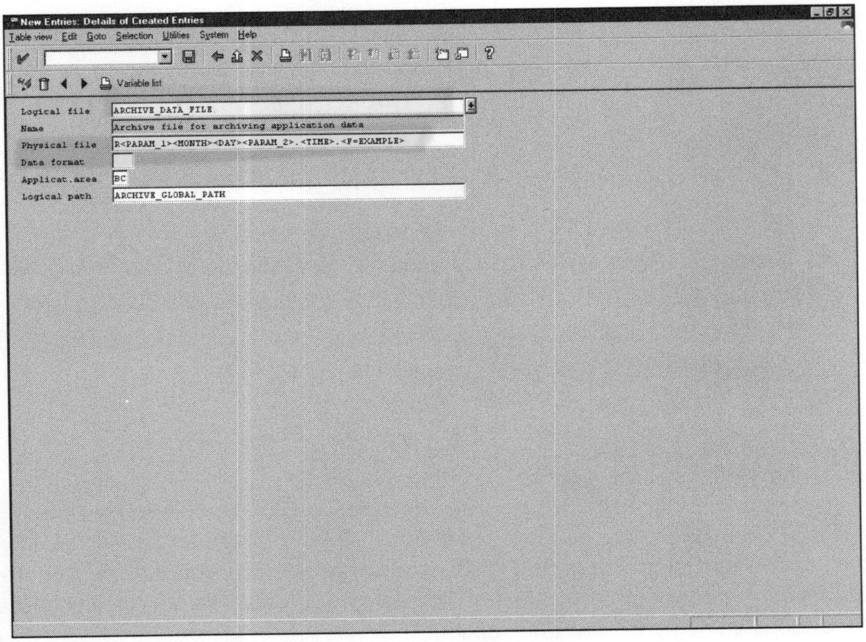

FIGURE 13-6 *Setting up the archive data file naming convention*

The default value of the file is set up as:

```
R<PARAM_1><MONTH><DAY><PARAM_2>.<TIME>.<F=EXAMPLE>
```

However, you can use other options as outlined in Table 13-3.

Table 13-3 **Archive Data File Naming Parameters**

Parameter	Description
<OPSYS>	Operating system in call
<INSTANCE>	R/3 application instance
<SYSID>	R/3 application name in SY-SYSID
<DBSYS>	Database system in SY-DBSYS
<SAPRL>	R/3 release in SY-SAPRL
<HOST>	Host name in SY-HOST
<CLIENT>	Client in SY-MANDT
<LANGUAGE>	Log on language in SY-LANGU
<DATE>	Date in SY-DATUM
<YEAR>	Year in SY-DATUM, 4-character
<SYEAR>	Year in SY-DATUM, 2-character
<MONTH>	Month in SY-DATUM
<DAY>	Day in SY-DATUM
<WEEKDAY>	Day of the week in SY-FDAYW
<TIME>	Time in SY UZEIT
<STIME>	Hour and minute in SY UZEIT
<HOUR>	Hour in SY UZEIT
<MINUTE>	Minute in SY-UZEIT
<SECOND>	Seconds in SY-UZEIT
<PARAM_1>	External parameter 1
<PARAM_2>	External parameter 2
<P=name>	Name of a profile parameter (see report RSPARAM for valid values)
<V=name>	Name of a variable (stored in variable table)
<F=name>	Return value of a particular function module (name convention for this function module: FILENAME_EXIT_name)

When you select one of the parameters from Table 13-3 for the file name, each one of them will have several valid values. Tables 13-4 and 13-5 illustrate two examples of valid values for the date and application formats.

Table 13-4 **Date Format Values**

Date values	Description
ASC	ASCII
BIN	Binary
DBF	DBASE format
IBM	ASCII with IBM code page conversion (DOS)
WK1	Spreadsheet format
DAT	ASCII data table with column tab

Table 13-5 **Application Area Format Values**

Application area values	Description
XF	Non-application-dependent from financial accounting view
AM	Asset management
BC	Basis system
CO	Controlling
FI	Financial accounting
GL	General ledger
HR	Human resources
IS	Industry solutions
MC	Logistics controlling
MM	Materials management
OC	Office and communication
PM	Plant maintenance
PP	Production planning

Table 13-5 Application Area Format Values *(Continued)*

Application area values	Description
PS	Project system
QM	Quality management
SD	Sales and distribution

Therefore, an example of a valid file format may be:

`<SYSID><APPLICATION>  <YEAR><MONTH><DAY>`

Setting Up Additional Parameters

◆ Additional parameters include the *technical settings,* which allow several variables (such as maximum file size, maximum number of data objects, commit counters, deletion options, and variants) to be set up. Figure 13-7 shows an example for the AM_ASSET archive object.

 NOTE

By default, the log.file name for the AM_ASSET object is set to FIAA_ARCHIVE_DATA_FILE. You will need to change this to ARCHIVE_DATA_FILE to adhere to your naming convention you set up earlier.

◆ The other parameter that requires setting up for the AM_ASSETT example is the maintenance of retention periods FI-AA, executed via the customizing button on the initial screen on transaction SARA, as viewed in Figure 13-8.

 NOTE

Each archive object will have different parameter settings—some will not have any.

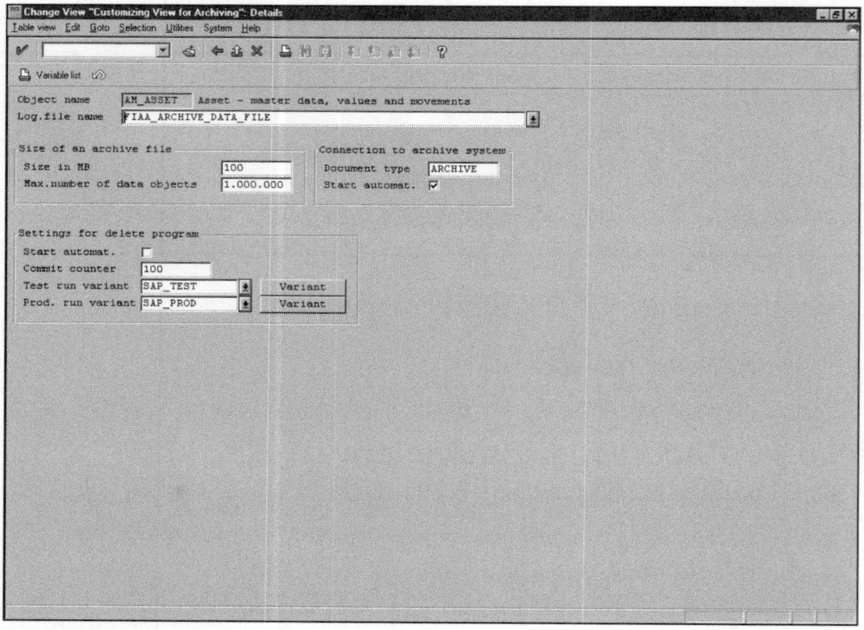

FIGURE 13-7 *Technical settings for the AM_ASSET*

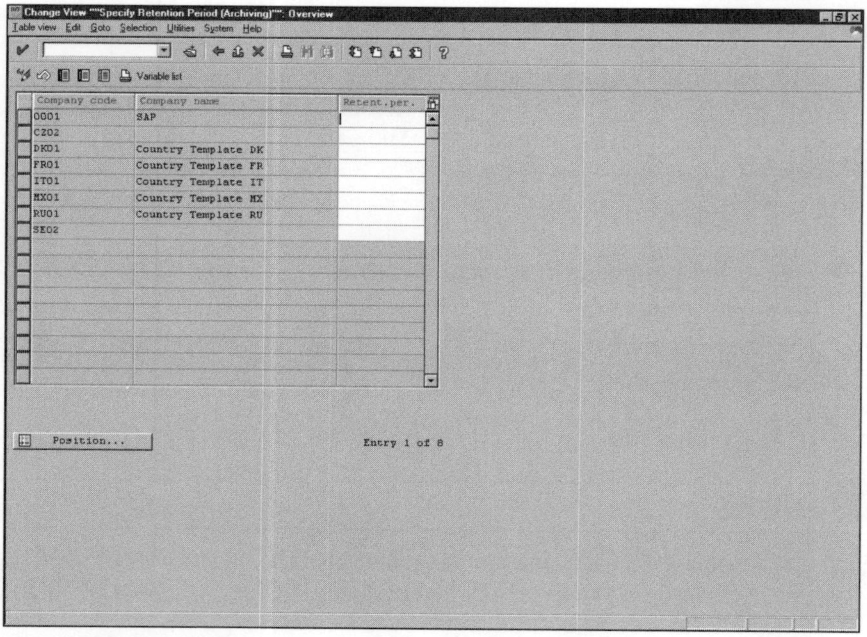

FIGURE 13-8 *Maintenance of retention periods for the AM_ASSET archive object*

STEP 2: Configuring the Archiving Object *(create custom archive object)*

The actual archiving is performed using the information provided in the archive object configuration setup in step 1. To further the AM_ASSET example, execute the transaction code **AOBJ** and select AM_ ASSET. You are now able to configure the object using the Navigation options, which include:

- ◆ Tables that are archived
- ◆ Tables in which deletions are made
- ◆ Maintain network graphic
- ◆ Customizing settings
- ◆ Archiving classes used
- ◆ Read program
- ◆ Customizing transactions
- ◆ Info tables for archive data
- ◆ Exit routine assignment in generation

With so many variation and combinations that can be set up, it would be more prudent to look at each of the configuration settings and see which one applies specifically for you and your company and leave the others at default. Then set up the configuration and perform the archive on a test box until you obtain the results that you require.

TIP

Once the changes have been made, it is a good idea to lock the AOBJ transaction code using the SM01 transaction code. This will stop unauthorized access to the archive configuration.

STEP 3: Performing the Actual Archiving

After executing the archiving transaction code **SARA**, you are presented with the main archiving menu with the three main operations:

- ◆ **Archive**—begin the archive process
- ◆ **Delete**—once the archive has been processed, you can then delete the data from the table

◆ **Management**—allows the management of the archived files

Several of the archive objects have additional operations that may be performed, which include the following:

◆ **Post-pr.**—perform post-processing steps after the archive.

◆ **Reload**—perform a reload of the data from a previous archive file. Please be cautious when using this option as it may introduce duplicate entries and other errors. Also, if an upgrade has been performed and table structure changes were introduced during the upgrade, data loss or incomplete data reloads may occur, thereby fragmenting the database.

◆ **Analyze**—perform preliminary checks and view the type of data that will be archived, enabling you to see what impact archiving has on the database.

◆ **Index**—allows you to create an index for the archive files. This will improve performance upon retrieval from the archive data bank.

◆ **Preparation**—some archiving objects require a program that prepares the data for archiving. This program flags data to be archived, but it does not delete any data from the database. Preparatory programs must always be manually scheduled and executed from archive management.

Figure 13-9 depicts the FI_DOCUMNT archiving objects with several of the archive options.

If, for example, you now click the archive button, you are presented with the screen in which you may set the start time to begin the archive, print the results to a printer (spool parameter), or create/maintain a variant.

Application Archiving Objects

To assist you in your archiving strategy, a table of application archive objects for the commonly used applications—FI, CO, MM, and SD—has been created. The tables will show you the type of data that will be archived, the archive objects involved, and the customizing requirements that are required to be performed, prior to the archive.

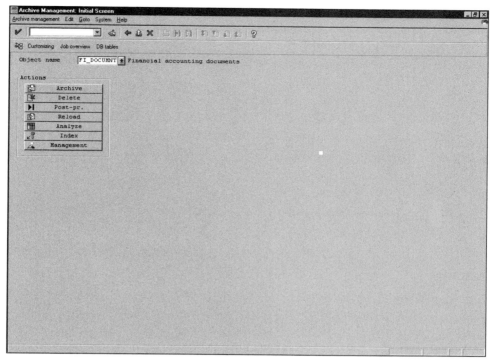

FIGURE 13-9 *Archive options for the FI_DOCUMNT object*

Financial Archive Objects

Table 13-6 maps out the type of documents that your business areas could archive with financial documents with respect to the archive objects. Several of the objects require additional customizing; for example, FI_DOCUMNT requires you to maintain the account type life and document type life.

Other document archive objects are accessed through their application menu paths, as shown in Table 13-6.

Table 13-6 **Financial Account Documents and Their Respective Archiving Objects**

Data type	Archive object	Customizing parameter	*Menu path*
Accounting documents	FI_DOCUMNT	Maintain account type life Maintain document type life	
Transaction figures (A/P, A/R, G/L)	FI_MONTHLY		
Checks (pre-numbered checks)	FI_SCHECK		
Customer master data	FI_ACCRECV	Mark customer for deletion (acctng)	
Vendor master data	FI_ACCPAYB	Mark vendor for deletion (acctng)	
General ledger master data	FI_ACCOUNT	Mark master record for deletion	
Bank master data	FI_BANKS	Mark bank for deletion	
Consolidation data (totals records and journal entries)	FLC-OBJEK	RW/RP reports for FI-LC archive	Accounting, Financial Accounting, Consolidation, Indiv.fin. stmts, Archiving, Create Archive, Customizing
Asset accounting data	AM_ASSET	Retention periods FI-AA	Accounting, Financial Accounting, Fixed Assets, Tools, Archiving, Edit, Customizing
Special purpose ledger	GLX-OBJEKT	Generate FI-SL archive DB reports Generate FI-SL archiving	Accounting, Financial Accounting, Special Purpose Ledger, Periodic Processing, Archiving, Create Archive, Customizing
Cash budget management	FM_BEL_CA		
Act. commitment line item—cash budget management	FM_BELEGA		

Accounting Documents (FI_DOCUMNT); Archive Customizing Example

As mentioned earlier in this chapter, the financial accounting documents require specific settings to be made via customizing, the account type life, and document type life (see Figure 13-10).

Define the Account Type Life

To access the application-specific customizing, either:

◆ enter transaction code **OBR7**, or

◆ follow menu path **Tools, Business Engineering, Customizing, Enterprise IMG, Financial Accounting, Financial Accounting Global Settings, Document, Accounting Document Archiving, Define Account Type Life,** or

◆ select the **Maintain Account Type Life** option in Customizing at the archive transaction **SARA**.

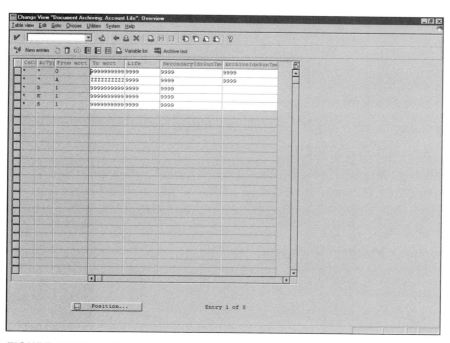

FIGURE 13-10 *Archive customizing options for the Account documents (FI_DOCUMNT)*

You then make changes to the following:

- **CoCd**—company code
- **AcTyp**—account type (Assets, Customers, Vendors, Material, or G/L Accounts)
- **from acct**—account number (used with the upper limit to create a range)
- **to acct**—account number (used with the lower limit to create a range)
- **life**—account type life (earliest period after which documents can be archived)
- **SecondaryIdxRunTme**—length of time secondary indexes to be held temporarily in the system.
- **ArchiveIdxRunTme**—length of time the archive index can be accessed from the database.

TIP

For testing purposes, the account life should be set to one day. After one day, the account will be cleared and it becomes a candidate for archiving.

Define the Document Type Life

To access the application-specific customizing, either:

- enter transaction code **OBR8**, or
- follow menu path **Tools, Business Engineering, Customizing, Enterprise IMG, Financial Accounting, Financial Accounting Global Settings, Document, Accounting Document Archiving, Define Document Type Life**, or
- select the **Maintain Document Type Life** option in Customizing at the archive transaction **SARA**.

You then make changes to the following:

- **CoCd**—company code
- **DocTyp**—document type (Asset posting, Accounting document, Net asset posting, Work order)

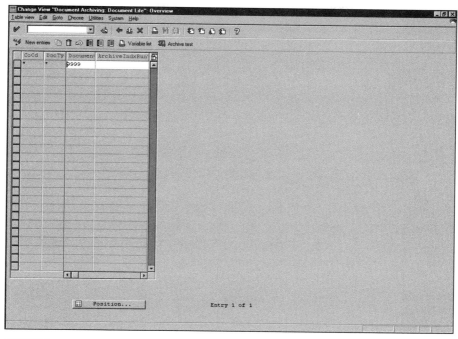

FIGURE 13-11 *Archive customizing options for the Account documents (FI_DOCUMNT)*

- ◆ **Document Life**—the earliest time documents can be archived
- ◆ **ArchiveIndRunTime**—Archive Index Run Time, length of time the index can be accessed from the database bank

TIP

Again, for test purposes, the document life should be set to one. These entries will require a longer period of time for production, defined by the application users

Controlling Archive Objects

Table 13-7 displays the controlling documents, which are accessed through the menu path **Accounting, Controlling, Cost Center, Environment, Archiving** and then select the object.

Table 13-7 Controlling Documents and Their Respective Archiving Objects

Data type	Archive object	Customizing parameter	*Menu path*
Cost center-all data (incl. Center master)	CO_COSTCTR		
Cost centers (actual)	CO_CCTR_ID		
Cost centers (plan)	CO_CCTR_PL		
Cost centers (line items)	CO_CCTR_EP		
Completely cancelled allocations:assessment, distribution, periodic reposting, and indirect activity allocation	CO_ALLO_ST		
Profit center accounting—totals records and line items in EC-PCA	PCA_OBJECT	RW/RP reports for EC-PCA archives	Accounting, Enterprise Controlling, Profit Center Accounting, Tools, Archiving, Create Archive

CO Cost Center Line Items (Co_CCTR_EP); Archiving Example

This object archives cost center accounting line items by client, controlling area, and fiscal year together with the total records in order to preserve the object relationships. However, the total records are *not* deleted from the SAP system.

To access the archive object, follow the menu path **Accounting, Controlling, Cost Center, Environment, Archiving, CCtr: Line Item** or execute transaction **SARA**, and insert the **Co_CCTR_EP object**. You will notice that there are no additional parameter settings required as with the finance FI_DOCUMNT object. You may therefore begin the archive operation.

Material Management Archive Objects

Table 13-8 lists the archive objects for purchasing, inventory management, material ledger, warehouse management, and invoice verification. Please note that unlike the financial archiving objects, *none* of these can be reloaded in the SAP

Table 13-8 Material Documents and Their Respective Archiving Objects

Data type	Archive object	Customizing parameter	Menu path
Material master records	MM_MATNR		
Purchase requisitions	MM_EBAN	C MM-PUR reorganization: requisition	
Purchasing documents Quotation, purchase orders, contracts, and scheduling agreements (not requisitions)	MM_EKKO	C MM-PUR reorganization RFQ	
		C MM-PUR reorg. scheduling agmts.	
		C MM-PUR reorganization PO	
Purchasing info records	MM_EINA		
Service master records	MM_ASMD		
Material and physical inventory document— Movement data only	MM_MATBEL	Change document retention periods	
Material ledger Period records from the material ledger	CO_ML_ML1		
Index material document: material ledger	CO_ML_IDX		

system. However, the documents may be viewed from the storage management system where they are stored.

As mentioned earlier, there is a sequence in which certain archives need to be performed to keep the integrity of the SAP system. This applies to archiving within modules too.

◆ Purchasing documents should be archived before vendor master records and material master records.

◆ Purchase orders should be archived before contracts.

MM—Purchasing Documents (MM_EKKO); Archiving Example

The purchasing documents' archiving objects are required to have tolerance limits set for archiving. Therefore:

◆ execute transaction code **OMEE**, or

◆ go to **Tools, Business Engineering, Customizing, Enterprise IMG, Materials Management, Purchasing, RFQ/Quotation, Define Tolerance Limits for Archiving**, or

◆ select the **C MM-PUR Reorganization RFQ** option in customizing at the archive transaction level via **SARA**.

Figure 13-12 shows two variables that can be set:

◆ Residence Time 1 is the number of days after which the archiving program may set the deletion indicator. For testing, set this indicator to 1; for production, this should be set to 30 or more calendar days.

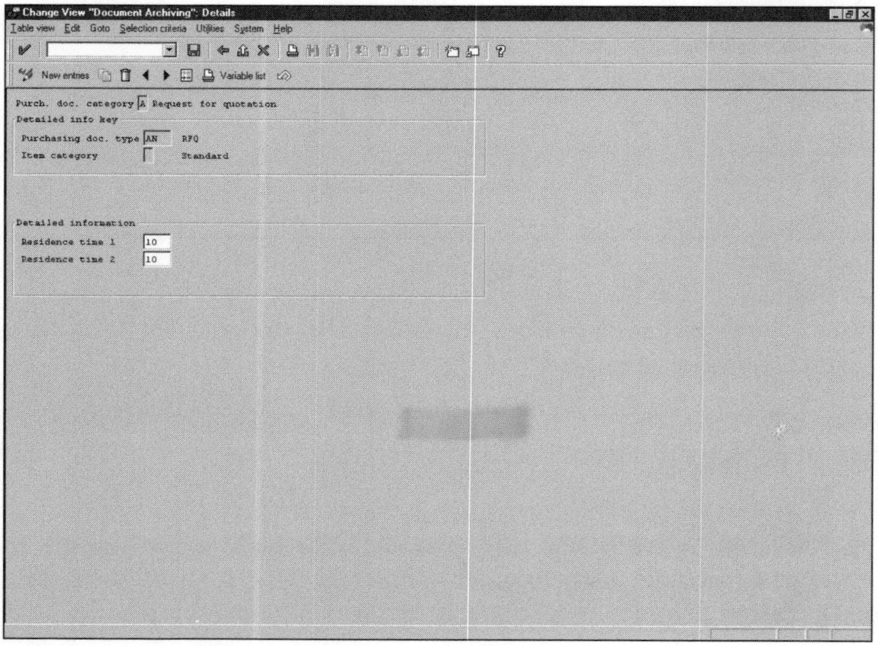

FIGURE 13-12 *MM_EKKO document archiving details*

◆ Residence Time 2 is the number of days after which the archiving program may delete documents that have the deletion indicator set. For testing, set this indicator to 1; for production, this should be set to 30 or more calendar days.

When you now set up the technical, you may set up the archive procedure as a one- or two-step process.

One-step Archiving

◆ The deletion indicator is set for a closed item.

◆ The item is archived and deleted at the same time.

For this process, the system checks the Residence Time 1 parameter.

Two-step Archiving

◆ The Deletion indicator is set for closed items in one run of the archiving program.

For this process, the system checks the Residence Time 1 parameter.

◆ The items with a Deletion indicator are then archived and deleted in the next run of the archiving program.

For this process, the system checks the Residence Time 2 parameter.

Now you may begin to archive the purchasing documents.

Sales and Distribution Archive Objects

Similar to other modules, Table 13-9 illustrates the archive objects for the sales and distribution module.

SD—Sales Documents (SD_VBAK); Archiving Example

Before archiving, the SAP system will check to see if the sales and distribution data is used in other SAP modules. If so, a dependency exists, and the data cannot be archived. The business areas therefore will require you to perform archives for the other modules before you begin the archiving for the Sales and Distribution module.

Table 13-9 Sales and Distribution Archive Objects

Data type	Archive object	Customizing parameter	*Menu path*
Agreements and conditions	SD_AGREEM		
Pricing condition records	SD_COND	Archiving Conditions V_T681H	
Sales documents	SD_VBAK	Archiving Control for Sales Doc.	Tools, Business Engineer, Customizing, Enterprise IMG, Sales and Distribution, Data transfer and Archiving, Archiving data, Archive control for sales documents
Sales activities	SD_VBKA	Archiving Control for Sales Activity	(same as above)
Billing documents	SD_VBRK	Archiving Control for Billing Docs	(same as above)
Shipment costs	SD_VFKK	Archiving Control Shipment Costs	(same as above)
SD Transport	SD_VTTK	Archiving Control for Shipments	(same as above)
Service notification	SM_QMEL		

Please note that change documents and texts are archived with sales and distribution documents and therefore do not influence whether or not a document can be archived.

Two factors determine whether or not a document can be archived:

◆ Status of the document
◆ Retention period

Therefore, to archive, the document should either be closed or flagged for deletion and the retention period expired.

◆ enter transaction code **VORA**, or

◆ follow the menu path **Tools, Business Engineering, Customizing, Enterprise IMG, Sales and Distribution, Data Transfer & Archiving, Archiving Control, Archiving Control for Sales Documents,** or

◆ select the **Archiving Control for Sales Doc.** option in customizing at the archive transaction level.

For the fields in Figure 13-13, you are required to maintain the entries for the SOrg (sales organization), SaTy (sales document type), ResidenceTime (residence time of sales document—that is, the number of days that must elapse in order to archive the sales document). Set to 1 for test purposes and greater than 30 (for production) and Rno (routine number). The particular data that is required for archiving will come from the application area experts.

Once you have gathered the information, you can then begin the archive as with the other functional areas and perform them in the test, quality assurance, and production systems.

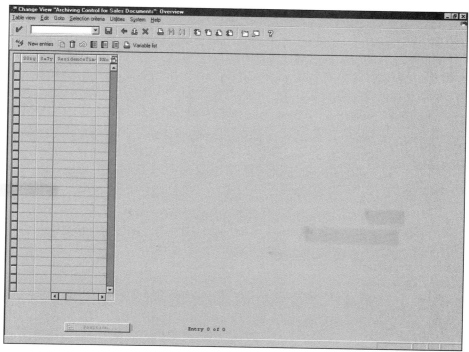

FIGURE 13-13 *Archiving control for sales documents*

Data Retention Tool (DART) *ABAP, financial data*

SAP's ADK (archive development kit) was developed for the storage of data that was inactive or closed and removed from the active SAP system. However, business code and government regulations have mandated that the above situation was inadequate, and thus SAP has developed DART—ABAP extraction tools, primarily focused on financial data—which creates a "flat" file and can be read using third-party tools.

There are four components of DART that can be used for your SAP system and ADK archive files. They include:

1. **Data extraction.** New data dictionary structure objects have been developed for the collection of the subset data from your SAP system. When the extraction tool is executed, data from specific tables and fields are copied to the new structure in a flat-file format. Data compression and conversion is performed to enable the creation of the file in a flat-file format.

   User exists are provided for custom requirements, which include the addition of new fields or new data sources.

2. **Data retrieval.** Previously archived data files, using the ADK method, may be retrieved using SAP's retrieval tool and "reloaded" into SAP tables that allow the extraction tool to correlate the required data. Once the extraction operation is completed, the reloaded tables can be cleared or emptied.

3. **Data merge.** If you set up the extraction tool to create monthly data extraction, the data merge tool may be utilized to combine the several extracted data files and ADK data files into a single data source.

4. **Query tools.** SAP provides two query tools. The first is a generic query tool to view the data in the extracted flat files. The second query tool is a view query tool that may be used with the SAP system and is used to create custom views by joining data segments from different SAP data sources into a single view.

The archive user profile will require specific DART authorizations as indicated in Table 13-10.

Note that the company code has been left blank—insert the company code you use within your company.

Table 13-10 Authorizations for DART Operations

Object class	Authorization object / Description	Values
Basis Administration	S_TABU_CLI Client-independent table maintenance	Authority to maintain client independent tables = X
	S_TABU_DIS Table Maintenance	Activity = 01-03 Authorization Group = TXWC
Cross Application	F_TXW_TFCF Data file configuration	Activity = 01-03
	F_TXW_TF Data files	Activity = 01-03 Company Code =
	F_TXW_TVCF Data view configuration	Activity = 01-03
	F_TXW_TV Data view queries	Activity = 01-03 Authorization Group = TXWC Company Code =
	F_TXW_RA Retrieve data from archive	Company Code =

DART may be accessed by executing the transaction **FTW0** or by following the menu path **Tools, Administration, Dart Retention Tool** on your SAP system. With the correct authorizations, you will be required to configure the global settings for the data file (menu path **Configuration, data files**) as shown in Figure 13-14 and select the data source from the transaction data configuration box.

Also, from the screen in Figure 13-14, you will be required to configure the directories and file path names for both the extraction and retrieval process. To configure the directories, click the Files directories button from the global parameter setting screen, and then click the create icon. When prompted, type in a name and description of the extraction session—in Figure 13-15, it is called **temp**. Now type in the volume id and the path. Figure 13-15 illustrates that three files will be created due to the size of the extraction (1500 MB), with volume ids 0, 1 and 2 and path /usr/sap/tmp/.

The file name is set by clicking the file path assignment in the global parameters setting screen, in which the file name options are shown in Figure 13-16. An example would be: /usr/sap/tmp/<CLIENT>/<FILENAME>.

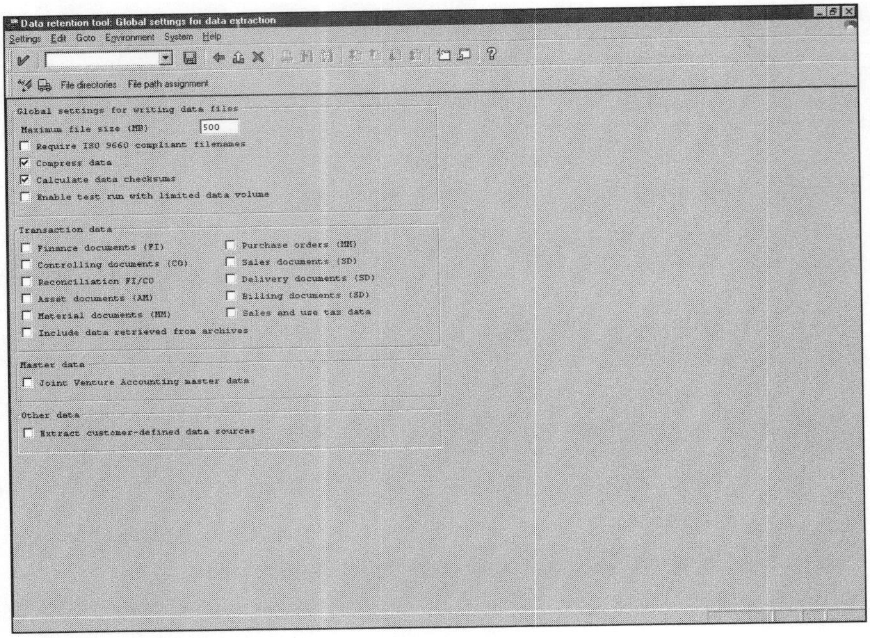

FIGURE 13-14 *Global settings for DART*

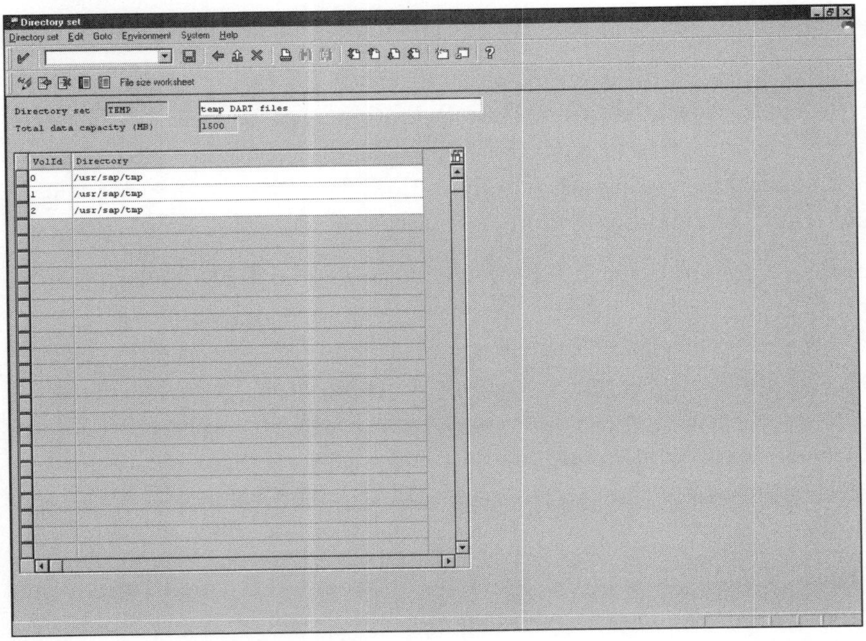

FIGURE 13-15 *File directories setup*

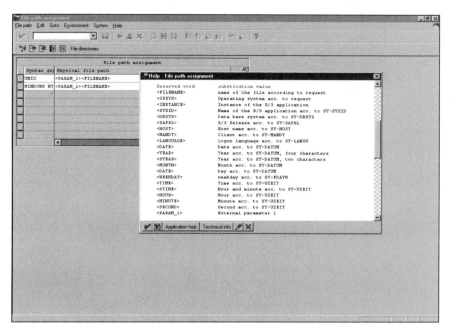

FIGURE 13-16 *File path assignment*

Once the configuration is completed, you are ready to perform the extraction, retrieval, merge, and query, in which you will be asked to input pertinent data for the operation and then allowed to execute the operation. Figure 13-17 shows the data inputs, marked by ?, for the extraction when all the transaction data is selected in the global parameter setting.

Summary

Listed in the following section is a quick step-by-step guide on performing the archive, deleting the data from the database, and post-archive processing. Also included are descriptions of the other options that may be available for some of the archive objects, such as analyze, prepare, index, reload, management, and the ArchiveLink.

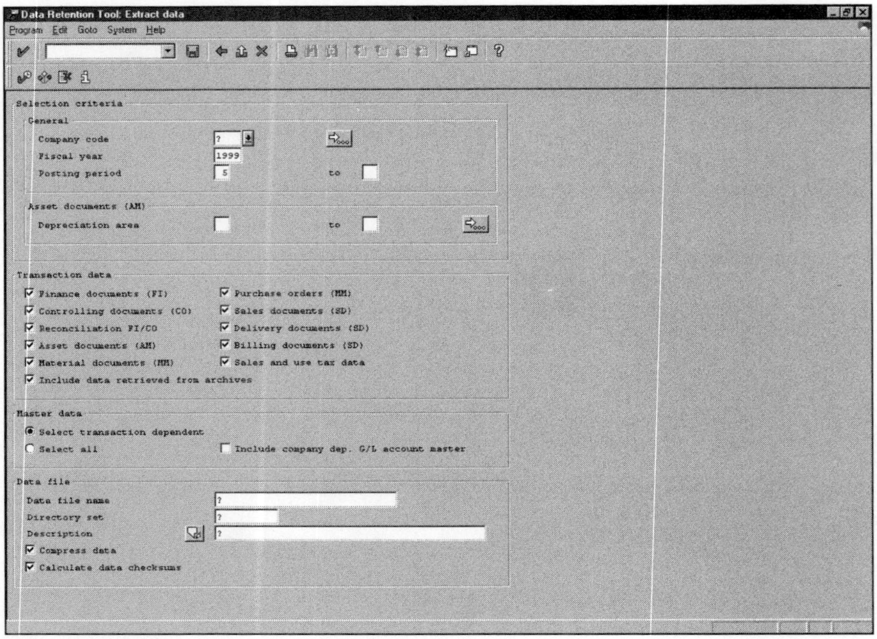

FIGURE 13-17 *Data extraction execution*

Archive

1. Start transaction code **SARA**, enter the object name, and click on Archive Action.

2. Set up the start time.

3. Set up spool parameters.

4. Create or maintain a variant.

5. Save the changes and execute the archive process—the message "New Archiving Job Generated" is displayed.

6. Check the job by following the menu path **Environment, Job Overview**.

7. Click on your job, and then click on Job Log to view the job status.

8. Click on your job, and then click on Spool List to view details of the archived files.

Deletion

1. Start transaction code **SARA**, enter the object name, and click on Delete Action.
2. Check the Test Run if you wish to run a test.
3. Set up Archive Selection (the job from the previous step).
4. Set up the start time.
5. Set up spool parameters.
6. Save the changes and execute the delete process—the message "New Delete Job Created" is displayed.
7. Check the job by going to **Goto, Job Overview**.
8. Click on your job, and then click on Job Log to view the job status.
9. Click on your job, and then click on Spool List to view details of the deleted files.

Post Processing

1. Start transaction code **SARA**, enter the object name, and click on Post Pr. action.
2. Set up the start time.
3. Set up spool parameters.
4. Insert the variant used in the archive process.
5. Save the changes and execute the Post-pr. process.
6. Check the job by going to **Goto, Job Overview**.
7. Click on your job, and then click on Job Log to view the job status.
8. Click on your job, and then click on Spool List to view details of the files.

The final check is to try and view a document that you have archived within your SAP system and verify that you receive a message stating that the document does not exist or that it has been archived.

Other Options

- ◆ **Analyze.** This option allows you to perform preliminary checks and view the type of data that will be archived, enabling you to see what impact archiving has on the database.

- ◆ **Preparation.** Some archiving objects require a program that prepares the data for archiving. This program flags data to be archived, but it does not delete any data from the database. Preparatory programs must always be manually scheduled and executed from archive management.

- ◆ **Index.** This option allows you to create an index for the archive files. This will improve performance upon retrieval from the archive data bank.

- ◆ **Reload.** Please be cautious when using this option as it may introduce duplicate entries and other errors. Also, if an upgrade has been performed and table structure changes were introduced during the upgrade, data loss or incomplete data reloads may occur, thereby fragmenting the database.

- ◆ **Management.** The Management function displays object-specific management information as a list that you can analyze. You have the following options:
  - determine or specify the location of the archive files
  - pass archive files and retrieve archive files from an archive system using the SAP ArchiveLink
  - make notes for archive files
  - set the management data delete flag
  - check the status of archive files (index, storage, and so on)

ArchiveLink

ArchiveLink is the SAP interface for the archive/storage and retrieval of archived objects either in file format or optical formats. Optically stored objects include scanned documents, outgoing documents, and print lists.

It may also be possible to display these archived documents and lists with ArchiveLink, but no analysis or reload may be performed using this tool.

Automatic passing of the files to ArchiveLink may be specified in the customizing of the archive object definition, or the archive files may be passed manually to ArchiveLink, as shown in the following:

1. Execute **SARA**, type in archive object name, and select Management.
2. Position the cursor on the archiving session.
3. Select Store. The Archive Management: Store via ArchiveLink.
4. Select Store Files.

To retrieve archive files that have been passed to ArchiveLink into the file system, follow these steps:

1. Execute **SARA**, type in archive object name, and select Management.
2. Position the cursor on the archiving session.
3. Select Store. The Archive Management: Store via ArchiveLink.
4. Select Get Files.

Chapter 14

An Administrator's Troubleshooting Guide

In This Chapter

- ◆ Analysis Tools
- ◆ Problem Diagnosis

In this chapter you will explore the various tools available to the Basis administrator to assist in the task of troubleshooting. You will also step through an example of diagnosing a problem and resolving the problem utilizing the tools you will learn about.

Troubleshooting is just one of the many varied tasks in a Basis administrator's daily activity. As a Basis administrator, you will always be the first person to be contacted when a system problem occurs. You have to analyze and determine whether this problem is of a functional nature. You will be able to diagnose and solve most technical problems fairly easily, but functional problems require extra experience and insight into the operations of SAP. Most people who report a problem take it for granted that the problem is of a technical nature and call the Basis administrator without really analyzing the problem. Therefore, you will have to analyze the problem by reproducing the conditions that caused it. If the problem is of a functional nature, you will first have to prove to the end user the cause of the problem. Thus, as a troubleshooter, you not only need to possess an excellent grasp of the technical aspects of SAP, but you must be equipped with a basic knowledge of most of the functional modules. Skills like creating quotes, sales orders, deliveries, month-end closures, production orders, MRP runs, and delivery due runs (to name but a few) are useful in areas in which you will be required to troubleshoot. These skills are not found in books or classes but are learned and perfected by aggressively facing each problem systematically. This chapter will expose you to some tools you have at your disposal to become an effective troubleshooter.

Analysis Tools

SAP provides a number of *analysis tools* you can use to determine what type of problem you're facing. The following tools are at your disposal:

- The system log
- The system process overview
- The ABAP dump analysis
- The update records monitor
- The lock entries monitor
- The system trace files
- Online Service System (OSS)
- The alert monitor

The System Log

SAP has extensive logging capabilities, which are utilized in the troubleshooting process. All application servers record the events in a local log. These events can be logged centrally if central logging has been configured in a distributed system. The application server records the events in a cyclic file. Once the log file reaches maximum size, the log is switched and the logging process starts overwriting the file from the beginning.

The *system log* is the place where most troubleshooting starts.

The system log functions are located through the menu path **Tools, Administration, Monitoring, Logs** or using transaction SM21. The System Log screen like the one shown in Figure 14-1 presents several input fields where you can narrow down your search by specifying the criteria.

The following search criteria are available:

- **From Date/Time** and **To Date/Time**. Specify the time interval for analysis.
- **User**. Enter the username you want to search for.

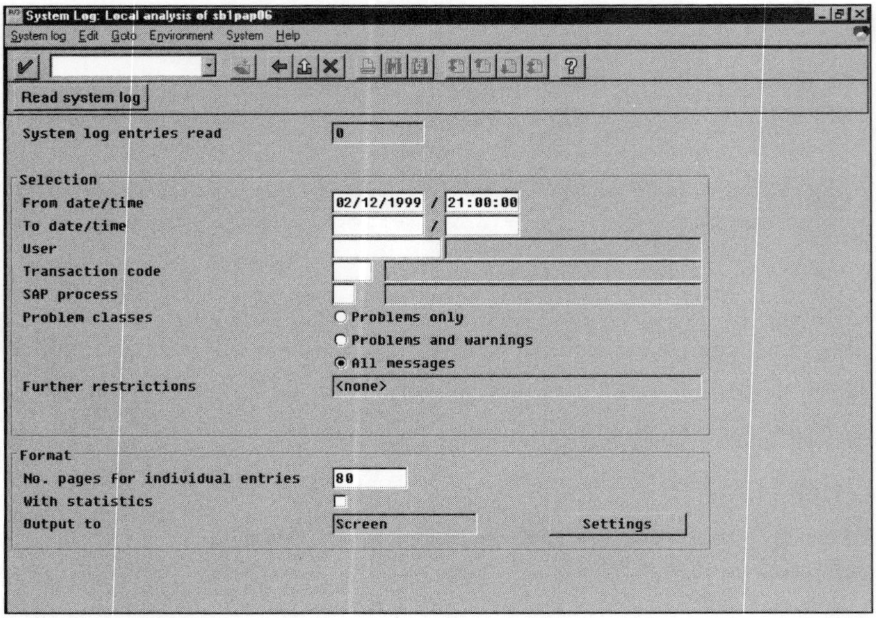

Figure 14-1 *The System Log screen*

◆ **Transaction Code.** Display the logs relevant for a specific transaction code.

◆ **SAP Process.** If you know the type of SAP you would like to troubleshoot, enter the type here.

DP	Dispatcher process
D<n>	Work process number
VB	Update process
V<n>	Update work process number
S<n>	Spool process
MS	Message server

◆ **Problem Classes.** This radio button group allows you to choose problems only, problems and warnings, or all messages. If there are many entries being produced over a short period of time, it would be useful to display problems only.

TIP

If the SAP system you are logged on to has a number of application servers, and you would like to scan all of the logs from all application servers, use the menu path **System Log, Choose, All Remote Logs** from the System Log main screen. This is of particular use if your system has quite a few application servers and you want to check for a certain criteria.

The system log includes an expert mode that allows additional selection modes. Expert mode is activated by using the menu path **Edit, Expert Mode.** Two additional button—Attributes and Message IDs—become visible. When you select Attributes, the system displays a new dialog box. This screen is extremely useful as a troubleshooting tool, as it allows you to restrict log events.

Figure 14-2 illustrates the input fields in the attributes selection button. The following fields are used to improve your search criteria:

> **SAP process**—the type of process can be selected, i.e. dialog, enqueue, batch, or update.
>
> **Programs**—the SAP program name
>
> **Problem class**—k—Basis problem
>> s—operational problem
>>
>> t—transactional problem
>>
>> w—warnings
>>
>> x—something else
>
> **Development class**—development class
>
> **Terminal name**—User terminal name.

Message Id can be used to exclude certain message codes from appearing in the log report.

 TIP

To obtain a list of the available system log messages, run the RSLG0011 report.

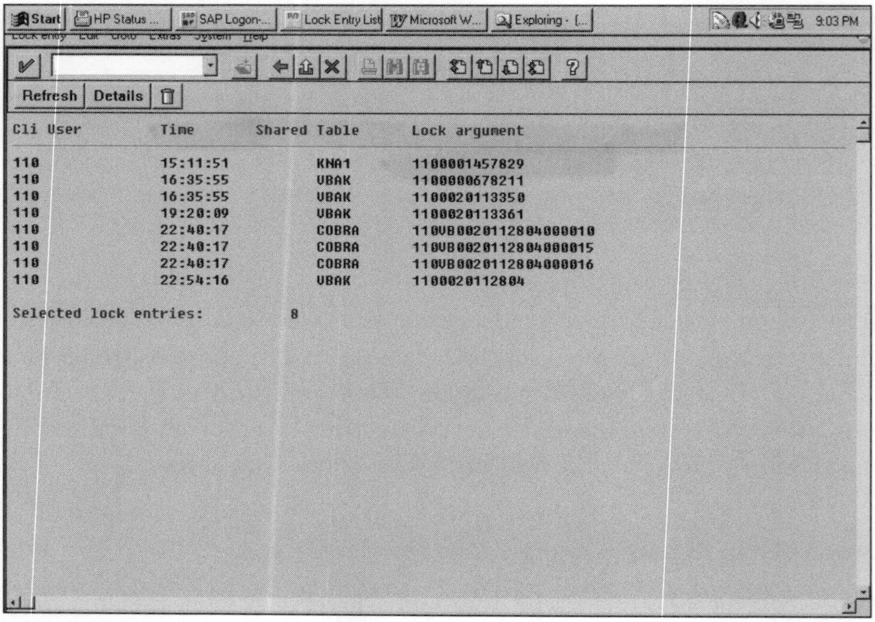

Figure 14-2 *The input fields in the attributes selection button*

The System Process Overview (SM50)

The *system process overview* displays the status of the work process on a particular application server. The system monitoring functions are located through the menu path **Tools, Administration, Monitoring, System Monitoring** or using transaction SM50. This screen is an ideal troubleshooting window into what is happening on a particular application server. The display is not real-time, so the Refresh button has to be pressed regularly to update the screen. The SAP work process corresponds to *Operating system* process. You are able to detect a number of problem areas by just monitoring this screen. If you would like to obtain more detailed information on a particular process, just select the work process and then click on the Detail Info button on top of the screen. In addition to the information from the overview display, the system will display which tables are being accessed, how much memory is being allocated, and how the database is being utilized.

TIP

This is an excellent troubleshooting display. From here you can see if the process is waiting for a gateway. By checking for sequential reads to the database, you can determine what was causing a long-running transaction.

A useful transaction that can be used in conjunction with the overview screen is transaction SM66. This transaction gives you a real-time view of which processes are active on a particular application server at a given time. This transaction is useful for tracing a process that is spawning other processes and causing the dialog processes to become flooded. An example of when this would happen would be if an ALE session was started and the person submitting the ALE session did not restrict the number of processes that would be spawned.

The ABAP Dump Analysis

The *ABAP dump analysis* is used extensively by the administrator to assist in analyzing the cause of program errors. A program that has serious errors causes the ABAP processor to abort the current program, and the development workbench generates an ABAP *short dump*. The short dumps are written to the database table SNAP.

CAUTION

The ABAP dump analysis contains invaluable data to be analyzed but can also cause serious system problems. If a large number of short dumps occur over a short period of time, the SNAP table could pose its own set of problems. The SNAP table could potentially fill up and reach maximum extents.

The SAP-supplied program RSSNAP00 should be scheduled to run daily to ensure that the SNAP table is reorganized regularly. This will ensure that there is sufficient space should a problem occur and a large number of dumps be written to the table. This can also be achieved from the dump analysis menu by selecting **Goto, Reorganize**.

When an error occurs, the system will generally advise the user that it is currently producing a dump by giving a system message in the startup bar. The user will be aware that an error has occurred and will probably call you. There are, however, situations where a short dump is produced and no system message is shown. Therefore, if you suspect a system problem, be sure to check the dump analysis by selecting **Tools, Administration, Monitoring, Dump Analysis** or using transaction ST22. Dump analysis can also be done from the system log (discussed earlier) and from the update records monitor (discussed later). Figure 14-3 shows the main screen for short dump analysis. The screen displays the number of short dumps that have been generated for the current day and the previous day. By selecting Today and clicking on the List Display icon, you'll see a list of dumps giving the time each occurred and indicating which user experienced the dump. Double-click to display the desired short dump just as it was displayed when the problem occurred.

The information displayed in a short dump can be divided into 20 different categories. The so-called short dump is in fact very long and contains many categories.

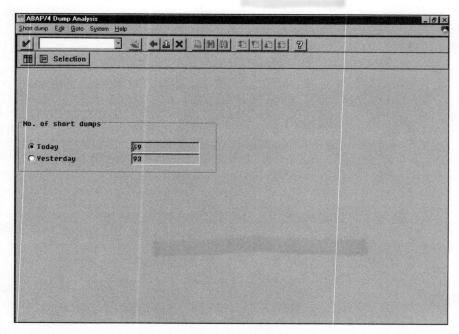

Figure 14-3 *The main screen for short dump analysis*

TIP

Be sure to educate your users to disregard the instruction to print out the dumps, for one dump can generate up to 50 pages. Explain that the dumps remain available on the system for you to view them.

By concentrating on the following categories, you will be able to accumulate all the data you need to troubleshoot your problem:

Category 1: What happened? Helps to define how the error occurred.

Category 3: Error analysis. Gives a technical analysis of the programs in which the error was occurring and why the error was occurring (e.g., a field in a structure was missing).

Category 4: How to correct the error. Provides search criteria if you need to search for reported errors in OSS.

Category 6: User transaction. Identifies both the transaction the user was executing and which server the user was logged on to.

Category 7: Info on where the termination occurred. Indicates the program where the error occurred as well as the main program if the failing program is an include.

TIP

Regenerating the programs mentioned in category 7 is a good starting point to your troubleshooting efforts. Sometimes includes are transported into a system, and because errors have occurred during the import process; regenerating the main programs solves the problem.

Category 8: Source code extract. Displays the source code where the error occurred, with an arrow at the line that failed.

TIP

It's wise to insert a breakpoint in the source code just before the error occurs when you start analyzing the problem in debug mode.

Developers and SAP experts who are doing more extensive analysis of a problem utilize the remainder of the categories.

The Update Records Monitor

The update work processes are responsible for ensuring that the database tables are updated with the data created by the user transactions. These update processes are processes that need to be checked during the troubleshooting process. The *update process* has transactions to monitor, check, and perform update operations on the update process, which is very useful when troubleshooting an update problem. When an error occurs, the user will receive an express SAP message indicating that the update process has been terminated. The update monitoring functions are located through the menu path **Tools, Administration, Monitoring, Update** or using transaction SM13. Figure 14-4 shows the main screen for the update records monitor. The screen displays the input fields and buttons for choosing update record selection criteria.

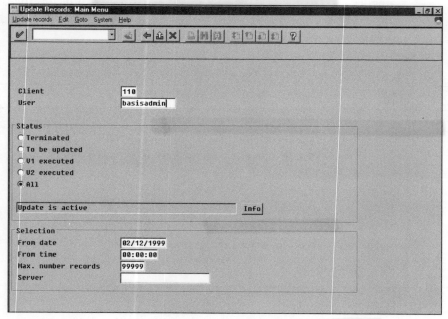

Figure 14-4 *Main screen for the update records monitor*

The approach to troubleshooting update record problems should be as follows:

1. Check the update transaction to list the update records in the error status. They will be displayed with the status "ERR" in a red boundary.

2. Double-click on the record showing the error. This results in a list of the update function modules that are processed during the update step.

3. Depending on the error message, resolve the problem and either repeat the update processing or repeat the transaction that failed initially.

4. The Status dialog box (as shown in Figure 14-5) displays the error message associated with the update termination message. The error text will be displayed with a preceding error code, which can be used to find more information on the error.

The error codes can be found by choosing **Tools, ABAP/4 Workbench, Development, Programming Environ, Messages** or using transaction SE91. The error message and code can also be used to look for associated problems in SAP OSS notes. The ABAP Short Dump button can be used to display the short dump

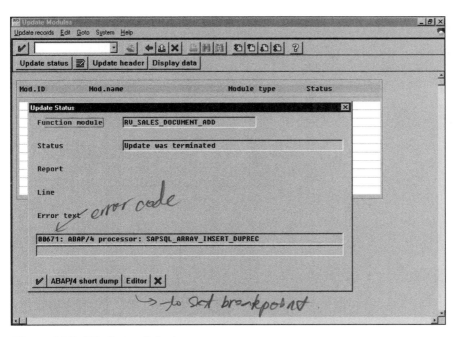

Figure 14-5 *The Status dialog box*

information if a short dump was generated. The editor key will take you to the code where the error occurred. This could be useful if you need to debug the program. This would be a good place to set a breakpoint before you try the erring transaction again.

The most common causes of update problems are database problems, such as tablespaces becoming full. It is always good practice to check the Update Records main menu screen and make sure that the field to the left of the Info button is reading "Update Is Active."

 CAUTION

When the database experiences tablespace problems, this field occasionally will switch to deactivated status. This status will occasionally have to be switched manually to start the update process. This is achieved by selecting **Update Records, Update, Activate** from the Update Records main menu.

The Lock Entries Monitor

The *lock objects* (also known as the *enqueue work processes*) are responsible for ensuring the integrity of the data by preventing multiple users from changing the same data simultaneously. This locking method, which is independent of the locking mechanism used by the underlying database, uses locking mechanisms defined in the data dictionary, which exercises locks over table data records. The lock-monitoring functions are located through the menu path **Tools, Administration, Monitoring, Lock Entries** or through transaction SM12. This screen allows for the selection of lock entries by table name, client, user name, and specific lock argument. Clicking on the Continue button will display the list of current lock entries.

The display includes the following columns:

CLI	Client number
User	The user locking the object
Time	The time the lock occurred
Shared	Indicates if the lock is exclusive or not
Table	The table with locked rows
Lock argument	Shows the data used by the lock object

Lock entries should be checked during the troubleshooting process. Normally, lock entries are deleted automatically by the system as the programs release the data objects. However, should a problem occur and a lock is not released, this could potentially block other users from updating the same information. The lock-monitoring transaction allows the manual deletion of unreleased locks. However, this should under no circumstances be done without a thorough investigation into the cause of the lock.

A lock can occur in a number of instances. If a user has lock entries and shuts down the workstation without logging off R/3, or if the automatic logout profile is active on the server, the user's sessions remain active in the SAP system. These lock entries cannot be released and will need to be manually deleted. To manually delete a lock entry from the lock entry list, select the entry holding the lock and click on the Delete icon from the application toolbar, or select **Lock Entry, Delete**.

Another example is if a user opens a delivery. All of the items in that delivery will be locked until the user exits the transaction. The only way to release the lock is to notify the user or manually delete the lock.

When experiencing problems in the update processing, locks can be created and not released because the update process was unable to complete. The update process problem will have to be resolved before the lock will be released. (Refer to the previous section on troubleshooting the update process.) Once the update problem is resolved, the lock should be released automatically.

The operation of the whole locking mechanism can be tested with utilities provided under the Extras menu on the Initial Lock menu. The available options are:

Statistics	Reports on lock statistics
Diagnosis	System tests the locking process and provides report
Diagnosis in update	System performs test with lock objects
Function Info	Information on how the lock process operates

System Trace Files

The R/3 system provides trace facilities that enable administrators to debug and track system problems. There are four types of tracing functions provided that can be utilized for problem solving and performance tuning of the system and ABAP code. The tracing functions are

- System traces   *troubleshooting*
- Developer traces
- SQL trace   *developer's tool*
- ABAP program trace   *check performance of indexes and matchcodes on database tables*

System Traces

The system trace-monitoring functions are located through the menu path **Tools, Administration, Monitoring, Traces** or transaction ST01. The SQL, system, and developer traces will be available. The ABAP program trace is located through the menu path **Tools, ABAP/4 Workbench, Test, Runtime Analysis** or transaction SE30. Developers analyze their code using the SQL and ABAP program traces. These traces are also used to check performance of indexes and matchcodes on database tables. The system trace and developer traces are used for troubleshooting.

Selecting the Switch Trace Edit button on the System Trace main screen configures the system trace. A new screen is displayed, from which the following trace options can be selected:

- **Trace types.** This is where you select the type of trace required. By clicking on the Authorization Check button it is possible to trace which authorizations are touched by a transaction. This will assist in determining security profiles.

- **General management.** There are two fields here:

     General filters. Allows you to filter the trace by process, user, transaction, or program.

     Write options. Allows you to decide where the trace will be written.

- **Status of the active system.** In the file selection field, enter any value (using 0 to 9 and A to Z). This value will be substituted in the variable as defined in profile parameter rstr/file.

The default value is /usr/sap/<SID>/<instance name>/log/TRACE*x*00, where the chosen letter replaces *x*.

The system trace files are written in circular files.

CAUTION

Always be sure to check that traces are switched off after you have completed your analysis. The trace writes to the /usr/sap/<SID>/<instance>/log directory. If this file system were to get full, you potentially could experience performance problems. Old trace files should be deleted once the analysis is complete.

Developer Traces

The developer traces contain trace information about SAP work processes. There is valuable troubleshooting information in these files, as they provide explicit technical detail about system errors. These traces can be viewed from the Monitoring menu. Actual operating system files are located under the following directories:

/usr/sap/<SID>/<instance>/work

/usr/sap/<SID>/<instance>/profile

To display the contents of the files, double-click or select File Display. The names of all the developer trace files start with "dev_" and are listed in Table 14-1.

Table 14-1 Developer Trace File Names

Trace	File name
Dispatcher	dev_disp
Work processes	dev_w<*n*> *n*= number of work processes
Dynpro	dev_dy<*n*>
Roll	dev_ro<*n*>
Paging	dev_pg<*n*>
Remote function calls	dev_rfc<*n*>
Message server	dev_ms
Database interface	dev_db<*n*>
Enqueue process	dev_eq<*n*>
System logging	dev_lg<*n*>

Online Service System

SAP provides a service system that contains invaluable information for troubleshooting problems in the SAP environment. This feature has made SAP one of the leaders in online support services. The wide range of features provided by the SAP Online Service System (OSS) includes the following:

- Searching for and entering trouble tickets to report system problems
- Downloading software patches
- The latest release, installation, and upgrade information

The OSS functions can be found through the menu path **System, Services, SAP Services** or transaction OSS1.

To obtain more information on the features of OSS, more details are discussed fully in Chapter 4. OSS is a very valuable tool to have in your troubleshooting arsenal. OSS can be referenced after receiving a short dump. The information supplied in a short dump can be used to search OSS to establish if the error is a known SAP problem. The chances are someone has encountered the problem before you, and reported it to SAP. By searching OSS you can eliminate the possibility that SAP has provided a fix for your problem.

To determine if a fix has been provided, a search of the OSS note database is necessary. This is achieved by logging onto OSS and using the menu path from the inbox screen **Gen. Functions, Find,** and in the free text area fill in the information provided by Category 4 of the short dump. Fill in the SAP release you are currently using in the search criteria selection box. This will narrow down the search of notes relating to your specific release of SAP. Select the find button, and this should provide a list of OSS notes that could possibly be related to your specific problem. We will cover this in more detail later in the chapter, in the "Diagnosing the Problem" section.

The Database Alert Log

Another invaluable tool is the alert log. Here all the activity that occurs at the database level is recorded and can be viewed to diagnose many problems that are not always visible at the SAP level of monitoring and logging. This file resides in the saptrace directory, which is under the home directory of the ora<sid> user. The saptrace directory includes two other directories: background and usertrace. The usertrace directory includes trace files generated by user processes, while the background directory contains the alert<sid>.log file. The alert file continuously collects all the database start, stop, backups, log switches, and error messages. This file is constantly updated and is not lost when the database is restarted. This file can be viewed from within SAP from the following menu path: **Tools, Administration, Monitoring, Performance, Database, Activity**. Click on the detailed analysis menu, then select Database message log.

Diagnosing the Problem

In all cases of troubleshooting, you have to first diagnose the problem before actually solving the problem. In the first part of this chapter we discussed the tools that were available to assist in the diagnoses of problems. You will now use a real-life example to step through the decision points, which you will use as a basis for all your problem diagnosing.

In the example, you receive a message from one of your end users that while creating a sales order, they received an express mail message indicating that the update process was terminated.

Is the Problem Reproducible?

The first step is to contact the end user and obtain the information to reproduce the problem. The system where the problem occurred, the client, the transaction, and finally the data, are needed by the transaction to reproduce the error. Once you have received all the relevant information, try and reproduce the error by re-entering the transaction data in the same manner the user described. For the purposes of this example, we will say that after re-entering the transactional data, you received the identical symptoms that the end user described.

You know that the problem still exists in your system and further investigation is necessary.

The first step, because the user reported an update terminated message, is to check the update records monitor, transaction SM13, to make sure that the update is still active. If the update is not active, that is your first clue. You now have to determine why the update is no longer active. The system log, transaction SM21, is a good place to start. Use the information provided earlier on how to use the system log to diagnose all the information provided by the end user and search the system log for clues. The ABAP dump analysis screen, transaction ST22, is also a good place to start diagnosing the problem. Check for dumps created by the end user and your login, because you both encountered the same error.

For the purpose of this example, say that you found a message in the system log relating to a table that had reached maximum extents. The error will mention the table and the amount of extents that had been reached. It will also mention that this problem will require intervention by the system administrator. To confirm your findings, you can log on as user ORA<SID> and check the alert log. The alert log can also be displayed from within SAP. Using the Alert log is discussed in detail in the first half of this chapter. You have now established why the update task was not active.

Problem Rectification

After diagnosing the initial problem, you will rectify the problem by allocating more extents to the table identified in the system log. Once the table has been extended, you will need to test the failing transaction once more. Try and post the transaction one more time, and this time you are able to post the transaction successfully.

Utilizing the diagnosis tools at your disposal, you were able to identify and isolate the area causing the problem and rectify the problem. This method of utilizing the analysis tools at your disposable and identifying the problems will make you invaluable to your company and end users.

Chapter 15

The Internet and SAP

In This Chapter

◆ Architecture and Administration

◆ Internet Application Components (IAC)

◆ ITS and Components

◆ WebReporting and SAP@Web Studio

◆ Security

A substantial number of companies are allowing access to their SAP systems by their remote users and by non-company staff. The benefit of doing so is to allow the users, typically sales staff and preferred vendors, access to real time data over a very cost-effective communications medium—the Internet.

This chapter will show you what hardware and software you require from SAP, how to configure it, what the implications are of allowing Internet access to your SAP system, and finally what users are allowed to perform on the system once they are logged on.

Architecture

As mentioned earlier in the book, SAP has a typical three-tier client/server model with the database server, the application server, and the presentation server. To allow the SAP system to be accessed over the Internet or an intranet (internal company Internet accessed by your company's employees) using a Web browser, an additional two layers—an ITS (Internet Transaction Server) and an (Hyper-Text Transport Protocol) HTTP server—are added to this three-tier model, with the Web browser acting as the presentation layer. Figure 15-1 illustrates a block diagram of the SAP system and the flow of the request and response from a Web browser.

The ITS and HTTP servers act as an interface between the presentation and application layers. The ITS is also able to link one or more HTTP servers with one or more SAP systems.

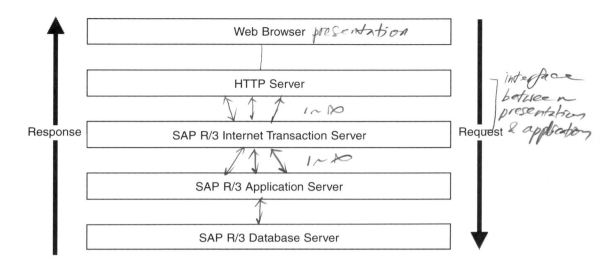

FIGURE 15-1   *A five-tier architecture allows you to access SAP over the Internet or an intranet.*

Installation Summary

This topic provides a quick guide to the steps that are required to install the ITS and its components. Please be aware that there are several new terms and acronyms introduced but are explained in greater detail later within this chapter.

Installation is achieved by means of several executable files that are FTPed (File Transfer Protocol) from SAP's SAPSERV3 or SAPSERV4 servers or copied off specially ordered SAP CDs. These files include:

- ◆ **Setup.exe.** For the physical installation of the software for the IAC (Internet Application Components), you are required to use Setup.exe first, as it will collate all the information required for the installation and the succeeding virtual ITS installations.

- ◆ **ITSInstall.exe & ITSDeinstall.exe.** These executables will copy or delete, respectively, the files required to create the AGate (application Gateway) and WGate (Web Gateway).

- ◆ **ITSVInstall.exe & ITSVDeinstall.exe.** These executables will copy or delete the files required to create one or more virtual ITS servers under the directory C:\Program Files\SAP\ITS\2.0\<Vitual ITS>\ and the following subsequent subdirectories:

...\Install	Install protocols
...\Logs	Install and access logs
...\Service	Service files
...\Templates	HTML business templates
...\Traces	Error logs

Administration

The operational administration of the servers is also controlled using executable files that include:

◆ **ITSVControl.exe.** Starts up or stops the virtual ITS and Web servers.

◆ **ITSVProtect.exe.** Administers the files access.

 NOTE

Using the service file and the parameter runtimeMode, you may place the server in either production mode (pm) or development mode (dm). Other parameters are also available to configure the security.

The Internet Application Components (IAC)

Basic networking knowledge is required to configure the ITS and IAC hardware and software components, which include:

◆ TCP/IP addressing, ports, and connectivity

◆ Bridges and Routers

◆ Domain Name Systems (DNS)

◆ Hypertext Transfer Protocol (HTTP)

◆ File Transfer Protocol (FTP)

◆ Remote connectivity and login (Telnet)

- ◆ Electronic mail (e-mail)
- ◆ Simple Mail Transfer Protocol (SMTP)
- ◆ World Wide Web (WWW)
- ◆ Universal Resource Locator (URL)

The components of the IAC can be broken down to each of their distinct levels, running their own part of enabling software.

- ◆ **Web Browser.** The browser should support HTML 3.2 or later. (Both Microsoft Internet Explorer and Netscape Navigator, versions 4.0 and higher, support HTML 3.2 and run on Windows 95/98 and NT.)
- ◆ **Server.** The ITS software will be loaded on top of either Microsoft Internet Information Server 4.0 or Netscape Enterprise Server 3.0 or Netscape Enterprise Server for UNIX.
- ◆ **ITS.** Depending on the version of the SAP software, you may use one of the following:

SAP R/3 3.1G	ITS 1.0
SAP R/3 3.1H	ITS 1.1
SAP R/3 4.0A	ITS 2.0
SAP R/3 4.0b	ITS 2.1

ITS and Components

The ITS software consists of five different elements:

- ◆ **AGate.** Application Gateway is the gateway that is used to connect to the application server on the SAP system.
- ◆ **DIAG.** Dynamic Information and Action Gateway is the protocol used to call the SAP transactions.
- ◆ **RFC.** Remote Function Calls are used to call SAP function modules.
- ◆ **WGate.** Web Gateway is the gateway that is used to connect to the HTTP server.
- ◆ **CGI.** Common Gateway Interface is used to communicate between the HTTP server and the executable program on the same server.

For technical reasons, the CGI requires that the WGATE software be installed on the same server as the HTTP server. This leads to the various server configurations that may be used to set up the Internet application components. For example, in Figure 15-2, the ITS and HTTP components are installed on the physical server, whereas in Figure 15-3, the two components are installed on separate boxes.

In all the scenarios depicted by Figures 15-2 through 15-5, each WGate should have one AGate; however, you may have two AGates running on one machine.

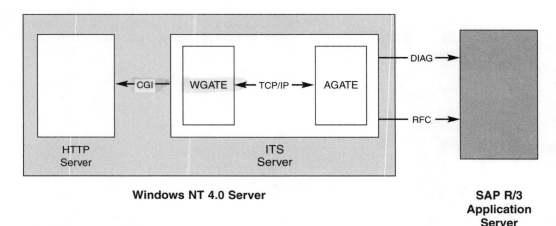

FIGURE 15-2 *ITS and HTTP components are loaded on the same computer.*

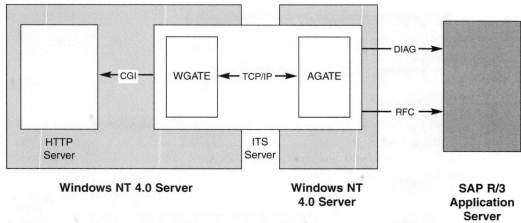

FIGURE 15-3 *ITS and HTTP components are loaded on separate computers.*

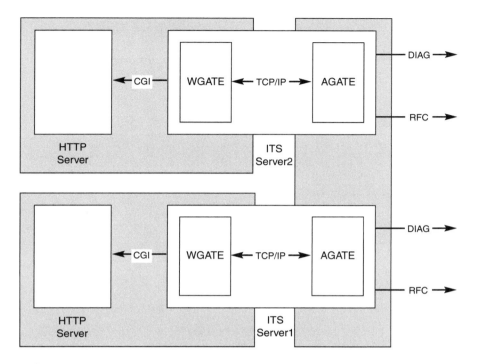

FIGURE 15-4 *One ITS and two HTTP components are loaded on separate computers.*

You may also have one or more SAP application servers communicating with one or more AGates!

Obviously, as more users are connected via the HTTP/ITS server and querying the SAP system, the more likely it is that degradation of performance will occur. The way to resolve this issue is to first add more memory, then faster CPUs, then increase the quantity of CPUs, and finally add more ITS servers.

ITS Project Directory and Service File

The project directory is one that is created upon the start of a project using the SAP@Web Studio tool. It may contain one or more WebTransactions and be used to upload (publish) to or download from the ITS or upload to an SAP system. This folder may also contain templates, text, and MIME files (e.g. graphic, video, sound, etc.).

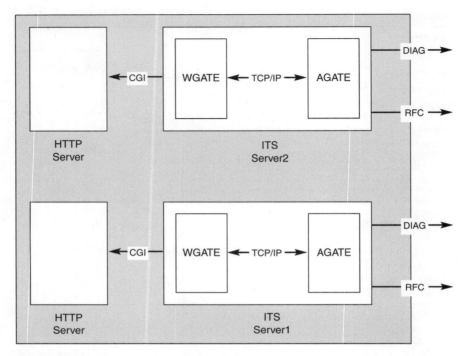

FIGURE 15-5 *Two ITS and two HTTP components are loaded on the same computer.*

An ITS service file is required for each Internet user in order to be able to access the SAP system using the URL format:

> **http://<server>/path/wgate/service/!**

An example:

> **http://nt01/scripts/wgate/1234/!**

The services file provides the following:

◆ Logon information

◆ Allowing the execution of a Transaction (WebTransaction) or Function Module (WebRFC)

◆ Conversion of SAP screens and data to HTML pages

The service files are ASCII files, with srvc file extensions, running on the AGate computer. The files should include data, such as:

~messageserver

~systemname

~logingroup

~appserver

~systemnumber

~client

~login

~password

~language

~transaction

~xgateway

[handwritten: ITS operation: { WebTransaction, Web RFC, Web Reporting }]

The SAP user data is held for Internet users in a file called global.srvc.

As mentioned earlier, the ITS software consists of five different elements: AGate, Diag, RFC, Wgate, and CGI. The ITS has three distinct operations:

- **WebTransaction.** Where certain SAP transactions are accessible with the use of a Web browser. It consists of three parts: a Web-enabled R/3 transaction, a service file, and an HTML business template.

- **WebRFC.** Where certain SAP function modules are executed via the ITS to display or change data.

- **WebReporting.** Where certain SAP ABAP programs generate reports and lists, including reporting trees.

Creation of WebTransactions

As just mentioned, WebTransactions are operations in which SAP transactions are accessible with the use of a Web browser. Each SAP transaction is required to be converted to HTML format, and even though SAP provides a large number of transactions that can be accessed over the Internet, not every transaction is available for access over the Internet. But, SAP is providing a large number of converted transactions in the HTML format on a daily basis. A WebTransaction consists of three parts:

- A Web-enabled R/3 transaction performed within SAP

- A service file created on the AGate computer

- An HTML business template—an HTML conversion of each SAP screen

SAP web-enabled transaction ⟷ BAPI ⟷ Business object interface

For an SAP transaction to be Web-enabled, two components are required:

◆ **BAPIs** (business application programming interfaces). A BAPI is an interface to create, change, or retrieve business objects within the SAP system business data and processes.

◆ **Business objects** (residing in the Business Object Repository). Business objects are a view of related SAP data and processes; examples include employee, invoice, customer, vendor, purchase order, and customer order.

Each object has components associated with it, including the following:

◆ Basic data   ◆ Attributes

◆ Interfaces   ◆ Methods

◆ Key fields   ◆ Events

An example of the attributes and methods for two common SAP business objects are shown in Table 15-1.

Table 15-1 Business Objects and Their Attributes

Business Object	Attributes	Methods
Customer	Name	Remove
	Shipping Address	Address Change
	Billing Address	
Purchase Order	Vendor	Create
	Date	Change
	Item list	Display
		Approve

NOTE

SAP provides close to 1,000 object types and 500 BAPIs for SAP Version 4.x.

To design a WebTransaction enabling an SAP transaction, you must follow five steps:

1. Identify your audience and data by answering the following questions:

   • Who will be your target audience?

   • What is your product?

   • What information are you making available?

- What are your hardware and software requirements to access the information

2. Design a flow map to identify the steps your audience takes to access information (i.e., login, dates, etc.)

3. Select existing BAPIs and business objects to use to set up WebTransaction.

4. Create the SAP transaction using the BAPIs and business objects to create screens, input fields, and so on.

5. Create the HTML business template using SAP@Web Studio.

Creation of WebRFC and WebReporting

WebRFC and WebReporting allow you to do the following:

◆ Execute special RFC-enabled function modules in SAP. Figure 15-6 illustrates a call to a WebRFC-enabled function module.

◆ Run an ABAP report using the WebRFC connection. Figure 15-7 illustrates a call to an WebRFC-enabled function module, calling an ABAP report.

◆ Display lists and trees using a Web browser.

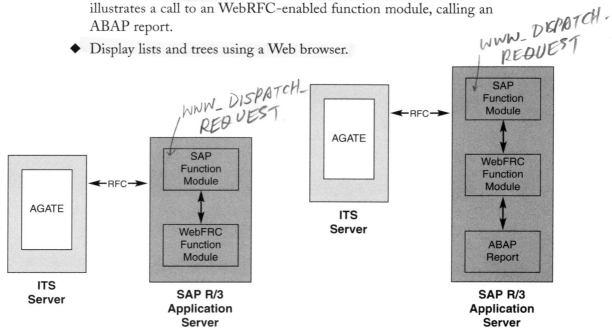

FIGURE 15-6 *ITS calling an SAP function module (WWW_DISPATCH_REQUEST), in turn calling a WebRFC-enabled function module*

FIGURE 15-7 *ITS calling an SAP function module, in turn calling a WebRFC-enabled function module, in turn calling an ABAP report for WebReporting*

Call the WebRFC with the following syntax:

```
../wgate/WebRFC/!?_function = <function module> [& <name> = <value>]
```

An example:

```
../wgate/WebRFC/!?_function = WWW_GET_URL
```

A list of function modules used by the WebRFC calls are shown in Table 15-2.

Table 15-2

Function Modules Used by the WebRFC Calls	
Function Group ALEW - ALE/Web Basis Function Group	WWW_USERTYPE_GET_WITH_ID WWW_USERTYPE_SELECTION_POPUP WWW_USER_AUTHORITY WWW_USER_AUTH_MESSAGE
Function Group AWRT - ALE via Web Runtime System	WWW_URLENCODE
Function Group SBWW - Display BOR	WWW_GET_BOR_TREE_LIST WWW_GET_BOR_TREE_NODE WWW_GET_BOR_TREE_OBJ_DETAILS WWW_GET_BOR_TREE_TYPEINFO
Function Group SHTM - Basis WWW Development	WWWDATA_DELETE WWWDATA_EXPORT WWWDATA_IMPORT WWWPARAMS_DELETE WWWPARAMS_DELETE_ALL WWWPARAMS_INSERT WWWPARAMS_MAINTAIN WWWPARAMS_MODIFY_SCREEN WWWPARAMS_MODIFY_SINGLE WWWPARAMS_READ WWWPARAMS_READ_ALL WWWPARAMS_UPDATE WWW_SETTINGS WWW_SETTINGS_CLEAR
Function Group SR2I - R/2 Connection to WebReporting	WWW_R2_GET_REPORT

Table 15-2 *(continued)*

Function Modules Used by the WebRFC Calls

Function Group SURI - SAP Internet Interactive	WWW_I_BEFORE_SELSCREEN WWW_I_GET_LIST_LEVEL_0 WWW_I_GET_LIST_LEVEL_N WWW_I_GET_STATUS_FUNCTIONS
Function Group SURL - SAP Internet	WWW_DISPATCH_REQUEST WWW_DRILL_DOWN WWW_ERROR_MESSAGE WWW_GET_HTML_OBJECT WWW_GET_MIME_OBJECT WWW_GET_NODE_LIST WWW_GET_REPORT WWW_GET_SCRIPT WWW_GET_SELSCREEN WWW_GET_TREE_LIST WWW_GET_TREE_NODE WWW_GET_URL WWW_HTML_ECHO WWW_HTML_FROM_LISTOBJECT WWW_HTML_MERGER WWW_ITAB_TO_HTML WWW_ITAB_TO_HTML_HEADERS WWW_ITAB_TO_HTML_LAYOUT WWW_LIST_BACK WWW_LIST_TO_HTML WWW_LOAD_OBJECT_ATTRIBUTES WWW_LOAD_TEMPLATE_ATTRIBUTES WWW_L_HTML_LIST_BUTTONS WWW_L_MERGE_LIST_WITH_TEMPLATE WWW_MODEL_MODULE WWW_PACK_TABLE WWW_PROCESS_EVENT WWW_SCREEN_TO_HTML WWW_SET_RETURN_CODE WWW_SET_URL WWW_URL_PREFIX

The WebRFC service file may include the following parameters:

```
~Xgateway
~RFCGatewayHost
~RFCGatewayService
~RFCSystemType
~RFCTimeOut
~RFCDebuggingOn
~RFCDetailError
```

WebReporting

To execute an ABAP report, you may use a function module as seen in the following example. You must ensure that the users have access to the authorization group that the function module belongs to as well as all other relevant authorizations.

```
../wgate/WebRFC/!?_function = WWW_GET_REPORT
                                    &_report = reportname
                                    &_variant = variantname
                                    &_template_set = templatename
```

for check boxes/radio buttons:

```
cboc_<name>
radc_<name>
```

for parameters:

```
par<type>_<name>
```

for select options:

```
sel<type>_<name> - low
sel<type>_<name> - high
```

For each of the function modules, please see the documentation that is provided within your SAP system (use transaction code SE37, type in the name of the function module, then press the F9 key).

WebReporting Browser

To view the SAP trees via the ITS server, you are required to use the same function module you used for the WebRFC WWW_DISPATCH_REQUEST, which in turn will call WWW_GET_TREELIST, which will then access the SAP ABAP reports and lists (see Figure 15-8).

Other WebReporting browser function modules include:

WWW_GET_NODE_LIST
WWW_GET_REPORT
WWW_GET_SELSCREEN
WWW_GET_TREE_LIST
WWW_GET_TREE_NODE

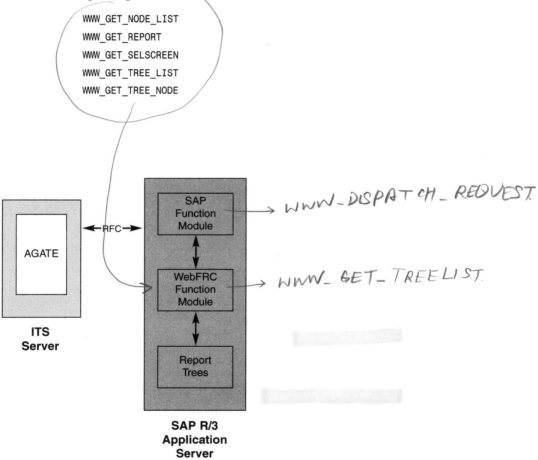

WWW-DISPATCH_REQUEST.

WWW_GET_TREELIST.

FIGURE 15-8 *WebReporting browser*

User Administration

Using SAP transaction code SU05, you are able to create the ID of a user, and define the type of user. Examples of user types are:

APPLICANT	Applicant
BUS1006001	Business partner employee
BUS1007	Debtor
BUS1008	Creditor
BUS1065	Employee
KNA1	Customer
PDOTYPE_PT	Attendee

You are then able to create, change, delete, lock/unlock, reset password, etc., as per any typical SAP user.

TIP

A user ID may be more than one type. For example, a user may be a creditor and a debtor.

Security

control access
— encryption.

Security can be implemented in the following ways:

◆ Controlled access to the network, directories, and files. This may be no access, read-only access, or full (read/write/change/delete) access by means of a logon ID and password.

◆ Encryption technology to protect communication across the Internet and/or secured networks. Includes different encryption standards such as RSA (asymmetrical encryption) or DES (symmetrical encryption).

Controlled Access

user ID, password.
IP

Access is enforced using a *firewall*, which protects your network and systems from outside intruders. Access is allowed either to users with approved IDs and passwords or to computers from known IP addresses and trusted (known) networks.

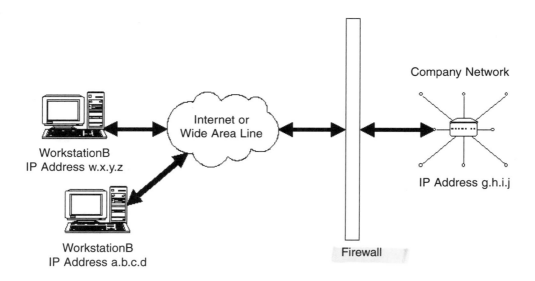

FIGURE 15-9 *Firewall protection is set up between your network and the Internet world.*

in coming only

The firewall stands as a barrier between your network and the Internet world, as shown in Figure 15-9. If the firewall is configured to allow only workstations with IP addresses a.b.*.*, then any workstation that has an IP address beginning with a.b will be allowed to pass through the network (IP components c.d are ignored). Therefore, workstation B is allowed to pass through the firewall but workstation A is blocked. As a second layer of defense, workstation B will still require user IDs and passwords.

A *proxy server* has two job functions. The first as a firewall to allow access from the Internet to your network, and secondly to allow computers on your intranet to access the Internet.

firewall — network ⟷ Internet
proxy server — network ⟷ internet.
↳ intranet.

Encryption Technology

Another security measure is to use the Secured Socket Layer (SSL) protocol, which resides between the TCP/IP protocol and application protocols to ensure authentication and encryption. *(presentation layer)*

To secure the IAC/ITS and its components, you need three layers of protection, as seen in Figure 15-10.

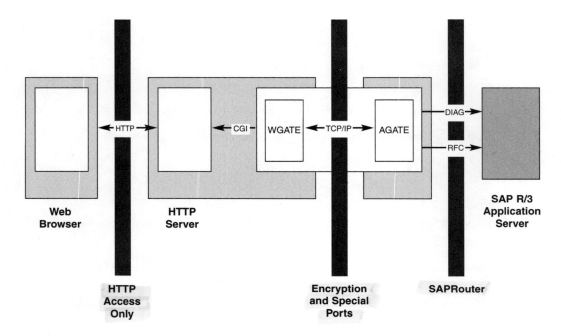

FIGURE 15-10 *Three areas where security can be enforced for ITS*

You can see that the HTTP firewall will only allow HTTP connections to pass through to the HTTP server. The second firewall will only allow encrypted connections via the ports to allow data to pass through to the AGate. The final firewall protects the SAP system via the SAPRouter connection, which is used in most SAP installations.

SAP@Web Studio

An ITS service is the set of service files, HTML templates, and other files used to call Web-enabled R/3 transactions from the Internet.

The SAP@Web Studio is a development tool that runs on your Windows NT PC, with which you can do the following:

- ◆ Create, change, or modify an ITS service
- ◆ Create, change, modify, generate, compile, or test HTML templates from R/3 screens

◆ Create, change, or modify language-support files to translate HTML pages

◆ Publish service and ITS files

You will need to download the SAP@Web Studio application from http://www.saplabs.com dependent upon your version of SAP. SAP releases:

◆ 3.1H and above is supported for ITS release 1.1

◆ 4.0A and above is supported for ITS release 2.1

◆ 4.5A and above is supported for ITS release 2.2

The SAP@Web Studio application also provides *wizards,* which offer step-by-step procedures for creating service files, HTML templates, and language-support files, as well as definitions of ITS sites, SAP connections, etc.

Summary

This chapter introduced the basic components required to set up the Internet Transaction Server and its components to not only be able to access your SAP system, but to execute business transactions as well.

It also introduced how to enable SAP transaction on the Web—either transactions converted to HTML by SAP or custom created ones using the SAP@Web studio.

The final area that was discussed was enabling security access to your Internet transaction server, and more importantly, your SAP system.

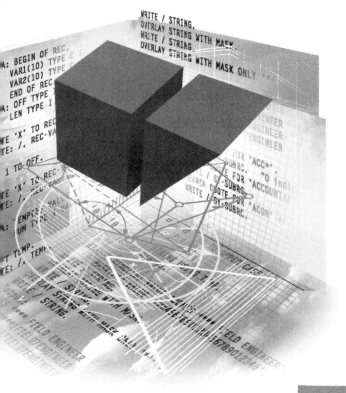

PART VI

Upgrading

16 The Administrator's Role in Upgrading R/3

17 Pre-Production Preparation for Administrators

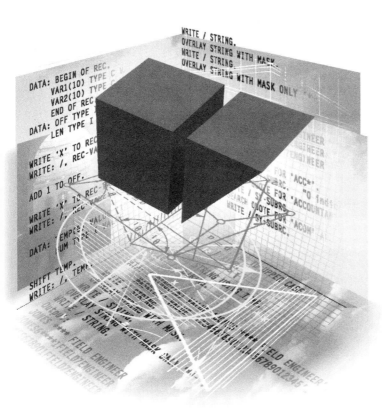

Chapter 16

The Administrator's Role in Upgrading R/3

In This Chapter

- ◆ When to Upgrade
- ◆ Planning the Upgrade
- ◆ The Technical Upgrade

An ancient Chinese curse says: "May you live in interesting times!" SAP upgrade times surely are interesting times.

An upgrade has two sides to it, namely the *Basis upgrade* and the *functional upgrade.* The Basis upgrade of a system without any special add-ons or industry solutions should take at the most two days per system. This means it should take only two days from the time you start **R3up** until you finish with the last Hot Package and post-upgrade tasks. The functional side of the upgrade is the portion that takes about three to six months, and it might take you a year if you were to rewrite SAP.

As Basis administrator, you will have to upgrade and upgrade again, keep track of transports, identify performance issues, and solve difficult problems for users and developers, to name just a few activities.

This chapter takes you through a high-level project plan pertaining only to the Basis administrator. You will be introduced to planning the upgrade, a few strategies, and finally the chapter will discuss the physical upgrade process for Development, Quality Assurance, and Production.

The Upgrade Process

Practice makes perfect! The same is true with an SAP upgrade. If you plan and document your upgrade very well and you do a few test upgrades on a research and development machine before you even touch the development, quality assurance, and finally the production systems, your upgrade will be very successful.

When to Upgrade

A better question than when to upgrade might be "Why do companies upgrade?" Companies might upgrade to a new release because:

◆ New and/or required functionality is built in.

◆ Known program bugs have been fixed.

◆ Performance improvements have been made.

◆ SAP stops supporting old releases.

◆ SAP harnesses the new functionality added to the hardware, operating systems and databases.

◆ Third-party software running on SAP requires a specific new release.

As for when to upgrade, do not upgrade the production system during an active business period. Active business periods are month-end, quarter-end, and year-end. The bottom line is that you need to plan your upgrade well and make it timely.

Planning Your Upgrade

As mentioned before, the Basis side of the upgrade is a very small portion of the complete upgrade timeline, but is nevertheless extremely important. The success of the upgrade project will largely depend on the planning and technical ability of the Basis administrator and that person's ability to communicate technical concepts and issues to the project team and the business.

Upgrade Project Phases

An SAP upgrade goes through a few phases. The success of the upgrade will depend on how well you plan and prepare for each of these phases, which are listed below:

1. Prepare the upgrade plan.
2. Perform upgrade on a research and development system.
3. Perform upgrade on the nonproductive systems (development and quality assurance).
4. Upgrade production.
5. Go live and support the business user community.

Upgrade Complexities

No textbook example exists for an upgrade. No two plans are the same, and for that matter, no two SAP environments are the same. If it were possible to only upgrade SAP, upgrades would be relatively easy; alas, operating systems, databases, and third-party software also need to be upgraded. Another problem with planning for an upgrade is that the development, quality assurance, and production environments are never the same (this includes hardware, software, and data in the database). Even if you have a research and development system, it probably will not represent production very closely. The ideal would be to have all your SAP environments the same, but because of budget constraints, this is highly unlikely.

A few things to keep in mind about an upgrade are as follows:

◆ SAP and all the software it interacts with need not be compatible and supported to function together. Is SAP supported on this version of the database or that version of the operating system? Are the tax software, the printer spooling software, the scheduling software, etc., supported?

◆ Industry solutions are not supported on all SAP releases. Industry solutions can complicate upgrades because sometimes you have to do two or more upgrades in order to get to your desired SAP version. The industry solution *ISSW*, also known as *Golden Gate*, is supported on SAP releases 3.0D, 3.0F, 3.1H AND 4.0B. If you have a system with SAP 3.0D installed and your goal is release 3.1H, then you will have to upgrade to 3.0F and then to 3.1H. The reason for this route is that the upgrade from 3.0D to 3.0F and from 3.0F to 3.1H are proven upgrades. In other words, it will work and you will find support for any errors you may encumber. Theoretically, it is possible to upgrade directly from 3.0D to 3.1H, but the upgrade path is unproven. My advice is to contact the industry solution vendor and confirm that the upgrade path you want to follow is feasible.

◆ The languages installed on the system and the functionality used to accommodate the installed languages should be taken into consideration. An example of this might be when MDMP (MNLS) systems are finally replaced with UNICODE systems. Chapter 4 discusses the issues around language installations. Briefly, when you eventually convert to UNICODE, all the characters used in your current environment need to be converted to UNICODE. If you are using blended code pages, it will still be possible to convert, but the process will be more complicated.

◆ The production system usually has some kind of high-availability software installed, allowing the SAP environment to move from a failing machine to another, functional machine, and thereby ensuring system availability. With SAP you have to make sure that your high-availability software is supported with the latest release of SAP. If not done properly, this little portion of the upgrade has the potential to drastically prolong the system unavailability.

◆ Another problem is that companies sometimes are in the middle of other development projects. The theory is that you have to freeze the environment. That is, no more changes are allowed until after the upgrade. Tell that to your manager who has committed that certain new functionality will be available at a given date and that you will have the upgrade complete. You have to develop an upgrade plan that will accommodate developers making changes without affecting your upgrade. A frequent complaint from developers is that the development system does not have sufficient business data for them to do initial testing of code. A client copy is a potential solution to this problem, but if you have a database with a size of 50GB, this is out of the question. Some companies copy their production environment to development and upgrade development. SAP upgrade material, however, states that you are never to copy your production environment over your development environment. Development contains all of your objects, changes, versions, and so on. It is your source for information if you have problems during your upgrade. Still, companies are obviously willing to take the risk. They copy the current development environment somewhere for reference. Then they copy production to development, upgrade the new development, and migrate all changes that they want from the old development to the new. They keep the old development environment around for a month or two for reference and to make sure they have everything they need. Eventually they back it up, place the backup in a safe place, and remove the old development environment entirely.

The question now is should you not copy production over development or should you take the risk doing as described above. The SAP documentation says just that you should not copy production over development. To expand on that: Do not copy production over development if you do not have a reference copy of development online and handy.

There are a few things that you have to consider when copying production over development, namely:

1. Make sure that the system that owns all your development objects remains the development system.

2. You will loose the version information on all the development objects. Make sure you have all relevant version information documented into the ABAP code.

3. Make sure you keep your IMG notes. You will have to export the notes from the old environment to the new environment. That is if you do not have these notes in production.

Prepare for the Upgrade

As Basis administrator and technical lead, you should have a role in making decisions during the initial planning phases of the project plan. This is a very important part of the upgrade. You are part of the decision-making process, which defines the upgrade organization, designates the resources required for the upgrade, determines the upgrade budget, compiles the project work plans, and so on. All of the above is beyond the scope of this chapter. If you want to know more about these concepts, get ahold of the ASAP methodology, which provides explanations in much more detail.

A Basis administrator's primary responsibility is the SAP hardware and software environment, and he needs to be aware of the following components within the SAP environment:

◆ **Capacity and resource planning.** The upgrade manuals (Manual R/3 Installation on <OS> - OS Dependencies and Upgrading to Release <Release> <OS>) suggest OS kernel settings and additional disk space requirements for the upgrade. (Replace <OS> with the operating system you use, for example HPUX, and replace <release> with the target SAP release you are upgrading to, for example 40B.) The *PREPARE* phase of the upgrade will also make resource recommendations. Since you are doing capacity and resource planning, you might as well extend it to include future resource and capacity planning. Analyze the existing system for performance and resource consumption. You can then budget for more CPU, disk, and memory, or maybe hardware that is more powerful.

◆ **Additional language support.** Each language installed on the system will require additional disk space and downtime that need to be taken into account.

◆ **Industry solutions.** Industry solutions are not supported with every SAP release. Some of them are supported on every other release, and if you are three or four versions behind with SAP, it will mean that you will have to do two or more upgrades. Each of these upgrades complicates matters, meaning that you will have to plan for additional downtime and disk space. Another problem with doing multiple upgrades is that it reduces the number of strategies you can use to upgrade the SAP environment.

◆ **SAP country-specific versions.** Some companies are lucky enough to be located in countries (like Brazil) that have very specific law requirements. SAP developed solutions for these companies that are not part of the standard SAP software.

◆ **Third-party products or add-ons.** An SAP environment is a combination of diverse software packages interacting with the standard SAP application from within and without. All these different software packages have different requirements. Some will have to be upgraded because their respective release versions are not certified to function correctly with the other software in the environment, including SAP.

◆ **Interfaces between R/3 and non-R/3 software.** SAP does not work isolated on its own. It interacts with the world outside (with other SAP environments, legacy environments, specialized applications, the Internet, and real-time systems, to name just a few). Each of these interfaces will require attention in order to keep it functioning in the new SAP environment.

◆ **Operating system release.** You have to verify that all your software packages running in the SAP environment are supported and certified to function correctly on your current operating system. If they are not, you will have to upgrade your operating system as well. You will also have to keep the operating patch levels current. Once you begin upgrading the operating system, you will have to account for the resource and downtime requirements for the upgrade and for upgrading any high-availability software packages (like MC Service Guard) running on the production systems.

◆ **Database release.** SAP has to be certified to run on the database release you are running or have to upgrade to. Both SAP and the database have to be certified to function correctly on the operating system that both are running on or will be running on. Upgrading to Oracle 8 or SQL Server will require downtime in order to convert the data from the old database format to the new. You might consider doing a complete database reorganization. All these factors need to be taken into account when deciding whether or not to do an upgrade.

The crux of the matter is that you have to compile an inventory list of all your hardware and software, along with a matrix containing the environment interdependencies and the resource requirements for each.

The worst case scenario is that you would have to upgrade SAP, the OS, database and all third party software, while the best case is that you would only have to upgrade SAP. Plan to upgrade the other components separately from SAP. This considerably lessens the impact and risks to the business community. It is difficult to suggest when an environment upgrade versus the SAP upgrade should take place. It will depend on the state of your environment. Sometimes you will be able to do SAP first, other times you will have to do the upgrades together, and other times you will have to do SAP last.

Taking all the above points into consideration, draw up a rough project plan with estimated time and resource requirements. A few factors you should note while putting together the time estimates include:

◆ The number of systems
◆ The number of clients on a system
◆ The number of languages
◆ The size of the database
◆ The power of the hardware

The project plan should include time estimates for development, quality assurance, and production. You should also decide on the strategy that you want to follow, namely A_SWITCH, A_ON, or A_OFF. The selected upgrade strategy will greatly affect both the run time and the downtime of the upgrade.

The objective with the different strategies is to provide companies with different options on the amount of upgrade time and the amount of production downtime. In a perfect world, production downtime would be zero.

The SAP upgrade manuals describe the different strategies (A_ON, A_OFF, and A_SWITCH) very well, so all that remains here is to quickly state the main difference between the different strategies. Each strategy is a trade-off between the total business downtime and the disk space required to accommodate the downtime. If you require the minimum downtime, you will require huge amounts of disk space and vice versa.

down time ↓ → disk space ↑
down time ↑ → disk space ↓

Planning the General Upgrade

Before attempting any upgrade, you have to do some serious research on how the upgrade should be accomplished. SAP provides a bunch of booklets explaining the upgrade process step-by-step; research these booklets and any additional updates SAP provides through OSS with care.

Your planning efforts will focus on both the general upgrade and the technical upgrade. The following sections discuss several steps that are involved in planning the *general upgrade*.

Review Upgrade Notes

Always download the latest OSS notes from the OSS servers. Here you will find suggestions and recommendations on possible problems that might occur during the upgrade. Each of these changes suggested by the different notes must be included in the technical upgrade plan. The technical plan should read like a recipe. Every step should be known and anticipated in advance. You should be able to follow the plan to know when to stop the upgrade in order to make corrections in advance before any errors occur. If unavoidable errors do occur, the solution should be part of the plan.

Following is a list of the different sources for additional upgrade information. You will find the information you require in the SAP upgrade documentation and the OSS system notes.

◆ *Release notes* containing release specific information

◆ *OSS notes* pertaining to upgrading to the new SAP release

◆ *Industry solution notes* describing the Industry solution upgrade process and specific errors pertaining the industry solution

◆ Notes explaining the training necessities for the new SAP release

◆ Notes explaining how the SAP authorizations for the new release should be changed

Put a Test Plan Together

Test plans should be developed for both the functional and technical upgrades. The Basis administrator should be involved with both. Everything in the environment that changes should be tested, and if a specific item cannot be tested, the reasons for this should be documented.

Basis-related testing includes the following areas:

◆ Interfaces are an integral part of SAP. Each of the different interfaces needs to be tested for connectivity as well as functionality. If you have a high-availability environment configured, you will have to test the interfaces in all the different fail-over states the high-availability environment offers.

◆ Printing and faxing are two of the windows users have on data within the SAP system. Printing and faxing orders, invoices, checks, and reports are very important components of the business workflow. You will have to test at least the printers critical to the business. Also, make sure that you have redundant printers and faxes for these critical business functions.

◆ The most important scenario that should be tested is the ability to recover from a disaster before, during, and after the upgrade. Test your backups and your ability to restore them.

◆ You have to test the high-availability functionality in your SAP environment. Compile a list with all the different failure scenarios that you can envision happening to the SAP environment and test each of those. Think of network problems, hardware problems, power failures, software problems, and so on.

◆ You have to put stress on the SAP environment. Normal day-to-day activity on SAP is usually not a problem. You need to know how the system will react during exception periods like month-end or quarter-end periods. You should tune and build the SAP system to deal with these situations.

◆ Identify the transactions that are business critical and are used often. Test these transactions by executing volumes of these transactions at the same time. This should indicate to you how many of a certain transaction can be executed at the same time without any negative effect on the SAP environment.

◆ As administrator you have a bunch of transactions within SAP to test. You also have to test your monitoring and alert procedures.

◆ Performance statistics gathering is not actually a test on its own, but it is an integral part of each of the tests. Gather and use these statistics to tune SAP and to make it a better system for all the users.

Postpone Existing R/3 Projects and Changes to the Environment

Postponing projects and changes usually requires something more than simply stating: "There shall be no changes to the environment henceforth." Not only should emergency changes be allowed, but you probably shouldn't stop all the other R/3 projects for the duration of a six-month upgrade project. The project team has to be creative, finding ways to simultaneously accommodate the upgrade and the other projects.

One solution is to stage the upgrade repeatedly on a research and development system, allowing developers and the business to continue in the normal development, quality, and production environments. Yes, while you are staging the upgrade, the business environment is changing, and the developers are probably introducing new problems into the upgrade. The objective is to find solutions to most of the problems and challenges during the technical upgrade. Once this goal is achieved, freeze the SAP environment (do not allow any more changes). Do a final staging upgrade, then move to development and upgrade it. Developers can then continue development, but they are not allowed to transport anything to quality or production. When development is done, move immediately to quality and after that to production. The goal with this plan is to move through development, quality, and production in the shortest possible time, allowing the developers to follow the upgrade with their changes through the SAP environment.

Whatever strategy you follow, it has to be communicated to the project team and the business community. Chance control procedures have to be in place and adhered to. *Change control* is a set of rules governing the way changes are made to your system.

Planning the Technical Upgrade

The following sections discuss several steps that are involved in planning the *technical upgrade*.

Reduce the Downtime for the Upgrade *(Reduce DB size by archive, reorganization, delete client)*

Choose the A_ON upgrade strategy from the three strategies discussed earlier. A_ON allows for the shortest downtime, but it requires huge amounts of archive space. The reason for the space requirements is that the upgrade is executed with the database archive mode on. A_SWITCH is the default upgrade selection that is a compromise between disk space requirements and the amount of downtime.

Archive old outdated application data out of the database. This should reduce the database size, speeding up the upgrade, especially if the tables that are being archived are used during table conversions. Archiving can be a very slow and time-consuming process. Preferably, all data should be archived long before the upgrade takes place.

Another time-consuming option is to reorganize the entire database. This option tends to become impossible for very large databases (VLDBs). A better proposition would be to identify only those database objects that require reorganization. Reorganize the database over time, perhaps by doing one tablespace at a time or maybe one large table at a time. Doing the database reorganization during the upgrade depends on your database size, hardware, and the available resources. Reorganizing the database can take weeks.

By now it should be obvious that in order to accelerate the upgrade process, you should attempt to reduce the database size. Yet another option is to delete clients that are not required anymore or clients that can be re-created after the upgrade.

Prepare to Adjust the Custom Changes Made to SAP

Why do you need to do modifications and adjustments? The answer probably is self-evident. Changes were made to SAP objects either by implementing OSS notes or by customers building their own functionality into the system. All these changes should be analyzed and reimplemented, if required, in the new upgraded SAP environment. Ideally, there should be no modification and adjustment phase, for the following reasons:

◆ Zero changes equate into zero modifications and adjustments. In other words, during upgrades, no effort is required by analysts and developers to find all the changes, reimplement the changes, and finally testing the changes. The ideal is not always possible, therefore you should always attempt to return as many objects as possible to the SAP standard.

◆ It greatly shortens the overall upgrade timeline. The development team will have to spend time analyzing and recoding every additional change in the system. These modifications then have to be tested. All these additional activities are time-consuming.

◆ A shorter upgrade is less expensive. "Time is money." During the upgrade, you will require additional resources to accommodate all these changes. The longer you have to keep these resources around and busy on an upgrade, the more expensive your upgrade will be.

◆ In theory, performance should be better. This is probably a dangerous statement to make. SAP codes its ABAP programs with performance in mind, and if the code does not perform the first time around, the customer community will complain and SAP will recode it. This is not necessarily true for custom developed code. Custom developed code, once coded, has a tendency not to stay optimized for performance.

◆ The SAP standard functionality is supported by SAP. SAP has a dedicated support team for its code, and it is easier and cheaper to contact SAP if you experience problems with its code. SAP does not support custom developed code.

Planning the modifications and adjustments was not really a feature in the SAP releases before 3.1H. Since Release 3.1H, SAP has included a set of utilities to assist the Basis administrator and the developers to identify modifications and adjustments before the actual upgrade takes place. In Version 4, this process of identifying modifications and adjustments is part of **PREPARE**.

You can do a complete test upgrade that will identify all the changed objects during the SPAD and SPAU phases. Currently, you are doing the planning for the technical upgrade. By executing a test upgrade, you are actually jumping ahead to the physical technical upgrade. The disadvantage is that you have to execute the upgrade while still in the planning phase. Typically, you want to do all your planning before executing the upgrade. The advantages obviously are that you know exactly what object conflicts to expect and you have completed the technical upgrade at least once. It is better to do early detection during a planning phase.

The following tools can be used to analyze changes to a standard SAP system. These tools are upgrade-specific; that is, if you start upgrading from a different SAP release, you will have to read the notes pertaining to that specific release.

- **RSTODIRS** identifies the release that a transport object was delivered with. Figure 16-1 displays an example of the output generated by this program.

- **RDDGETGT** identifies if a particular modified object must be adjusted. Figure 16-2 displays all objects that have a conflict with the objects being delivered.

- **RSTODIRD** identifies used SAP objects that were deleted. Figure 16-3 lists the objects that were deleted between two different releases. In this example there are no deleted objects

- **RDDGETMO** lists conflicts that exist between modifications in the current SAP release and the target SAP release. Figure 16-4 is an example of such a list.

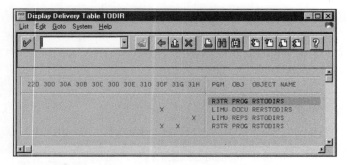

FIGURE 16-1 *Display delivery table TODIR*

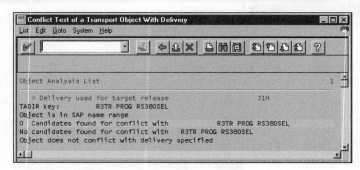

FIGURE 16-2 *Conflict test of a transport object with delivery*

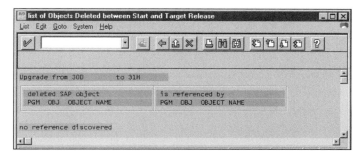

FIGURE 16-3 *List of objects deleted between start and target release*

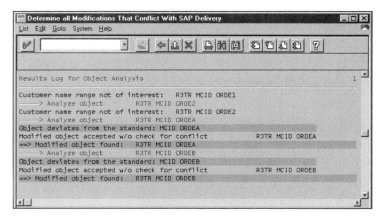

FIGURE 16-4 *Determine all modifications that conflict with SAP delivery*

◆ RDDFINFO identifies objects that do not have an entry in TADIR (see Figure 16-5).

◆ ADIRACCESS is a table that contains all objects that were registered for change in OSS. Figure 16-6 is an example listing of objects registered for change.

Get Ready to Upgrade Third Party and non-SAP software.

Upgrading just the third party, the database, or the operating system alone is a potential upgrade project by itself.

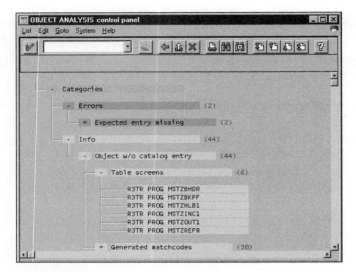

FIGURE 16-5 *Object analysis control panel*

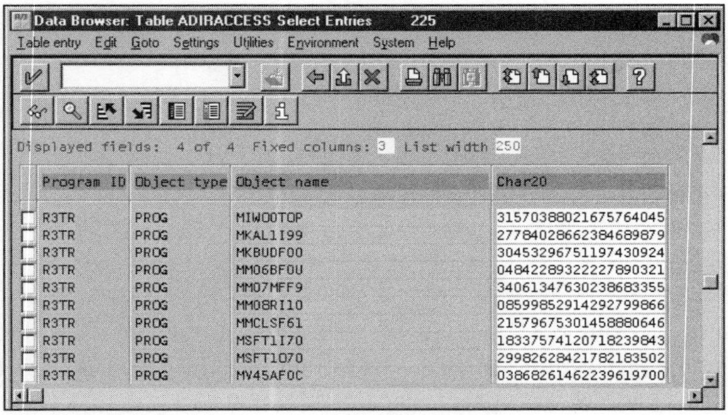

FIGURE 16-6 *Objects registered for change with OSS*

SAP is not an island. It reacts to and interacts with its environment. All the different software functioning together is interdependent. If you upgrade one software package to a new release, you have to check each of the other components for compatibility.

Most of the time, you can upgrade SAP without touching the other software in the environment, and you should endeavor to do just that. Upgrade only SAP, and plan to upgrade the rest of the software some other time, maybe sometime before or after the actual SAP upgrade.

Changing the whole environment at once will have a huge impact on production downtime. A very nice solution, if you have to do everything at once, is to combine the entire upgrade with the installation of new and more powerful hardware. Build the environment completely on the new hardware, and when D-day finally arrives, stop production, move it to the new hardware, and start production with minimal downtime.

Plan the Front-End GUI Rollout

Installing the new front end is part of the upgrade project that nobody wants to do, especially if there are thousands of users in different buildings, cities, countries, and continents. It requires a massive effort to identify all the different environments and to roll the front end to each of these environments without any problems.

Although installing the front end is the unwanted child, it is one of the most important steps during the upgrade. All the front ends have to be upgraded before the SAP system goes productive. You cannot run a release 3.1F SAPGUI on a 4.0B SAP release, but you can run a 4.0B release SAPGUI on a 3.1F SAP release.

Plan the Installation of New or Additional Hardware

During the lifetime of your SAP system, you should routinely do *capacity planning.* Always be on the lookout for disk space requirements and for CPU and memory bottlenecks. It is important that you do the same before an SAP upgrade. Calculate the additional resource requirements introduced by upgrading all the different software components. All this new software might also require a more powerful hardware platform to run on.

Plan to install the new hardware (that is, additional disk space, maybe more memory or additional CPUs) before you attempt the upgrade. These additional resources might speed up the upgrade process, so by installing them before the upgrade, your anticipated upgrade downtime might be less.

Ensure the CTS Environment is Consistent

All the systems in the SAP cluster need to be consistent as far as transportable objects and customizing are concerned.

In order to compare transported objects, list table **E070** on all systems and analyze them for any inconsistencies between the different systems.

To compare the customizing differences between two systems, use the programs **RSTABL00** and **RSKEYS00**. Figure 16-7 and Figure 16-8 display the introduction screens for both these programs.

The utilities displayed in figures 16-7 and 16-8 enable you to compare the contents of tables on different systems. **RSTABL00** exports a table from one system into a sequential file, and **RSKEYS00** compares the contents of the file with the equivalent table from another system. The documentation that comes with each

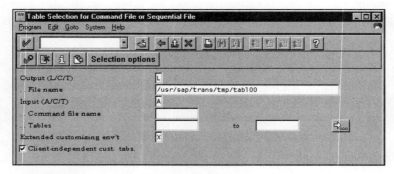

FIGURE 16-7 *RSTABL00 exports the contents of tables to a file.*

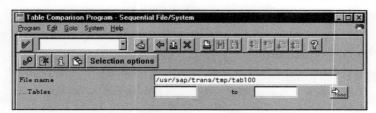

FIGURE 16-8 *RSKEYS00 compares the contents of a table with the contents of the file exported by RSTABL00.*

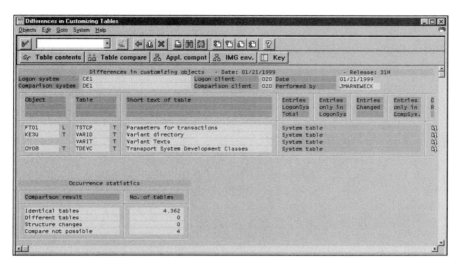

FIGURE 16-9 *Customizing differences between two different clients*

of these utilities describes in detail the functionality of each. **RSKEYS00** displays a report describing the differences between the tables in the different systems.

The utility **RSTABCMP** (as portrayed in Figure 16-9) is used to display the customizing differences between two different clients in an SAP system.

Last Few Planning Steps

Once everything is planned and analyzed, the only remaining thing is to update the project with the required time, utilities, and resources. Negotiate these requirements with the upgrade team, the business users, and management, and obtain approval for the required downtime on each environment—especially production!

The Technical Upgrade

Figure 16-10 shows a timeline of an upgrade. This is not the only way to do your upgrade. Different projects and business environments have different requirements.

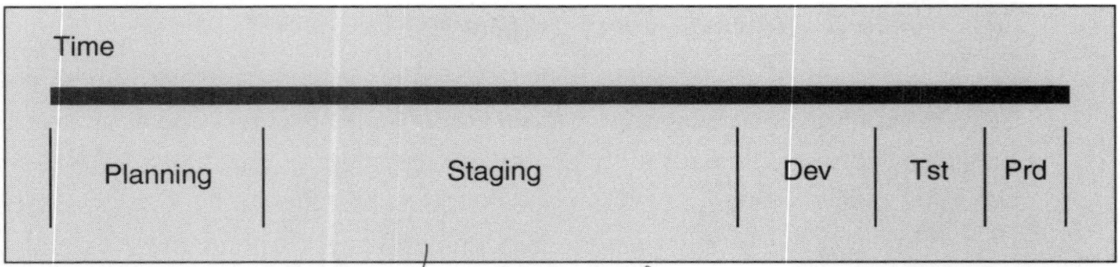

FIGURE 16-10 *Upgrade timeline*

[handwritten annotations:] → research and development
→ 2nd instance on development machine
→ another machine

The company that made use of the above-mentioned timeline wanted the minimum impact to its business environment. The company had other projects running and did not want to freeze the SAP environment for any prolonged period of time. The requirement was to move through development, quality, and production in the shortest period of time possible. Additionally, the company wanted an option to back out of the upgrade at any point in time without having time-consuming back-out procedures.

The only way to accomplish this is to know as much as possible about the upgrade. The best way to obtain this level of knowledge is to do the upgrade on a research and development machine. This research and development environment might be a second instance on the development machine or, if money is not an option, another machine altogether. Between each upgrade, you allow the business analysts and developers to identify and adjust any modification conflicts. They rebuild the system until it is functional, capture the changes, and test the system, all while documenting each of the steps required to build the new upgraded SAP version. Once it's built, the Basis administrator wipes out everything and starts the process again; this continues until confidence is high that most of the conflicts have been resolved.

Finally, you move to development and freeze the SAP environment (only emergency changes are allowed). You verify all the environments for consistency and upgrade development. Correct any fallout on development that was missed because the business did not want to freeze the environment while the stage upgrades were in progress. Allow the users to test the functionality one last time (a very short test period), unfreeze development, and then upgrade quality and production immediately.

Upgrade the Front-End Software

As was mentioned in the planning phase, the front-end software on all presentation servers has to be upgraded before the upgrade begins. The SAP front-end is backward compatible with all SAP releases. In other words, the SAP Release 4.5B front end will work on, say, the 3.1H SAP server release. This has the advantage that if the upgrade project is aborted, the front-end rollout does not have to be undone.

Start the installation process of the front-end software on each of the workstations in the environment, doing so either automatically or manually.

The SAP front end has five important files. These files get updated either by the **SAPLOGON** utility or by the Basis administrator. The advantage of having the Basis administrator create a few versions is that this needs to be done only once. These files can then be distributed across the organization. The following list elaborates on each of the front-end configuration files.

- **saplogon.ini** should not be maintained manually. It is better to use the **SAPLOGON** utility. Save all the shortcuts to the different SAP environments in this file and distribute it all over the organization. The sapmsg.ini and the saproute.ini files are used within this utility. The entries you see in Figure 16-11 are saved in the saplogon.ini file.

FIGURE 16-11 *SAPLOGON Front-end Utility*

◆ **sapmsg.ini** is used in the **SAPLOGON** utility when a new connection is created. When you press either the Group or the Server Selection buttons, a screen requesting an SAP System ID will appear. The system ID is D01, Q01, P01, or O01. Select the Down arrow to open the selection box. All the available IDs should be displayed. (This list is the entries in the sapmsg.ini file.) Select one, and the *Message Server* entry should be filled out automatically. The following displays the contents of sapmsg.ini—it contains a list of all servers that are running the message service:

```
[Message Server]
D01=sapdev.company.com
Q01=sapqas.company.com
P01=sapprd.company.com
O01=oss001.wdf.sap-ag.de
```

◆ **saproute.ini** In some environments, it is not possible to directly connect to an SAP system. The SAP OSS environment is an example of this. You have to jump from one machine that is running the SAP Router to another. The development machine and the sapserv4 machines are running the SAP router. You have to connect through development and sapserv4 in order to reach OSS.

On the same window as discussed with sapmsg.ini, you will see an option to select an *SAP Router*. These entries are obtained from the saproute.ini file. You only need this file when your SAP environment is not on the same network as the rest of your organization. The following displays an example saproute.ini:

```
[Router]
OSS Connection=/H/sapdev.company.com/H/sapserv4/H/
```

◆ **sapdoccd.ini** resolves requests for SAP help. It identifies the path to the help documentation on the network. You are allowed to define the path to global help documentation. The global help documentation is available to everybody. You are also allowed to specify help per instance. You might have one set of documentation files for development and another for production. This typically starts to play a role when the company decides to implement custom documentation. The following shows sample contents for sapdoccd.ini:

```
[global]
docucdD=\\docu_server\German_Docu
docucdE=\\docu_server\English_Docu
docucdF=\\docu_server\Frensh_Docu
[SID]
SID=XXX
docucdD=\\docu_server\German_Docu
docucdE=\\docu_server\English_Docu
docucdF=\\docu_server\Frensh_Docu
[SID]
SID=D01
docucdD=\\docu_server\German_Docu_dev
docucdE=\\docu_server\English_Docu_dev
```

◆ The **services** file contains, among others, the port numbers for the SAP services. The following lists the contents of the services file:

```
...
sapmsD01      3601/tcp
sapmsQ01      3601/tcp
sapmsP01      3601/tcp
sapdp00       3200/tcp
...
sapdp99       3200/tcp
sapgw00       3300/tcp
...
sapgw99       3399/tcp
sapsp00       3400/tcp
...
```

◆ The **hosts** file is only required if you do not make use of DNS name resolution. The file contains TCP/IP addresses and their associated host names and aliases.

Install the Upgrade Assistant

SAP introduced a new feature into SAP upgrades, namely the Upgrade Assistant. The Upgrade Assistant is a Java-based server that has to be installed together with the message server on the central instance. The Upgrade Assistant interfaces with R3up and it allows more than one user to monitor the upgrade process. The first user to log on is the upgrade administrator; all the other users are observers.

The other part of the Upgrade Assistant is the Upgrade Assistant GUI. More than one GUI is allowed to interface with the Upgrade Assistant server.

This feature is only available with an upgrade to Release 4.0X. In the old 3.1X days, you had to write a little UNIX script that would page you when the upgrade stopped for whatever reason, and only one person was able to monitor the process.

The upgrade manuals describe in detail the requirements for the Upgrade Assistant and how to install it. Details about the upgrade administrator are as follows:

- The Upgrade Assistant allows only one administrator.
- The administrator requires a password.
- The administrator has full control over the upgrade.
- The administrator can become an observer at any time during the upgrade.

Details about the upgrade observer are as follows:

- The Upgrade Assistant allows multiple observers.
- An observer can become the administrator.
- An observer is only allowed to monitor.

Upgrade Development

The upgrade process for development is very much the same process as for upgrading the research and development environment. For this reason, we will only discuss upgrading the development system.

Perform PREPARE

The **PREPARE** utility has to be executed before the actual upgrade takes place, and it has to complete error-free. **PREPARE** can be executed as many times as the upgrade administrator sees fit, but it never should be executed after **R3up**.

All the utilities associated with an SAP upgrade have changed. **PREPARE** 4.0X is no exception. SAP included more mandatory as well as optional tests into the **PREPARE** utility. The **PREPARE** script is divided into different phases that have five different execution statuses, namely Initial, Succeeded, Failed, Ignored, and Canceled. **PREPARE** can only proceed with the next phase if the current phase completes successfully or is ignored, and the only way to ignore an error is to provide a password.

PREPARE can be executed on a production system without affecting the production environment. This means that **PREPARE** can be executed during the initial planning phase of the upgrade, assisting the project team with identifying potential upgrade issues.

The **PREPARE** utility before Release 4.0 was a sequential script running through all the tests, capturing any errors in a log file called CHECKS.LOG. With Release 4.0 the strategy has changed. The **PREPARE** script is more interactive; some checks are mandatory while others are optional, and checks can be repeated selectively.

PREPARE consists of different modules, each providing specialized functionality. When **PREPARE** is executed, it runs sequentially through the mandatory modules, *Parameter Input, Initialization, Import,* and *CD Read,* and then it displays a window allowing the administrator to select any of the modules *General Checks, Activation Checks, Necessary Checks for Conversions, Optional Checks for Conversions, Modification Support,* and *Pre-processing* for execution. Each of these selection options is associated with help documentation explaining that module's exact functionality.

Baseline Backup of the SAP Environment

Depending on the upgrade strategy selected, a baseline backup should be performed on the system. Make sure that you are able to revert to the old environment in case some kind of disaster occurs. (An offline backup is the safest.)

You need to back up the following:

◆ The operating system
◆ The database
◆ Non-SAP software
◆ SAP kernel and related files

Perform Non-SAP Software Upgrades

During the planning phase, you determined if the operating system, the database, or any other software required upgrading before SAP was to be upgraded.

Follow the detailed plans you compiled to upgrade each of these software components and bring all the versions to the desired levels. Once this is done, run **PREPARE** again and consider making another backup.

TIP

The OS, database, and Kernel patch level can all be upgraded before the start of the upgrade to prepare the environment for the pending upgrade.

Perform R/3 Upgrade

Everything is ready, so the only thing left now is to execute **R3up** in order to upgrade SAP from the old release to the new release. You will notice that this is the end of the chapter. This is exactly how the upgrade is. Most of the work is done during the initial stages of the upgrade. The final upgrade of each of the systems does not require a lot of effort.

The upgrade consists of a number of phases, and these phases are grouped together in five groups:

- ◆ Initialization
- ◆ Data transfer
- ◆ Basis adjustments (import)
- ◆ Application adjustments (SPPD)
- ◆ Completion (SPAU)

After the successful execution of all the phases within these groups, you will have to perform the post-upgrade steps.

Initialization

The upgrade initialization phases do the following activities:

- ◆ The administrator is required to enter system- specific information regarding the upgrade.

- **R3up** does a database check using the **tp** utility.
- Check RFC functionality again.
- Check to see if a batch server is configured.
- Check for open repairs.
- Do a space check.

Data Transfer

This group gets the data and the environment ready for the upgrade. Listed below is a summary of the activities that take place during the phases in this group.

- Import the upgrade shadow tables into PSAPESXXX and PSAPELXXX. "XXX" denotes the SAP upgrade release number (e.g., 40B).
- Lock the development workbench.
- Import upgrade command files.
- Copy local development into shadow tables.
- R3load imports exchange tables.

Basis Adjustments

This group of phases initializes the Basis environment for the upgrade.

- Lock the R/3 environment using **tp locksys** and **unlocksys**.
- Upgrade the central Basis system; that is, **R3up** loads the labels and reports required by the new kernel.
- Swap the old kernel with the upgrade kernel. This only happens if the upgrade kernel is newer than the existing kernel.
- Temporary profile modifications are made. One of the changes is to point the transport directory to /usr/sap/put.

Application Adjustments

During the execution of this group of phases, the upgrade will request the administrator to adjust the data dictionary.

- Require the administrator to execute SPDD in order to adjust modified data dictionary objects. If adjustments are required, these adjustments can be captured in a transport request that can be used in subsequent upgrades.

Completion

The final activities that the upgrade executes:

◆ Remaining language imports are done.

◆ Development workbench is unlocked.

◆ Adjust non-data dictionary objects using SPAU. These changes can also be captured in a transport request for subsequent upgrades.

◆ The upgrade logs are saved.

Post-upgrade Activities

Last, you have to execute the manual post-upgrade activities. You are actually just getting the system ready for normal productive operation. The typical things you have to do are the following:

◆ Resolve messages noted in the log file LONGPOST.LOG.

◆ Run the load generation report RDDGENLD.

◆ Do incremental conversions.

◆ Install online documentation.

◆ Import extended online help.

◆ Apply Hot Packages.

◆ Perform ABAP adjustment.

◆ Reschedule background jobs.

◆ Run database optimization tools.

◆ Do a post-upgrade system backup.

◆ Unfreeze existing R/3 projects on development.

◆ Do the upgrade configurations and customizations.

◆ Adapt the environment to accommodate any changes to authorizations.

◆ Adapt any interfaces.

◆ Perform unit testing.

Upgrade the Quality Assurance Systems

All the preparation work is done. To complete the QAS upgrade you will execute most of the steps you already did during the development upgrade. Here follows a very brief summary of the high level steps required to upgrade QAS.

- ◆ Perform **PREPARE**.
- ◆ Perform pre-upgrade backup.
- ◆ Perform non-R/3 software upgrade.
- ◆ Perform R/3 upgrade.   *R3up*
- ◆ Perform post-upgrade maintenance.
- ◆ Import new change requests from development.
- ◆ Perform post-upgrade QAS backup.

Upgrade the Production

Finally, the end is in sight. You reached the final upgrade. You have practiced for this upgrade so many times now, you should be able to do it with your eyes closed. Listed here is a summary of the high level steps required for the production upgrade.

- ◆ Execute **PREPARE**.
- ◆ Perform pre-upgrade system backup.
- ◆ Perform non-R/3 software upgrade.
- ◆ Perform R/3 upgrade.
- ◆ Perform post-upgrade maintenance.
- ◆ Import new change requests from development.
- ◆ Perform post-upgrade system backup.
- ◆ Perform monitoring during turnover in PRD.
- ◆ Unfreeze existing R/3 projects.
- ◆ Support the go-live SAP environment.

Summary

The SAP upgrade is a very complex procedure. The various permutations for different upgrade plans are unlimited. This chapter could never do justice to the complexities of a real upgrade. The most important thing that you should realize is that you need a well thought-out plan and that you should prepare for the upgrade in the finest detail. When you finally upgrade production, you should have a systematic list of steps describing when and how to perform each of them. Running the **PREPARE** and **R3up** utilities is easy because they prompt you for input. Even using ~~SPAD~~ and SPAU is easy. Identifying the adjustments and testing the functionality is the hard part.

SPDD

Chapter 17

Pre-Production Preparation for Administrators

In this Chapter

This chapter introduces some of the steps that are required to be performed prior to going live with either a big-bang new implementation or a next-phase roll out. This covers the hardware, the SAP software, SAP functionality, data migrations and conversions from legacy systems, SAP performance and monitoring, and disaster recovery.

Resource Planning

Earlier in the book (Chapter 2) you saw a breakdown of the roles and responsibilities for each member of the Basis support team, though the number within a support team naturally depends on the size of the implementation. A quick summary shows that the:

◆ **Operating system administrator** will ensure that during pre-implementation, the hardware, and operating system are functioning correctly and the script jobs have been created for performance monitoring.

◆ **Database administrator** will ensure that the database is fully functional during pre-implementation and is optimized for performance. The database will require complete attention as data migrations are being carried out from the legacy systems to SAP.

◆ **SAP R/3 system administrator** will ensure that the complete SAP system is fully functional during pre-implementation and is optimized for performance. This will include network connectivity, SAPGUI installation, printer setup, implementation of transport management, operation modes setup within CCMS, and so on.

A more complete listing of these functions are provided at the end of this chapter.

◆ **SAP R/3 security administrator** will ensure that all the security profiles have been created and tested by and approved by a member of the functional team. The external audit company, or the internal audit group and the project manager will sign-off on the successful implementation of the security environment.

As the nature of the SAP and the lines between the operating system, database, and Basis are merged, each of the administrators is required to be cross-trained in each of the functions to effectively manage and administrator the system. This allows a successful extraction of the external consultants upon the initial implementation completion of the project.

The next few topics will address specifically the procedures for performing these pre-production checks.

Test and Measurement

A number of tests and measurements need to be performed prior to going live, and most involve the system administrator(s) and the application experts. Typically, either an SAP automation tool, such as CATT (Computer Aided Test Tool), or third-party vendors tools are used to perform the tasks outlined in the following section. Examples of some of these tools include Mercury Waverunner and the AutoTester tool.

Volume Test

Volume testing is performed to ensure that the SAP system is able to manage the large critical R/3 business processes and key transactions and to ensure the system performs well over a set period of time—typically a day. The volume test plan should include the SAP application modules, core transactions volumes, core transaction functionality, reporting, queries, online modes (dialog), background modes, interfaces, and batch processing.

Volume Test Plan Example

Typically, this plan is created by the application leaders from information provided by your company with respect to your current business processes and business transactions.

For example, a volume test may include the creation of a customer order using transaction VA01 for 10 users totaling 1,000 orders per day (see Figure 17-1). The automated tool should re-create this scenario, and you as the Basis administrator should evaluate the system performance, while the application experts should ensure the quality of the orders.

Module	Business Process	R/3 Transaction	Online/Background /Interface/CPIC	Priority Low/Medium/ High	Response Time (Seconds)	No. Of Users	Volume Data (per day)
SD	Create customer order	VA01	Online	High	1.5	10	1000

FIGURE 17-1 *An example of a volume test plan*

Stress Test

Stress testing is used to confirm that the configured hardware production environment is ready for productive operational use for all business processes and transactions. It is also used to identify potential improvements to system performance prior to going live and for the final integration testing (see Figure 17-2).

Pretest Checks

Before carrying out the stress test, ask yourself the questions for each bullet point. Only you (or your project team) will know the answers because each implementation is unique in its own way:

◆ **System configuration.** Configure the stress test system identically to reflect your future productive operating conditions (i.e., the database server size; number of application servers; number of dialog, background, and batch processes; logon load balancing; and distribution of users). You may even perform these tests within the actual production environment. Once performed, return the system back to its pre-test configuration.

◆ **System setup.** Set up all components (parameters of the operating system, database server and application servers, SAP parameters, etc.) of the server to their optimal configuration. These may require adjusting as the tests are performed.

◆ **Backup and restoration.** Perform a complete off-line backup of the system to restore the production system's previous condition prior to the stress test.

◆ **Functional readiness.** Gain approval from the functional teams to ensure all business procedures and transactions are fully set up and the system is configured the way you eventually want to run it in production.

◆ **Simulated operation.** Ensure you either have identified end-users to perform their potential daily tasks or you have configured an automated testing tool to simulate the users.

Server	Test #	Disk Space (Gb)	Memory (Gb)	Applications	# Users	# Dialogs /Background	Comments
PRD	1	50	2.5	FI / CO / MM	25	10 / 5	

FIGURE 17-2 *Stress test example*

◆ **Measurability.** Understand what measurements are to be made, what measurement procedures are to be used, and how will you analyze the results. You may require the assistance of your SAP consulting partner to interpret the data.

Perform Tests

As you perform the tests, observe the following:

◆ **System performance.** Monitor certain business processes and transactions that cause system resources to fluctuate in performance (for example, CPU I/O, disk I/O, database throughput, application server behavior, network traffic, etc.) Also, understand that different types of processes (online, batch, background, etc.) and the time of day can adversely effective system response.

◆ **User behavior.** Monitor the business procedures under test conditions and gauge whether the tests are carried out at a realistic speed by the users. For instance, do the end-users input purchase orders every minute in a real-life example or are there peak and slow times during the day?

Reporting Results

After the tests, report on the following aspects:

◆ **End-users.** Gather feedback from users and their reactions to the system and its performance. Have the users identify problems with particular business procedures or transactions.

◆ **System behavior.** Graph and chart over the test period how the system behaved and note the system parameters.

◆ **System performance.** Identify any significant performance problems. Diagnose and resolve any issues. In certain circumstances, you may not know how to resolve the particular performance problems. You may then require the assistance of the SAP Early Watch team.

Test #____123____

# Users	Appl(s)	Trans	# Dia/Btc/Up	Av. Resp Time	Av. Wait Time	Av. DB Time	CPU Load	Comments
10	FI/CO/MM/SD	VA01	10/5/1	0.5	0.25	0.11	50%	

FIGURE 17-3 *Stress test example*

System Administration Tests

This task is to simulate the system administration procedures for the production environment using a similar or actual environment. This would include tests of each procedure and task listed as follows and described in the next sections:

- ◆ Job scheduling management
- ◆ Database management (database administrator's task)
- ◆ Database backup and recovery management
- ◆ Transport Management System (TMS)
- ◆ SAP system alerts and logs
- ◆ Spool and fax management
- ◆ Daily monitoring activities
- ◆ Disaster recovery

If any of the tasks failed, you will be required to take corrective actions, which may include parameter changes, altering thresholds, performing additional backups, and so on.

As you perform each test, it is recommended that you keep complete documentation of the procedures, roles, responsibilities, and tasks performed and changes logged. Develop and test a suitable escalation procedure first through your corporate management and also to your consulting firm and/or SAP.

Job Scheduling Management

This task schedules the daily, weekly, and/or monthly system clean-up jobs that are required to run in order to keep the production system operational and also to schedule business processes jobs.

Before the business processes jobs are scheduled, they will require documentation from the application groups providing details, such as:

◆ Frequency of the job

◆ Priority (A, B, or C, with A being the highest)

◆ Estimated duration

◆ Output requirements

◆ Person to be notified in case of failure

Once you have the information, you may begin to create a timetable of the jobs that require scheduling. Once you have set up the jobs, you may see SAP's representation of the scheduled jobs through CCMS.

SAP's clean-up and reorganization reports are responsible for removing data, print jobs, system logs, and so on, that are no longer needed in the system. This process will assist in the maintenance of the production system as well as regain a significant amount of disk space (see Figure 17-4).

Job	Description
RSBTCDEL	Clean up **background** jobs that have expired a set number of days Using the batch administrator user id, execute this program **daily** during off-peak hours .
RSPO0041	Clean up spooling objects Execute program **daily**, also depends on number of spool object created
RSBDCREO	Clean up the batch input session logs Execute program **daily**, but this depends number of logs created
RSSNAPDL	Clean up **ABAP/4 run-time error dumps** logged from within the system. Used in conjunction with RSNAPJOB
RSNAPJOB	The function of this job is to automatically schedule RSSNAPDL to run. The report RSNAPJOB requires that there is a variant called "DEFAULT." The initial start time will be 1:00 a.m. **daily**
RSBPCOLL	This program calculates the **job run-time statistics** information. Execute program **daily**, however it does not require a variant as the program produces statistics on jobs that have completed successfully.
RSBPSTDE	Clean up the job **run-time statistics** information. Execute program **monthly** to delete the statistics that have not been updated since the specified date or number of days.
RSCOLL00	This program **collects performance data** across all production R/3 servers. Execute program **hourly**
RSM13002	Clean up the **process update requests** Execute program **daily**

FIGURE 17-4 *The cleanup jobs that are required to run on the SAP system*

Table 17-1 Names for All Cleanup Jobs, Programs, Variants, Frequency and Client-Dependency

Job Name	Program	Variant	Frequency	Client Dependent
SAP_COLLECTOR_FOR_PERFMONITOR	RSCOLL00	NO	HOURLY	NO
SAP_COLLECTOR_FOR_JOBSTATISTIC	RSBPCOLL	NO	DAILY	NO
SAP_REORG_JOBS	RSBTCDEL	YES	DAILY	YES
SAP_REORG_SPOOL	RSPO0041	YES	DAILY	YES
SAP_REORG_BATCHINPUT	RSBDCREO	YES	DAILY	YES
SAP_REORG_UPDATERECORDS	RSM13002	NO	DAILY	NO
SAP_REORG_ABAPDUMPS	RSSNAPDL	YES	DAILY	NO
SAP_REORG_JOBSTATISTIC	RSBPSTDE	YES	MONTHLY	NO

These programs are set up using the background job transaction (SM36) and the status/logs viewed using transaction SM37. Most of these job programs require a variant, which is a set of parameters used when executing the job. These variants are created using ABAP.

Client-dependent indicates that some of the jobs are client-specific objects and will therefore have to be scheduled in all clients created. Jobs that are not client-dependent perform a reorganization in all clients, and they do not require special authorizations or special usernames.

Database Management

This task determines the necessary technical database tasks required to be performed on a regular and periodic basis. The frequency of each task will be dependent upon the activity of the production system and thus the activity on the database.

The tasks involved with the performance and monitoring of database-related areas mainly revolve around maintaining the alert and performance information of the system. For example, during the data migration prior to go-live, the database will require constant attention, particularly the tablespaces and indexes.

Once in production, take corrective action when alerts and error logs are created (such as tablespace extension requirements), monitor the database growth on a daily basis to forecast additional hardware requirements, move large data files onto separate disks to increase performance, and reorganize data files after archiving, or large changes further increase performance and regain lost disk space.

Database Backup and Recovery Management

This task tests the backup and restore procedures to be used within the production environment. This may include several data corruption scenarios, such as database corruption, disk failure, CPU failure, and other hardware failures.

As you perform each test, it is recommended that you keep complete documentation of the procedures, roles, responsibilities, and tasks performed and changes logged to create a "how-to" manual on recovering a database.

This test also provides some valuable data on the time required to perform these tasks and the impact on the production environment, especially if the system has to be available 24 hours a day, seven days a week.

Verify Data Written to the Backup Medium

The SAP SAPDBA, BRBACKUP, and BRARCHIVE tools can be executed with the "-v" option to read the data written to tape and to compare it with data on the disk. This simple procedure will verify that data on the backup medium can be read and will confirm the quality of the backup.

This test will extend the time of the backup but will ensure recoverability of the system in the event that there is a failure. It should also be performed on a regular basis as part of your operational procedures.

Backup and Recovery

To ensure that a backup and recovery may be performed, follow these steps:

1. Back up database files
2. Back up log files
3. Restore database files and log files
4. Recover the database

The last two steps simulate a recovery from a disk failure. First, restore the files from the backup medium to the disk. Then adapt the data files to the last consistent status before the disk failure using the log files. Last, perform the recovery of the database.

Transport Management System (TMS)

Configure and test the transport management system to ensure that changes to the productive environment may be made only through the TMS. Prior to going live, there are cases where changes are made in the production directly—bypassing the usual transport hierarchy of **DEV, QAS, PRD**—but these are only in emergency instances and are documented and approved by the application and technical team leads and project manager. A quick check would include ensuring that the:

◆ Transport management system was configured correctly
◆ Production client closed to accept changes directly
◆ Production client only accepts changes via transport
◆ Check the options for system change options in transaction code SE06

SAP System Alerts and Logs

Viewing the SAP system alerts and logs should be part of the daily monitoring activities; however, from a testing perspective, you will be required to check that all the alerts have been configured and thresholds set using the CCMS, and to ensure that they work during the volume and stress tests.

Printing and Fax Management

Test the printing and fax functions, which include volume printing/faxing, selective printing/faxing, and special printing/faxing (e.g., check printing, bill of material printing), as well as any related administration procedures, as outlined in the following:

- Printing and faxing large print jobs
- Volume printing and faxing
- Printing and faxing various output types on various types of printer and fax devices
- Printing and faxing administration

Daily Monitoring Activities

Test the daily monitoring activities necessary in maintaining the SAP R/3 environment. These include:

- System log analysis and correction
- Dump analysis
- Database lock analysis
- CCMS monitors
- Trace and runtime analysis
- User/password locks and resets
- Developer traces

Daily Transactions

The following is a recommended list of transactions that need to be executed on a daily basis to monitor the performance of your SAP system. As you become more familiar with SAP, you will begin to perform new tasks and may decide to add them to the list too. This is a bottom-up approach, where you begin by checking the operating system first, then the database, and finally the SAP R/3 system.

- **Network Monitoring.** You may perform basic monitoring of the network if the network collector process has been activated for your operating system (see Table 17-2).

Table 17-2 **Network Alert Monitoring Transactions**

ST08 / ST09	Network Alert Monitor	Alerts should be acknowledged, analyzed, corrected and documented.

◆ **Host Operating System.** You may perform basic monitoring of the operating system using the transactions in Table 17-3.

Table 17-3 **Operating System Monitoring Transactions**

AL16	OS Alert monitor	All alerts should be acknowledged, analyzed, corrected and documented.
OS03	OS Parameter changes	The SAP system monitors all operating system kernel changes.
OS06	OS monitor	All alerts should be acknowledged, analyzed, corrected and documented.
TP	OS level TP command	All warnings and error messages should be analyzed and corrected.

◆ **Database.** Table 17-4 shows you the database monitoring transactions.

Table 17-4 **Database Monitoring Transactions**

AL02	Database alert monitor	All alerts should be acknowledged, analyzed, corrected and documented.
DB02	Storage management	Monitor database growth.
DB03	Parameter changes	The SAP system monitors all database profile changes.
DB12	SAPDBA logs	Verify success of backups Verify free space in log directory Monitor table and index growth and fragmentation.
ST04	Database logs	Monitor the database error log daily Monitor total logical and physical read/writes to track workload Monitor expensive SQL statements.

SAP R/3 System Administration

Some of the administrative transactions that will assist in the performance and monitoring the SAP Basis components are listed in Table 17-5.

Table 17-5 SAP Basis Monitoring Transactions

RZ01	Graphical job monitor	Administrators should monitor run-time statistics for each job to ensure best background schedule.
RZ02	System monitor	Ensure all systems are functioning and using correct operation mode.
RZ08	SAP alert monitor	All alerts should be acknowledged, analyzed, corrected and documented.
SE01/ SE09/ SE10	Transport logs	All alerts should be acknowledged, analyzed, corrected and documented.
SM04	User overview	Ensure users belong to logon groups, check locked user and passwords failures, check authorization failures.
SM12	Lock entries	All old lock entries should be analyzed and corrected.
SM13	Update records	Check aborted updates, should not occur in production—otherwise analyze and correct.
SM21	System logs	All warnings and error messages should be analyzed, corrected and documented.
SM35	Batch input logs	Batch input logs should be checked after each run and errors corrected.
SM37	Job log overview	Any jobs that did not run should be analyzed, corrected and documented.
SM50/ SM51/ SM66	Process overview	Long running background jobs and runaway reports should be analyzed, corrected and documented and killed with the user's permission.
SP01	Spool request overview	Failed print jobs should be restarted, old print jobs deleted and Temse area cleaned up.

Table 17-5 SAP Basis Monitoring Transactions *(continued)*

SP12	Temse administration	Check file system and database for large/mass print jobs. Check Temse consistency (RSPO0043) run daily, prior to spool reorganization (RSPO0041).
ST02	Buffer analysis	Monitor the buffers and make changes accordingly.
ST03	Workload analysis	Check, track and graph data. Reading the statistics will come with experience.
TU02	Profile parameter changes	History of all profile changes.

Disaster Recovery

This task tests the procedures described in your disaster recovery plan for the productive environment. This initiative may be performed by internal company resources or by a third-party provider, and you will need to test its services and responsiveness too.

Ensure that the entire technical infrastructure can be reproduced, including the network, system hardware, performance, printing, user configuration, and so on, in a timely manner. This test will provide data on the time required to recover from a severe disaster and will help define the roles and responsibilities of each member of the recovery team.

Worst-case scenario: complete destruction of your primary site of work, with personnel injuries. Some of your steps may then include what's described in the following sections.

Disaster Recovery Procedure

◆ Simulate the conditions for disaster recovery.

◆ Determine the severity of the disaster (i.e. can a backup system be used on site or do you need to move off-site, perhaps to your supplier's recovery site)

◆ Contact all respective partners to participate in the testing (hardware, software, networks, telecommunications, third-party disaster recovery provider, etc.).

◆ Collect all tapes and backup units required (stored off-site).

◆ Complete step-by-step documentation to ensure that anyone with the right skills may perform the recovery, tasks, and tests.

Recovery and Test

◆ Test SAP connectivity from all sites.

◆ Test application functionality.

◆ Test integration to other applications.

◆ Test batch jobs.

◆ Test interfaces.

◆ Test print jobs.

◆ Test procedure to return to regular operation.

Document Findings

◆ Determine the actual disaster recovery elapsed time.

◆ Determine escalation and de-escalation procedures.

◆ Determine success criteria.

Pre-production Data Migration and Data Loads

Prior to go-live, "legacy" data has to be transferred to the SAP database from the older systems that it would be replacing. The general topic of data migration and data loads should have been addressed early in the SAP project lifecycle by the project teams to be able to determine the schedule and conversion methods. These steps would have included:

◆ Identifying what data needs to be transferred from legacy systems to your production system

- High-level specifications of how to transfer the data
- High-level specifications of the data itself, for example:
    - File type transfers and relation to SAP (transaction)
    - Number of files
    - Quality of data
    - Complexity of data
    - Time estimate
- Detailed conversion definition
    - Data transfer method (direct input method, call transaction, batch input)
    - Determine data fields
    - Determine file structure
    - Determine fields in flat file
    - Map legacy data to R/3
- Detailed conversion programs
    - Using ABAP programs
    - Using mapping tools
    - Data transfer programs
    - Legacy formatting tools
- Test and migrate conversion programs to QAS and PRD
    - Executing the conversion programs on limited data file
    - Checking the conversion
    - Migrating the programs to QAS and repeating above procedure but with a larger data set (check results)
    - Migrating the programs to PRD and repeating above procedure but with a larger data set (check results)
    - Resetting production prior to the limited data conversion test

The above is a summary of some of the steps that you should check while being assembled over the period of the project by the respective project teams so that you have adequate time to create these programs and perform several trial tests.

Pre-production Checklist

A final summary for the pre-production of the SAP production system has been put together for you, as follows:

◆ Approval of the production system:

Back up production system.

Resolve open issues from the final integration tests.

Verify the data conversion is complete and approved.

Document changes in the production system and create a report.

Inform SAP about your planned go-live dates.

◆ Secure productive environment:

Create operating system and database user level access with sufficient security for project team members, reports, interfaces, and data transfers to ensure the integrity of the SAP environment and production data.

Ensure sufficient security for the operating system users, database users, and SAP administrators, and securing the password for the following users:

Operating system users:	root, <SID>adm, ora<SID>
Database users:	sapr3
SAP users:	SAP* and DDIC

◆ Verify that SAP user Ids, passwords, and their authorizations have been created:

Verify that all users have been set up and profiles have been tested for correct access to SAP business processes and transactions.

Ensure that power users have been identified so that users know whom to contact for security-related questions.

Check with power users and team leaders to make a final check with users to be sure that they have been adequately trained to start using the production system.

◆ Transaction checklist:

Review initial transactions in the productive system, and verify processing.

	UNITS	Day 1 - Mon 02/05			Day 1 - Tues 02/06		
	#	PLAN	ACTUAL	VAR.	PLAN	ACTUAL	VAR.
1. Business Processes							
Customer Orders	#	100	98	-2	110	110	0
Shipments	#	60	60	0	60	65	5
Billings	$	175000	174750	-250	192500	192700	200
2. System Performance							
Transaction Response							
Order Entry VA01	sec	1.5	1.5	0.0	1.5	2	0.5
Batch							
Backorder Rescheduling	hrs	0.5	0.75	0.25	0.5	0.5	0.0

FIGURE 17-5 *Checklist of daily and weekly transactions*

Checklist for end-of-first-day business processes and system performance.

Checklist for end-of-first-month business processes and system performance.

Checklist for end-of-first-quarter business processes and system performance.

Checklist for end-of-first-year business processes and system performance.

Stabilization of the Production System

Creating a relatively stable yet growing production environment is the "holy grail" for the SAP system administrator, especially during the initial days upon going live. However, if you have sized the SAP system correctly and set up your system parameters optimally, if the SAP application experts have configured the business processes optimally, and if the ABAP programmers have created efficient code, then there is no reason why your system should not function correctly.

If not correctly configured, then users will see long delays on the execution of transactions and business processes. In order to resolve the situation, you will require input from the application, programming, and technical experts—the whole project team.

As the users become more familiar with the SAP system, their activity level will increase, and you will be required to tweak the SAP system parameters. This will be an iterative process in which you will change *one* parameter at a time and then check the results. For example, if performance of the system is poor and it is determined that it is a system-related issue, then change *one* of the start-up parameters and reboot the system. The next day, check to see if the system operates more efficiently; if not, change another parameter and repeat the process. (Please see Chapter 11 relating to system performance for specific parameter changes.)

Other topics related to stabilizing the system are external "forces" placed on the SAP environment, such as:

◆ Hot Packages or Legal Patches (introducing code, table, or security changes)

◆ New functionality introduced in existing modules

◆ New phase of SAP implementation—perhaps the introduction of new modules

◆ New company, plant, or warehouse using the SAP production system (additional SAP project phases and users)

These all have an impact on the way the SAP environment operates and how it performs and grows.

Summary

As a Basis resource, you are required to work very closely with the business processes/application group in order to understand what is the time frame of your SAP project. From there you will be able to gauge the activities that will be performed prior to going live.

◆ You will be involved with the system testing to ensure that the SAP system is able to handle the SAP configuration and transaction volumes.

◆ You will configure the system to its best setting from data provided from the previous tests.

◆ You will perform data conversions and setup interfaces from your legacy systems.

◆ You will set up users and their authorizations to ensure that they have the correct access to perform their day-to-day tasks.

◆ You will test and prove that the SAP system is recoverable from minor problems (database crash) and major disasters.

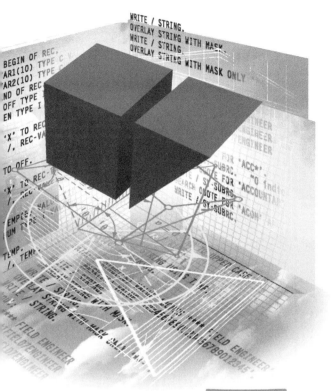

PART VII

Appendixes

A **Understanding the EDI Architecture**

B **Understanding Ready-to-Run R/3**

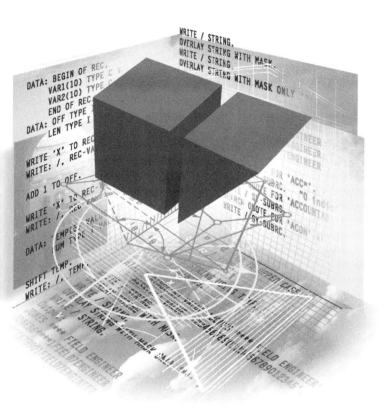

Appendix A

**Understanding the
EDI Architecture**

In This Appendix

- ◆ Basic EDI Components
- ◆ Triggering of the SAP EDI Transaction
- ◆ Selection of Your EDI Subsystem
- ◆ Certification
- ◆ X12 Transaction Set (v3040)

This material gives a quick introduction to some of the electronic data interchange (EDI) tools, techniques, definitions, processes, and concepts as related to SAP. It will provide you with a high-level appreciation of EDI and assist in the decision-making process of implementing EDI, in your quest to leverage this tried, tested, and true standard business tool.

TIP

The topics addressed here are all covered extensively in *ALE, EDI, & IDoc Technologies for SAP* by Arvind Nagpal (Prima Publishing, 1999), which includes comprehensive coverage of the ALE and EDI processes within SAP.

EDI enables you to electronically transfer documents, such as purchase orders, sales orders, quotations, bill of materials, and so on, from an SAP R/3 system to other systems (including other SAP R/3 systems) and also enables you to receive documents from other systems. The EDI architecture consists of the following elements:

- ◆ EDI-enabled SAP application — *capable of generating and receiving IDOC*
- ◆ EDI interface translator
- ◆ EDI subsystem

CSP

Typically, the translator and the subsystem consist of the same software/hardware combination provided by a certified SAP Complementary Software Provider.

TIP

Information on CSPs and their certification status is available directly from SAP.

Figure A-1 illustrates a typical system setup of SAP and the EDI subsystem communicating to a second EDI subsystem and SAP system via a value-added network (VAN) communications network provided by a specialty provider. It provides a virtual connection for the two remote systems using a network supporting the EDI protocol, EDIFACT and/or ANSI X12. At the end of this chapter, a complete list of the ANSI X12 standards is provided as a reference guide.

At present, IDocs are not a standard approved for transmission over the VAN and therefore require an EDI translator to remap the document to EDI standards. This remapped document is then transmitted over the VAN and received at the EDI subsystem. If the receiving system is an SAP system, then the document is remapped again into an IDoc document. In the example, the transmitted document is a purchase order that is received as a sales order.

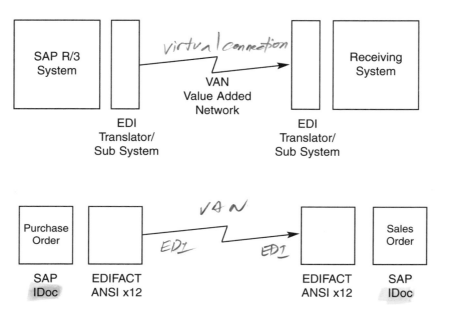

FIGURE A-1 *EDI Architecture*

What Is an EDI-Enabled Application in SAP?

The SAP system uses a standard that is unique to SAP for moving the documents generated within SAP to other components within SAP known as *intermediate documents, (IDocs)*. An EDI-enabled application within SAP is capable of generating IDocs data from SAP documents and of reading IDocs data to create SAP documents. The flow of the documents will determine the type of process, namely an outbound or inbound process.

In the standard SAP system, a large number of EDI-enabled applications are capable of generating and processing IDoc data, but not all EDI documents are supported. However, SAP provides a comprehensive set of tools for developing IDocs and programs to "EDI enable" an application. With each upgrade of the SAP software, the list of supported IDocs and EDI-enabled applications grows considerably.

If the standard process does not meet your requirements, you can extend the standard IDocs and enhance the standard programs to meet your business needs. SAP provides user exits at strategic points in the IDoc process to facilitate the addition of your custom code. Enhancements are supported when you upgrade your SAP system as SAP guarantees the location of any given user exit and the context in which it is invoked.

You can also develop new business scenarios as you encounter the need to create new IDoc structures and programs to create or process those IDocs. After you develop the IDoc and the programs, you can configure the interface to recognize your newly created programs and IDocs. The standard monitoring and testing tools can be used for your custom-defined scenarios.

As mentioned earlier, there are two EDI processes, which will be discussed in the following sections.

Outbound Process

The *outbound process* sends documents from the SAP system to your business partner (e.g., customer, vendor, or bank) and consists of the following steps:

1. **Application IDoc creation.** This is the routine part of executing an SAP transaction to create an application document, such as a sales or purchase

order document. If the creation of the application documents is SAP-standard EDI-enabled processes, then the EDI process begins. (Some configuration will be required, as explained later.) The document is converted to an IDoc format, which can now be processed by the EDI components.

2. **Exporting the IDoc to operating system.** The IDoc created in the previous step needs to be extracted from the SAP database repository and passed down to the operating system layer as an IDoc-formatted text file, for processing by the EDI subsystem.

3. **IDoc to EDI conversion.** The IDoc-formatted text file has to be converted into an EDI standard format. Third-party software known as a *translator* (SAP refers to translators as *EDI subsystems*) carries out the conversion and provides status information to the SAP system.

4. **EDI transmission.** Once converted to an EDI standard format, the document is transmitted to a trading partner based on the partner's setup.

5. **EDI subsystem status.** The EDI subsystem should be set up to report the state of processing at various stages back to your SAP system. This ensures complete visibility of the process from within SAP.

Inbound Process

The *inbound process* simply reverses the steps of the outbound process. The inbound process receives an EDI document (e.g., payment information or a sales order) from a business partner (such as a bank or a customer) and creates an SAP document. The inbound process consists of the following steps:

1. **EDI document received.** EDI documents are received from a business partner over the VAN in one of the EDI standard formats and deposited in a common repository for the EDI subsystem.

2. **EDI to IDoc conversion.** The document is converted into an IDoc at the EDI subsystem level.

3. **Transfer of IDoc to SAP layer.** The IDoc is stored as a text file at the operating system layer, where the subsystem executes an inbound program that reads the IDoc text file and creates an IDoc in the SAP repository.

4. **Creation of application document.** The IDoc is passed to a posting program that creates an application document (such as a shipment notice or invoice) that is appropriate for use in the SAP system.

5. **View application document.** The application document created via EDI may be used like any other document within the SAP environment, just as though it had been created using a standard SAP transaction on the system.

Basic EDI Components

The EDI component is enabled with your SAP system; however, it requires configuration with your company process details (business partners, customers, vendors), components configuration (port definition, partner profiles, process codes), and the types of messages (EDI transactions) you wish to exchange. The proceeding subtopics will break down each of the configuration stages.

EDI Configuration Setup

The configuration settings for the EDI process are performed within the IMG (*Implementation Guide*) and in the area menu of the EDI system, accessed as shown below.

Implementation Guide (IMG)

The EDI customizing settings are accessed via the IMG, executing transaction **SPRO** and then following the path **Cross-Application Components, IDoc Interface/Electronic Data Interchange, IDoc Interface—Basis** (as seen in Figure A-2).

Several IMG configuration steps include:

1. **Setting the number ranges for IDocs.** Each IDoc created (either inbound or outbound) is assigned a 16-digit number from 0000000000000001 through 9999999999999999 that uniquely identifies the IDoc in the system. Typically, all you do is to ensure that this number range is set in the manner, which happens to be default.

2. **Coupling IDoc creation to IDoc processing**. Using the menu path **SPRO, Cross-Application Components, IDoc Interface/Electronic Data Interchange, IDoc Interface—Basis,** Activate Event Coupling for IDoc Inbound. The process of creating IDocs from the input file is separated from the processing of the IDocs, and thus the two processes need to be coupled for EDI process flow. This is accomplished by using

FIGURE A-2 *IMG configuration setting for EDI setup*

the workflow concept of *publish* and *subscribe* and is maintained via an event-linkage table. When an IDoc is created, it raises an event, which is the publishing portion to inform the system about the creation. The subscriber process starts automatically when the corresponding event is published, and processes the IDoc.

3. **Communication settings.** These settings are made only once and are independent of both the transaction and the business partner and used via the menu path **SPRO, Cross-Application Components, Distribution (ALE), Communication.**

Configuring an RFC Destination

An RFC destination is a logical name used to identify a remote system on which a function needs to be executed. You define the RFC destination system with a host name and the program or function name to be executed. For the EDI subsystem, an RFC destination is required as it logically resides on an external system from your SAP system irrespective of whether it physically resides on the same system as SAP or on a separate system. Ideally, connection between the systems are via TCP/IP and a "trusted user" ID on each system, to ensure that each can execute programs on the other system. The subsystem vendors are required to write their programs using RFC protocols; however, the rfcexec program shipped with the SAP system circumvents this problem. SAP may start the subsystem by calling the function RFC_REMOTE_EXEC, which is implemented in the program rfcexec and passes the name of the shell script, to allow the RFC_REMOTE_EXEC function to execute the shell script.

Setting Up Trusted User IDs

The trusted user ID setup allows the SAP system to trigger rfcexec remotely. The following example illustrates how to set up these users in both the SAP (system-SAP) and EDI (systemEDI) systems:

1. Ensure the systems are configured at the TCP/IP level to communicate with one another (you may execute the *ping* command at the OS level to verify communication).

2. Set up a user on the systemEDI system with the same name as the SAP user ID at the OS layer on the systemSAP system, which would be <Sid>adm.

3. Create a home directory for this user on systemEDI. This should be the same as the home directory on systemSAP.

4. Create an .rhosts file, with permissions 600, in both systems to allow trusted users to be created.

5. Edit the .rhosts file on systemEDI and enter systemSAP; likewise, edit the .rhosts file on systemSAP and enter systemEDI.

6. To verify that the trusted users are set up correctly, execute the OS **remsh systemEDI date** at the OS from systemSAP and it should return the date from the systemEDI system. Similarly, enter **remsh systemSAP date** from systemEDI and it should start a session for the systemSAP system.

Setting Up an RFC Destination in SAP

From the menu path Tools, Administration, Administration, Network, RFC Destination or executing transaction SM59, set up RFC destinations that EDI using TCP/IP to connect to the subsystem. The default RFC destination (SERVER_EXEC) is shipped with SAP, where SERVER_EXEC starts the rfcexec server program on the SAP application server. Figure A-3 depicts a typical setup of an RFC connection setup, where:

◆ **RFC destination**—Unique name for your RFC destination.

◆ **Connection type**—Use type "T" to indicate TCP/IP.

◆ **Activation type**—Use the Start button.

◆ **Start on**—Select either Application Server or Explicit Host, depending on where the subsystem is installed.

◆ **Program**—Enter **rfcexec** for the RFC server program.

Clicking on the Test button will test the connectivity to the rfcexec program. If successful, then you can successfully connect to the system that has or will have the EDI subsystem; otherwise you will have to determine the error in your setup.

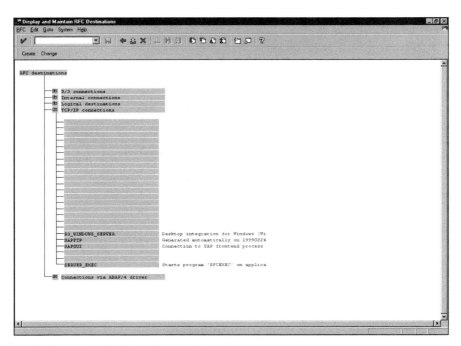

FIGURE A-3 *TCP/IP RFC destinations*

Area Menu of the EDI System

Other EDI settings are accessed via the Area menu of EDI, executing transaction **WEDI** (or menu path **Tools, Administration, Administration, Process Technology, Idoc, IDoc Basis**), as seen in Figure A-4.

An example of area menu configuration is the setting up of the EDIADMIN table, by executing transaction **WE46** or menu path **Tools, Administration, Administration, Process Technology, Idoc, IDoc Basis, Control, Idoc, Administration**. The EDIADMIN table is where global variables used in the EDI process are set up. These include:

- ◆ MAXSYNERR—Maximum number of syntax errors the IDoc interface should log
- ◆ EDIADMIN—IDoc administrator notified in exceptional situations
- ◆ SEGDVCLASS—Development class for the segment editor
- ◆ TESTPORT—Port for testing the IDoc interface

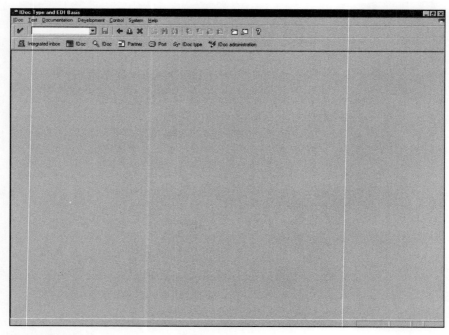

FIGURE A-4 *IDoc Type and EDI Basis screen*

EDI Component Configuration

Port Definitions

The port defines the technical characteristics of the connection between SAP and the subsystem and the medium in which data is exchanged between the two systems. You are required to set up the ports via the transaction **WE21** or menu path **Tools, Administration, Administration, Process Technology, IDoc, Port Definition.**

The IDocs are transferred to external systems via ports, and depending on the type of system to which you are connecting, you may select one of the following four types of ports:

- ◆ **tRFC port**—ALE communication
- ◆ **File port**—EDI
- ◆ **R/2 system port**—R/2 system
- ◆ **Internet port**—Internet applications

Figure A-5 illustrates the initial port definition screen, where:

- ◆ **Port name**—Name to uniquely identify the port

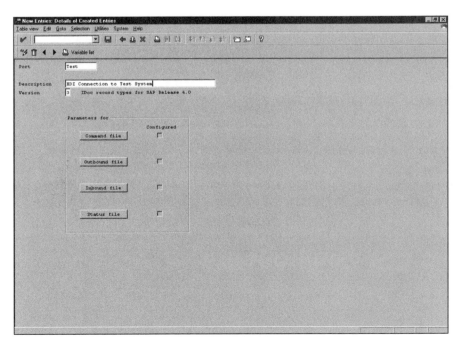

FIGURE A-5 *Attributes for a file port definition*

◆ **Description**—Description of the port

◆ **Version**—Release level of the IDoc being generated by SAP for backward compatibility

A port definition is client-independent and has the following parameters:

◆ **Command file.** The command file parameter specifies the path to the command file of the subsystem, usually in the form of a shell script or batch file, provided by your subsystem vendor. In Figure A-6:

> **Automatic start possible**—Allows the subsystem to be started by SAP

> **Logical destination**—Name of the RFC destination defined in previous step

> **Directory**—Directory path of the subsystem shell script

> **Shell script**—Name of shell script supplied by the subsystem vendor

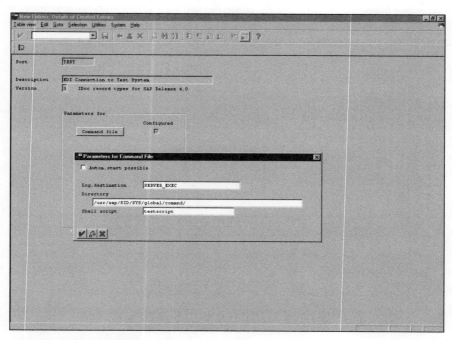

FIGURE A-6 *Command parameters for port definition*

◆ **Outbound File.** The outbound file parameters specify the name and location of the IDoc file generated for an outbound process. As seen in Figure A-7, and where:

Directory—Directory path where the IDoc file is to be generated.

Outbound file—Specify a file name for your outbound IDocs if you are performing tests, as the files are overwritten every time you create an outbound document. (Leave blank to use dynamic file names as described below.)

Function module—SAP provides a dynamic file-naming option, which generates a unique file name at run time. Execute transaction WE55 to add your custom function module for naming the files.

◆ **Inbound file (optional).** The inbound file parameters specify the name and location of the IDoc file for an inbound process. Typically, these parameters are not used, as the subsystem provides a path name and file

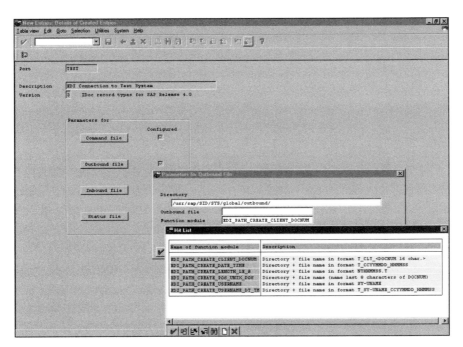

FIGURE A-7 *Attributes of the outbound IDoc*

name when it triggers the inbound process via startrfc. See Figure A-8 as an example, and where:

Directory—Directory path where the IDoc file resides.

Inbound file—Specify a file name for your inbound IDocs if you are performing tests, as the files are overwritten every time you create an inbound document. (Leave blank to use dynamic file names as described below.)

Function module—SAP provides a dynamic file-naming option, which generates a unique file name at run time.

◆ **Status file (optional).** The status file parameters specify the name and location of the status file used to pass status information for an outbound IDoc. Typically, these parameters are not used, as the subsystem provides a path name and file name when it triggers the process via startrfc. See Figure A-9, where:

Directory—Directory path where the status file resides.

Status file—Specify a file name for your status file if you are performing tests, as the files are overwritten every time you create an inbound document. (Leave blank to use dynamic file names as described below.)

Function module—SAP provides a dynamic file-naming option, which generates a unique file name at run time.

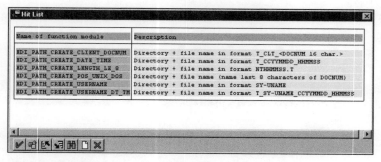

FIGURE A-8 *Attributes of the inbound IDoc*

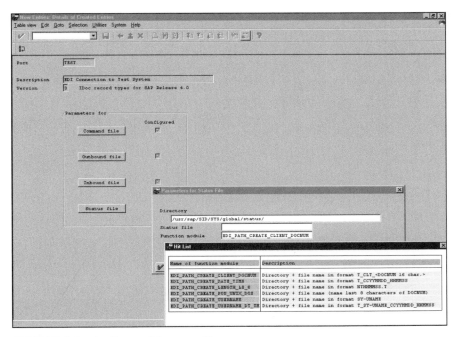

FIGURE A-9 *Attributes of the status files*

Partner Profile

A partner is defined as any business partner with whom you conduct business and exchange EDI documents. In SAP the partner profile maintains parameters specific to the IDoc process. A partner profile in the subsystem maintains parameters specific to the EDI process, which include the following:

◆ Unique partner number

◆ Partner type

◆ Standard used (EDIFACT, ANSI X12, etc.)

◆ Version of the EDI standard

◆ EDI message exchanged (850, 860, ORDERS, ORDCHG)

◆ Functional acknowledgment flag

Triggering of the SAP EDI Transaction

The subsystem creates a status file to report the status to SAP every time the inbound or outbound process is triggered using startrfc, a generic program supplied by SAP. The syntax for the startrfc command is as follows:

```
        startrfc              -3 <R/3 system>
-d <system id>
-u <userid>
-p <password>
-c <client>
-l <language>
-h <App. Server>
-s <system number>
-g <gateway host>
-x <gateway services>
-t <file name>
-E <port name>
-F <function module name>
```

Triggering of Inbound Process

The EDI subsystem is responsible for triggering the inbound process upon receiving an inbound EDI transmission and for creating an IDoc file. SAP provides startrfc to start any RFC-enabled function module from the OS level. For the EDI process, the subsystem uses startrfc to trigger the function module EDI_DATA_INCOMING using the -F option.

The following conversions and translations are carried out for both the outbound and inbound processes:

♦ Creation of control record for inbound

♦ Stripping of control record for outbound

♦ Data translation from IDoc format to EDI format for outbound

♦ Data translation from EDI format to IDoc format for inbound

♦ Bundling and unbundling of IDocs

Reporting Status to SAP

In an outbound process once an IDoc has been transferred to the EDI subsystem, SAP is unable to follow the process. However, it maintains visibility by the subsystem reporting status back to the SAP system. The subsystem reports the status codes shown in Figure A-10 to SAP depending on the state of the process. When the subsystem has status information to send to SAP, it creates a status file and triggers the SAP system using startrfc. The startrfc program calls the EDI_STATUS_INCOMING function module to start the processing of a status record in SAP. These status codes are attached as status records in SAP.

Error Handling

Sometimes it may be necessary to retransmit EDI documents because they are either lost or have errors during transmission. The EDI subsystems provide tools to retransmit a document.

In the outbound process, the subsystem reports errors (translation errors, syntax errors, transmission errors, connectivity issues, etc.) back to SAP.

Status Code	Description
4	Error within control information of EDI subsystem
5	Error during translation
6	Translation OK
7	Error during syntax check
8	Syntax check OK
9	Error during interchange handling
10	Interchange handling OK
11	Error during dispatch
12	Dispatch OK
13	Retransmission OK
14	Interchange Acknowledgement positive
15	Interchange Acknowledgement negative
16	Functional Acknowledgement positive
17	Functional Acknowledgement negative
22	Dispatch OK, acknowledgement still due
23	Error during retransmission
24	Control information of EDI subsystem OK
36	Electronic signature not performed (timeout)

FIGURE A-10 *Status codes passed to SAP by the EDI subsystem*

In the inbound process, the subsystem is responsible for reporting and managing the errors until an IDoc is created. It provides necessary monitoring and recovery tools to handle the errors.

Archiving

The EDI subsystems provide data archiving and management options for documents transmitted to and from your trading partners for audit and liability issues.

Selection of Your EDI Subsystem

There are a number of EDI subsystems on the market, and each basically carries out the main functions with the following major components:

◆ **Definition component**. This is where mapping definitions are created—mapping data in IDoc format to/from documents in EDI standard format. Typically, this component has a GUI with easy drag-and-drop capability to create structures of the application document and IDocs. The various functions carried out on the definition component are:

> Definition of the source and destination structure
>
> Mapping of fields in the source structure to the destination structure
>
> Compilation of maps for other platforms
>
> Mapping tests
>
> Utilities to upload/download document structures and maps

The software vendors usually license this component on a per-user basis.

◆ **Execution component**. This is where the complete environment for executing the maps, trading partner relationships, and other server-related functions are performed. The following are some common tasks performed on the server:

> Map execution
>
> Maintenance of trading partner agreements
>
> Configuration of the environment
>
> Maintenance of log information

Archiving

Tools for monitoring the process

Tools for restart and recovery of failed transactions

Scripts for connectivity with VAN

The execution component is usually licensed on a per-installation basis.

How Much Will It Cost?

Prices vary from hundreds of dollars for simple one-function products to several thousands of dollars for full-function applications. The price is dependent upon several factors:

◆ Difficulty of training and implementation

◆ Initial cost of the software and hardware

◆ Maintenance fees for the software and hardware, including software updates, standards updates, technical support, and customer service

◆ Training costs

◆ VAN charges for transmitting data and connection time

◆ Mailbox costs including a monthly fee for maintaining a mailbox on their network (billing may be per document transmitted or according to the number of characters in each document)

Certification

The certification process is endorsed by SAP, regarding the connectivity and ability to exchange data between the two systems in an IDoc format. With the internal structure of the IDoc changing with every major release of SAP, SAP certifies the subsystem vendors on a per-release basis.

 TIP

Check with your vendor to learn the exact SAP releases for which they have been certified.

SAP has developed standard test scenarios that have been recorded using the CATT (Computer Aided Test Tool) system, where the results are verified. The certification process requires the subsystem to pass the following tests:

◆ **Connectivity test scenarios.** An outbound IDoc is created and the shell script provided by the subsystem vendor is executed, and if successful, then the test of outbound connectivity is successful. For an inbound IDoc, the subsystem calls the startrfc program to pass an IDoc file or a status file to the SAP system. It calls the EDI_DATA_INCOMING function module for IDoc files and EDI_STATUS_INCOMING for status files. If the function modules are started correctly, the test is considered successful.

◆ **Handle IDoc format test scenarios.** Two business scenarios are implemented in SAP to test the ability to handle IDocs:

1. SAP creates a purchase order for a vendor, which is passed to the subsystem as an IDoc file. The subsystem converts the IDoc into an EDI standard format and reports the status of the IDoc to SAP. The outbound purchase order is then sent to SAP as a sales order from a customer.

2. A sales order response is created in the SAP system and passed to the subsystem as an IDoc file. The subsystem converts the IDoc into an EDI standard format and reports the status of the IDoc to SAP. The outbound sales order acknowledgment is then sent to SAP as a purchase order acknowledgment for the purchase order created in the first step.

These steps are repeated for several vendors and using different types of purchase orders (single-line item and multi-line item).

Complete details of the certification process can be obtained from the SAP Web site (**http://www.sap.com**).

Summary

SAP supports the EDI process by providing EDI-enabled applications that are capable of sending and receiving IDoc messages. The IDoc is SAP's proprietary format for exchanging data between business applications but is based on EDI standards and has a flexible structure to accommodate business rules for representing data. IDocs are mapped to an EDI standard format by EDI subsystems, which are third-party tools certified by SAP for their connectivity and ability to handle IDoc messages. One IDoc can be mapped to one or more business transactions.

SAP provides a complete development and enhancement environment for extending and creating new IDocs or EDI transactions along with various tools to configure, monitor, and troubleshoot the system.

X12 Transaction Set (v3040)

104	Air Shipment Information
110	Air Freight Details and Invoice
125	Multilevel Railcar Load Details
126	Vehicle Application Advice
127	Vehicle Baying Order
128	Dealer Information
129	Vehicle Carrier Rate Update
130	Student Educational Record (Transcript)
131	Student Educational Record (Transcript) Acknowledgment
135	Student Loan Application
139	Student Loan Guarantee Result
140	Product Registration
141	Product Service Claim Response
142	Product Service Claim
143	Product Service Notification
144	Student Loan Transfer and Status Verification
146	Request for Student Educational Record (Transcript)
147	Response to Request for Student Educational Record (Transcript)
148	Report of Injury or Illness
151	Electronic Filing of Tax Return Data Acknowledgment
152	Statistical Government Information
154	Uniform Commercial Code Filing
161	Train Sheet
170	Revenue Receipts Statement
180	Return Merchandise Authorization and Notification
186	Laboratory Reporting

190   Student Enrollment Verification

196   Contractor Cost Data Reporting

204   Motor Carrier Shipment Information

210   Motor Carrier Freight Details and Invoice

213   Motor Carrier Shipment Status Inquiry

214   Transportation Carrier Shipment Status Message

217   Motor Carrier Loading and Route Guide

218   Motor Carrier Tariff Information

250   Purchase Order Shipment Management Document

251   Pricing Support

260   Application for Mortgage Insurance Benefits

263   Residential Mortgage Insurance Application Response

264   Mortgage Loan Default Status

270   Health Care Eligibility/Benefit Inquiry

271   Health Care Eligibility/Benefit Information

272   Property and Casualty Loss Notification

276   Health Care Claim Status Request

277   Health Care Claim Status Notification

290   Cooperative Advertising Agreements

300   Reservation (Booking Request) (Ocean)

301   Confirmation (Ocean)

303   Booking Cancellation (Ocean)

304   Shipping Instructions

309   U.S. Customs Manifest

310   Freight Receipt and Invoice (Ocean)

311   Canadian Customs Information

312   Arrival Notice (Ocean)

313   Shipment Status Inquiry (Ocean)

315   Status Details (Ocean)

317   Delivery/Pickup Order

319   Terminal Information

322   Terminal Operations Activity (Ocean)

323   Vessel Schedule and Itinerary (Ocean)

324   Vessel Stow Plan (Ocean)

325   Consolidation of Goods in Container

326   Consignment Summary List

350   U.S. Customs Release Information

352   U.S. Customs Carrier General Order Status

353   U.S. Customs Events Advisory Details

354   U.S. Customs Automated Manifest Archive Status

355   U.S. Customs Manifest Acceptance/Rejection

356   Permit to Transfer Request

361   Carrier Interchange Agreement (Ocean)

404   Rail Carrier Shipment Information

410   Rail Carrier Freight Details and Invoice

414   Rail Carrier Settlements

417   Rail Carrier Waybill Interchange

418   Rail Advance Interchange Consist

419   Advance Car Disposition

420   Car Handling Information

421   Estimated Time of Arrival and Car Scheduling

422   Shipper's Car Order

425   Rail Waybill Request

426   Rail Revenue Waybill

429   Railroad Retirement Activity

431   Railroad Station Master File

440   Shipment Weights

466   Rate Request

468   Rate Docket Journal Log

485   Ratemaking Action

490   Rate Group Definition

492   Miscellaneous Rates

494   Scale Rate Table

511   Requisition

517   Material Obligation Validation

527   Material Due-In and Receipt

536   Logistics Reassignment

561   Contract Abstract

567   Contract Completion Status

568   Contract Payment Management Report

601   Shipper's Export Declaration

602   Transportation Services Tender

622   Intermodal Ramp Activity

805   Contract Pricing Proposal

806   Project Schedule Reporting

810   Invoice

811   Consolidated Service Invoice/Statement

812   Credit/Debit Adjustment

813   Electronic Filing of Tax Return Data

815   Cryptographic Service Message

816   Organizational Relationships

818   Commission Sales Report

819   Operating Expense Statement

820   Payment Order/Remittance Advice

821   Financial Information Reporting

822   Customer Account Analysis

823   Lockbox

824   Application Advice

826   Tax Information Reporting

827   Financial Return Notice

828   Debit Authorization

829   Payment Cancellation Request

830   Planning Schedule with Release Capability

831   Application Control Totals

832   Price/Sales Catalog

833   Residential Mortgage Credit Report Order

834   Benefit Enrollment and Maintenance

835   Health Care Claim Payment/Advice

836   Contract Award

837   Health Care Claim

838   Trading Partner Profile

839   Project Cost Reporting

840   Request for Quotation

841   Specifications/Technical Information

842   Nonconformance Report

843	Response to Request for Quotation
844	Product Transfer Account Adjustment
845	Price Authorization Acknowledgment/Status
846	Inventory Inquiry/Advice
847	Material Claim
848	Material Safety Data Sheet
849	Response to Product Transfer Account Adjustment
850	Purchase Order
851	Asset Schedule
852	Product Activity Data
853	Routing and Carrier Instruction
854	Shipment Delivery Discrepancy Information
855	Purchase Order Acknowledgment
856	Ship Notice/Manifest
857	Shipment and Billing Notice
858	Shipment Information
859	Freight Invoice
860	Purchase Order Change Request—Buyer Initiated
861	Receiving Advice/Acceptance Certificate
862	Shipping Schedule
863	Report of Test Results
864	Text Message
865	Purchase Order Change Acknowledgment/Request—Seller Initiated
866	Production Sequence
867	Product Transfer and Resale Report
868	Electronic Form Structure
869	Order Status Inquiry
870	Order Status Report
872	Residential Mortgage Insurance Application
875	Grocery Products Purchase Order
876	Grocery Products Purchase Order Change
878	Product Authorization/De-authorization
879	Price Change
880	Grocery Products Invoice
882	Direct Store Delivery Summary Information

888   Item Maintenance

889   Promotion Announcement

893   Item Information Request

894   Delivery/Return Base Record

895   Delivery/Return Acknowledgment or Adjustment

896   Product Dimension Maintenance

920   Loss or Damage Claim—General Commodities

924   Loss or Damage Claim—Motor Vehicle

925   Claim Tracer

926   Claim Status Report and Tracer Reply

928   Automotive Inspection Detail

940   Warehouse Shipping Order

943   Warehouse Stock Transfer Shipment Advice

944   Warehouse Stock Transfer Receipt Advice

945   Warehouse Shipping Advice

947   Warehouse Inventory Adjustment Advice

980   Functional Group Totals

990   Response to a Load Tender

996   File Transfer

997   Functional Acknowledgment

998   Set Cancellation

Appendix B

Understanding Ready-to-Run R/3

In This Appendix

♦ Benefits of Ready-to-Run R/3

♦ Technical Attributes of Ready-to-Run R/3

♦ System Administration Assistant

♦ Ready-to-Run R/3 Process Description

♦ Accelerators for SAP Application Areas

Due to SAP's wide range of design, flexibility, and scalability—which proved to be a time consuming and expensive process that required extensive experience and knowledge—SAP developed the Ready-to-Run R/3 (RRR) solution.

An SAP R/3 implementation could be considered as two distinct stages: the *technical setup* followed by the *configuration stage*. In the technical setup, you have to consider a number of technical questions to allow you to configure your technical infrastructure for your SAP system to its fullest potential. Each of these questions have to be addressed separately, and then with training and experience, you make each piece work together as a single unit. Some of these technical questions include:

♦ What are your network requirements? (LAN/WAN and remote connectivity)

♦ What will be your hardware size?

♦ How will the hardware be set up and configured?

♦ How will the SAP system be set up and configured?

♦ What are your SAP system's operational setup and performance criteria?

These questions can be answered simply and easily by using the SAP RRR solution.

What Is Ready-to-Run R/3?

Ready-to-Run R/3 (RRR) is a program developed jointly by SAP and its hardware vendors to offer customers a jump start on their SAP projects by providing them with the initial technical setup specific to their projects' requirements. It is by all definitions a pre-sized, pre-installed, and pre-configured SAP R/3 system turnkey solution delivered to the client "project ready." It is designed to be a simple but robust solution suited for most small and mid-sized organizations. Figure B-1 illustrates the main components of the SAP RRR solution, which include the network, the SAP systems, management tools, the front-end PCs, and other third-party applications.

The Ready-to-Run R/3 solution is completely aligned with SAP's Accelerated-SAP (ASAP) implementation methodology, where the SAP Basis customizing steps have already been performed. The Ready-to-Run R/3 solution may also be complemented with additional SAP R/3 accelerated module implementation packages.

The SAP Ready-to-Run R/3 methodology provides a PC tool known as the QuickSizer, in which the client or project manager will input the modules being implemented, the approximate number of users, and the activity level (low, medium, or high), after which the QuickSizer tool will automatically size the SAP R/3 test and production machine. Typically, the development machine is used by a small number of technical and customizing team members.

The QuickSizer tool may be utilized in one of two ways. The first is based on the number of users for each application module and sun module and their level of activity. Figure B-2 shows the user-based screen capture of the QuickSizer.

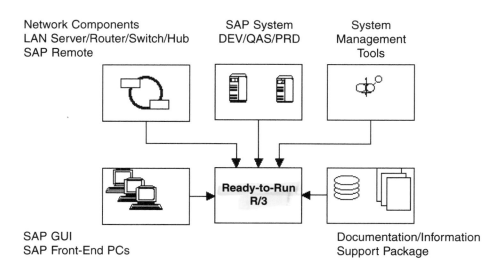

Network Components
LAN Server/Router/Switch/Hub
SAP Remote

SAP System
DEV/QAS/PRD

System
Management
Tools

Ready-to-Run R/3

SAP GUI
SAP Front-End PCs

Documentation/Information
Support Package

FIGURE B-1 *Components of the SAP Ready-to-Run R/3 solution*

The second way is based on SAP transaction volumes (including both online and batch transactions).

Figures B-3 and B-4 illustrate the *transaction quantity* sizing screens for online (dialog) and background (batch) transactions.

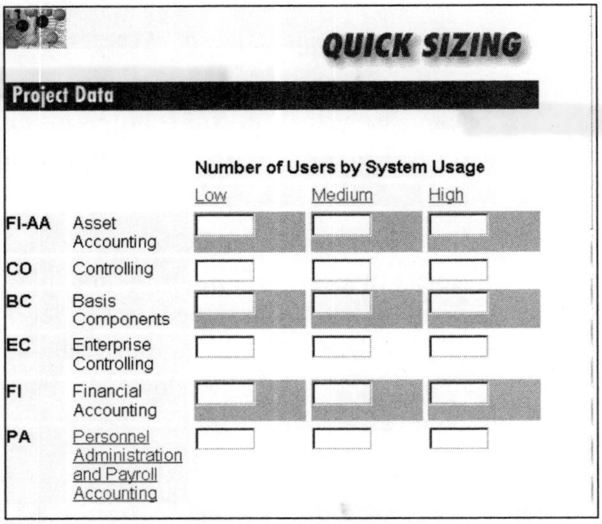

FIGURE B-2 *QuickSizer user based sizing screens*

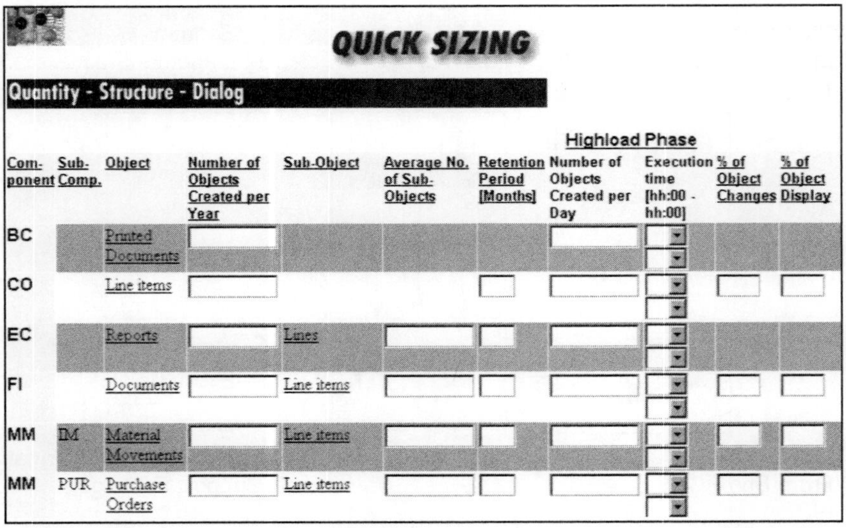

FIGURE B-3 *QuickSizer transaction based sizing screens used in conjunction with the QuickSizer batch based.*

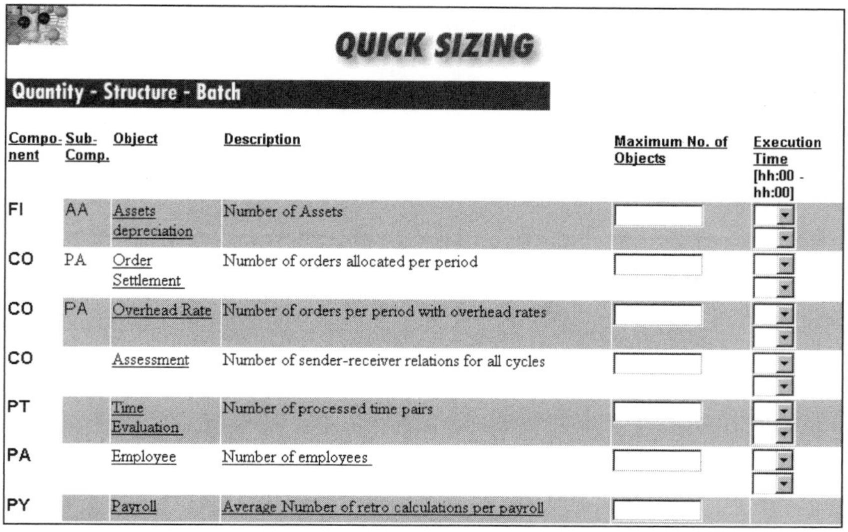

FIGURE B-4 *QuickSizer batch based sizing screens*

For example, use the user based sizing method of the QuickSizer tool and the data in Table B-1 to size your machine.

Table B-1 User Based Data to Quick-Size a Production System

Application	Number of users/Activity Levels		
	Low	Medium	High
FI-AA			30
CO			30
BC			5
FI			30
PA		12	
PD		12	
MM			10

The results would be similar to those shown in Figure B-5.

The actual calculations are very simple, and you may even perform them using a spreadsheet. SAP provides the load factor per module and the load factor per user type, as shown in Table B-2.

Table B-2 Load Factors for the Application Area and the Activity
Level of the Users

Module	Load Factor
AM	0.6
CO	1.2
BC	0.8
EC	0.8
FI	0.2
HR-PA	0.2
HR-PD	0.6
MM	0.6
TR	0.2
PM	1.2
PP	1.2
PS	1.2
QM	0.6
SD	1.0
SM	1.2
WM	0.4

User	Load Factor
Low	0.1
Medium	1.0
High	3.0

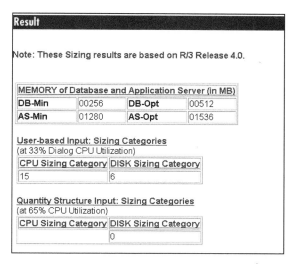

FIGURE B-5 *QuickSizer results*

Therefore, extending the example in Table B-2, the total load on the system is 183.6 as calculated in Table B-3.

Table B-3 Load Factor Calculations

Users	Calculation	Total
30 High level FI-AA users	30(users) x 3.0(user load factor) x 0.2(application load factor)	18.0
30 High level CO users	30(users) x 3.0(user load factor) x 1.2(application load factor)	108.0
5 High level BC users	5(users) x 3.0(user load factor) x 0.8(application load factor)	12.0
30 High level FI users	30(users) x 3.0(user load factor) x 0.2(application load factor)	18.0
12 High Medium PA users	12(users) x 1.0(user load factor) x 0.2(application load factor)	2.4
12 High Medium PD users	12(users) x 1.0(user load factor) x 0.6(application load factor)	7.2
10 High level MM users	10(users) x 3.0(user load factor) x 0.6(application load factor)	18.0
	Total	183.6

To determine what the total system load relates to a specific SAP system requirement, SAP provides a corresponding Excel spreadsheet that will determine the package type required according to your results. This spreadsheet is found on SAP's Web site at:

http://www.sap.com/service/rrr_over.htm

NOTE

The QuickSizer tool is used for sizing up to a certain user and/or transaction limit. Most hardware vendors size their systems up to a maximum of 250 to 300 users.

All you have to do is to decide the platform of your choice (hardware and database vendor), that relates to the package number required for your project. A complete list of the vendors and their respective hardware and software may be found again at SAP's Web site.

Upon ordering the SAP system, you will receive a fully configured, tested, and integrated solution that contains all the components required for running your SAP project for maximum performance. This includes:

◆ Server(s) hardware

◆ Operating system

◆ Database system

◆ SAP R/3 system software

◆ Configured network components

◆ Backup units and tapes

◆ Printers

Typically, the Ready-to-Run R/3 solution is available in models suitable for system sizes from approximately 15 to 300 concurrent users.

Benefits of Ready-to-Run R/3

Ready-to-Run R/3 decreases the total cost of ownership (TCO) of the SAP project by:

- Starting the implementation upon the delivery of the pre-configured SAP R/3 system and its components
- Reducing technical setup and consulting by 20 to 30 days in accordance with the specifications of SAP's ASAP methodology
- Providing a System Administration Assistant (SAA) to speed up administrative tasks
- Taking advantage of SAP and its partners' "best practices" embodied in the Ready-to-Run R/3 configuration
- Providing full and complete documentation of all operating, technical, and system processes and configuration

Technical Attributes of Ready-to-Run R/3

The SAP system setup, configuration, and customizing of the Basis component is performed by experienced SAP consultants from SAP's hardware, database, and technical partners to provide you with the optimum setup for your environment. Examples of the setup, configuration, and customizing provided by the Ready-to-Run R/3 concept include:

- SAP system parameters and configuration setup for optimal performance

    System setup (system name, host name, TCP/IP address, etc.)

    Uninterrupted Power Supply (UPS) setup

    Optimizing operating system performance

    Optimizing database disk performance for efficient reads and writes

    Database tuning (indexes setup)

- SAP system parameters setup
- SAP buffer setup

◆ SAP language(s) loaded

◆ SAP client setup

Test system

Client 000—SAP standard client

Client 001—SAP standard client with data

Client 010—Customizing client

Client 020—Test client for customizing

Client 030—Training, play, and test client

Client 066—SAP Early Watch client

Production system

Client 000—SAP standard client

Client 001—SAP standard client with data

Client 010—Production client

Client 066—SAP Early Watch client

◆ SAP routine clean-up jobs

◆ SAP correction and transport system (TMS)

◆ SAP users/profiles and authorizations (sample activity groups provided) including the setup of the profile generator

◆ SAP day/night operation modes

◆ SAP printer and spool setup

◆ SAP database backup strategy preset through CCMS

◆ SAP alert monitor configured

◆ SAP R/3 SAPGUI preloaded on the presentation clients

◆ OSS (online support service) connection and its network components (WAN connection, routers setup, firewall setup, Internet access, etc.)

◆ SAP Early Watch

The SAP Ready-Run R/3 network setup is delivered as shown in Figure B-6.

Production System

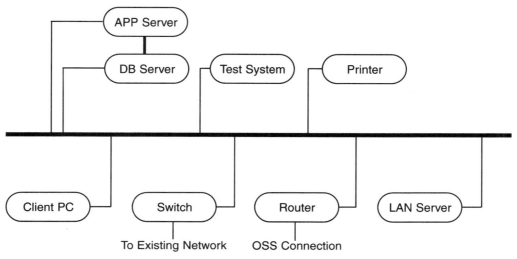

FIGURE B-6 *Network infrastructure for RRR*

System Administration Assistant

Optimal management of the SAP system is ensured through the use of a specially developed online tool for the system administrator, known as the System Administration Assistant (SAA). Using proven operation concepts, the SAA specifies exactly what the system administrator needs to do on a daily, weekly, and monthly basis. The SAA is a hypertext checklist from which the system administrator can directly start the required R/3 transactions and programs and is also able to display context-sensitive help.

You may download the SAA tool directly from SAP's Web site: **www.sap.com**.

Ready-to-Run R/3 Process Description

The requirements to implement Ready-to-Run R/3 may be expressed as a series of steps:

1. **System sizing.** The SAP project manager will run the QuickSizer to determine the SAP system requirements (accessed through SAPnet at **http://sapnet.sap-ag.de/rrr** where you will be required to type your SAP OSS id and password).

Figure B-7 illustrates a simple flowchart of the RRR process.

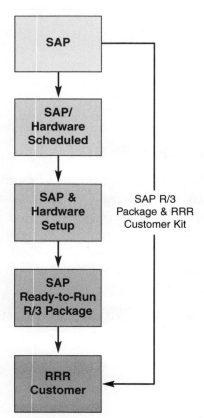

FIGURE B-7 *Flow chart of the Ready-to-Run R/3 process.*

Deliver SAP RRR Package

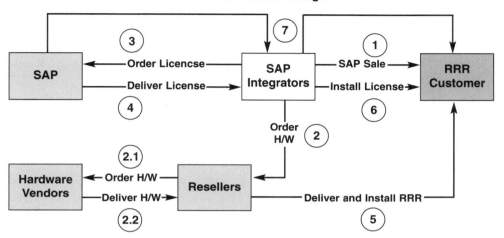

FIGURE B-8 *Process flow of Ready-to-Run R/3*

2. **Delivery of SAP system and its components.** Based on the SAP system's requirements, SAP will send the package on to the hardware partners to set up the test and production SAP R/3 systems from guidelines provided by SAP and the hardware vendors' consultants.

   Another variation on Figure B-8 is to have the Ready-to-Run R/3 SAP systems delivered in either one or two shipments as follows:

   • Deliver the whole system (test and production) in one delivery.

   • Deliver the test system first and the production system later.

   Once the Ready-to-Run R/3 systems have been delivered, the hardware vendor will set up and test the complete environment and hand ownership of the SAP system over to you with complete documentation.

3. **Ready-to-Run R/3 workshop.** Once the hardware has been set up and the documentation provided, a workshop (typically one to three days long) is conducted for the following purposes:

   • To demonstrate SAP concepts, the SAP R/3 system, and its settings and tools

- To introduce the Ready-to-Run R/3 Administrative Assistant
- To provide hands-on administrator training through examples and exercises
- To perform configuration training (OSS connection, SAP license setup, CCMS alerts, operation modes, etc.)

4. **Handover**. The system is formally handed over to the client, with each party signing a checklist (provided by SAP).

5. **Additional SAP training**. The administrators are required to attend additional training for day-to-day operation support. This may be in the form of SAP formal training, computer-based training (CBT), or a workshop.

Accelerators for SAP Application Areas

Complementing the AcceleratedSAP (ASAP) implementation methodology and the Ready-to-Run R/3 (RRR) program, SAP has developed accelerators for the application areas. These include:

◆ Preconfigured FI clients, activity groups, and print forms

◆ Preconfigured CO clients and product costing scenarios

◆ Preconfigured HR clients, activity groups, and print forms

◆ Preconfigured MM clients, activity groups, and print forms

◆ PP master setup, work center data transfer, and product costing scenarios

◆ PM data transfer

◆ Preconfigured SD clients, activity groups, print forms, and wizards

These configurations and related documentation may be downloaded from SAP's R/3 Simplification Web site at **http://207.105.30.51/simpweb** and used as a starting place for your customizing of the application areas.

Index

/$ST transaction, 298
/sapmnt directory structure, 81
/usr/sap directory structure, 81
/usr/sap/trans, 81

A

ABAP
   authorizations, 175–176
   development tools, 15–16
   dump analysis, 435–438
   errors, 322–323
   queries, 153–154
      deleting, 153–154
   Runtime Analyzer, 349–354
ABAP Data dictionary, 15–17
ABAP development, client 750, 55
ABAP Development Workbench, 15–16
ABAP Editor, 15
ABAP Query, Basis layer, 7
ABAP Repository, 15
ABAP Repository information system, 15
ABAP Runtime Environment, Basis layer, 6
ABAP Workbench, Basis layer, 6
access, client copy and, 136
accounting documents, archiving and, 411–413
acknowledging alerts, 335–336
activity groups, profile generator, 178–180
AGate (Application Gateway), ITS, 451
AIS (Audit Information System), 187–192
AIX users, 66–67
AL08 (logged users) transaction, 326–327
ALE (Application Link Enabling), 126

alert monitor, 333–337
alerts
   acknowledging, 335–336
   resetting, 335–336
   transactions, 337
allocation fault rate, redo log buffer and, 272
allocation retries, redo log buffer, 272
analysis tools, troubleshooting, 431–445
application archive objects, 408–419
application area format values, 404
application exits, 12
Application layer, 8
Application Link Enabling (ALE), 126
Application server, 7, 32
   software installation and, 82
   tuning and, 245
architecture, 5–6
   client, installation planning, 46–47
   client/server, 7
   hardware, tuning and, 249
   Internet access and, 448–449
   tiered, 7–8
Archive (ARCH), 275
archive mode, 143–144
archive objects, 393–398
   application archive objects, 408–419
   configuration, 407
   controlling, 413–414
   cost center accounting, 414
   financial, 409–417
   material management, 414–415
   purchasing documents, 416–417
   sales and distribution, 417–419

archiving, 390–427
application area format values, 404
applications, upgrades and, 480
authorizations, 392–393
DART, 420–423
date format values, 404
file names, setup, 400–405
global archive path, setup, 398–400
logs, monitoring, 332
overview, 391–395
performing the archive, 398–408
strategy development, 392
asynchronous disk I/O, 262–263
Audit Information System. *See* AIS
audit report tree, 187
audits
business audit, 187, 190–191
system audit, 187–190
Authority-Checks, 177
authorization classes, 159–168
authorization fields, 159–160
authorization objects, 159
authorization profiles, 164–166
authorizations
ABAP, 175–176
archiving, 392–393
critical combinations, 191–192
naming, 163
security, 159–177
table authorizations, 171–175
transaction SU53, 180

B

background processes, client copy and, 137
background user type, 168
backup solutions, 26
backups. *See also* recovery, 361–370
database backup, 363–364

databases, pre-production preparation, 507–508
environment, baseline backup, upgrade and, 493
full, 364
logical, 361
logs, monitoring, 332
offline (cold), 362–363
online (hot), 362
partial, 364
physical, 361
tablespace, 364
users, 145–147
restoring, 148–149
utilities, 370
BAPIs (business application programming interfaces), 5
bar alert indicators (alert monitor), 334
Basis layer, 6–7
Basis module, 5
Basis roles, 37
Basis Services/Communication Interfaces, Basis layer, 6
Basis upgrade, 470
batch instance, tuning and, 245
batch jobs, 324–325
batch servers, dedicated, 27
Batch service, 241
BDC (batch user) user type, 168
blended code pages, 88, 91–92
bottlenecks, 344–348
buffer cache, memory, 260–261
buffer management, 304–313
buffers, 310
data block buffer cache, 266–267
generic, 313
partial, 311–312
resident, 313
SAP, 307–308
shared memory buffers, 310
ST02 transaction, 322

statistics, 304

synchronization, 305–307

business audit, 187, 190–191

Business Engineer, Basis layer, 6

Business Management, Basis layer, 6

business process (client 775), 56

business structure, archiving and, 391

busy waits, 267–268

BWP (Business Information Warehouse Patches), 117

C

C Type transport, 224, 225

caches, SAP Cursor Cache, 309

calls, 275–277

parses, 276–277

recursive, 276

capacity

planning, 371, 485

upgrades and, 474

Category, Table T000, 128

CCCFLOW.SAP, 132

CCMS (Computer Center Management Tools), 340

monitoring transactions, 340–341

CD

copying installation software, 63–67

registration, 111

CDINST installation tool, 74

CDP files, 105

central instance, 244–245

Central System, OSINST installation tool, 71

CGI (Common Gateway Interface), 451

Change & Transport system, Basis layer, 6

Change control, 13–14

upgrades and, 479

changes, custom, upgrades and, 480–483

Checkpoint (CKPT), 275

classes, authorization classes, 159–168

cleanipc utility, 296

client 700 (customizing), 54

client 725 (quality assurance), 54–55

client 750 (ABAP development), 55

client 775 (business process), 56

client architecture, installation planning, 46–47

client strategy, system landscape, 53–57

client-dependent objects

changes, 128–129

transports, 128–129

client-independent objects, changes, 129

client/server architectures, 7

clients, 124

copy profiles, 133–135

copying, 130–131, 147–148

background process, 137

checklist, 140–141

consistency protection, 138

log analysis, 132

online, 136–137

paging memory and, 138

prerequisites, 136–138

rollback segments and, 137

utilities for, 138–139

variants and, 137

creating, 124–154

deleting, 133, 144–145

exporting, 132, 149–151

importing, 132, 133, 151–152

usage, 125–126

cluster tables, data dictionary, 16

code pages

blended, 88, 91–81

CDP files, 105

standard, 89

cold backups, 362–363

commit call, 275

commit work, paging memory and, 138

Communication Interfaces, Basis layer, 6

complete recovery, 365

Component Integration/Installation Windows Components, Basis layer, 6

composite profiles, 165

Computer Aided Test Tool (CATT), ABAP, 16

Computing Center Management System, Basis layer, 6

CONFFILE installation tool, 79

configuration
    objects, archive objects, 407
    OSS, 109–111
    TMS, 228

connections, service connection, 113–114

Consolidation environment, 13

Consolidation system, 53

control files, backups, restoring database, 368–369

control panel alert monitor, 336

control tables, CTS and, 231

controlled access, security, 462–463

copy profiles, clients, 133–135

copying
    clients, 147–148
        background process, 137
        checklist, 140–141
        consistency protection, 138
        log analysis, 132
        online, 136–137
        paging memory and, 138
        prerequisites, 136–138
        rollback segments and, 137
        transaction SCC0, 130
        transaction SCC9, 130–131
        transaction SCCL, 130
        transport requests, 131
        utilities, 138–139
        variants and, 137
    databases, 380–388
    overwrite protection, 129

correction and transport system. *See* CTS

corrections, 223
    online support, 116–117

cost center accounting, archiving, 414

CPIC (interface user) user type, 168

CPU load, monitoring, 328–329

CPU time, response time and, 346

critical authorization combinations, 191–192

CRTs (Conflict Resolution Transport), 116

CTS (Correction and Transport System), 13, 50, 221–237
    control tables, 231
    environment maintenance, 236–237
    environment, consistency, upgrades and, 486–487
    initialization, 233–236
    object types, 226–227
    parameter files, 231
    UNIX level setup, 229–233

cursors, SAP Cursor Cache, 309

custom changes, upgrades and, 480–483

Customer Masters, access, 185

Customer Name Range, 14

customization, 11
    client 700, 54
    client 700 and, 54
    projects, 12

Customizing Master, 125

D

daily monitoring, pre-production preparation, 509–512

daily transactions, monitoring, 509–510

DART (Data Retention Tool), 420–423

data access and retention, archiving and, 391

data block buffer cache, 266–267

data consistency, 305–307

data dependence, archiving and, 391

data dictionary, ABAP, 16–17

data elements, data dictionary, 16

Data load, 125

data loads, pre-production preparation, 513–514

data structures, data dictionary, 16–17

database administration, 356–388

database alert log, troubleshooting and, 444–445

database backup, 363–364

Database Interface, Database Platforms, Basis layer, 6

Database layer, 8

database management, pre-production preparation, 506–508

Database server, 7
  selecting, 29–30
  tuning and, 244

Database Writer (DBWR), 273–274

databases
  ABAP Runtime Analysis, 349–350
  backups, pre-production preparation, 507–508
  capacity planning, 371
  copying, 380–388
  distribution, tuning and, 251–257
  extents, monitoring, 332–333
  file systems, monitoring, 331
  free space, monitoring, 332–333
  installation, 357
  layout, 30–32
  localization, TCP0D language table, 98–100
  logs, monitoring, 331
  monitoring, 330–333
  Oracle, installation, 31
  recovery, pre-production preparation, 507–508
  relational, 6
  reorganizing, 361, 375–380
  sizing, 30
  software, installation, 80–87
  startup, ORAINST utility and, 71
  tuning, 264–282

ARCH, 275
busy waits, 267–268
calls, 275–277
CKPT, 275
data block buffer cache, 266–267
DBWR (Database Writer), 273–274
LGWR (Log Writer), 274–275
PGA, 265–266
PMON, 282
redo log buffer, 271–273
redo logging, 277–279
SGA, 265
shared SQL pool, 269–271
SMON, 282
sorts, 281
table scans, 279–281
upgrades, 357

date format values, archives, 404

DDIC, special user account, 169

dedicated batch servers, 27

default profile, language profile parameters, 102–103

deleting
  clients, 133, 144–145
  queries, ABAP, 153–154

Delrina Winfax software, 208–211

DEV (development server)
  security, 158
  system landscape and, 24

developer traces, 443

developers, registration, 14, 110

development
  environment, 53–57
  management, 357–361

development system, upgrading, 492–496

developments, multiple, 13

DIAG (Dynamic Information and Action Gateway), ITS, 451

dialog instance, tuning and, 245–246

Dialog service, 241

dialog user type, 168

dictionary cache, shared SQL pool, 269–271

disaster recovery, 512–513

disk I/O monitoring, 262–264

disk space

    checking, 142–154

    client copy and, 136

    software installation and, 80

dispatch time (response time), 344

distribution, tuning and, 242–248

    databases, 251–257

    software, 251–255

domains, data dictionary, 16

downtime, upgrades, reducing, 480

E

Early Watch service, 17, 109

em/initial_size_MB (extended memory parameter), 288

encryption technology, ITS, 463

enhancements, 12

Enqueue service, 241, 320–321

enterprise resource planning (ERP) application. *See* ERP

enterprise structure, archiving and, 391

environments, 13

    backup, baseline, upgrade and, 493

    production, 56–57

    quality assurance, 56

ERP (enterprise resource planning), 4

esmon utility, 293

Ethernet, 34

exits, 12

exporting clients, 132, 149–151

extended memory, 287–288

extents, databases, monitoring, 332–333

F

fax management, pre-production preparation, 509

faxing, 208–220

FCS (First Customer Shipment), 116

FDDI, 34

FDDI rings, 243

Fiber Optic, 34

fields

    authorization, 159–160

    data dictionary, 16

file names, archives, setup, 400–405

file systems

    databases, monitoring, 331

    installation preparation, 65

    monitoring, 329–330

    raw devices and, 250–251

    setup, FSINST and, 73–74

    tuning and, 249–251

files

    permissions, modifying, 66

    sapconf, 65

filters, ABAP Runtime Analysis, 349–350

financial archive objects, 409–417

Financial Management module, 4–5

firewalls, security, 462

flexibility, 9

formats

    application area values, 404

    date values, 404

free space, databases, 332

Front End Services, Basis layer, 6

front-end

    software, technical upgrade, 489–491

    upgrades, 485

FSINST installation tool, 73–74

full backups, 364

functional upgrade, 470

G

Gateway service, 241

gateways, 327

generic buffering, 313

Get ratio (SQL area), 271

global archive path, setup, 398–400

Global Database Alert Monitor, 333–337

graphical user interface, 9. *See also* SAPGUI

group hit list (ABAP Runtime Analyzer), 353

groups, UNIX, 66

    CTS and, 231

H

hardware

    architecture, tuning and, 249

    installation, upgrades, 485

    lifetime, 23

    outsourcing, 43

    scalability, 23

    size, 27

        installation planning, 44–45

    tiers, 25–26

hardware independence, archiving and, 391

hardware platform, selection, 22–27

hardware requirements, 22–28

    future growth plans, 28

    implementation, 23

    IT department and, 27

    servers, 27–28

    system landscape, 23–24

headers, segment headers, 268

heap (memory), 289–291

heterogeneous systems, 8, 25

hierarchy display (ABAP Runtime Analyzer), 354

hit list (ABAP Runtime Analyzer), 352

homogenous systems, 8

hot backup, 362

Hot Packages, 11, 116, 327–328

    distribution, 119

    installation, 117–119

    LCP-HR Legal Patches, 117

    patch queue, 118–119

HP-UX printer installation, 198–199

HTTP (HyperText Transport Protocol), 448

Human Resources module, 5

I

IAC (Internet Application Components), 450–451

IDocs (intermediate documents), 127

implementation

    hardware, 23

    modules, 23

    rolling releases, 57–58

importing

    clients, 132, 133, 151–152

    languages, 106–108

    queries, 154

    variants, 152–153

incomplete recovery, 365–369

initialization

    CTS, 233–236

    language tables, 90

installation

    available space, 65

    database software, 80–86

        Application Server, 82

    databases, 357

    file system preparation, 65

    hardware, upgrades, 485

    ITS, 449–450

    language tables, 94–102

    languages, 93–102

installation *(continued)*

Oracle

database, 31

ORAINST utility, 68

ORAINST utility, 67–71

planning checklist, 44–48

print drivers, 200–202

printers, 197–207

HP-UX printers, 198–199

SAP level, 199–200

Windows NT, 199

SAPcomm/TOPCALL, 212–217

software, copying from CD, 63–67

tools, 71–79

UNIX and, 63–67

users, 66

Upgrade Assistant, 492

Installation Tools, Basis layer, 6

instances

installation, SAPINST and, 79

language profile parameters, 103–105

integration, 5

Integration environment, 13

Integration system, 53

Interactive program debugger, ABAP, 16

intermediate documents (IDocs), 127

internal tables, ABAP Runtime Analysis, 349–350

Internet

architecture, SAP access and, 448–449

IAC, 450–451

SAP@Web Studio, 464–465

security, 462–464

Internet Application Components (IAC), 450–451

Internet Transaction Server (ITS), 448

Internet transaction server. *See* ITS

IPC resources, KCHECK and, 76

ipcrm command (UNIX), 297

ipcs command (UNIX), 297

IS (industry specific) solutions, 10–11

ITS (Internet Transaction Server), 26, 448, 451–454

administration, 450

encryption technology, 463

installation, 449–450

project directory, 454–460

service files, 454–460

WebReporting, 460

WebReporting Browser, 461–462

WebRFC, 457–460

J

job scheduling management, 504–506

K

K Type transport, 223, 225

KCHECK installation tool, 76

kernel, 6

Kernel Components, Basis layer, 6

kernel parameters, operating system tuning, 257

kernel patches, 327–328

kernel, UNIX, 67

L

language tables, 94–102

languages, 87–108

blended code pages, 88

CDP files, 105

classifying, 95

importing, 106–108

installation, 88–90, 93–102

profile parameters, 102–105

RSCP utilities, 107–108

support, upgrades and, 475

tables, initializing, 90

UNICODE, 88, 92

LANs (local area networks), 33–34

layout, databases, 30–32

LCP-HR Legal Patches, 117

Legal Patches, 11

lifetime of hardware, 23

light alert indicators (alert monitor), 333–334

load balancing, 326

tuning and, 246–248

locales, 93

lock entries monitor, troubleshooting and, 440–441

Lock Manager, 320–321

lock objects, 440–441

locking users, 148

log files, redo, 277–279

log switch, 278

Log Writer (LGWR), 274–275

logical backups, 361

logical system, Table T000, 126–127

logon groups, load balancing, 246

logs

analysis, client copying, 132

archive mode, 143–144

monitoring

archives, 332

backups, 332

databases, 331

operating system, 330

pre-production preparation, 508

long tables, scans, 280

M

maintenance, scheduled, 370–388

Manufacturing and Logistics module, 5

mass printing, 196

master records, users, 166–168

matchcodes, data dictionary, 17

material management archive objects, 414–415

MDMP (Multi-Display/Multi Processing), 87, 91

MDSP (Multi Display/Single Processing), 88, 90–91

MEMLIMITS utility, 296–297

memory

amount used, 302–303

buffer cache, 260–261

data block buffer cache, 266–267

disk I/O monitoring, 262–264

extended, 287–288

heap, 289–291

monitoring, 329

page memory, 289

parameter values, 291

physical, 258

private, 261–262

random access, 258

roll area, 286–287

roll memory, 284–286

shared, 261–262, 287–288

shared memory buffers, 310

swap space, 258–259

usage, monitoring, 303

virtual memory, 260

memory management, 283–304

operating system tuning, 258–259

tools, 292–304

Menu Painter, ABAP, 15

Message Server service, 241

messages, OSS, 112

metadata, ABAP Development Workbench, 15

migration, pre-production data migration, 513–514

Mixed Native Language Support (MNLS), 88

MNLS (Mixed Native Language Support), 88

modules

Financial Management, 4–5

Human Resources, 5

implementation, 23

logon groups, 246

Manufacturing and Logistics, 5

Sales and Distribution, 5

monitoring, 318–337

    daily monitoring activities, 509–512

Multi-Display/Multi Processing. *See* MDMP

N

naming

    authorizations, 163

    conventions, 14

Native Language Support (NLS), 88, 90

network installation, database software, 86–87

networks

    architecture, tuning and, 242–248

    printing and, 195

    requirements, 33

NLS (Native Language Support), 88, 90

O

Object Access Key, repairs and, 222

objects

    archive

        application archive objects, 408–419

        configuration, 407

        financial, 409–417

        material management, 414–415

        purchasing documents, 416–417

        sales and distribution, 417–419

    authorization, 159

    changes to, 11

    client-dependent

        changes, 128–129

        transports, 128–129

    client-independent, 129

    corrections, 223

    registration, 14, 110–111

    repairs, 222

    transporting, consolidation system, 223

    transports, types, 223–225

    types, CTS, 226–227

    version management, 14

OCS (Online Correct Service), 109

offline backups, 362–363

online backup, 362

online client copy, 136–137

Online Correction Service (OCS), 109

online correction support, 116–117

online redo log files, 277–279

Online Service System (OSS), 108

operating system

    administrator, 38–397

    language installation, 93–94

    monitoring, 328–330

    selection, 29

    tuning, 257–264

Operating System Platforms, Basis layer, 6

operation modes, 299–300

ORABUILD installation tool, 76–77

ORABUILD_PRO installation tool, 78–79

Oracle

    databases

        control files, 83

        installation, 31

        ORABUILD and, 76–77

    directories, database software installation, 82

    installation, ORAINST utility, 68

    SYSPROF and, 75

    tuning SAP, 264

    users, creating, 360

ORAINST utility, 67–71

    database startup and, 71

    procedure, 69

ORALOAD utility, 77–78

ORAUNLOAD installation tool, 78

OS

print process, 197–198

printer setup, 198–199

OS-Blocks written, 279

OS06 transaction, 300–302

OSINST installation tool, 71–73

OSS (Online Service System), 108–111

configuration, 109

general functions of, 114–115

messages, 112

registration, 110–111

troubleshooting and, 444

outsourcing, 43–44

overwriting, protection by copying, 129

P

page area, 323–324

page memory, 289

paging memory

client copy and, 138

commit work and, 138

paging, monitoring, 329

parameters

files, CTS and, 231

kernel parameters, operating system tuning, 257

pctincrease, 372

setup, archive processing, 398–406

storage, changing, 371–372

values, 291

parses, 276–277

partial backups, 364

partial buffering, 311–312

passwords, 169–171

patch queue, 118

patches, distribution, 119

pctincrease parameter, 372

performance. *See also* tuning

bottlenecks, 344–348

goals, determining, 342–348

monitoring, 322, 340–354

tuning, 282–313

permissions

files, modifying, 66

UNIX, CTS and, 231

personnel roles, 38–43

PGA (Process Global Area), 265–266

phases of upgrades, 471

phasing implementation, 57–58

physical backups, 361

physical memory, 258

physical reads, 267

physical writes, 267

Pin ratio (SQL area), 271

planning upgrades, 471–487

platforms, hardware, selecting, 22–27

PMON (process monitor), 282

pool tables, data dictionary, 16

post-upgrade activities, 496

PRD

security, 159

server, system landscape and, 24

upgrades, 497

pre-production preparation

checklist, 515–516

daily monitoring activities, 509–512

database management, 506–508

job scheduling management, 504–506

production system stabilization, 516–517

resource planning, 500–501

testing, 501–504

TMS, 508

PREPARE utility, upgrades, 492–493

Presentation Layer, 7

Presentation server, 7, 32–33
SAPGUI, 9
Primary Development, 125
print drivers, installation, 200–202
printers
automatic definition, 197
installation, 197–207
HP-UX printers, 198–199
SAP level, 199–200
Windows NT, 199
print drivers, installation, 200–202
setup, operating system, 198–199
types/needs, 196
printing
mass printing, 196
print process at OS level, 197–198
remote, 195
troubleshooting, 202–207
user information, 147
printing management, pre-production preparation, 509
private memory, 261–262, 289–291
problem resolution, 17
process-local storage (heap), 289–291
processes, 325–326
Production client, 125
Production Environment, 56–57
Change control, 13
production system, stabilization, 516–517
profile generator, 177–180
authorizations, 164
profile parameters, languages, 102–105
profiles
authorization profiles, 164–166
composite, 165
maintenance, 299–300
users, modifying, 66
project directory, ITS, 454–460

projects, custom, 12
proxy servers, 463
purchasing documents archive objects, 416–417

Q
QAS (quality assurance)
environment, 159
server, system landscape and, 24
upgrades, 497
quality assurance
client 725, 54–55
environment, 56
queries
ABAP, 153–154
importing, 154
QuickSizer, 27
module implementation, 23

R
R/3 standards, 9–14
R/3 upgrades, 494–496
R3SETUP utility, sapconf file, 65
R3up, 494–496
RAID technologies, 249–250
random access memory, 258
raw devices, file systems and, 250–251
RDDIMPDP, 236
reads, data block buffer cache, 267
rec/client = OFF/ALL, 143
Recipient system, 53
recording changes, 128–129
tables, 143
records, master records, users, 166–168
recovery. *See also* restore
complete, 365–369
databases, pre-production preparation, 507–508
disaster recovery, 512–513

incomplete, 365–369

recursive calls, 276

redo log buffer, 271–273

redo log writes, 279

redo logging, 277–279

registration

    developers, 14

    objects, 14

    OSS, 110–111

relational databases, 6

release dependence, archiving and, 391

reloads/pins, 271

remote printing, 195

remote support connections, 36

Remote Support service, 17

reorganizing databases, 361, 375–380

repairs, 222

    System Change Options, 223

    transports, 224

reporting test results, pre-production preparation, 503–504

Reporting, Basis layer, 7

reports, audit report tree, 187

resetting alerts, 335–336

resident buffering, 313

resource planning, pre-production preparation, 500–501

resource planning, upgrades and, 474

resource requirements, 37–44

responsibilities, security, 184–187

restoring

    databases, 368–369

    user backups, 148–149

restrictions, Table T000, 129–130

RFC (Remote Function Calls), ITS, 451

roles, security, 184–187

roll area, 286–287, 323–324

roll memory, 284–286

rollback segments, client copy and, 137

rollbacks, 275–276

rolling releases, 57–58

ROOT.SH, 69–71

RSCCEXPT utility, client copy, 140

RSCCPROT utility, client copy, 140

RSCLCCOP utility, client copy, 139

RSCLICHK utility, client copy, 140

RSCLICOP utility, client copy, 138

RSCLIEXP utility, client copy, 138–139

RSCLIIMP utility, client copy, 139

RSCLTCOP utility, client copy, 140

RSCP utilities, languages, 107–108

RSMEMORY utility, 292

RSTXR3TR utility, client copy, 138

RZ03 (control panel) transaction, 336

RZ03 (thresholds) transaction, 304, 335

RZ10 (maintenance) transaction, 298–299

RZ11 (maintenance) transaction, 298–299

S

sales and distribution archive objects, 417–419

Sales and Distribution module, 5

Sand Box, 125

SAP

    Basis monitoring transactions, 511–512

    changes to, 11–12

    database administrator, 39–40

    printer installation, 199–200

    printing, troubleshooting, 207

    security administrator, 42–43, 186–187

    system administrator, 40–42

    tuning, 282–313, 283–304

SAP AG convention, 53

SAP Archive Link, Basis layer, 6

SAP Business Workflow, Basis layer, 7

SAP Cursor Cache, 309

SAP GUI, 5–6

SAP Knowledge Provider, Basis layer, 6

SAP Office:Mail and Archive System, Basis layer, 7

SAP R/3

    monitoring, 318–333

SAP Script, Basis layer, 7

SAP USA convention, 53

SAP*, special user account, 168

SAP@Web Studio, 464–465

SAPcomm/TOPCALL, faxing and, 211–219

sapconf file, 65

SAPconnect, faxing, 219–220

sapdba, 373–375

SAPDBA utility, 84

SAPGUI (SAP graphical user interface), 9

SAPINST installation tool, 79

SAPLOGON utility, technical upgrade and, 489

SAPPFPAR utility, 293–295

SARA (archiving), 391

scalability, 9

    hardware, 23

scheduled maintenance, 370–388

Screen Painter, ABAP, 15

SE06, initialization, 234

searches

    matchcodes, 17

    system log, 431–432

security, 156–192

    administrator, 186–187

    AIS (Audit Information System), 187–191

    Authority-Checks, 177

    authorizations, 159–177

    controlled access, 462–463

    DEV, 158

    firewalls, 462

    Internet access and, 462–464

    passwords, 169–171

    PRD, 159

    profile generator, 177–180

    QAS, 159

    roles and responsibilities, 184–187

    SAP security administrator, 186–187

    traces, transaction ST01, 180–182

    users

        master records, 166–168

        special user accounts, 168–169

Security, Basis layer, 6

segment headers, 268

servers

    application server, 7, 32

    database server, 7

        selecting, 29–30

    dedicated batch servers, 27

    presentation server, 7, 32–33

    requirements, 27–28

service connection, 113–114

service file, ITS, 454–460

services, 241

SGA (System Global Area), 265

shared memory, 261–262, 287–288

shared memory buffers, 310

shared SQL pool, 269–271

short tables, scans, 280

single-system landscape, 51

size

    databases, 30

    hardware, installation planning, 44–45

    redo log buffer, 272

    shared SQL pool, 269–271

SM04 transaction, 303

SM12 (lock manager) transaction, 320–321

SM13 (updates) transaction, 325

SM21 (system log) transaction, 321–322

SM37 (batch jobs) transaction, 324–325

SM39 (batch jobs) transaction, 324–325

SM50 (processes) transaction, 325–326

SM50 (system monitoring) transaction, 300, 434

SMGW (gateway) transaction, 327

SMLG (load balancing) transaction, 326

SMON (System Monitor), 282

software

    CD, CDINST and, 74

    database software, installation, 80–86

    distribution, tuning and, 251–257

    front-end, technical upgrade, 489–491

    non-SAP, upgrades, 483–485, 494

    third-party, upgrades, 483–485

software release strategy, 48

software requirements, 29–36

    database server, selecting, 29–30

    LANs, 33–34

    networking requirements, 33

    operating systems, selection, 29

sorts, database tuning and, 281

source code, OSS, registration, 110–111

SPAM updates, 116

SPAM utility, 117

Spool service, 241

SQL, traces, transaction ST05, 183–184

ST01 (trace) transaction, 180–182

ST02 (buffers) transaction, 322

ST02 (roll and paging) transaction, 323–324

ST02 transaction, 304

ST03 (performance) transaction, 322

ST03 transaction, 302–303

ST05 (SQL Trace) transaction, 183

ST05 (trace switch) transaction, 324

ST22 (ABAB errors) transaction, 322–323

startup, databases, 71

STAT transaction, 304

storage parameters, changing, 371–372

storage, tuning and, 249–251

stress test, 502–503

STUN (performance-monitoring window) transaction, 340

subroutines, ABAP Runtime Analysis, 349

SWAP partitions, database software installation, 85

swap space, memory, 258–259

SWAP space, setup, 64–65

synchronous disk I/O, 262

SYSPROF installation tool, 75

system administration tests, pre-production preparation, 504

system alerts, pre-production preparation, 508

system audit, 187–190

System Change Options, 223

system landscape, 23–24, 50, 51–53

    client strategy, 53–57

    installation planning, 45

    single-system, 51

    three-system, 52–53

    two-system, 52

system layout, tuning and, 242–248

system log, 321–322

    troubleshooting and, 431–434

system monitoring, 318–337

system name

    installation planning, 46

    selecting, 63

system process overview, troubleshooting and, 434–435

system requirements, hardware requirements, 22–28

system trace files, troubleshooting and, 441–443

system traces, 442–443

T

T Type transport, 225, 234

T002C language table, 95–96

table authorizations, 171–175

table monitoring (buffering), 310–313

table scans, 279–281

Table T000

    Category, 128

    logical system, 126–127

    restrictions, 129–130

tables

    ABAP Runtime Analyzer, 352–353

    changes, recording, 143

    cluster tables, data dictionary, 16

    data dictionary, 16

    language tables, 94–102

        initializing, 90

    matchcodes, 17

    online documentation, viewing, 174

    pool tables, data dictionary, 16

    view tables, data dictionary, 16

tablespace backups, 364

TASYS table, 234–235

TCB0B language table, 96

TCP/IP, 34

TCP09 language table, 101–102

TCP0C language table, 97–98

TCP0D language table, 98–100

TCPDB language table, 100–102

TDEVC table, 234

technical questionnaire, installation planning, 44

technical upgrades

    development system, 492–496

    front-end software, 489–491

    performing, 487–497

    planning, 479–487

    Upgrade Assistant, 492

Test client, 125

test plans, upgrades, 478–479

testing, pre-production preparation

    reporting results, 503–504

    stress test, 502–503

    system administration tests, 504

    system performance, 503

    user behavior, 503

    volume testing, 501–502

third-party products

    upgrades, 483–485

    upgrades and, 475

three-system landscape, 52–53

threshold values (alert monitor), 335

tiered architecture, 7–8

TMS (Transport Management System), 227–228

    configuration, 228

    pre-production preparation, 508

TOPCALL, faxing, 211–219

TPPARAM, 234

    CTS and, 231–233

trace switch, 324

traces

    SQL, transaction ST05, 183–184

    transaction ST01, 180–182

transactions. *See also* WebTransactions

    /$ST, 298

    AL08 (logged users), 326–327

    alert transactions, 337

    CCMS monitoring transactions, 340–341

    execution times, 342–343

    OS06 (operating system), 300–302

    RZ03 (control panel), 304, 336

    RZ03 (thresholds), 335

    RZ10 (maintenance), 298–299

    RZ11 (maintenance), 298–299

    SAP Basis monitoring transactions, 511–512

    SCC0, local or remote client copy, 130

    SCC3, client copy log analysis, 132

    SCC5, deleting clients, 133

    SCC7, client import, 132

    SCC7, client import/export, 131

    SCC8, client export, 131

    SCC9, remote client copy, 130–131

SCCL, local client copy, 130
SECR - audit report tree, 187
SM12 (lock manager), 320–321
SM13 (updates), 325
SM21 (system log), 321–322
SM37 (batch jobs), 324–325
SM39 (batch jobs), 324–325
SM50 (processes), 300, 325–326
SM50 (system monitoring), 434
SM51 (memory), 300
SM66 (memory), 300
SMGW (gateway), 327
SMLG (load balancing), 326
ST01 (trace), 180–182
ST02 (buffers), 304, 322
ST02 (roll and paging), 323–324
ST03 (performance), 322
ST05 (SQL Trace), 183
ST05 (trace switch), 324
ST05 - SQL Trace, 183–184
ST06 (operating systems), 300–302
ST22 (ABAP errors), 322–323
STAT, 304
SU53 - authorization check, 180
transport domains, 228
configuration, 228
transport requests
SCC1, client copy, 131
SCC2, client copy and transport (import and export), 131
SCC6, client import, 133
Transport system, installation planning, 47–48
transports
exporting clients, 132
objects
client-dependent, 128–129
consolidation system, 223
types, 223–225

troubleshooting, 430–446
ABAP dump analysis and, 435–438
analysis tools, 431–445
database alert log, 444–445
diagnosis, 445–446
lock entries monitor and, 440–441
OSS (online service system) and, 444
printing problems, 202–207
system process overview, 434–435
system trace files and, 441–443
update records monitor and, 438–440
TSYST table, 234
tuning
application server and, 245
batch instance and, 245
central instance and, 245
database performance, 264–282
database server and, 244
dialog instance, 245–246
distribution and, 242–248
file systems and, 249–251
guidelines, 348
hardware architecture and, 249
load balancing and, 246–248
network architecture and, 242–248
operating systems, 257–264
planning, 240–264
SAP, 282–313
software distribution, 251–255
storage and, 249–251
system layout and, 242–248
two-system landscape, 52

U

undo block, 268
undo header, 268
UNICODE, 88, 92

UNIX, 62–119
   commands
      ipcrm, 297
      ipcs, 297
   CTS setup, 229–233
   groups, 66
   installation, 63–67
   kernel, 67
   users, 66
Until cancel (restoring database), 368
Until time (restoring database), 368
update records monitor, troubleshooting and,
   438–440
Update service, 241
updates, 325
Upgrade - general, Basis layer, 6
Upgrade Assistant, technical upgrades, 492
upgrades, 470–498
   Basis upgrade, 470
   capacity and, 474
   change control, 479
   complexities of, 472–474
   CTS environment consistency, 486–487
   custom changes and, 480–483
   databases, 357
   downtime, reducing, 480
   environment baseline backup, 493
   front-end, new, 485
   functional upgrade, 470
   hardware installation, 485
   language support and, 475
   non-SAP software, 483–485, 494
   phases, 471
   planning, 471–487
   post-upgrade activities, 496
   PRD, 497
   preparing for, 474–487
   protection against, 130

   QAS, 497
   R/3, 494–496
   resource planning and, 474
   reviewing notes, 477
   technical
      development system, 492–496
      front-end software, 489–491
      performing, 487–497
      planning, 479–487
   test plans, 478–479
   third-party software, 483–485
   when to do it, 471
user calls, 275
User Master, 125
user master records, 166–168
user response type, 343–344
user-exits, 12
USERPROF installation tool, 75
users
   AIX, 66–67
   backing up, 145–147
   backups, restoring, 148–149
   context switching, roll memory and, 284
   locking/unlocking, 148
   number of, hardware selection, 23
   printing information, 147
   profiles
      modifying, 66
      USERPROF and, 75
   special user accounts, 168–169
   types, 168
   UNIX, 66
      CTS and, 231
utilities
   backups, 370
   cleanipc, 297
   client copy, 138–139
   esmon, 293

MEMLIMITS, 296–297
ORAINST, 67–71, 69
PREPARE, 492–493
RSMEMORY, 292
SAPPFPAR, 293–295
SPAM, 117

V

variants
    client copy and, 137
    importing, 152–153
vendor support, 26
version management, 14
view tables, data dictionary, 16
virtual memory, 260
volume testing, 501–502

W

wait time (response time), 344
WANs (wide area networks), 35–36
WebReporting Browser, ITS, 461–462
WebReporting, ITS, 457–460
WebRFC, ITS, 457–460
WebTransactions, 455–457
WGate (Web Gateway), 451
Windows NT printer installation, 199
Winfax, 208–211
Workbench Organizer, 11–12

Z

ztta/roll_extension (extended memory parameter),
    288

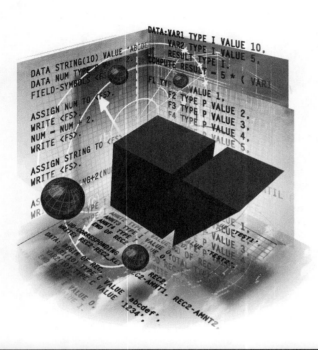

FREE SUBSCRIPTION FORM

To receive a FREE *SAP Technical Journal*, complete and return this form.

Please answer all questions, sign and date the card.

❑ **YES!** I wish to receive my FREE subscription to *SAP Technical Journal*.

❑ NO, I don't wish to subscribe

Signature (required)_____

Date (required)_____

Name_____

Title_____

Company_____

Address_____

City_____ State/Province_____

Country_____ Zip/Postal Code_____

Telephone_____ Fax_____

E-mail Address_____

1 What is your relationship to SAP? (check only one)
- 01 ❑ Customer
- 02 ❑ Third-Party vendor
- 03 ❑ Development partner
- 04 ❑ Consulting partner
- 05 ❑ Hardware partner
- 06 ❑ SAP Employee
- 07 ❑ Other_____

2 If a customer, is your R/3 System live?

Currently	Within the next 6 months
08 ❑ Yes	10 ❑ Yes
09 ❑ No	11 ❑ No

3 How many years have you been working with SAP products? (check only one)
- 12 ❑ Less than 1 year
- 13 ❑ 1 - 2 years
- 14 ❑ 2 - 5 years
- 15 ❑ Over five years

4 What is your current job function? (check only one)
- 16 ❑ Analyst/Program Analyst
- 17 ❑ Application Consultant
- 18 ❑ Application Developer
- 19 ❑ Basis Consultant
- 20 ❑ Basis Developer
- 21 ❑ Business Operations Manager
- 22 ❑ Design/Development or R&D Engineer
- 23 ❑ Network Engineer
- 24 ❑ Process Engineer
- 25 ❑ Product Manager
- 26 ❑ Quality/Reliability Manager
- 27 ❑ Software Engineer
- 28 ❑ Test Engineer
- 29 ❑ Web/Internet Professional
- 30 ❑ Other_____

5 Which SAP release(s) do you currently work with? (check ALL that apply)
- 31 ❑ R/2
- 32 ❑ R/3 3.x
- 32 ❑ R/3 2.x
- 34 ❑ R/3 4.x

6 Do you have Internet/intranet applications connected to SAP R/3?

Currently	Within the next 6 months
35 ❑ Yes	37 ❑ Yes
36 ❑ No	38 ❑ No

7 What SAP R/3 functionality do you use? (check all that apply)
- 39 ❑ Financial Accounting (FI)
- 40 ❑ Controlling (CO)
- 41 ❑ Asset Managment (AM)
- 42 ❑ Project System (PS)
- 43 ❑ Workflow (WF)
- 44 ❑ Industry Solutions (IS)
- 45 ❑ Human Resources (HR)
- 46 ❑ Plant Maintenance (PM)
- 47 ❑ Quality Management (QM)
- 48 ❑ Production Planning (PP)
- 49 ❑ Materials Management (MM)
- 50 ❑ Sales and Distribution (SD)

8 Which best describes your industry? (check only one)
- 51 ❑ Aerospace & Defense
- 52 ❑ Automotive
- 53 ❑ Banking/Insurance
- 54 ❑ Chemicals
- 55 ❑ Consumer Products
- 56 ❑ Consulting & Professional Services (please specify)_____
- 57 ❑ Computer Dealer (Reseller/Vendor)
- 58 ❑ Data Processing
- 59 ❑ Education
- 60 ❑ Entertainment/Tourism
- 61 ❑ Engineering & Construction
- 62 ❑ Healthcare
- 63 ❑ High Tech & Electronics
- 64 ❑ Media
- 65 ❑ Oil & Gas
- 66 ❑ Pharmaceuticals
- 67 ❑ Public Sector
- 68 ❑ Real Estate
- 69 ❑ Retail (not computers)
- 70 ❑ System House-Integrator or VAR/Systems/Integrators
- 71 ❑ Transportation
- 72 ❑ Telecommunications
- 73 ❑ Utilities
- 74 ❑ Other_____

9 What SAP R/3 infrastructure do you work with? (check ALL that apply)
- 75 ❑ OS/390
- 77 ❑ Windows NT
- 76 ❑ OS/400
- 78 ❑ UNIX

10 Which tools/languages do you use for SAP R/3 and SAP R/3-integrated solutions? (check ALL that apply)
- 79 ❑ ABAP
- 80 ❑ Active X
- 81 ❑ ALE
- 82 ❑ Batch
- 83 ❑ C/C ++
- 84 ❑ Cobol
- 85 ❑ COM/DCOM
- 86 ❑ CORBA
- 87 ❑ Delphi
- 88 ❑ DHTML
- 89 ❑ EDI
- 90 ❑ HTML
- 91 ❑ Java
- 92 ❑ JavaScript
- 93 ❑ PERL
- 94 ❑ PowerBuilder
- 95 ❑ SQL
- 96 ❑ Visual Basic
- 97 ❑ Other_____
- 98 ❑ None of the Above

FAX TO:
1-615-377-0525 or
SUBSCRIBE ONLINE
www.saptechjournal.com

11 What tools/topics are you interested in? (check ALL that apply)

- 099 ❑ Archiving
- 100 ❑ Application development tools
- 101 ❑ Application Link Enabling
- 102 ❑ Enterprise Management
- 103 ❑ Information Management
- 104 ❑ Internet/intranet
- 105 ❑ Middleware
- 106 ❑ Modeling
- 107 ❑ Performance Management
- 108 ❑ Reporting
- 109 ❑ Systems Management
- 110 ❑ Testing
- 111 ❑ Workflow
- 112 ❑ Other_____

12 How many total employees does your company have?

- 113 ❑ Under 100
- 114 ❑ 100 to 249
- 115 ❑ 250 to 499
- 116 ❑ 500 to 999
- 117 ❑ 1,000 to 4,999
- 118 ❑ 5,000 to 9,999
- 119 ❑ 10,000 or more

13 What is your company's total sales volume?

- 120 ❑ Under $10 million
- 121 ❑ $10 - $50 million
- 122 ❑ $50 - $250 million
- 123 ❑ $250 - $500 million
- 124 ❑ $500 million - $1 billion
- 125 ❑ $1 billion - $5 billion
- 126 ❑ Over $5 billion

PLEASE MAKE SURE YOU'VE:
- ☞ **Signed and dated the form**
- ☞ **Filled out the form completely**
- ☞ **Applied postage**
- ☞ **Folded form in half and taped closed (do not staple)**

FOLD HERE FOR MAILING

SAN FRANCISCO CA 94105-3912
55 HAWTHORNE ST STE 600
CIRCULATION DEPARTMENT

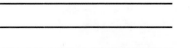

SAP TECHNICAL JOURNAL

PLACE STAMP HERE